Excellence in Education: the making of great schools

Cyril Taylor and Conor Ry

D1338238

DISPOSED OF
BY LIBRARY
HOUSE OF LORDS

David Fulton Publishers

David Fulton Publishers Ltd
The Chiswick Centre, 414 Chiswick High Road, London W4 5TF

www.fultonpublishers.co.uk

First published in Great Britain by David Fulton Publishers 2005

10 9 8 7 6 5 4 3 2 1

David Fulton Publishers is a division of Granada Learning Limited, part of ITV plc.

Copyright © David Fulton Publishers 2005

Note: The right of Cyril Taylor and Conor Ryan to be identified as the authors of their work has been asserted by them in accordance with the Copyright, Designs and Patents Act 1988.

British Library Cataloguing in Publication Data
A catalogue record for this book is available from the British Library.

ISBN: 1 84312 213 8

All rights reserved. No part of this publication may be reproduced, stored in a retrieval system or transmitted, in any form or by any means, electronic, mechanical, photocopying, or otherwise, without the prior permission of the publishers.

Typeset by RefineCatch Limited, Bungay, Suffolk
Printed and bound in Italy by Rotolito Lombarda

Contents

This book is dedicated to the many outstanding head teachers who are leading the quiet revolution that is transforming English schools. 'They are the bows from which our children as living arrows are sent forth.' – Kahlil Gibran

Preface

This book is written for all those who have an interest in education: parents, teachers, school staff, head teachers, governors, government officials, policy makers, the media, local councillors and Members of Parliament. The lessons taken from it can be used by all of these people to help schools raise their own standards. It is primarily about the experience of secondary schools, though many of the techniques and case studies will have a resonance with primary schools too.

The last 15 years have seen a remarkable change in education in England. This quiet revolution has made a significant difference to the workings of hundreds, if not thousands, of individual schools. Amid the hubbub of teachers' conferences, the justified complaints of excess bureaucracy, the shrill newspaper headlines of crises, or the inevitable political knockabout, the turnaround has rarely gained the attention it deserves. This book tries to redress that balance. It tells the stories of schools that have succeeded against the odds. It shows, in practical terms, how schools have used the changes to improve the life-chances of millions of young people.

Two views are commonly taken about the English education system. One is a counsel of despair which argues that nothing has gone right in our education system, and all our ills could be cured if we simply turned back the clock by 50 years. The other argues that nothing has gone right in our education system since schools started to account for themselves to taxpayers and parents, and all our ills could be cured if we simply scrapped tables, targets, testing and inspections. We believe both views to be mistaken.

There is much happening in schools that is good. And the evidence is that much of the improvement that has occurred has been a direct result of applying sound leadership, management and organisational techniques, alongside good teaching and learning. Governments of both political persuasions, from that led by

Margaret Thatcher to today's government led by Tony Blair, deserve credit for allowing and fostering these changes, often in the teeth of vocal opposition from vested interests. Kenneth Baker introduced the National Curriculum, testing and local management of schools. He introduced the first City Technology Colleges. The current government with an unrivalled Prime Ministerial commitment to education, has thankfully withstood siren calls and devolutionary diversions to scrap tests or abandon the publication of exam results. David Blunkett, as Education Secretary, introduced greater accountability and began the expansion of specialist schools that has proceeded at a rapid pace under Estelle Morris and Charles Clarke.

As part of the research for this book, we surveyed many successful schools, to see what techniques and methods they were using to succeed. The results of this survey, with a perceptive academic analysis from Dr Anthony Green and Ayo Mansaray from the Institute of Education at the University of London, are included in Appendix 2. But what they showed was something that we found from our own interviews, visits and experience over the years. There are common factors between good schools, there are similarities between what makes great schools. Leadership and management and good teaching are clearly important. But so are factors like good use of data and targeting, Information and Communications Technology (ICT), clear behaviour policies, new approaches to teamwork and, for some schools, the organisation of the school building and the timetable. These are all contributing to the growing success of many schools.

But there is a lot more that needs to be done to tackle the all too many secondary schools which still fail to provide their pupils with the education they deserve. Too many children still transfer from primary to secondary school without mastering the basics of literacy and numeracy. There is more that should be done to provide genuine school choice for families from every background, not just the affluent middle classes who can vote with their mortgage. Vast improvements have been made in the use and application of data, but it has not been used as effectively as it might be. And there is still far too little written about the practical ways in which some schools have made a difference, whether on discipline, organisation of the school day and term, or the structure of school buildings. It is also the case that bureaucracy has sometimes been excessively burdensome; teachers have been expected to do too much paperwork; and there has on occasion been too little clarity in some of the initiatives that have been introduced. Radical change, such as has happened to English education, is never easy.

But, pupil and school level targets have been vital to the recovery of hundreds of schools. The data now provided to schools by Ofsted and the Department for Education and Skills (DfES) makes it possible for schools (some of which we feature in this book) to foster personalised improvement and to provide individual programmes of learning in a way that would have seemed a mere pipedream a decade ago. Specialist status, academies and programmes such as Excellence in Cities have helped many schools to improve far faster than the national average (a trend which, incidentally, casts doubt on those who argue that exams have systematically got easier to pass, since improvements have been far from uniform). Ofsted inspections, which are now being streamlined, have shed a powerful and invaluable searchlight on schools, and, through their fearless identification of failure, have helped ensure that more youngsters gain a decent education.

It is not popular to paint such a picture of progress in so many of our schools. Teaching unions will say that it misses the point: we should instead be adding to the popular chorus of complaint, about over-tested children, damaging performance data, intrusive inspectors or disillusioned teachers. The Government's critics will say that it glosses over New Labour's 'failure' to reform the public services. Parents, especially in cities where there are still too few good schools, may not recognise the type of schools we present. And they are entitled to say so. The system may be a lot better than it was, but it is clearly not as good as it can and should be.

But, we are at a crossroads. Within two years, the vast majority of secondary schools are likely to have specialist status. There are significant resources being invested in the rebuilding and new building of secondary schools. Teachers have far more support, and are better paid, than ever before. Major changes may be in the offing with 14–19 education, and have already been announced for apprenticeships. Schools are also being trusted with greater independence than they have had for at least 20 years. ICT is finally beginning to show its potential as a tool of learning. And through it, pupils are being offered the possibility of a far more personalised journey through secondary education than before.

All these developments should be welcomed and embraced. But, as they come to fruition, schools will still need to keep their eye on their main purpose: to develop well-educated, rounded and active citizens who can support themselves and their families throughout their lives. Meeting this ambition is easier said than done in schools where a multiplicity of disadvantages militates against achievement and aspiration. Yet there are so many schools which have made it a reality now that there can be real hope that what works for the best can spread to the rest.

Our insularity sometimes leads us to believe that the problems we face – or their solutions – are peculiarly British. The reality is far from it. The United States public school system, despite some pockets of successful reform, has been trying to emulate many of the techniques which have been employed in schools here. Some Australian state governments and New Zealand have been ahead of us. Other European countries have been closely examining our reform programme and independent inspection system. There is a problem across much of the developed world with education, and many of the solutions that work here have been found to work in other OECD (Organisation for Economic Co-operation and Development) nations.

This book is about what makes good and great schools. The schools we have chosen generally are successful comprehensives which have introduced notable improvements, as a result of strong leadership and clear strategies for improvement. Or, they are secondary schools which have done things differently, and we feel that others could learn from how they have made a difference. Their success owes most to the individual schools themselves, and those that lead, teach, study in, or support them. But these schools also share many common characteristics: they set targets (usually for each student individually); they often involve parents beyond statutory requirements; they use ICT creatively and effectively; they craft their timetables imaginatively; they offer an innovative but purposeful curriculum; and they maintain a very clear set of sanctions for discipline. In some cases, the schools already spread their good practice to others in formal or informal partnerships. Others clearly have the potential to do so.

And they are more than just isolated success stories. Their number is growing. We hope that their stories can help to inspire others, particularly those who are leading or working with schools, whether as members of staff or governors, parents or external partners.

We would like to thank all those schools, principals and teachers who shared their stories with our readers, as well as officials in the DfES, particularly Professor David Hopkins; the Chief Inspector of Schools, David Bell; Liz Reid, Chief Executive of the Specialist Schools Trust; Christine Prentice and Ron Jacobs; Helen Wadsworth and Jane Ware, for their research, ideas and support for the project; and to our publishers Nigel Ward, the CEO of Granada Learning and Christopher Glennie, the Publishing Director of David Fulton Publishers. Naturally, any responsibility for errors or omissions lies solely with the authors. And the views expressed are, of course, our own, and do not necessarily reflect those of any of the views who helped us along the way.

Cyril Taylor and Conor Ryan
October 2004

1

What makes a great school?

Before we can determine what makes a great school, we must first agree on our definition. Success in examination results is clearly one indicator, but it is not the only one. The *Concise Oxford Dictionary* defines education as the giving of intellectual, moral and social instruction. Perhaps G. K. Chesterton put it more attractively when he wrote 'Education is simply the soul of a society as it passes from one generation to another.'[1] Or, we could put it more simply: good schools produce good citizens.

Sometimes, the debate about education creates false dichotomies. Some argue that education is about the acquisition of knowledge for its own sake. Certainly, there is much to be said for broadening the mind and awakening creative impulses. But it would be naïve to suggest that education is not also an economic imperative. The needs of a highly competitive global economy require all our young people to be challenged to perform to the maximum of their potential. Digby Jones, the Director General of the Confederation of British Industry recently said that 80 per cent of the jobs in the UK economy will soon require five or more good GCSEs or their vocational equivalent.[2] Yet, in 2003, almost half of young people finished compulsory education at age 16 without achieving this (though some will reach this standard by the age of 19 at further education colleges). There will soon be little work for those with too few skills.

If these are the purposes of education and schools, which institutions are most likely to provide this happy combination to their students? One way of looking at it would be to say that good schools are also happy schools, where a high

---

[1] *Illustrated London News* (5 July 1924), cited at http://www.dur.ac.uk/martin.ward/gkc/books/quotes.html.
[2] Confederation of British Industry News release, (17 February 2004).

proportion of dedicated teachers are committed to their success and remain in post for a considerable time. As a result, they enable every pupil, whatever their background, to achieve their full potential, and prepare them for the challenges they will face in later life.

There are perhaps seven ways in which we can identify a good school.

- They perform well in exams, both on an absolute and a value-added basis (the latter is discussed in greater detail below);
- A high proportion of pupils stay on in full-time education or training at age 16. For schools with post-16 provision this would include those progressing to the sixth form;
- For age 11 to 18 schools, a high proportion of their pupils go on to university or other post-secondary education as well as achieving good A Level results;
- They have few permanently excluded children, indicating high standards of order and discipline;
- There is a low turnover of staff;
- They have a large number of applications for places from parents;
- They make substantial provision for extra-curricular activities including sports, the arts, voluntary activities and other after-school activities.

Having established these criteria, we are now in a better position to determine *why* good schools perform so well. Throughout this book, we will draw extensively on individual case studies. We will not draw exclusively on the success of specialist schools, because many of the characteristics which successful specialist schools use have been adopted by other secondary schools. But, given that national education policy in England is geared towards the rapid expansion of schools which specialise in one of ten subjects, or a combination of some of them, the experience of those who were early to specialise is of particular interest. To some extent, our account is influenced by two important pieces of research commissioned by the Specialist Schools Trust: *The Seven Habits of Highly Effective Schools* by James Tooley and Andy Howes,[3] and *High Performing Specialist Schools: What makes the difference?*, written by a team of researchers led by Peter Rudd from the National Foundation for Educational Research (NFER).[4] (These will be referred to as the Tooley and Howes study and the NFER study, respectively.) Their findings may be familiar to many in the academic world, who have

---

[3] J. Tooley and A. Howes, *The Seven Habits of Highly Effective Schools: Best Practice in Specialist Schools* (London, Technology Colleges Trust, 1999).

[4] P. Rudd, S. Aiston, D. Davies, M. Rickinson and L. Dartnall, *High Performing Specialist Schools: What makes the difference?* (London, NFER, 2002).

identified similar factors in successful schools here and abroad, but they are no less significant for that. Both studies indicate that successful schools share common characteristics. The success factors are not particularly surprising in themselves, but a key finding of both studies is the interconnectedness of these qualities of excellence. In other words, the studies conclude that all the essential factors for a successful school must be implemented together in a coherent and joined-up way. Moreover, this in itself is one of the most important requirements for a school to be successful, and such joined-up thinking will produce an ethos of achievement and endeavour.

Qualities of excellence

From the two studies, we can identify a number of common characteristics in high-performing schools:

- A good leadership team of the head teacher, heads of department and governing body;
- Their ability to attract and retain good teachers;
- A focus on the basics such as literacy and numeracy;
- The setting of targets and use of data to monitor progress;
- Discipline and order;
- Curriculum innovation, which may include vocational awards and/or the International Baccalaureate;
- Extensive use of information communications technology (ICT) including linked wireless laptops and whiteboards;
- Consideration of a longer school day and non-traditional term dates;
- A focus on individual learning to create an ethos of achievement for all;
- The support of parents and the use of older students as mentors.

Let us consider these factors in greater detail.

The need for competent, inspirational leadership

A good school's most important requirement is to have an inspiring, highly respected leader. But it is also vital that he or she is backed up by a strong team of deputies and department heads, and that they are in turn supported by a good governing body. Mythology has grown up around the notion of the 'hero head' who battles to succeed against everybody else in the school, but those who are most likely to succeed will have the backing of others in the school's leadership team, as well as the school governors. Good leadership can be driven by an inspiring individual. But that alone is not enough: it also requires teamwork.

While successful head teachers have many different leadership styles, the NFER study found that the group of 20 head teachers they studied all shared certain characteristics:

- They all believed that they understood how to improve their own schools: 'You've got to believe in yourself to start with';
- They were very focused on their goals and committed to bringing about success in their schools;
- Many were unconventional and prepared to take risks in trying new ways to encourage learning;
- They were seen as being approachable, enabling new ideas, generated by management teams and teachers, to be taken on board;
- They were entrepreneurial, especially in finding sources of extra funding and in taking new opportunities, such as bidding for specialist status.

NFER determined that whatever their leadership style, each leader of the successful schools they visited had a clear vision of what they wished to achieve. It did not matter whether a school was urban or rural; nor whether it was in a deprived inner city area or a socially advantaged location. The vision of the head teacher was the most crucial factor in the school's success.

But successful head teachers must also be able to impart their vision for the school to their senior managers, teaching staff and pupils alike. The NFER study cited a number of head teachers:

'Having a first-class set of staff, who are extremely committed and who share the vision as deeply as I do.' Another talked, not about leadership on its own, but about a 'spirit of leadership' which 'permeates' the whole school. Yet another talked about 'climate' rather than 'spirit'. Teachers as well as senior managers talked about a feeling that 'success breeds success' and a belief that 'success is ingrained in the school'.

The NFER looked at a number of successful specialist schools, which they didn't name. In one school, they reported how the vision of the head teacher was crucial in carrying the school forward; she was prepared to challenge conventions where necessary and to 'do her own thing wherever this was perceived to be important for her students' success'. This meant being brave with the curriculum in the school, so that a vision centred around 'achievement and success' could be turned from words to reality. Flexibility was key here. 'The big thing is not to have a curriculum in which kids are bound to fail, but to have a flexible curriculum in which they'll achieve,' she told the researchers. But, of course, she couldn't do it alone, so she had recruited a number of young, energetic teachers to fulfil the school's specialist remit. Like other interviewees, she felt that rigorous recruitment was vital and that the whole school community (staff, parents, pupils and other partners) needed to share a vision. Efforts were made to ensure that the vision was transmitted to, and shared throughout the whole school community.

NFER's researchers visited another school, an urban school where about a quarter of students were eligible for free school meals and where all those they interviewed, including one of the student discussion groups, talked about the head teacher's leadership skills and how he had passed on a vision for the school. 'He leads from the front,' seemed to be a common verdict in this case. But once more, this was truly a team effort. The head may have developed the vision, but he did so first in partnership with the Senior Management Team in the school, his deputies and the senior heads of subject departments. He gained the backing of the school governors and then communicated to the staff. Once the staff were 'on board', the vision was then communicated to the children, so that everyone had ownership. The NFER reports that this head was highly regarded by staff and students. He was said to keep the school at the forefront of initiatives and had a drive to bring extra funding into the school wherever possible. According to teachers interviewed by the researchers, he trusted the staff, recognising their quality and had the ability to explain why decisions were made, why particular approaches were important. And crucially, he ensured that his staff were involved in decision-making processes and that their opinions were valued. Students liked and respected him, noting that he maintained a high profile around the school. Students felt that he knew all of them by name, which they appreciated. When asked what was good about the school, one student said: 'Mr X, our head teacher, he's the best, he's really influential.'

Approachability is not about 'letting it all hang out' in the caricature of some TV comprehensive schools. Rather it is about being open to new ideas and to the sharing of good practice. In some of the schools visited by NFER, this was felt to empower teachers: 'There's no "us and them" divide . . . [Senior Management are] very approachable and very forward looking and open to new ideas,' was one view. This democratic style of management appeared, in some institutions at least, to have reinforced the sense in which the whole staff were working towards the same goal. One head teacher has tried to 'create an empowering process that holds people to account, but in a supportive way'. Another head teacher, echoing this view, was clear about his aim to both support and challenge his staff: 'You need to transmit the fact that things can improve throughout the staff, but you need to do this in a way that does not frighten them [teachers] to death . . . we try to light the fire within, not the fire below.'

Discussions with students in some schools also highlighted the extent to which they felt a sense of belonging in the school. They often felt privileged to attend the school and proud of what they were achieving. A Year 10 student commented: 'There's a school council, we do get our say. We can say what the school can do to improve.' Yet another key characteristic of effective leadership in schools which can be seen elsewhere, in the private sector or in the Civil Service, was the empowerment of key staff such as department heads. Flat rather than hierarchical management structures often work best. Department heads are encouraged to make decisions. Time spent in meetings was kept to a minimum with clear, timed agendas, recommended action and minutes being taken with follow up of agreed action. There was good communication between senior managers, between senior management and subject leaders and with the governing body.

But if a good head is crucial to success, an obvious question that arises is the extent to which a school becomes dependent on the individual. This was another issue examined by the NFER study: what happens when a good school loses its outstanding head teacher?

Governors have a crucial role

Here the role of the governors is crucial. And their involvement and ownership of the initial vision can ensure that the factors that contributed to the school's success don't disappear with their initiator. Moreover, if a rigorous open selection process to find an able successor is put in place, the chances of success will be greater. In a really successful school, there will already be a strong senior management team in place to provide continuity. There will be proven systems in such areas as target setting and tracking the performance of individual children so that changes in leadership will not lead to standards falling back.

The importance of a good governing body to a successful school is significant in many other ways. Sadly, too few schools have strong governing bodies. This is partly because the system used to appoint governors, as well as some of the responsibilities they are assigned in law, can lead to weak governing bodies, which concern themselves with micro-management of trivial issues, rather than setting overall goals for achievement. Governors should focus on monitoring progress towards a school's goals and ensuring that the head teacher has both the resources and the support to succeed. Many specialist schools have the good fortune to enjoy the services of sponsor governors, who have experience of board membership of large enterprises and know the function of a good board of directors.

Changes in recent years have rightly given parents a strong role on governing bodies, and efforts have been made to encourage more people from business and the wider community. But the role of governors remains too broadly defined.

Perhaps a simpler set of responsibilities could be developed. The Association of Governing Boards of Universities and Colleges in the USA gives trustees and governors the following advice on the role of a governing body:

1 To select the Principal or Headteacher;
2 To monitor the Principal's progress in achieving goals agreed by governors;
3 To determine the mission of the institution;
4 To approve financial budgets including capital expenditure;
5 To ensure financial solvency;
6 To defend the autonomy and independence of the institution;
7 To enhance the public standing of the institution including helping with fundraising;
8 To serve as a court of final appeal.[5]

These might define the essential role of governors. But, the English governor has many other statutory functions such as admissions, including appeals, exclusions, and health and safety. The extent to which they can carry out all their legal duties is varied, and there are real difficulties in recruiting sufficient good governors in many schools. A limited and clear definition of the governors' role is important and good governing bodies will appropriate this role for themselves and will use their powers to develop and maintain the school's strategic vision, particularly at a time of change at the top.

Schools must be able to attract and retain good teachers

If good leadership is essential, the ability to attract and retain good teachers, especially in key shortage subjects such as mathematics, science and modern languages, is no less important. The latest subject skills survey by the Department for Education and Skills (DfES), as well as a number of Ofsted reports, have confirmed that an unacceptable proportion of teaching, especially in many schools facing challenging circumstances, is done by teachers without specialist degrees. Moreover, because of vacancies, supply or substitute teachers teach a significant amount of lessons, particularly in urban areas, though their numbers have started to fall. One way of solving the problem, which was pioneered by some of the country's most successful schools, is by employing teaching assistants and other administrative staff to relieve qualified teachers of administrative burdens such as taking attendance or photocopying; and thus improve their productivity as well as

---

[5] J. L. Zwingle, *Effective Trusteeship: Guidelines for board members*, 3rd edn (Washington, USA, Association of Governing Boards of Universities and Colleges, 1984).

persuading them to remain in post. This is now a key part of the Government's workload deal with teachers.

In his curriculum review of 1993–4 Ron Dearing found that many teachers were only spending half their time preparing for class, teaching and marking, with the balance being spent on administrative chores or attending meetings. For example in order to take the attendance register manually by reading out the names of pupils in a form it can take an average of 20 minutes a day per teacher. In a typically sized school of 1,000 pupils in 35 form groups this will require the equivalent of two full-time teaching positions. Teachers themselves reported a similar balance in the use of their time in more recent studies for the School Teachers' Review Body, and this was one of the factors which led to the workload deal.

Successful schools have been ahead of the game. Harris City Technology College (CTC), in Norwood, South London, now employs 40 teaching assistants to help 70 qualified teaching staff. Some of these teaching assistants may be graduates seeking Qualified Teacher Status (QTS) through the Graduate Teaching Programme (GTP) under which the Teacher Training Agency pays a £13,000 salary grant plus a £4,000 training payment for recent graduates enrolled in a GTP programme. Others will be parents of children at the school, and others still will bring experience from other work to the life of the school. Kemnal Technology College in Sidcup, Bromley, has taken the use of teaching assistants a step further by creating large classrooms capable or seating 60 to 75 pupils. Contrary to the alarmist newspaper stories that appear whenever such innovations are mentioned, these groups are not the norm, but special masterclasses. They are not seen as a substitute for smaller classes for most lessons, but an opportunity to gain exceptional insights into new knowledge. Very able teachers have been recruited to teach the class, and they are supported by up to three teaching assistants.

Teaching assistants can complement good teachers. They are not a substitute for them. But the truth is that good teachers will stay in schools where their skills and talents are used to the maximum extent, and where they receive the support they need to do their job well.

There is a strong focus on literacy and numeracy

The extent to which children have been taught in the basics is another key issue, one which we discuss in greater detail in Chapter 2. Those with poor standards of literacy and numeracy can find it particularly difficult to make the transition from primary to secondary school. While the Key Stage 2 tests have at least brought some standardisation to primary school testing, many schools find it useful to re-test pupils after their summer holidays to help determine whether further help

is needed. An increasing number of secondary schools now gives their incoming Year 7 pupils a literacy test such as the London or Richmond reading test, and a numeracy test. Pupils with poor reading skills are identified at an early stage, perhaps in a one-or two-week orientation programme given to incoming pupils in August. These pupils are then given intensive remedial support. As the former Education Secretary David Blunkett said in 1997, 'A child who can't read can't learn.' To be fair, substantial progress in literacy has been made in recent years. When the first national test results were published in 1995, more than half of the children entering secondary school in inner city areas were two or more years behind in reading. Now the figure is perhaps a quarter, though there is clearly scope for further improvement.

Use of targets and monitoring progress through databases

Many of the most improved schools in the country have specialist status. One of the reasons for this success is their use of targets for individual children, year groups and subject areas at both Key Stage 3 and GCSE. Targets have been criticised in recent years, partly because there were too many. Targets proliferated beyond those that really matter to pupil achievement, a situation that has since been reversed. But the evidence from specialist schools is that appropriate targets do make a difference, and that they can translate the vision of a good head teacher and the dedication of good teachers into tangible results. Carefully set, realistic targets are required to obtain specialist status in the first place. This skill in target setting has been developed to such an extent that it is transforming education through a process of personalising learning such that each child has a realistic goal for every year in the key subject areas. Sophisticated computer systems allow teachers to access the school database from anywhere in the school. Every child, whatever his or her starting point, can be challenged to the maximum of their potential.

The monitoring and evaluation of performance data is a key ingredient in a successful school. The NFER study suggests that the following aspects of monitoring and evaluation are important:

- Detailed use of value-added data to determine which departments are doing well and which are not.
- Data used extensively and not just collected. This requires that every teacher is comfortable in accessing and manipulating computer-stored data.
- Regularity in tracking student progress. At a minimum this will be done on a termly basis. Some schools now issue monthly reports to parents on their child's progress.

- Student involvement in the use of data. Teachers meet regularly with their pupils to review progress.
- Monitoring and evaluation of staff and increased accountability. Value-added data is especially useful in identifying weaker departments and taking appropriate action. As Jim Collins said in his book *Good to Great*, 'Good-to-great leaders *first* got the right people on the bus . . . and the right people in the right seats.'[6]

How data is communicated to parents and the wider community has been controversial ever since the Government decided to publish the GCSE results of every school in 1988. These figures are converted by newspapers into league tables, which when viewed in isolation can seem to tell you more about the admissions policy of the school than its standards. Nevertheless league tables of raw examination results are an important accountability tool, especially in measuring basic competence in literacy and numeracy. The addition of information showing how much schools have improved (or otherwise) in recent years offers additional context. But it is now also widely accepted that comparisons of the examination results of schools should also allow for the differences in their intakes of ability, particularly for secondary schools at age 11. These comparisons are called value-added measures.

Many inner city secondary schools have a large proportion of pupils with literacy and numeracy difficulties upon entry at age 11. Others receive a large number of excluded pupils from other schools with many having severe emotional and behavioural difficulties. Still more have a high degree of mobility or a high concentration of socially and economically disadvantaged families, often with only one parent. Many schools also have a large number of pupils whose native language is not English. The use of a value-added measure allows them and us to have a more complete picture of the performance of schools in such circumstances. Critics of raw league tables used to argue for simply introducing a poverty indicator such as the proportion of pupils on free school meals or the number of those in single parent families. But there is a danger of this becoming an excuse rather than a motivator. It is surely far better and fairer for all schools to be judged with reference to the previous educational attainments of their pupils. This will still in part reflect free school meal levels in primary schools but in the context of a specific education indicator of prior attainment.

At Thomas Telford School, a city technology college, regarded by many as the most successful comprehensive school in the country, every 16-year-old regularly

---

[6] J. Collins, *Good to Great: Why some companies make the leap . . . and others don't* (New York, Harper Collins, 2001), p. 13.

obtains not just five good grades at GCSE, but ten such grades. These raw results are remarkable in themselves. But the value-added score is also high. Using an index developed by Professor David Jesson for the Specialist Schools Trust[7] (described in more detail in Appendix 1), the percentage of pupils achieving five good grades at GCSE in 2003 was 13 points higher than the predicted percentage of 87 per cent good grades.

Some schools achieve particularly impressive value-added scores. Table 1.1 shows the ten specialist schools with the highest value-added scores in the country.

On this basis, inner city schools such as Sir John Cass Foundation and Redcoat Church of England Secondary School in Tower Hamlets, Selly Park Technology College for Girls, Birmingham and All Saints School, Barking out-perform even Thomas Telford. Many of the case studies we use in this book are schools that add value and achieve significant improvements, as well as those who achieve very high raw scores. But, even the analysis of examination success on a value-added basis does not tell the whole story on how a school is performing. We must, therefore, examine other important indicators of success even though it is difficult to find statistical measures for them.

Examination league tables do not give information on such important matters as the number of pupils excluded each year; the average attendance (a much better figure than the amount of authorised absence which can be the subject of manipulation); the number of applications for each place available (parents are usually well informed on which local schools are best); the proportion of pupils staying on in the school at age 16 if there is post-16 provision or the proportion of 16-year-olds who transfer to a post-16 institution if the school is only for 11 to 16-year-olds; and finally if the school has post-16 provision, the proportion of pupils going on to post-secondary education together with their A Level results. Wise parents will seek the answers to these other performance measures before applying for a place for their son or daughter. Some schools publish this information. Ofsted reports, which are available online (www.ofsted.gov.uk/reports), also contain some of this information and are a good introduction to many schools' achievements.

Maintaining good discipline and order

A child can only learn properly in a disciplined and orderly school environment. Yet there are too many schools where order has broken down. William Atkinson, head teacher of the Phoenix School in Hammersmith has turned around a previously failing school where only 6 per cent of the children got at least five good

---

[7] By starting with the average Key Stage 2 points per pupil of the 11-year-olds entering the school, Professor Jesson's formula predicts the likely GCSE grades for the school five years later. This is described in more detail in Appendix 1.

Table 1.1 Comparison of ten specialist schools with the highest value-added scores for 2003 (*Source:* Compiled by the Specialist Schools Trust 2004)

| Rank | School name | LEA | Specialist status | Average KS2 points per pupil, 1998 | Pupils with 5+ A*–C grades at GCSE, 2003 | | Gross difference, better or worse |
					Predicted (%)	Actual (%)	
1	Sir John Cass Foundation and Redcoat Church of England Secondary School	Tower Hamlets	LC[a]	23·4	30	79	49
2	Selly Park Technology College for Girls	Birmingham	TC[b]	24·1	41	82	41
3	All Saints Catholic School and Technology College	Barking and Dagenham	TC	25·5	50	89	39
4	The Cardinal Wiseman Roman Catholic School	Ealing	TC	25·9	55	93	38
5	Loxford School of Science and Technology	Redbridge	TC	23·4	30	65	35
6	Greensward College	Essex	TC	26·0	55	88	33
7	Ernest Bevin College	Wandsworth	SC[c]	23·8	29	60	31
8	The Hathershaw Technology College	Oldham	TC	22·6	22	52	30
9	Small Heath School	Birmingham	TC	23·5	31	60	29
10	Seven Kings High School	Redbridge	TC	25·3	49	78	29

[a] LC, Language College.
[b] TC, Technology College.
[c] SC, Sports College.

GCSE grades. Twenty-five per cent reached the GCSE standard in 2003, but no less significantly, the school has become a more orderly environment. His school has many refugee children of diverse ethnic origins who do not speak English at home. And it is an inner city school with its own particularly difficult challenges. To change the school discipline was crucial. Among the techniques Mr Atkinson uses is a strong emphasis on teaching and learning. He believes if the students have minds focused on learning, it leaves less room for misbehaviour. This is combined with a zero tolerance of physical violence and bullying. Mr Atkinson and his senior staff patrol the corridors and are linked by walkie-talkies so that staff resources can be concentrated where need arises.

Despite the best efforts of many over the years, there are still around 50,000 primary and secondary pupils who skip school without permission on any given school day. More than 9,000 pupils were also permanently excluded from school in 2003. Truancy is not just a problem for the pupils who miss vital lessons. It is also a sign that a school is not succeeding. This is why successful schools set themselves the challenge of maximising attendance. They insist on regular attendance so that children can keep up with the work in class. An increasing number of schools use smart cards to take attendance not only in the mornings and afternoons but also for every class. Lord Harris, sponsor of 12 city technology colleges (CTCs), academies and specialist schools, believes that attendance is key to improving performance. When the Sylvan School in Croydon became Harris CTC in 1990, attendance was poor. Today it is 97 per cent and results have improved from 11 per cent of pupils achieving five good grades at GCSE to 93 per cent in 2003.

The school uniform has also come back into fashion, and with good reason it is now required in most schools. Besides helping to create a sense of community and pride in belonging to the school, the use of uniforms also makes it easier to spot children absent from the school in neighbouring streets and shopping areas. In addition, school uniform removes competitive dressing pressures where children show off expensive clothing, which sometimes creates behavioural problems.

To instil a caring yet disciplined ethos takes time and considerable dedication. On a visit to Bacon's CTC one of the authors was told by a Year 13 student, who had been at the school since before it became a CTC, that bullying was a serious problem in the old school, and the older children were often the perpetrators. He said that it had taken a number of years to change the ethos. Now the older children act as mentors to the younger children. Norham Community Technology College in Newcastle instituted a hugely successful initiative called 'Be a buddy not a bully' which has been copied elsewhere.

One of the greatest causes of failure in inner city schools is the placing of large numbers of excluded children in unpopular and under-subscribed schools, which because they rank low on parental preference, have places available. This places an intolerable burden on these schools. While violence cannot be tolerated and may lead to permanent exclusion, without proper alternative provision, it can simply export the problem to another school. There is now more provision in pupil referral units, but pupils are frequently moved on after a short while. In the absence of such alternatives, one can understand why some, like Tim Brighouse the former Director of Education in Birmingham, discouraged schools from permanently excluding children since this led to a high concentration of pupils with behavioural problems in a few schools.

A key ingredient in fostering good discipline is developing good relationships between staff and pupils. As the Tooley and Howe study put it:

> At Brooke Weston CTC, the building design has contributed to the development of a self-regulating school. There is no staff room, no 6th form block, no secret coffee hole to which staff escape from the mêlée. But there is no mêlée. Computer areas are built into the corridors as open learning spaces for the use of both students and staff. There are no remote staircases as stairs are located at the major junctions of each floor, close to high traffic areas such as reception, auditorium and dining areas.

In other words, trust in students is at the heart of the educational philosophy driving the school. This may sound unreal to some head teachers of underperforming schools in socially challenged areas – and it is true that the fundamentals need to be tackled first. But recognising that school organisation and structures influence behaviour is an important next stage.

Drug dealers can be a particularly malign influence on schools. The sad experience of a previously successful technology college in the Midlands, which was badly affected by local drug dealing is a cautionary tale. The school had the misfortune to be located in an area taken over by drug dealers. Two drug dealers were shot and killed near the gates of the school, in a dispute over territories. The resulting uproar badly affected the perception of the school by prospective parents. Standards then declined and the school lost its specialist status. Schools not only need to work with the police to combat this scourge, they need students and parents actively to take a stand against the incursion of drugs into the school. On a practical level, CCTV to monitor any drug dealers near the school and improved measures to make a school's perimeter secure both have a part to play. It is hardly surprising that many schools now employ permanent security at their gates.

Parents are crucial in restoring discipline to a previously failing school. Most parents care passionately about the education of their children. The fault in the past has been to make it difficult for parents, especially those from ethnic minorities who do not speak English, to work with their school. St Paul's Way School in Tower Hamlets dramatically improved its performance when its principal until

2003, Martyn Coles, decided that he would work closely with the majority of his parents, who were Bangladeshi, a significant number of them one parent families who did not speak English. By employing Bangladeshi speaking receptionists and giving English classes to the mothers in the evening, Martyn Coles gained their support and the performance of the school improved dramatically.

Active sports and after-school programmes also play an important role, particularly in boys' schools. Some successful schools now open at 7.30 in the morning to allow working mothers the opportunity to bring their children to school before work and remain open to 6.00 in the evening to avoid children being turned onto the streets when their parents are still working.

Being innovative with the curriculum

One of the early successes of the CTCs was to introduce cross-curricular dimensions to learning. In other words, they recognised that it is possible to learn aspects of one subject through another subject; and that doing so strengthens the teaching of both. This can either be done by incorporating facets of mathematics or English, for example, into each subject, as the Key Stage 3 strategies for 11–14-year-olds recommend. Or, it can mean setting aside time for special projects or activities at a time in the week or term when the regular curriculum is suspended. For example, the first CTC, Kingshurst in Solihull, suspends normal classes for a week twice a year so that each year group can work on a team project. In one such week, a number of teams in each year group designed model bridges. This involved them in three subjects: science, mathematics and design technology. The team whose model bridge withstood the simulated weight of goods vehicles crossing the bridge won the prize. This cross-curricular approach brought theoretical physics, mathematical formula and design technology to life. The early CTCs, being independent schools, were also exempt from regulations, which prevented the teaching of BTEC (Business Technology) National Diplomas in schools. These courses were soon modified to become the General National Vocational Qualifications (GNVQs) in such subjects as business, science and information technology (IT). These became so popular that in 2003 15 per cent of the entire GCSE cohort of 600,000, that is, 100,000 children, took a GNVQ qualification.

Thomas Telford School has produced an online version of GNVQ IT (accessible via http:www.ttsonline.net), which has proved so successful that with the profits earned from the sales of the course, Telford has been able to sponsor two academies and 70 specialist schools. The Telford approach teaches the use of IT across the curriculum, believing it to be a tool to assist learning rather than a subject by itself.

Many sports colleges use PE to develop students' wider skills and performance in all areas of the curriculum and school life. Students' leadership skills are developed and enhanced, for example through a range of challenging outdoor and adventurous activities, through taking responsibility for supporting and guiding younger pupils' learning in the playground and by being given a clear student voice. In addition, PE is successfully combined with many other curriculum areas to give exciting opportunities, such as designing and making the next trainer shoe in D&T, monitoring the associated physiological changes of an elite athlete in science and preparing our journalists of the future with a range of sports reporting opportunities.

Perhaps the most innovative development of the curriculum in recent years has been in after-hours activities, which have been actively supported with government and lottery grants in many schools. Many specialist schools arrange supervised after-class activities in the 3.00 to 5.00 period in the afternoon. But such activities are also scheduled at breakfast and in the lunch times. The most popular types of extra-curricular activities reported by the NFER in their study were:

- Computer clubs and other ICT activities;
- The arts: drama, music and dance;
- Language clubs, trips and exchange programmes;
- Sports clubs and activities;
- Duke of Edinburgh award scheme;
- Optional lunchtime classes and breakfast clubs;
- Summer schools;
- Classes for the gifted and talented;
- After-hours homework classes.

One student interviewee in the NFER study was very enthusiastic about the variety of opportunities in his school, 'There is a club for everything,' he said.

The use of ICT, wireless technology and the wonderful world of the Internet

The last ten years have seen the transformation of education through the use of computer-based learning and the Internet. The early technology colleges pioneered the use of ICT in schools and learned through hard experience what works and what fails. Millions of pounds were invested in both hardware and software, and a significant proportion of it was ineffectual. However, lessons have been learned. In the first place, it was necessary to train teachers in the effective use of ICT. Even with recent progress, a quarter of secondary school teachers still say that they are not confident in the use of ICT in the classroom, and many more rarely realise its potential.

But the gains can be extraordinary. Cornwallis Technology College, a former secondary modern school in Kent, now a successful technology college and Microsoft Partner School, is a leader in the use of ICT and has transformed its results. Every teacher is competent in the use of multimedia projectors and linked wireless laptops. Year 7 pupils are given intensive instruction in the use of the computer. Laptop trolleys, which can be moved easily from classroom to classroom, ensure every child has access to a computer. The use of wireless technology has removed the need for expensive hardware to maintain fibre optic cables. Students have become avid users of the Internet. The Cornwallis has twice won national awards for its website.

Thomas Telford CTC uses TypeQuick learning materials for learning keyboard skills so that within a few weeks of arrival, its Year 7 pupils have acquired basic competency in touch-typing – a skill which will prove invaluable throughout their lives. John Kelly Girls' Technology College in Brent has pioneered the use of the American SUCCESSMAKER literacy and numeracy software which has had excellent results in improving both reading and mathematics skills. This method was originally developed by Pat Suppes at Stanford University for use in US prisons; it is now used in 6,000 schools worldwide. A teacher who has been trained in the use of the software can supervise as many as 15 pupils at a time, each at a different level of attainment. Schools using SUCCESSMAKER for just 30 minutes a day per pupil report that reading skills increased dramatically in just three months.

Brooke Weston CTC ensures every child has access to a computer at home linked by broadband to the school's central server. Homework assignments can be completed online and more advanced students can progress at the speed which suits them. Wireless technology will in a short time bring the benefits of the use of the Internet to all schools, even those in remote areas. But considerable investment will be required if the full benefits of the Internet are to be made available to both teachers and pupils.

Changes to the working day and the length of terms

When the National Curriculum was introduced in 1988 there were widespread complaints that there would not be sufficient hours in the week to allow all ten subjects to receive adequate attention. This concern was aggravated by the gradual reduction which had taken place over the years in the number of hours each pupil spends in class each week. One of the authors attended St Marylebone Grammar School in the fifties, when pupils arrived at school at 8.30 a.m. and left at 4.30 p.m., with a 15-minute break in the morning and a 45-minute lunch break. All the rest of the 35 hours a week was spent in class apart from one afternoon devoted to sports and a daily assembly of 15 minutes. While the situation is improving, many schools today spend fewer than 25 hours a week in class. Until recently there was no legal requirement on the number of hours of lessons which each child must be given each week, although all schools are required by national regulations to meet no less than 380 half sessions a year. This allows for 70 days of school holidays a year excluding weekends. Happily there is now a minimum requirement of 24 hours of class time per week for secondary school pupils.

By contrast the industrious Japanese secondary pupils both spend more hours in class per day (typically seven against five in England) and attend school for more days in the year (typically 240 days against 190 in England). Richard Lynne (*Educational Achievement in Japan: Lessons for the West*) estimates that in a school year, the Japanese child will have as many as 1,500 hours of lessons compared to 950 for the English child.[8] This is not to argue that Japanese educational methods should be adopted wholesale: the pressures there are extreme. But it is to suggest that a better medium should be reached – and some schools have shown that this can happen.

The City Technology Colleges pioneered the use of both longer school days and five eight-week terms compared to the usual longer three terms. Increasingly schools organise breakfast clubs and after-school activities. Many pupils benefit from Supplementary Schools, which recently received the welcome recognition of the DfES. Summer and Easter activities are increasingly common. And the potential for change has been further enhanced by the radical proposal of the Local Government Association for a six-term year, which many local education departments have already adopted.

By focusing on individual learning, schools can create an ethos of achievement for all

A focus on achievement for every pupil is probably the most valuable attribute of a high performing school. This general focus on achievement creates an ethos of high expectation for every pupil and huge pride in achievement. In the NFER study, the researchers were told again and again that a focus on individual learning helped to create an ethos of valuing achievement.

> This focus on achievement and high expectation for all was very much centred on the individual *per se* but also on all students regardless of academic ability. As one school prospectus outlined: 'All girls and staff are encouraged and enabled to develop their skills, talents and potential to the full regardless of nationality, ethnicity, ability – both intellectually and physically – social circumstances, age, gender or religion.'

---

[8] R. Lynn, *Educational Achievement in Japan: Lessons for the West* (London, Macmillan/Social Affairs Unit, 1988).

The Government has recognised the importance of this approach in what the School Standards Minister David Miliband calls 'personalised learning'. By demonstrating that all pupils are capable of doing well in something, schools can remove, especially among boys, the anti-learning culture from many inner city schools. By making it 'cool' to work, high performing schools remove embarrassment about academic success and discourage abuse between students about being a swot.

In one school cited by the NFER study, the head teacher emphasised that changing staff expectations of students was a very important factor behind their success. He noted that when he first arrived at the school, there were certain students who were not entered for any examinations. He set about changing the culture of the school to one in which it is expected that every student could be entered for examinations. He stressed that the school's ethos was to convince students that they can and will achieve, and to share the student's aspirations. He remarked to the NFER researchers: 'They seem to buy into that culture.' This was a view reinforced by one of his teachers, who said: 'There's an ethos of high standards . . . we expect everyone, whatever their ability, to do ten GCSEs and they do!'

The sense that everyone can succeed was reflected in the students' comments. For example, one student emphasised: 'If you're willing to work and you're motivated then they'll help you to get to where you want to go. Or if you want to do better in subjects, then they're willing to sit down [with you]. Even if you're not so well motivated, they'll still push you to your full potential; they won't let it lie.' As another student put it: 'It's such a well-rounded school. If you're not good at an academic subject, you could be good at something else. Your teachers will push you to achieve your potential in everything.'

Another head teacher interviewed by the NFER stressed that building students' confidence and self-esteem is key. 'We use specialist status as a way to boost self-esteem for the whole school.' Individual target setting provides every pupil with the goal to achieve and this is linked to their ability level. But some pupils used to failure will find this approach challenging. One pupil commented to an NFER researcher 'It's made it quite hard sometimes when I haven't done well. I thought I was a failure but I am getting over that now and I have started to think that if my teacher says I can do it then I can succeed.' Intrinsic to this focus on the individual is the use of mentoring and tutor groups. Some schools use a house system instead of a year group system. This means that students have the same house form tutor through their time at school. Students value friendship and trust with their teacher. Concerns that this will undermine the teacher's authority have proved to be unfounded. Rather the reverse seems to be the case; the evidence is that it actually strengthens a teacher's authority and respect. Students appreciate the work teachers undertake on their behalf. A student commented to a NFER researcher:

'You see how hard the teacher works so you think you should work hard as well.'

Relationships between pupils are important in fostering a peer-group culture that supports success and hard work. One student emphasised that, in her school, doing well was not frowned upon by her friends, but celebrated. 'Your friends are proud of you,' she said. 'They encourage you to go for things like prefect or monitor.'

The support of parents and the use of older pupils as mentors

As we have seen, St Paul's Way School in Tower Hamlets dramatically increased its success by involving parents in the school. While a small minority of parents fails to support their children's schooling, most care passionately about the education of their children. And this is no less true in the inner cities than in the leafy suburbs. Indeed, most parents of inner city children know only too well that success in today's intensely competitive job market place requires the skills which modern jobs demand.

But schools are often unsure about how best to involve parents. The most important way to do so is by removing any blockages in the system. This means going beyond the statutory and often sterile parents' evening. Parents should be trusted with regular updates of their children's progress – examples of which we see in Chapter 6. They should be able to visit the school freely, without the need to make appointments. There should be an active parent–teacher association and strong parent governors. Indeed, parents can play an even greater role. One school has outsourced the catering and cleaning of the school to a parents' co-operative. Not surprisingly, both the quality of service is outstanding and, more importantly, the feedback given by the parents' co-operative to the head teacher about what is going on in the school is invaluable. The days of a bureaucratic local education authority (LEA) which conspired with some of the teaching unions to make state education a secret garden are over. Parents have indeed a right to know what is going on. They can give invaluable support to their child's education.

Older students can give similarly valuable support. The state of Georgia in the USA, under the leadership of its then governor, now US Senator, Zell Miller, developed two exciting initiatives which offer valuable lessons. Under his HOPE Scholarship program,[9] the proceeds of a state lottery were used to provide

---

[9] HOPE is an acronym for Helping Outstanding Pupils Educationally – the website address is www.gsfc.org/HOPE/Index.cfm.

free higher education on a means-tested basis to students maintaining at least a B average in their studies. A condition of this support is that such students must provide mentoring once a week to one or more high school students at risk of dropping out. This use of peer-group mentors has proved very successful. Another effective measure to raise standards is the Georgia P–16 Initiative.[10] P stands for educational programmes mainly in literacy and numeracy in rural areas to pre-school pupils and 16 stands for the last year of the four year US undergraduate degree course. By encouraging secondary schools to support primary schools and further and higher education to support secondary, the state of Georgia has raised its educational standards considerably. In a similar way, the then Education Secretary, David Blunkett in 1997 transformed the specialist school movement by requiring specialist secondary schools to work closely and support their feeder primary schools. The use of sixth formers to mentor and to help Year 7 and 8 pupils is also now becoming increasingly widespread. Not only does this help the younger children, it also helps the sixth former to develop a sense of responsibility.

On the next pages are included a self diagnosis and checklist for schools to determine whether or not they qualify for great school status.

---

[10] More information on the Georgia P–16 Initiative is available at education.gsu.edu/p16/p16overview.html.

How does your school measure up on the NFER criteria?

This is a checklist for head teachers and governors, which goes beyond the league tables, to determine whether or not their school is a great school.

1 Examination results

    (a) What was the average Key Stage 2 points per pupil of your GCSE cohort when they entered as Year 7 pupils five years ago? ....

    (b) Using David Jesson's value-added formula (see Appendix 1), what should be the percentage of pupils obtaining 5+ A*–C at GCSE or equivalent for the same group of pupils?..%

    (c) What was the actual percentage of pupils obtaining 5+ A*–C grades or their equivalent at GCSE?..%

    (d) What was the value added for your school (compare the actual results with the predicted)?...

2 Are incoming Year 7 children given reading and numeracy tests and if necessary remedial support in these areas?..

3 Does each child in every year group have specific targets for achievement in each subject?..

4 Is your school oversubscribed? Yes ☐ No ☐

    (a) Number of places available...

    (b) Number of applications for Year 7 entry for latest year...............

5 Exclusions

    (a) How many pupils were permanently excluded from your school last year?...

    (b) Is the number of permanent and fixed-term exclusions falling? Yes ☐ No ☐

6 What is the percentage of pupils staying in full-time education post-16 (either by staying on in the school or elsewhere)?......................................%

7 If your school has post-16 provision, what is the percentage of 18-year-olds gaining entrance to university or other post-secondary education?...........%

8 What is the annual percentage turnover of your
(a) teaching staff?...%
(b) support staff?..%

9 How extensive is your school's programme of extra-curricular activities (tick one)?
(a) More than 10 hours a week ☐
(b) 5–10 hours a week ☐
(c) Less than 5 hours a week ☐

10 School opening hours
(a) School premises open at...a.m.
(b) School premises closed to pupils at....................................p.m.
(c) Breakfast is offered Yes ☐ No ☐

Most great schools will have both a positive value added and be able to answer most of the above questions in a positive way.

Improvement techniques

Which of the practices listed below are used in your school?

1 Strong and effective leadership team Yes ☐ No ☐

2 Strategies to attract and retain good teachers and support staff Yes ☐ No ☐

3 Administration by secondary school of reading and numeracy tests for incoming Year 7 children with rigorous implementation of support programmes as required Yes ☐ No ☐

4 Setting of specific targets for achievement in each subject/for each child/for every year group Yes ☐ No ☐

5 Maintenance of discipline and order producing high standards of behaviour through strategies which include involvement of parents, support staff and use of older pupils as mentors

Checklist	Yes	No
Involvement of parents	☐	☐
Use of support staff	☐	☐
Use of older pupils as mentors	☐	☐
Use of sanctions	☐	☐
Use of incentives	☐	☐
Specific measures to stop bullying	☐	☐
Anti-drug and substance abuse measures	☐	☐

6 Innovative teaching techniques, including use of non-traditional awards and examinations Yes ☐ No ☐

7 Use of information communications technology as a learning tool

Checklist		
	Yes	**No**
Access to broadband width	☐	☐
Wireless access to the Internet	☐	☐
Teachers trained in the use of ICT	☐	☐
Number of laptops available to teachers		
Number of laptops available to pupils		
Number of classrooms with whiteboards		

8 School day
  (a) Do you use a longer school day? Yes ☐ No ☐
  (b) What is the typical average number of classroom teaching hours per pupil per week (the national average is 25)?——
  (c) How many days in class are given each year (the typical length is 190)——
  (d) Use of longer terms. Do you use a 3-term year ☐ 5-term year ☐ 6-term year ☐ other ☐

9 Is there a clear focus on personalised learning to encourage a school-wide ethos of achievement? Yes ☐ No ☐

10 Active involvement of parents in the school? Yes ☐ No ☐

2

Starting out: the transition from primary to secondary school

To any 11-year-old, the shock of leaving a primary school, which usually has fewer than 400 pupils (and is sometimes far smaller), for a large secondary school with more than 1,000 pupils, and sometimes as many as 2,000, should not be underestimated. After all, at primary school, not only does everyone know everybody else, but pupils usually work with a single teacher who covers the whole curriculum. To move from the comparative safety of that often comfortable and reassuring atmosphere into what can seem like the rough and tumble of a secondary school can be traumatic. Not only is a pupil going from being an older child at their former school to being among the youngest at the new school, there is a new approach to learning introduced at the same time. There are usually different teachers for each subject. Pupils often have to move between classes after every period. Homework is more demanding. The expectation that you will take a more rigorous approach to study can come as a shock. Students are drawn from much larger catchment areas, and it can take far longer to get from home to school. On top of all that, the sheer physical size of 18-year-olds, especially boys, compared to 11-year-olds is itself daunting, particularly in those schools where there is still a culture of bullying. And after a summer break, children who are tested in English and mathematics are often found to have regressed significantly from the achievement recorded both in the national Key Stage 2 tests and their primary school teacher's own assessment. It is hardly surprising that many head teachers have started to experiment with new ways to make the transition from primary to secondary school easier.

This is why wise secondary school head teachers are paying increasing attention to this potential trauma for their incoming Year 7 pupils. The best secondary schools address the problem well before the age of transfer. They develop close links with their feeder primary schools, making contact with children and their families long before they enter the secondary school rolls. Through masterclasses and opportunities to meet their new teachers and classmates, they are able to break down the barriers which militate against successful transition. Of course, this is not an entirely altruistic gesture: not only does sensible transition planning help youngsters to adjust to a new environment, it also makes them more willing to learn, and to do so in a disciplined manner. So, the school can gain through more productive Year 7 lessons and a more orderly environment.

John Kelly Girls' Technology College

One school which has taken this issue seriously is John Kelly Girls' Technology College in Brent, which employs a part-time member of staff to work closely with the school's feeder primary schools. Children from the primary schools are invited to John Kelly Girls' to use the SUCCESSMAKER literacy laboratory. Kathy Heaps, the school's head teacher since 1990, says there is a wide range of measures which she employs to tackle stress associated with moving from primary to secondary school.

'We begin seriously to address transition in Year 5, when the pupils are about nine years of age, though we do work with younger students in our specialist subjects when the pupils are as young as six or seven,' she explains. 'But we complement this work as children are starting their final year of primary schools by arranging a series of visits to our feeder schools. Our incoming head of Year 7 will visit our main feeder schools in early September, and she will be accompanied by two students who can talk about what life is really like starting in John Kelly Girls'. Their job is to "sell" the school to the primary, but it is also to answer questions honestly about life in Year 7. We find this is extremely effective as the girls have just completed one full year with us and their memories of the early days in Year 7 are still very real. The pupils in the primary school appreciate hearing from students as well as teachers what the school is like. They find it easier to ask the sort of questions they want answered, and to have their fears and concerns addressed.' But links between John Kelly Girls' and its feeder primaries are not confined to these 'welfare visits', important though they are. Indeed, there is a menu of activities here from which any secondary school could benefit. The links permeate a whole range of activities, from masterclasses to a special homework club. There are masterclasses in four subjects, which are geared at nine to 11-year-olds in the school's feeder primaries, offering pupils the chance to learn more about mathematics, science, design and technology and information and communications technology (ICT). The classes are offered to gifted and talented students in Years 5 and 6 from the main feeder schools on Saturday mornings. Ms Heaps says they are very popular with students and their families. And while such provision is an important part of the community focus in specialist schools, the classes are rewarding not only for the pupils who participate in them, but also for the staff who teach them.

Another activity which can be shared between a primary and secondary school is homework provision. The John Kelly Girls' Homework Club is not only open to all the students at the secondary school, it is also attended by girls in Years 5 and 6 from the main feeder school, Braintcroft Primary. It helps that the primary school is just across the road from its secondary sister school, and the practical arrangements involved for such links are obviously easier where schools are close together. Nevertheless, this link can prove a great introduction for children to their future school. 'If they come here as students as some have, they find it far less intimidating,' says Kathy Heaps, who also makes a point of giving extra support to any pupils who are underachieving or in need of particular help, and ensuring that gifted and talented students are given the chance to use their talents. But such programmes need not just be about giving girls a quiet place to study. John Kelly Girls' lays on extras that include story-telling, creative writing courses and computer projects. The club is staffed by teachers, classroom assistants, administrative staff and sixth form students, with the school's Learning Resources Manager taking overall responsibility for keeping it going.

The John Kelly Girls' example is instructive in other ways too, for it embodies many of the activities which other successful schools have tried in part. Specialist schools have a particular advantage – and an extra duty – when it comes to developing such links. Some language colleges develop primary languages programmes, for example, which have given local youngsters a taster of European languages well before they started in secondary school. Such activities will be increasingly important as the Government seeks to encourage language learning to start at Key Stage 2 across the country. There are similar opportunities with all the specialisms, as part of their community focus, to build such links. As part of John Kelly Girls' specialist work, technology teachers spend a part of every week teaching pupils from Year 6 in one of the main feeder schools. 'Sometimes this is team-teaching with the class teacher; sometimes it will allow the primary teacher to have a very valuable free period,' explains Ms Heaps. 'The primary school pupils also get the opportunity to come to the college to use specialist equipment in information and communications technology, or design technology. The school's technological resources are also put to good use when, in the spring and summer terms, pupils from Braintcroft Primary come over to the college to use the SUCCESSMAKER program, which is one of the best computer programs for teaching reading and mathematics, on our network. This gives them a much appreciated boost in literacy and numeracy, ahead of their national Key Stage 2 tests.'

Such links need not simply be confined to the school's specialism. Primary schools often find it difficult to lay on the extra arts and music classes that children and parents want. John Kelly Girls' has met this gap by offering art lessons to Year 5 students from its main feeder schools. There is also a popular Saturday music school, which caters for 200 students, bringing together pupils from the feeder primary schools, John Kelly Girls' and the neighbouring secondary school, John Kelly Boys' Technology College. Students receive three hours of tuition, for which they pay a very reasonable £12 a week. They get the chance to use solo instruments, to do ensemble and choral work, to learn to use keyboards and to learn more about the theory of music. Although the lessons are open to secondary and primary pupils, they are particularly popular with younger students, and around 90 per cent come from the feeder primary schools. Needless to say, the school is also immensely popular with the parents, since it is effectively looking after their children from 9.00 a.m. until 1.00 p.m. every Saturday, a time when many of them want to get their weekly shopping done.

So, many potential students gain some familiarity with the school through a lively series of learning opportunities. These activities are not confined to term time. One of the earliest innovations of the new Labour government in 1997 was to support the establishment of summer schools, based at secondary schools for pupils from local primaries. The original schools focused on literacy and numeracy, targeting those needing remedial help. More recently, the programme has included a much wider range of activities for the more able students. John Kelly Girls' runs a summer school for those pupils who are starting at the college in the autumn. It also offers taster days and an induction day.

There are three summer schools every year at John Kelly Girls' Technology College, which like most summer schools run for between eight and ten days. Schools can run them at any time during the summer holidays – John Kelly Girls' offers them immediately after the secondary school breaks up in July. The pupils, who have done their national tests in May, receive between 40 and 50 hours of tuition. Two of the summer schools are geared at those who did not gain a level 4 in English or mathematics, so they focus on literacy or numeracy. A third school caters for the more able students, the gifted and talented strand. Timing is something that should be discussed not only with staff, but also with potential students and their families. 'There is always a difficult choice to be made about when you run the summer schools, because families will want to plan holidays, as will our own staff who teach at the schools,' explains Ms Heaps. 'We have tried many variations. At one stage we did five days in July with a further three at the very end of August just before the students join us. But after much deliberation, we have now settled on up to ten days as soon as we break up in July. We offer 25 places in each school, so we can accommodate half of those who will join us in the autumn. We would really like to run the provision for the whole cohort but these are not funded.'

Taster days are a good way of giving potential students the chance to experience a small sample of life at their new school. At John Kelly Girls', they take place in June and July every year, and are open to Year 5 pupils from the main feeder schools. The pupils spend a whole day at their potential new school. Not only do they see the school's facilities, they are taught by some of the staff, and are looked after in the playground and the dining hall by Year 8 girls who have been designated as welfare representatives. 'We've found that the day is very valuable in giving them a real insight into life at John Kelly Girls' just when they and their families are starting to think a lot more about their choice of secondary school,' says Ms Heaps. These taster days can be reinforced by an induction day to introduce pupils to school life. John Kelly Girls' does this in the July before they start. 'We find that doing this before the summer holidays can allay many of their concerns which might build up over the summer, as their first day in secondary school approaches,' explains Ms Heaps. All the new students spend a whole day at their new school, gaining the chance to meet their future classmates and to be introduced to the teachers who will be teaching them in the autumn. They also meet girls from Years 8 to 11. Those attending the induction day will also receive two booklets. One is produced by the college for parents and carers and the other has been produced by existing students for the new girls. At the same time, the head of Year 7 will spend time with Year 6 class teachers in the feeder primaries to exchange information about the newcomers, so that the school can have the fullest picture about their strengths and weaknesses.

Timetabling is always an important issue, as we shall see in later chapters. At John Kelly Girls' the transition between years (after Year 7) is helped by starting the new year's timetable in July rather than September. The school believes this makes it far easier to make a productive and flying start in the first week back after the holidays.

Once children start in their new school, the transition process needs to continue. Another good idea is to give new pupils the run of the school for a day before their fellow pupils return from their holidays. This can help them to find their own way around before the whole place appears too crowded. 'Day one in September is different for the new students,' Ms Heaps explains about what happens in John Kelly Girls'. 'They come in a day earlier so they have the building to themselves and they can get used to the geography of a large secondary school, which can be daunting even if they have been here for other activities or the induction day. And it is certainly a new challenge coping with a timetable which means they have to move between six different classrooms a day, when they are used to their own desk in primary school. So, on this first day, they will spend a good deal of time with their new form tutor and will also have help from their own Welfare Representative, one of around 15 who are selected on merit from the students and serve throughout Year 8.'

Many schools re-test pupils to assess whether or not they need extra help or stimulation. The Key Stage 2 tests can offer some information, but many schools also use other tests such as the London Reading Test. John Kelly Girls' does this in the first week of the September term. 'We used this before SATs were introduced, and we continue to use it as it allows us to compare new data with that on our intakes dating back to 1993,' says Ms Heaps. 'We find it provides the most accurate record of any shifts in our cohort.'

Despite recent progress from the National Literacy Strategy, about one in four 11-year-olds arrive in secondary schools without having achieved level 4 in Key Stage 2 English. Many inner city schools report that for their own intakes, the proportion of 11-year-olds behind in reading is substantially greater. This is one reason why schools like John Kelly Girls' do their own testing of each new intake. As well as the London Reading Test, new girls are also tested in their cognitive ability, using tests that are taken by most schools that are part of the Government's Excellence in Cities programme of urban school reform.

All these tests give the school a valuable body of data from which it can monitor and measure progress. They also help to identify which students need remedial help and which could benefit most from gifted and talented programmes. In schools which use setting by subject ability or streaming, it can help to identify which might be the most appropriate initial sets and streams, too, providing additional indicators to other information. And they solve a problem which the Qualifications and Curriculum Authority (QCA) needs to address, the late arrival of valuable individual data from the Key Stage 2 tests.

'We don't receive all the KS2 data in time for it to be useful,' says Ms Heaps. 'Some still has not arrived by half-term, and we also find that tests taken with no prior teaching or revision give a more accurate representation of the students' actual ability levels in the areas being tested. We sometimes have students for example, with a level 4 in Science but with a low level 2 in English and we wonder how can they access the questions in Science? We use the results of these tests to inform teaching in Year 7 and to direct support both for students with learning difficulties and gifted and talented students.'

But it should not all be about testing, of course. It is remarkable how quickly the links between the old and new schools can be severed. Yet, there is surely no reason why this should be so. Indeed, it is the almost total severance of such links that can make the transition so difficult for some students. This is why John Kelly Girls' are asked to write back to their Year 6 class teacher and their head teacher, and invite them to come to a tea-party at John Kelly Girls'. 'That keeps the link and helps them to move on,' explains Ms Heaps. 'On the day, the girls proudly show their former teachers the work they have been doing at John Kelly Girls' and they usually put on a display of music or drama. They absolutely love seeing their teachers arrive and are most disappointed if any can't make it. They also continue the process they benefited from, by writing letters to the Year 6 class at their old school to tell them about John Kelly Girls'.'

Another feature of John Kelly Girls' that is particularly valued is the school's Breakfast and Homework Club, which runs from 7.30 a.m. on school mornings. 'We open early to provide homework support in the Learning Resources Centre and breakfast for girls who leave home without eating,' says Ms Heaps. 'The Homework Club is staffed by an experienced teaching colleague who also happens to be a year manager. We find that the majority of students who attend in the early mornings are the younger students whose parents have to leave for work and naturally don't want their daughter to be left alone at home.'

How other schools tackle primary to secondary transition

The activities offered by John Kelly Girls' are in many ways exemplary. By getting to know their Year 7 pupils before they arrive, secondary schools can also do other crucial assessment tasks. John Kelly and many other schools use cognitive reasoning tests to more closely identify the range of ability in their incoming class. They then use this data to assign pupils to tutor groups as well as determining which pupils should be in the first track sets for each subject and those requiring remedial help. Many schools use the diagnostic data to set achievement targets for each 11-year-old in the key subjects of mathematics, science and English and if a specialist school, their specialist subject. Sophisticated databases ensure that every teacher has easy access to this data. Progress is reviewed at frequent intervals. Some schools produce monthly written reports to parents on the progress of their child, which means that parents can feel fully involved in their children's learning from day one. Schools like St Paul's Way School encourage parents, especially those of Year 7 children, to 'drop in' without appointment to discuss the progress of their children.

But their need to re-test students after they start in secondary school suggests that improvements may be needed in the Key Stage 2 tests nationally. For John Kelly Girls' is not alone in its concerns. The Government was surprised and a little embarrassed when some students at its early summer schools appeared to have fallen back once they were re-tested in the autumn, despite intensive tuition at the summer schools. Many other schools use the London Reading Test or similar tests to assess their own intake. When they are using setting by subject ability, this can be particularly important. But it also identifies quickly where remedial tuition may be needed to ensure that pupils can keep up with their classmates in the secondary curriculum.

Some of those head teachers at those secondary schools which have been concerned about the validity of Key Stage 2 tests, believe that it would be better if secondary schools administered the tests themselves. They believe this would solve two problems. First, it would ensure that the secondary schools had immediate access to the test data. Currently many schools complain that they do not receive the Key Stage 2 data for up to one third of their pupils (either directly from the primary school or from the LEA) until November. Secondly, having the test administered by the secondary school, with external marking and validation to ensure standards and to avoid pupils being marked down in order to improve value-added scores, would also give greater confidence in the validity of the test results. There is a concern that there is too much coaching for Key Stage 2 tests. Accountability for the primary school could still be maintained by requiring the secondary school to report back to the DfES the Key Stage 2 test results by primary school, which would allow primary school performance tables to continue to be published. As every child now has a unique computer number this should be possible to do.

The myriad activities at John Kelly Girls', of course, can be seen at other schools around the country, many of which have been developing innovations of their own. Slough Language College seconds some of its language teachers on a part-time basis to teach in the primary schools. Thomas Telford CTC also organises an induction programme in the autumn term. One unusual feature of this programme is that new pupils are taught to touch-type, making it far easier for them to work with computers in the college. Thomas Telford uses TypeQuick learning materials (Comprix is the UK distributor of the Australian company TypeQuick). Pupils learn elementary keyboard skills so that they should be able to type around 30 words a minute after ten hours of instruction. This acquisition of keyboard skills proves invaluable throughout secondary school. And with the ubiquity of computers in universities and the workplace, it is equally useful in higher education and employment.

Such programmes clearly ensure that 11-year-olds arrive for the start of term already knowing their new school and feeling confident of making a successful adjustment. Good attendance habits are also instilled in the first year. Many schools now use smart cards or other computer-based attendance records to take attendance. These schools track average actual attendance which sometimes average as much as 97 per cent rather than the more widely used measure of the proportion of pupils not in school for either authorised or unauthorised absence. Again, the support of parents is invaluable. While home–school agreements setting out the school's expectations of pupils in terms of attendance, behaviour and homework, are used by most schools, and have been a legal requirement since 1998, there is usually no requirement that parents sign such an agreement. Indeed the admissions rules governing state schools militate against such requirements. So, there is little sanction when it is broken, beyond the courts for persistent truancy or temporary exclusions for constant bad behaviour. Without a sense that these documents are serious agreements, they are often seen as being of too little practical value. This is why some CTCs, which are not bound by the same rules as other non-fee paying schools, require the parents of incoming Year 7 pupils to agree in writing to support the school's code of conduct.

A typical agreement might include:

- not arranging holidays during term time;
- a willingness to purchase a school uniform and ensuring the child comes to school wearing this uniform (many schools provide financial assistance for parents to purchase school uniforms and most schools work to keep costs down);
- ensuring that the child arrives punctually and attends regularly;
- helping children with their homework;
- agreeing to regular meetings with the child's tutor; and
- reporting problems such as bullying.

In return good schools agree to involve parents in the life of the school and to report at regular intervals on the progress being made by the child.

All of these preparatory steps help ensure a smooth transition from primary to secondary school. The secret is not just to ensure that when the important day arrives and the nervous 11-year-old, accompanied by an equally anxious parent, arrives at 'big' school for the first day of term, they get a special welcome. It is in building up those relationships in the months and years before, so that the big day is still one to remember, but it is not nearly so traumatic. And with the high mobility rate in inner city areas this sort of welcome and induction help is particularly important for those children transferring into the school during the term or in later year groups. One of this book's authors, Cyril Taylor well remembers his own traumatic experience in transferring from a school in Leeds to another in London at age 12. Due to a confusion about the date of the start of term, he arrived a day late. There were no arrangements for mentoring or help to learn what to do.

Year 11 pupils can also play a vital role in easing the transition. It is, after all, not so long since they made the same move themselves. Many schools now use sixth formers and older students to mentor Year 7 children. The system of mentoring has several advantages beyond the obvious one of helping younger pupils to adjust to 'big' school. Asking an older child to look after a young one helps to teach a sense of responsibility. It also counters any tendency of older children to bully younger ones.

Getting the transition right is the first stage in ensuring that pupils will have the chance to thrive in secondary school. That many schools now see it as an integral part of their activities can only be welcomed. And there is no doubt that a measure of the way in which a school is a good school is the extent to which it is willing to help its newest students.

Key points in this chapter

Plan the transition: It is important to plan the transition carefully, using a mixture of opportunities for new pupils and their families to experience life at their new school. Moving from small to large school environments can be traumatic, and has been identified as one reason why many pupils appear to fall back in Year 7. Such planning can start with Year 5 pupils from local primary schools.

Develop linked learning: By developing opportunities, such as homework and arts clubs, where older primary school pupils can benefit from the resources and facilities at the secondary school, they can gain an early insight into their new (or potential) school. These activities can relate to a school's specialism, and are often one way in which schools can meet their requirement to develop a community focus.

Visits and induction: Give new pupils the chance to get to know their new school, by offering them the chance to spend a day experiencing teaching and learning opportunities there. It can also be a good idea to have an induction day before school breaks up for the summer, to ease any concerns that may develop among new pupils over the holidays.

Make day one special: Consider opening the school to Year 7 a day before the rest of the pupils return. This will give them an opportunity to settle in without the threat of older, larger pupils. It is also an opportunity to give pupils an uninterrupted introduction to their timetable and curriculum, as well as school rules and activities.

Start gathering data early: Consider supplementing the data from Key Stage 2 tests (if you have it at pupil level) with other reputable tests, so that you can assess which pupils may need extra help, and which may benefit from gifted and talented programmes. Such assessments can also help to determine which sets may be appropriate in subjects which are set by subject ability. It will also help you to monitor and measure progress. The Government should consider ways of improving the flow of information from Key Stage 2 tests to secondary schools, perhaps even giving them the chance to administer the tests.

Don't break the link: Offer opportunities for students to keep in touch with their old primary school, at least in Year 7, perhaps by inviting former teachers or writing to Year 6 pupils. This not only helps them to move on without the break being too severe, it can also help to reassure those who will follow them.

Home–school agreements: There is a case for schools to make full use of home–school agreements, setting out the obligations and rights of parents, pupils and schools, covering issues such as homework, behaviour and attendance. But the Government should consider giving more schools the chance to attach sanctions where the agreement is being consistently broken, so that they are taken more seriously.

3

The drive for continuous improvement

In 2003, there were still 253 secondary schools in England where fewer than one in four of their pupils gained five good GCSE grades. Though this was a significant improvement on three years before, when the total had stood at 436, it was a reflection of how far some schools still need to travel to offer their students a decent standard of education. Perhaps unsurprisingly, many of these schools are located in socially disadvantaged areas. A high proportion of their pupils is eligible for free school meals and many have English as a second language. Raising standards of achievement certainly requires considerable determination. But for these students, more than any others, it is vital. And despite the urgency of raising standards, time is essential. Although improvement can start quickly, it will usually take several years to raise standards significantly.

Nor should we just be concerned about those schools with low overall GCSE results. An equally serious problem lies with those schools which are called the 'coasters': those that don't achieve as well as they should, given the ability of students entering the school. On average 53 per cent of pupils achieve five or more good GCSEs, a figure that includes selective and independent schools. But, despite faster than average improvements in many comprehensives, too many schools still have intakes of ability which would warrant much greater success than the national average. These schools too need plans of action to bring their performance closer to the achievement level which their ability intake would indicate.

This chapter looks at a wide variety of standard improvement techniques, some of which may be used by all schools; others are more appropriate to schools in areas of social disadvantage. In this chapter we will look at four schools in detail, because their stories offer lessons with wider potential application: Harris City Technology College in Norwood in the London Borough of Croydon, Archbishop Holgate's Science College in York, All Saints Technology College in the London

Borough of Barking and Dagenham and Kemnal Technology College in the London Borough of Bromley. In the next chapter, we will look specifically at how several failing schools have recovered, sometimes in a relatively short space of time, by adapting the most frequently used techniques for school improvement to their own cases. In Chapter 1 we identified ten common principles for a successful school:

- A good leadership team of the head teacher, heads of department and governing body;
- Ability to attract and retain good teachers;
- A focus on the basics such as literacy and numeracy;
- Setting of targets and use of data to monitor progress;
- Discipline and order;
- Curriculum innovation including use of vocational awards and International Baccalaureate;
- Extensive use of Information Communications Technology including linked wireless laptops and whiteboards;
- Consideration of a longer school day and/or non-traditional term dates;
- A focus on individual learning to create an ethos of achievement for all;
- Support of parents and use of older students as mentors.

But how does a school achieve these ten qualities of excellence? Clearly different circumstances require different approaches. Survey data from leading schools in the country indicated there are a number of common techniques. In this chapter, we will see how some schools used some of these techniques to great effect.

Using data and targets to foster improvement

The first step is the setting of challenging but realistic targets for improvement. This requires a careful audit of a school's strengths and weaknesses. What are the literacy and numeracy levels of incoming Year 7 pupils? Every teacher knows that children who cannot read cannot learn, yet it is surprising how many schools do not tackle this problem in a systematic and focused way. Targets for improvement cannot just concentrate on GCSE results at age 16 or A Level point counts at age 18. Possibly the most crucial period is Key Stage 3 – the period between age 11 and age 14. Successful schools will almost always set targets for improvement between Key Stage 2 and 3 in the key subjects of mathematics, science and above all English. A key part of a successful improvement plan will be its timescale, since very few schools can achieve instant results. Indeed, it may take five years before significant GCSE improvement is made – the same period from Year 7 to Year 11 when pupils take their GCSEs – and schools may face a damaging effect on morale if targets are missed in the interim, which highlights the importance of setting realistic targets in the first place. But they should also be reasonably challenging, or they are not worth setting.

The importance of data

Use of data is key to raising standards. Harris City Technology College in Croydon regards the communication of and access to accurate student performance data as crucial to raising pupil performance and spreading good practice. Harris uses the Central Management Information System (CMIS) supplied by Serco Learning. This keeps data on a central system under the following headings: students (including personal details, contacts, family information, 'events', examinations, attendance, exclusions and so on); staff; assessment (known as HARS – Harris Assessment Recording System); attendance (taken electronically twice a day); options; reports; applications; examinations; returns; timetable and cover. All the data is linked and any update to the data in one part of the system will feed through to other areas. No data has been lost in the past three years. Student data is kept up to date by two members of staff in the Student Information Centre. Other people have responsibility for other parts of the system. The data can be accessed by all staff, with various security levels in place. The system also has a web-based presence so it can be accessed remotely and the plan is to open access to students and parents, again with security levels. The power of the system is that the data can be viewed in a variety of ways – by individual, by tutor group, by year group and so on.

Assessment, recording and reporting

The key use of the data for school improvement lies in the assessment, recording and reporting system. For assessment to work in a coherent way there must be common criteria across the curriculum, and these should be applied across the college. Comparisons of student and teacher performance across subjects will inevitably throw up issues of variable performance. To measure performance the Harris system uses national norms: National Curriculum levels, subdivided into points for Key Stage 3, GCSE grades for Key Stage 4 and points again for Key Stage 5. The recording of the data feeds into the reporting of this information to management on a regular basis which enables them to formulate action plans, thus linking assessment directly to improvement strategies. Among other things, it highlights areas of underachievement. 'The use of data is objective, it removes subjective assessment and leaves no room for "excuses" because it is based on performance.'

Measuring pupil progress at Harris CTC

So, how does the system work for an individual pupil? Harris does its own entry level testing for each pupil before they start in the school at the age of 11 to establish a baseline. It is worth stressing that as a CTC, the college selects from the full range of ability of applicants in accordance with the criteria embodied in the Funding Agreement between the schools and Secretary of State for Education. Harris uses an NFER test to assess ability and take a predetermined number of students from nine bands of ability who have demonstrated the greatest aptitude for mathematics, science and technology. The college draws students from five London boroughs, providing a minimum of 90 places to Croydon residents and the remaining 90 places to Bromley, Lambeth, Southwark and Lewisham – and over 70 primary schools. The Key Stage 2 data from the primaries arrives at the college too late to be useful, so the college does its own tests – using the NFER non-verbal reasoning and London Reading tests. Pupils are then put into rank order by individual subject. Four bands are established: Band A (15%); Band B (35%); Band C (35%) and Band D (15%). At Key Stage 3 it is assumed that Band A pupils should progress by one National Curriculum level each year and so by three National Curriculum levels over the Key Stage. Other bands have a similar 'default' position, so there would be five points for Band B, four points for Band C and three points for Band D. Individual students are measured against these 'default' positions. The progress of each student is measured and recorded in half-termly units, requiring data input six times a year. As well as measuring progress in National Curriculum terms, marks are awarded on a scale of 1–5 for effort, presentation and ICT capability, represented by symbols such as circles and triangles on the report.

Reporting progress to parents

Keeping parents informed is an important part of the drive for continuous improvement. It helps to reinforce the messages being delivered in the school, and to enlist parental co-operation with teachers in raising standards. Harris goes far beyond the statutory requirement of reporting to parents once a year on their child's progress. Two computer-generated performance profiles are sent home each year plus one handwritten 'summative' annual report. The data in these reports are used to set targets. They are also used to inform choices at the end of Key Stage 3 when pupils preparing to do their GCSEs can either choose the Yellow Route (GCSE) or the Green Route (GCSE and double award GCSE).

The involvement of parents in this process is considered crucial. At the beginning of each academic year parents receive a curriculum synopsis as to what their children can be expected to learn over the coming year. There is a particularly detailed explanation of the system used for recording and monitoring progress at the beginning of Year 7. They also receive a Key Stage 3 booklet. Parents are invited to parents' evenings where they will meet up to a dozen staff. They are also invited to attend twice yearly individual 'academic tutoring' sessions with their child at which performance is analysed and targets set.

By 1996 the school was already popular, but parents really appreciate the additional information provided by CMIS and their involvement in their children's progress. Of course, all this has made the school even more popular. There are 1,200 applications for 180 Year 7 places but through the use of the NFER non-verbal reasoning test and its banding system, the school still maintains a comprehensive intake. Pupils appreciate regular information on their progress and they like the 'rank order' and banding, which helps to motivate them. They now understand achievement issues and the data they receive. Boys, for the first time, think it is 'cool' to excel in their studies.

Although this extensive reporting might appear to put a heavy burden on staff, all are trained in its use and most information is generated electronically. It is not a time waster because it highlights issues and areas of concern so clearly. Carol Bates, Principal and Chief Executive says: 'The system is very popular with staff, parents and pupils and has an elegant simplicity.' The key point of the data collected by the CMIS and HARS, and its reporting both internally and externally, is to highlight issues which need to be addressed, especially underperformance.

In the case of Harris CTC, back in 1999, the most important of these was the performance of boys, whose achievement levels lagged 18 per cent behind the girls. The difference nationally is still 10 per cent. Carol Bates, who is a believer in the value of Steven Covey's 'seven habits'[1] approach – which stresses the importance of ethos, leadership, student learning, innovation, quality control, organisation and structures, parents and community links – adopted a variety of strategies to address this issue. She devoted a whole INSET day for all college teaching and non-teaching staff to raise awareness of the issue and to look at the different learning styles of boys and girls. This training is repeated annually. Literacy was identified as a key issue for boys. Ways of making the curriculum more 'boy friendly' were considered and embedded in schemes of work. Issues such as coursework and time management were also addressed. Male underachievers were identified through HARS. Parents of these pupils (plus the parents of a much smaller number of girl underachievers) were invited to a 'raising achievement' evening. This is now a

---

[1] S. Covey, *The Seven Habits of Highly Effective People; Powerful lessons in personal change* (New York, Free Press, 1989).

regular event and attracts very good attendance. An intensive study skills day for Year 11 underachievers has been established as an annual event during the February half term. This is in addition to the existing revision sessions held after college, on Saturdays and during the holidays. Other college systems such as academic tutoring, senior management team progress reviews and feedback to parents, were also utilised to address the issue. By 2002 the proportion of boys achieving five good GCSEs at Harris was just 1 per cent behind that of girls, a significant improvement on the national achievement gap between the genders.

Other lessons from the Harris CTC story

Before it became a CTC in 1989, the secondary school which became Harris had been a deeply unpopular, failing comprehensive school. Only 12 per cent of its pupils achieved five or more A*–C grades at GCSE and there were no first-choice applications to the school. All the 450 pupils in the original school transferred to the new Harris CTC together with most of the staff, but there was an immediate change of head teacher with Lyndon Jones being appointed Principal. It took six years to turn the school around. But by 1996, 57 per cent of pupils were gaining at least five good GCSE passes, a figure significantly above the then national average. That result improved further in 1997, when 64 per cent of pupils achieved at least five good GCSE grades. But the results then entered a plateau, and dipped significantly in 1998 and 1999, before regaining some momentum in 2000 (Table 3.1). This presented a real challenge for the school: how to move significantly further forward.

In the early days, the school's chief sponsor, Lord Harris of Peckham, played a crucial role, with Lyndon Jones, in inspiring the staff and pupils to improve standards. When Carol Bates took over as Principal and Chief Executive of Harris CTC in September 1999 she had a clear challenge – to raise achievement and, in particular, to lift the percentage of pupils gaining five or more A*–C grades from 50/60 per cent closer to 90 per cent.

Table 3.1   GCSE progress at Harris CTC 1997–2003

Year	Pupils achieving 5+ A*–C grades (%)
1997	64
1998	53
1999	57
2000	68
2001	90
2002	91
2003	92

Carol Bates met the challenge using four techniques. We have looked in some detail at how she used performance data to identify key issues; and we have seen how that enabled a strategic focus on key areas such as the performance of boys. Equally important were raising awareness of the challenge among the whole-school community, particularly with parents; and the continuing professional development of staff. The introduction of GNVQ Part One in 1999 provided a valuable and innovative approach to teaching and learning which addressed the needs of those students not able to undertake 11 traditional GCSEs.

Ms Bates believes that success in raising standards comes from focusing on the key issues. 'The staff are constantly on the case,' she says. 'It's about never being complacent, about never taking your eye off the ball.' Getting staff, pupils and parents to agree a common approach to school problems is key to tackling issues and raising achievement. Ms Bates does this through constant communication and the use of data. Issues around particular subjects and the issue of literacy, which could be sensitive, are addressed in the context of the national agenda. The staff are involved at every stage in the process. Each staff member has an ongoing training programme, with special provision for all new staff joining the college. Where issues of staff performance arise, these are principally addressed by additional support and professional development. The college believes that its approach, including the use of data, improves professional and student performance.

The approach seems to work. A remarkable 90 per cent of Harris CTC pupils achieved five or more A*–C grades at GCSE in 2001, making it the most improved school in the country and one of the highest achieving comprehensives. The level of achievement was maintained in 2002 (91%) and 2003 (92%). In terms of value added, Harris scores +16 on the value-added scale developed by Professor David Jesson for the Specialist Schools Trust.[2] For the first time, in 2004, three students were offered places at Oxbridge, something of which the college is very proud. Harris CTC has turned a failing school into one of the most popular and successful comprehensive schools in the country.

Dame Enid Bibby, Head teacher of Wood Green Sports College in Sandwell puts the Harris philosophy another way. 'Be consistent, insistent, persistent in your drive to raise standards,' she says.

Having the right staff

Jim Collins, author of the best-selling American management book *Good to Great* says that when his researchers started their work, he expected to find that the first step in taking a company from good to great would be to set a new vision and

---

[2] See Appendix 1 for a full description of how Professor David Jesson calculates his data.

strategy, and then get people committed and aligned behind the new director. He found, by contrast, that executives in outstanding American companies who ignited the transformation from good to great did not first figure out where to drive the bus and then get people to drive it there. No they '*first* got the right people on the bus, the wrong people off the bus, and the right people in the right seats – and then figured out where to drive it'.[3] Moving on staff who are not pulling their weight in underperforming schools is easier said than done.

The Government has made it easier for schools to remove failing teachers. Yet, a government-funded study by academics from Manchester Business School shows that while formal procedures to remove an incompetent teacher averaged five months, a considerable improvement on before, most cases were still dealt with less formally and could involve up to two years of informal procedures before formal procedures were invoked.[4] Moreover, the European Union has imposed on the public sector (and now even the private sector) in the UK the TUPE (Transfer of Undertakings (Protection of Employment)) regulations. This effectively says that when, for example, an Academy (non-fee paying independent schools similar to CTCs) takes over a failing school it must also transfer to its employment all the existing staff of the previous school. Clearly this presents a problem, especially if the head teacher is also not up to the job. Fortunately, the rules do not give incumbents the absolute right to keep their jobs. They can be persuaded to leave, particularly if there is funding available to pay for redundancy. It may seem perverse to provide a pay-off for somebody who is incompetent, but the alternative is worse. If a school has a weak head teacher it will be very difficult to improve its performance. But the same applies to senior managers. Without a good team of competent managers no enterprise, least of all a school, will perform well. Governing bodies have an important responsibility in this area. If there is weak leadership in a school, the governors must take the necessary action.

Archbishop Holgate's Science College

Archbishop Holgate's Science College in York, founded in 1546, is an interesting case study on the importance of getting the right staff in place. When John Harris was appointed Head of Archbishop Holgate's School in York in 1992, the situation was dire. Indeed, if things had not changed the school could have closed within a few years. Rolls were falling rapidly. There were only 450 pupils in the school.

---

[3] J. Collins, *Good to Great: Why some companies make the leap . . . and others don't* (New York, Harper Collins, 2001), p. 13.

[4] J. Earnshaw, E. Ritchie, L. Marchington, D. Torrington and S. Hardie, *Best Practice in Undertaking Teacher Capability Procedures* (London, DfES, 2002).

Behaviour was poor with violence a common occurrence. Staff numbers were being cut each year as the funding dropped. Not surprisingly, staff morale was crumbling and parental support had all but disappeared. Just 16 per cent of pupils were gaining at least five good GCSE passes. With other good schools in York to choose from, only 72 parents applied for Archbishop Holgate's 150 places that year, and many were not first preference choices.

Mr Harris realised it was going to be a long haul to first stabilise and then improve the situation. 'It was a bit like a tanker going on to the rocks,' he recalls. 'First the school had to change direction, albeit slowly, before it could sail to safety.' So, how did he tackle what was essentially a crisis? First, he looked at external factors. Could the catchment area be changed, and would changing transport to school arrangements help? Mr Harris quickly concluded that trying to change the 'externals' was not the answer. He had to look after the pupils he had and they deserved a good quality of teaching and pastoral care. 'The quality of pastoral care had to come first and was the most urgent, because you have to have order before you can learn,' he explains. 'If parents feel their children are well cared for at school, if the vibes going home via the children are good then the school will receive crucial parental support. You can never overestimate the importance of the parental grapevine.' So, the early priority was to create an ordered environment, a positive ethos and a situation where pupils were happy to come to school and where relationships were positive. In short, as he puts it, 'a context within which quality teaching and learning could flourish'.

All this took time and Mr Harris is keen to emphasise that there is no single, quick answer to school improvement and no easy quick fix – if there were then everyone would be doing it. Having established a degree of order through a lot of hard work, Mr Harris's explanation of the remarkable improvement the school achieved over the next 12 years has two main threads. 'My first lesson was that whatever we did, we had to do it well and do it with serious conviction,' he says. 'You have to get all the pieces in place and get them right one at a time. If you can do that there comes a point where enough is right and the whole enterprise surges forward.'

For Mr Harris, the pieces include:

- clear strategic aims;
- quality of teaching;
- strong, proactive pastoral care;
- staff appointments;
- effective levelling, teaching and target setting;
- a listening senior management team;
- displays;

- a whole-school setting policy;
- furniture;
- transparent evaluation structures;
- regular and meaningful homework;
- positive ethos;
- a proactive policy on attendance and punctuality;
- seating plans;
- an effective system of rewards;
- marking policy;
- effective partnership with the LEA;
- relationships with governors;
- time for staff;
- the tone of the newsletter to parents;
- effective lunchtime supervision;
- the smile on the face of the receptionist.

In fact the list includes 'absolutely everything'. It matters what colour the walls are. It affects morale if the boilers don't work or the toilets are in a bad state. And it is a sign of poor organisation if the queues are too long at lunchtime. Once you get pieces in place of 'serious quality' then you up the stakes, start moving forward and everyone sees this and wants to be part of the growing success story. 'The key is – if you do it, do it with "passionate conviction" and get it right,' says Mr Harris. 'If the timing isn't right, wait until it is.' So while he was happy to take part in a Key Stage 3 national pilot, he has turned down other initiatives because he was not sure the school could get it right.

Get the staffing right

All these ingredients matter. But when Mr Harris prioritises one piece of the jigsaw above all others it is staffing – staff appointments, staff induction, staff expectations and staff support. He believes that the single most important thing you can do is to make sure you are appointing the right people. To do this you have to be very clear in yourself about your aims and values and present them in a way which will encourage the right people to work at the school. 'You need to devote a great deal of time to the appointment process,' he says. 'If I am not certain about the applicants for a post, I will happily re-advertise rather than appoint. While York is quite a good area for recruitment, it is getting harder, but I would rather put a short-term solution in place than make a bad or even average permanent appointment.'

Mr Harris looks for good or better teachers who subscribe to the aims, values, aspirations and ethos of the school and who create an ordered working atmosphere – the last being non-negotiable. 'I want teachers who can make a real difference to pupils,' he says. 'So, the appointment process includes not only the usual tour of the school and interviews, but also an observed taught lesson where we look for rapport with pupils, a good knowledge of their subject and, above all, an ability to manage a classroom effectively.' He feels it is essential to set expectations when appointing so that feedback and staff development are in process before a new teacher starts work at the school. There is then further induction and ongoing feedback and support.

Eighty per cent of the staff of the school have been appointed since Mr Harris took up post so the current team is essentially his creation. In the early years, some difficult decisions had to be made – and this sometimes meant redundancies. 'My basic approach is to try to take people with me at an appropriate pace, while all the time keeping my eye on the ultimate vision for the school,' he says. 'I did meet some staff resistance, but we worked through this, had patience – always aware that the vision would only be achieved if the staff implemented it. Gradually a higher percentage buy into your aims and values and they become the majority rather than a minority.' Rising rolls in recent years have also provided the opportunity to appoint people and put in structures according to the 'school of his dreams'. The structures are actually quite traditional and a new leadership team of four which shares the head's vision is now in place.

These changes did not happen quickly. It took Mr Harris over six years to turn things around at Archbishop Holgate's. League tables are by definition always 'ancient history', reflecting past Year 11 performance rather than the improvements coming through. It is difficult to persuade parents to send their children to a school with poor results even if they like the feel of the place. In the case of Archbishop Holgate's only 42 per cent of pupils come from a local catchment, so the school is competing with other schools in York, the general standard of which is very good. The school is now over-subscribed however, and twice yearly parental surveys show very positive parental attitudes. The improvement in the percentage of pupils achieving five or more A*–C grades has been dramatic in recent years. In 2000, just 39 per cent of pupils achieved that standard. By 2003, that proportion had risen to 75 per cent.

Archbishop Holgate's intake is average on most measures such as ability and social deprivation, but nevertheless the school is adding serious value to its pupils' performance. The Jesson research for the Specialist Schools Trust shows that it achieves 12 percentage points higher at GCSE than expected. Moreover, it is one of the ten most improved schools in the country. Other indicators also show success. A very good Ofsted report in 2001 only identified three areas of weakness, all of which have now been addressed. Mr Harris reports that unfortunately only one parent considering the school for their child requested a copy of the report –

perhaps proving his point that the parental grapevine is the important thing in changing perceptions.

The attitude and commitment of pupils has changed with a more 'school-minded' approach, better punctuality, more focus on work and excellent attendance at Saturday morning classes. Pastoral care has moved from the 'reactive' to the 'proactive'. Teachers are no longer fire fighting, but are able to concentrate on encouragement and achievement among pupils. There have been no permanent exclusions in the past three years. Specialist science college status was achieved in September 2002 – something the school sees as a recognition of its achievement and a 'speeder' to the improvement process.

The school's reputation within York has changed dramatically. Villages outside of the city, which in the past would (and did) fight hard not to be in the catchment area, are now happy to be linked with the school. It is the most inclusive school within the city and has the highest ethnic mix and number of refugee children although, given the context is York, the figure is not high overall in these measures.

So, how does John Harris sum up the achievement? 'In short, fulfilled pupils, fulfilled staff and improved results, without changes in external factors,' he says. 'Gradually more and more people share the vision and values – that number increases until you reach the point where enough buy into the aims and values for the others to want to catch up as the school moves forward. It is the same with pupils. They see the direction and they are brought along. So, the centre of gravity moves.'

All Saints Technology College, Dagenham

Des Smith, head teacher of All Saints Technology College in the London Borough of Barking and Dagenham, has had a similarly uplifting experience since he took up the headship of the (then) all boys Bishop Ward School in 1984. Mr Smith regards himself as very privileged to have held this position for the past 20 years. The school, meanwhile, is virtually unrecognisable from the one he joined. It is not only the name which has changed, the whole school has been completely transformed. Mr Smith is now a 'critical friend' to the head teacher of another challenging school, the new Academy in Bristol. So, what has changed at All Saints and what made it happen?

Mr Smith begins to explain the transformation by describing the school's 'geo-political' context. 'All Saints is the only voluntary-aided school in the London Borough of Barking and Dagenham and, as a Catholic school, comes under the Brentwood Diocese,' he says. 'Barking and Dagenham is a tough area in which to work. For example, it has the lowest number of graduates per household in the whole of England and Wales. Numbers staying on in education post-16 have been historically low. The Brentwood Diocese, meanwhile, includes several former grammar schools and high-achieving comprehensives, particularly in Havering and Brentwood. All Saints has historically been the "Cinderella" of the Diocese, not the school of choice for many Catholic parents.'

When Mr Smith took on the headship of Bishop Ward School in 1984, results were very low, the roll was around 75 pupils in each year group and the atmosphere was 'depressed and violent'. 'The first job was to stop the decline,' he recalls. 'The nature of the school changed somewhat when it became co-educational, through merging with Sacred Heart Girls' School in 1992. It is true that the school's intake improved at that time, but the boys still outnumber girls by 60/40.' In terms of ability, the intake has also improved, but Ofsted in 2003 still described it as 'below average'. 'I would say that we are now properly comprehensive,' says Mr Smith. 'And unlike many voluntary-aided schools, we do not interview potential pupils.'

It took a long time to raise standards at All Saints. The school was one of the first schools to achieve specialist status in 1994 when just 31 per cent of pupils gained five or more good grades at GCSE. Progress was slow but steady for the first five years with results improving to 42 per cent in 1999. Then all the improvement measures which had been put in place suddenly took hold. In the next four years results improved at a rapid rate, so that by 2003, 89 per cent of pupils were achieving five good GCSEs.

Hardly surprisingly, in 2003 it was the second most improved school in the country and had a value-added score of +39. Now, around 50 pupils go on to university each year. And the school is very popular with parents with two first-preference applications for every place. To what does Mr Smith ascribe this success?

Getting the ethos right

'My first task was to end the violent atmosphere in the school and instil an ethos of non-violence, care and pastoral support,' he says. 'In my first few years, that meant winning the hearts and minds of my pupils and their parents.' The work continues today, with assemblies which have the atmosphere of a Methodist revival meeting. He and his senior management team are highly visible around the school, particularly during break and lunch times when they are always on duty. The atmosphere during lunch is lively, even noisy, but completely non-threatening and once lessons start a silence descends over the building. There were no permanent exclusions in the last academic year. Ofsted said in 2003 'Pupils' attitudes, behaviour and relationships are consistently very good; pupils want to learn.'

Pupils variously described the school as 'strict on behaviour', 'anti-bullying', 'safe', 'friendly' and a school they felt lucky to be a part of.

Recruitment of staff

Mr Smith believes that good order must always come first, but it is closely followed by improving teaching and learning. 'The best way to do this is to recruit gifted teachers,' he says. 'That means having the right subject leaders and getting good Heads of Department.' As Ofsted put it: 'Recruitment and induction of teachers is excellent; arrangements for staff development and performance management are very good.' One part of this is involvement in Initial Teacher Training (ITT). Mr Smith regards the school's involvement in ITT as crucial to recruiting and keeping good staff. He thinks it is good for his existing staff to be involved in training others and his 30 trainees each year include some of his best recruits. But he also admits that changing the staff culture was difficult initially. 'There is now a more loyal and positive attitude, which is based on our success.'

Partnerships with parents

The school has worked hard to involve parents. Regular parents' evenings attract the attendance of a remarkable 90 per cent of parents (one Year 11 parents evening in early 2004 attracted 96 per cent, something of which Mr Smith is particularly proud). Their success owes something to the enormous amount of preparation which goes into them. Mr Smith doesn't confine parents to formal evenings. He has an 'open-door' policy as far as practicable and he offers additional practical services such as signing passports and applications for driving licences. Parents are fully informed of curriculum changes such as the introduction of the GNVQ ICT course.

Building momentum

With these strategies in place, a momentum of improvement has built up over the years. Some of the GCSE improvements are readily acknowledged to be due to the introduction of the GNVQ ICT course, which is equivalent to four GCSE passes. But the school believes this course has a great deal of validity in its own right, a view endorsed by local employers and the pupils themselves. 'Success breeds success and I strive to ensure that all departments move forward without any great variations between them,' says Mr Smith. Difficult questions are asked of 'non-performing' departments and some difficult decisions have been taken along the way, which have meant that some staff have had to move on.

Mr Smith's analogy is that of a dam: 'If the dam is a barrier to achievement then once it is breached everything rushes through,' he says. The result is that All Saints (and, incidentally, the two Catholic schools in neighbouring Newham) are no longer the 'Cinderellas' of the Diocese – and in the case of All Saints 35 per cent of its pupils come from outside of the Borough of Barking and Dagenham. All Saints, the school once shunned by parents, has become a school of choice.

Strategies for improvement: specialism and the Key Stage 3 strategy

All Saints was one of the first schools in the country to achieve technology-college status back in 1994 and Mr Smith describes the impact as 'enormous'. At the time only 31 per cent of pupils were getting at least five good GCSE grades, but the new status changed perceptions of the school. Prestigious sponsors, including the HSBC banking group, became involved. The school felt it was part of a 'new breed' of schools whose reputation was not just based on academic considerations. Overall capacity was increased and Mr Smith, who recognises the importance of public relations, made sure that parents and the local community were fully aware of the changes. He pays tribute to the work of the Specialist Schools Trust in promoting schools such as his.

Mr Smith also attributes some of the school's success to an emphasis on work in Key Stage 3, with pupils aged 11–14. One of the most important factors is an induction programme for Year 7 pupils in their first seven weeks in the school. This programme includes 'away days' and immersion into the school's culture. Echoing a famous tenet of Jesuit philosophy, he says that if you 'capture the hearts and minds of these pupils in their first seven weeks you have them for their school career'.

All new pupils are tested on entry and given Cognitive Ability Test (CAT) scores. They are tested again in Year 9, and there is a separate programme for those with significant literacy problems. To improve continuity with the school's 17 feeder primary schools, the children bring in their primary workbooks, enabling staff to see what they have been working on and to what standard.

There are two further elements crucial to All Saints' improvement strategy: Mr Smith regards the support from his governors as 'critical' and he believes a good physical environment is crucial, not least because of the messages it conveys. He has been very active in securing new buildings for the school – Ofsted commented positively on 'the pursuit of new buildings to house science, music and drama' as well as the sixth form block and this was also commented on by pupils.

Overall this eight-pronged strategy – ethos, staff recruitment and teacher training, partnership with parents, building momentum, specialist status, Key Stage 3 strategy, governor support and improving the physical environment – has resulted in a very successful and confident school.

Improving a boys' school: the Kemnal story

Nationally boys underperform girls by ten points at GCSE. So, the story of Kemnal Technology College, an all boys 11–18 comprehensive in Bromley, Kent is particularly interesting. When it achieved specialist status in 1994, only 30 per cent of Kemnal's boys achieved five good grades at GCSE. Progress was painfully slow in the early years, when its results remained below 40 per cent, but in 2002, with a particularly strong GCSE group, 56 per cent of pupils gained five or more good GCSEs and, in 2003, 49 per cent did so. More significantly, this meant that, given the school's intake, the school was providing an advantage of 17 per-centage points in 2003 on the Jesson value-added scale (and even higher the year before).

So what made the difference? John Atkins, the head teacher, says that in 2001 the school adopted a much more radical approach to improvement. 'The remodelling of Kemnal Technology College has taken two years,' he says. 'We have taken an holistic approach. Many schools argue that they are working at full capacity. That is why when new initiatives are suggested they are sometimes greeted with concern as schools try to "bolt on" initiatives to a system already working at full capacity. The way forward is to rebuild the school with a different model appropriate to the twenty-first century and create capacity. It can be done.'

The results speak for themselves. The school is an 11–18 boys comprehensive with 1,300 pupils on roll. Twenty-one per cent of pupils are eligible for free school meals, significantly above the national average and 60 per cent of the intake have reading ages below their chronological age. Thirty per cent are on the Special Educational Needs (SEN) Register. Yet, Key Stage 3 results are now, for the first time, above national average for boys. GCSE results are also above the national average for boys for the second year running. According to Ofsted's scale, these results are A/A*compared to other similar schools. The school was hoping that 60 per cent of pupils would gain at least five good GCSEs in 2004 against a predicted score from Key Stage 2 data of 32 per cent. If it succeeds, this would mean a value-added score, on the Jesson scale of +28.

Mr Atkins summarises the process as follows: 'You need to create capacity for teachers, which allows them to focus on the detail of teaching and learning and so raise standards. On average, each teacher has a limit of eight hours of workload "capacity" each day. This "capacity" needs to focus on the essentials and the detail of teaching and learning and not on administrative detail.' Mr Atkins views part of his job as head teacher as protecting teachers from anything which might divert them from their main task – that includes questionnaires from the Government or the LEA. The only time consideration will be given to anything not directly focused on raising standards among the boys at Kemnal is during 'planning time' towards the end of the summer term. Mr Atkins sensibly has no hesitation in challenging demands made by outside bodies, however powerful. So, the agenda is to transform the workforce to increase the capacity of teachers to teach. A series of strategies is employed.

The role of e-learning and data management at Kemnal

Technology has been a crucial component in increasing capacity. All teachers use interactive whiteboards and have laptops and desktop computers. Even the most techno-phobic teacher has been converted to the power of new technology. Electronic lesson preparation and the sharing of resources across the college has improved teamwork. And students are more focused as the lessons become more interesting. Vivienne Hughes, the school's deputy head teacher, calculates that an extra ten minutes of learning time has been created in each lesson.

Like Harris CTC, Kemnal uses Central Management Information System (CMIS). This has transformed the way pupil data is kept. Pupils are registered electronically, morning and afternoon and for every lesson, and parents, as well as the Attendance Officer, can access this information in 'real time' for their child. Student attendance now stands at 93 per cent, up from 91 per cent in the past two years. The system also keeps data on teacher assessment, pupil results and targets, which parents can also access at any time. A tutor comment is added once a term. No other teacher reports are required, so the teacher workload is reduced. Parents without computer access are given hard copies or can use the school's computer facilities. The data can be transferred to the virtual learning environment, including student planners and homework timetables. Another application of technology is Learning Activity Management System (LAMS), a tool to promote the use of cognitive skills to improve learning by engaging whole classes in reflective questioning and answering.

In short, e-learning is used to improve teaching and learning, to save on administrative tasks and to free up time to tackle the raising of standards. Baseline data is used to track every student in college and tackle underachievement straight away. One example Mr Atkins quotes is the consideration given by the leadership team to Year 11 GCSE performance. 'There are 200 boys in Year 11, who between them have 1,400 GCSE entries,' he says. 'Using the data kept on CMIS the leadership team met every teacher in every subject and considered these entries. They identified 150 boys underachieving in 300 entries and put in intervention strategies for each of these.'

Supervision and using staff time effectively

Mr Atkins felt that having to cover lessons for absent staff was bad for staff morale and that there was often minimal teaching and learning taking place in these lessons. 'We now employ five cover supervisors who work in departments when not required to cover lessons,' he says. 'They undertake all cover as and when required, using prepared lessons on the college's shared drive. They are people from the local community whom we employ on the basis of their classroom management skills. The result is that Kemnal teachers are no longer required to cover for absent colleagues and the standard of cover has improved.'

People from the local community are also employed to manage the canteen as well as all break and lunchtime duties. The fact that they are drawn from the local community means that they are able to establish effective relationships with the pupils. Teachers are no longer involved, although the senior management team and key staff are linked to the supervisors by walkie-talkies in case of incidents. 'The truth is that the ancillary staff manage the students far better than the teachers ever did,' says Mr Atkins. Ancillary staff are also used as invigilators for examinations alongside teaching staff.

Accommodation for the staff means rethinking traditional school organisation. So, there is no longer a single staff room, for the simple reason that on a large site this meant long walks for a cup of coffee. Instead, there are six satellite areas offering refreshments and other facilities for staff. These rooms are serviced by what Mr Atkins describes as 'life style managers for teachers' – staff whose contribution helps teachers to achieve a better balance between work and life – reducing time wasted and stress for teaching staff.

The staffing profile of Kemnal has changed dramatically over the years as a result of these changes. In 2000, for a school with 1,000 students, there were 74 teachers and 46 other adult employees. In 2004, with 1,300 students, there are 65 teachers and 100 other adult employees. Any job or task which does not need a qualified teacher is carried out by support or administrative staff. This has also had a positive effect on staff morale. Staff attendance was 99 per cent in the 2003 autumn term and there has only been one staff resignation since February 2003. All ancillary staff and assistant teachers are following the draft Higher Level Teaching Assistant guidelines, issued by the DfES, and the school regards staff development and training as essential for all staff. All adults employed by the school are treated with equal respect and have equal status.

Using teachers to best effect – double classes

A new staffing structure and the effective use of ICT should allow some rethinking of the traditional classroom model. Yet, all too often, sensible experimentation becomes unnecessarily controversial. The idea of bringing students together for shared or double classes is regularly highlighted by some of the teaching unions as something which will undermine the status of teachers. The experience of Kemnal, which is piloting the idea of 'double' classes, suggests that the critics are somewhat wide of the mark.

Kemnal's initiative, which has attracted national attention for its double classes in mathematics and ICT, involves a teacher taking a class of up to 80 students, supported by three assistant teachers. The classes take place in specially built classrooms, equipped with three whiteboards and wireless technology so that pupils can easily use laptops. The teacher prepares the lesson, introduces it and conducts the plenary part of the lesson. The assistants call the register (online), help students during the lesson, give out equipment and do the marking. Examination results from these double classes are above the college average. Mr Atkins reports that contrary to the views of some critics, there is a much calmer atmosphere in these lessons. He attributes this to the presence of more adults and the differing roles they play. Classroom assistants have also been used as intervention tutors to work with 30 students in Year 9 to raise their national test results at Key Stage 3 from level 4 to level 5.

Challenging assumptions

One of the secrets of schools which strive for continuous improvement, is their ability to challenge received wisdom. So, Mr Atkins has not only challenged traditional staffing structures – indeed the deputy head teacher, Vivienne Hughes, was herself a classroom assistant only a few years ago – he has also taken a different approach to meetings and parents' evenings. Regular meetings have been largely dropped, with just one meeting of one hour per week given over to teaching and learning issues. Parents' 'evenings' occur during the day, twice a year and the school closes for that day. The head teacher believes it is unreasonable to expect teachers to teach for five hours, talk to parents for four hours and then deliver good quality lessons the next day.

Another commonly held assumption is that, unless virtually all teachers are automatically given performance pay increases, schools will become impossible to manage. This has become an article of faith in many schools and has forced the Government to restructure the third upper pay scale and create a new grade of excellent teacher. Kemnal has seen performance management as the foundation of the school's transformation, the glue that holds it together. And it has been rigorous in its application. It is often the 'tough end' of the process where hard decisions have to be made, but Mr Atkins regards it as essential. The process has enabled the college to raise the performance of its staff. Unlike many schools which moved all their teachers up the performance pay scale, only three teachers moved from UPS1 to UPS2 at Kemnal. Those that were unsuccessful asked what they had to do to reach this standard. They were set rigorous and challenging targets. The approach is far closer to what the Government had hoped would happen with performance management than what happened in practice. But while teachers are disappointed not to get the extra pay, there have been no resignations.

There are two other ways in which Kemnal has challenged received wisdom. First, it has been willing to look at a system where stage is more appropriate than age, restructuring the 'year system' so that it is more appropriate for the remodelling agenda. It has also been fairly tough in removing any 'blockages' in the system which may be hindering progress. Sometimes younger staff become frustrated because their prospects of promotion are limited by existing staff. To combat this concern, four members of the leadership group were moved aside in 2003, with their salaries and pensions protected. This strategy has provided 15 internal promotions and the leadership group now has four members of about 30 years of age, the 'young guns'. In summary, schools should challenge all assumptions because the pupils only have one chance.

Conclusions

Schools and researchers have found many common characteristics that can help schools continuously to improve their achievements. Schools often find themselves in two phases of development: shifting from very poor results to matching the average; and then seeking to move from average to good or excellent. The real challenge for schools that have come through the first phase is moving to the second one, and that requires renewed effort and commitment. It also needs strong leadership, good teamwork, excellent information (and its application) and a willingness to challenge some aspects of conventional wisdom. The schools we have seen in this chapter all exhibit such tendencies. We shall now consider how schools have moved through that first phase in more recent years, using a variety of techniques.

4

How to turn around a failing school

We have seen how some schools have not only recovered from a poor reputation and performance, but have gone on to develop a culture of continuous improvement. In this chapter, we will look in more detail at how some schools specifically lifted themselves from Ofsted's list of failing schools. We will hear from people like Dexter Hutt who, when he became head teacher of Ninestiles School in Birmingham, faced an uphill task. Just six per cent of students gained five good GCSEs. The recently designated technology college had a poor record in the local area: it was 'perceived as a tough school, unloved and unwanted by thoughtful parents'. Five years later, not only did almost three quarters of the students reach the GCSE standard, but Ninestiles had successfully turned around another Birmingham school and had started to help a second school to improve. Dexter Hutt was knighted in the 2004 New Year's Honours List. A year after Sir Dexter started his drive for improvement in Birmingham, Hugh Howe took the reins at Fir Vale School in Sheffield in September 1999. Fir Vale had an unimpressive record as Earl Marshal School. The school was one of 18 to be controversially 'named and shamed' by the new Labour government in 1997. Fir Vale was not the sort of school which might expect a visit from the Queen and the Duke of Edinburgh. Yet just before the school was ready to celebrate over a third of its pupils gaining five good GCSEs in 2003, Mr Howe proudly welcomed these royal visitors, and showed them around his new school. They saw a school outwardly transformed with new buildings and equipment, but more importantly they experienced a school reborn as somewhere that pupils, many of them from Sheffield's poorest areas, can hope to achieve their full potential. It is also one that parents actively choose and openly support.

These schools show that failing schools can and do recover. We have seen in the previous chapter some of the techniques that have been shown to work. We now have the evidence of ten years of Ofsted to back that up. Yet there is often a sense of despair in the public discourse about failing schools, a feeling that nothing improves. For some schools, failure does lead to closure. In the years since Ofsted first started inspecting schools in 1992, over 100 primary and secondary schools have been closed after attempts to turn them around failed. But consider this remarkable fact: for every failing school that is forced to close, another eight are successfully turned around and placed on the road to recovery, sometimes within little over a year (though embedding such improvements can take longer, as we have seen). And in the years since Ofsted started to place schools in what it calls 'special measures', some 800 primary and secondary schools across England have travelled this journey. Their story is one that offers hope to those who find themselves in these difficult and challenging circumstances.

Before Ofsted, whose future we will consider in Chapter 11, there was little consistency in how often inspections occurred. Schools could go for several decades without being visited by Her Majesty's Inspectorate. And therefore there was often little indication of the extent to which some schools were failing, or indeed the extent to which others were succeeding well beyond expectations. Sometimes local inspectors intervened when matters had blatantly got out of hand. But schools could not expect a regular national inspection; now they are visited at least once every six years. And despite the verdict of Ofsted, it can still be difficult to persuade teachers and governors that radical measures are needed.

When Lady Marie Stubbs took over St George's School in Maida Vale, North West London, at the behest of Westminster Council, she did so in the wake of a terrible event. Philip Lawrence, a previous head of the inner city Catholic comprehensive, had been killed trying to break up a fight at the school's gates. The school had been placed in special measures. Yet there was a sense of denial all around. Lady Stubbs describes her first meeting with the governing body:

> Ofsted, I told them, has described St George's as being 'at the bottom end of limited progress' and I was seriously concerned about the state of the school. I described in detail the dreadful attendance, poor behaviour and low staff morale, the parlous state of the school's finances, the lack of essential teaching materials, the absence of vital data and of a proper administrative infrastructure – in short all the mechanisms for maintaining a good school. After painting this devastating picture I paused . . . But there was barely time to draw breath before the Chairman thanked me and suggested the meeting moved on to sorting out the various committees.[1]

As her inspiring account showed, Lady Stubbs overcame such attitudes to turn around the school, so that within 15 months it had moved from being damned by Ofsted to earning the inspectors' praise. And the time it takes to turn around a

---

[1] Marie Stubbs, *Bottom of the Class* (London, John Murray, 2003) p. 48.

failing school, which in its early days could amount to five years, has been reduced to between one and two years. That doesn't mean necessarily that the GCSE results will be touching the national average, but that there is at least a sense of purpose back in the school where its pupils are clearly making progress.

Of course, there are few staffrooms where an Ofsted inspection is welcomed with open arms. The wait for the visit is often more traumatic than the inspection itself. And it is because Ofsted can declare a school to be failing that there is such concern. Yet despite such tensions, regular inspection means that it is much easier to spot where a school is really improving, simply coasting or sinking into decline. Where performance tables give a snapshot, inspections should offer a more rounded judgement. Ofsted has used two categories to differentiate the degrees of decline: 'special measures' and 'serious weaknesses'. The most serious is to say that a school 'requires special measures'. In other words, the school is failing – or likely to fail – to provide its pupils with 'an acceptable standard of education'. More recently, the inspection regime has been toughened to the extent that poor leadership can be deemed to be reason for failure even where other aspects of the school are considered to be satisfactory. No longer can a school be said to be satisfactory while it has a poor head teacher. This change pushed up a little the proportion of schools failed in 2002–3 and is likely to do so in subsequent years. A school may be more likely to go into special measures now than before, and schools which might previously have been said to suffer from serious weaknesses (or given 'notice to improve' in the new terminology) are being placed in special measures. In total, around three per cent of schools are placed in special measures after an inspection, though the overall number of such failing schools had been falling from 1997–2002. There were 280 primary, secondary and special schools in this category at the end of the 2002–3 school year, 31 of them secondary schools. That figure hides a big turnover. One hundred and fifty-three schools improved sufficiently during the year to be removed from special measures and a further 14 schools were closed. But 159 schools were added to the list, including 19 secondary schools.[2]

There were 518 schools in special measures at the end of 1997–8 and this number had fallen to 274 by the end of 2001–2. However, the introduction of tougher leadership requirements by Ofsted has led to a higher number of failing schools more recently, with the number of secondary schools in special measures rising from 19 in 2001–2 to 31 in 2002–3, and an increase in the number of failed pupil referral units and special schools. It is also the case that failing schools are being turned around more quickly than before so the rise in overall numbers has been less dramatic. Moreover, some schools which might previously have been

---

[2] Figures provided by the DfES Press Office.

defined as having 'serious weaknesses' are being placed in special measures to emphasise the need for stronger leadership.

Other schools are said to face challenging circumstances. Of the 3,114 maintained mainstream secondary schools in England, the Government places around 600 schools in this category: these are schools where 25 per cent or fewer pupils achieved five or more good GCSE grades in one or more consecutive years over a three-year period, or where more than 35 per cent of pupils are entitled to free school meals. The Government expects no school to have fewer than 25 per cent of pupils achieving five good GCSEs by 2006. Many of these schools have not been placed in special measures. And many have improved considerably partly as a result of the extra support that has gone with this designation, including many where fewer than a quarter of pupils gained the requisite five good grades. However, some of these schools will either be in special measures or have been judged after inspection to have 'serious weaknesses'. Around five per cent of schools – just over 200 a year – are deemed to fit this category. Their most common deficiencies, according to the Chief Inspector of Schools, are a poor head teacher, poor teaching (where 10–20 per cent of lessons are said to be unsatisfactory) and limited improvement since the previous inspection.

Ninestiles School and Waverley School – the federation approach

For any school facing these challenges, the success of schools like Ninestiles and Waverley is an inspiration. As we have said, when Sir Dexter took over Ninestiles School in 1988, just six per cent of pupils gained five or more good GCSE grades. By 2003, the proportion had risen to 76 per cent, far higher than a predicted outcome based on the school's intake at age 11 of just over 40 per cent. Ninestiles is now a thriving mixed school with 1,500 students of all backgrounds. There are four applicants for every place at a school which was once seen as the local 'tough school'. Sir Dexter is no less proud of the school's achievement in other scores: virtually every pupil now achieves at least five A–G passes, whereas in 1998 only 44 per cent did so and a staggering 32 per cent of pupils left without a single GCSE pass. Having learned things the hard way at Ninestiles, he and his team were in a strong position to apply the same formula when Birmingham LEA invited him to lead a School federation after Waverley School had experienced a highly critical inspection report. In 2001, just 16 per cent of pupils at that school had gained five or more good GCSE passes; by 2003, the proportion had risen to 51 per cent.

'There was no vision and there were low expectations in April 1998,' recalls Sir Dexter. 'Teachers were happy, with no sense of failure, because of a strong belief that they were doing all that was possible. They felt they couldn't overcome the area. There were abysmal social relationships with fighting, swearing and racist abuse prevalent. Pupils were locked out for an hour at lunchtime, and as a result pupils with statements were being chased around the school. There was very little if any discussion about teaching and learning. And reports home included [grade] As even for bottom set pupils.'

So, how did he do it? 'The school improvement strategy we tried at Ninestiles was a risk,' admits Sir Dexter. 'We tried out each aspect of it very carefully. It was important for the changes to gain credibility with the staff. While initially they were wary of change, our staff are now far more receptive to it. They associate change with progress. So when we were sent in to Waverley, we had a package that had been tried and tested.' By December 2000 Ofsted was reporting that 85 per cent of lessons were good or better at Ninestiles, whereas the average for English secondaries at the time was just 57 per cent. The school has also gradually moved towards a more comprehensive intake, attracting a wider mix of students. The proportion in receipt of free school meals is now 25 per cent compared to 47 per cent in 1998, though the 2003 exam group had a higher proportion than the overall school population from poorer backgrounds.

Ninestiles has been a specialist technology college since September 1997. With specialism has come clear targets and the development of what the school sees as 'a genuine learning community with the capacity for continuous change'. Training of teachers is a crucial part of the Ninestiles strategy. The school places a premium on professional development, with 15 advanced skills teachers, a national record, and having become the only school in the region allowed to train and qualify graduates as teachers. A huge investment has been made in information technology, with the school having 1,000 laptops on site and over 800 12–14-year-olds having their own laptop as well as there being computers on every teacher's desk. The school is an accredited Cisco academy, for IT training.[3] Sir Dexter says a crucial factor is that each innovation is interlocking, with their combined effect much greater than the sum of their individual parts.

Sir Dexter put his then deputy Christine Quinn in as head teacher of Waverley in February 2001, initially for 18 months, with that contract now extended to 2005. She moved schools with just two weeks' notice. Sir Dexter remained 'executive head' of what became known as the 4Start Federation. There was a £200,000 grant provided from the council and the DfES to help make the necessary changes, a sum Sir Dexter recalls had not been available to him when he set about changing Ninestiles, although he had benefited from the £120,000 annual premium that went with being a specialist school.

---

[3] This means it provides internationally respected online ICT courses.

In February 2001, the existing head at Waverley, a 600-pupil inner city comprehensive with a largely Muslim intake, resigned after school inspectors found a school with real problems. Birmingham LEA asked Sir Dexter to take charge. By Easter, six weeks later, the new team was in place and change started to happen very rapidly. Since discipline had broken down at Waverley, a new behaviour system was introduced, known as Discipline for Learning, which like other similar packages codifies the way teachers respond to poor behaviour. In this case, students move from an initial warning, through a second warning, an hour's detention after school and where previous warnings have failed, isolation in a separate room where they must stay for classes and their lunch break. The warnings system is circumvented and stricter punishments are used for more serious misbehaviour, particularly any involving fights or violence. 'It's a consistent policy, similar to a magistrates' bench,' says Sir Dexter. 'Teachers may have different ways of interpreting the system but they do so within a consistent framework which is understood by staff, parents and pupils.'

Targets were set for rapid improvement. In fact, the target of 38 per cent of pupils to achieve five A–C grades for 2003 was overshot by 13 percentage points. Pupils were introduced to a more vocational curriculum, with many taking the Information Technology GNVQ. There were plenty of meetings with the staff to give them a sense of ownership of the new mission, to allow them to adapt measures that had succeeded at Ninestiles and to bring them on board at a time when they were feeling somewhat battered by the changes. Crucially, big changes were made in the school's middle management, which Sir Dexter and Ms Quinn felt to be one of Waverley's biggest weaknesses. New expectations of middle management's role were made clear. All schemes of work were examined and lessons with pace and structure were introduced, along the lines of the Key Stage 3 strategy, where they didn't already exist. And there was a physical improvement to everybody's environment too, with the school painted and carpeted. Pastoral changes were made and daily assemblies introduced to reintroduce a sense of community. Within ten months HMI was reporting that 'the outlook of and for the school has been transformed'.

Ninestiles also boasts one of the most advanced wireless systems of internal school communications in Europe. And this system, which allows teachers to adapt the technology to the needs of each individual subject, was brought into Waverley. Trainers from Seattle, where such technology is at its most advanced, were flown in to help staff adapt. Ninestiles sees information technology as essential in making lessons more varied and more interesting. But as Sir Dexter adds: 'It is not a substitute for poor teaching. You need good teaching for it to work properly.'

The link with Ninestiles also allowed a partnership to develop between departments at both schools. Links between teachers were an important part of this approach. Teachers from Waverley could visit their colleagues at Ninestiles and observe the school's best teachers in action. Advanced skills teachers worked in their partner school. Ninestiles introduced a philosophy of enabling those who want to teach to do so, providing training and access to courses where necessary. Few teachers at Waverley left as a result, though there are always some staff members who are not willing to face up to the necessary changes in a failing school. The job for the leadership team in those circumstances is to recognise that fact and be prepared to find ways to replace them. Because the procedures to remove incompetent teachers remain lengthy (and head teachers are often resistant to using fast-track procedures) this can involve encouragement to move on, sometimes helping teachers to change career. And Sir Dexter says what he calls a 'no blame' culture cannot be absolute: 'We only blame teachers who are not doing their job well if they don't care. A few teachers at Waverley chose to move on, but most welcomed the change in climate.' And any initial resentment there may have been over what must have seemed like a takeover disappeared in time once teachers felt ownership of the new structure, and even started to modify it. That last point is crucial: teachers needed to feel the goals and targets are their own.

As is often the case, the parents whose children were still at both Ninestiles and Waverley when the schools were underachieving had become used to lower standards and aspirations. Persuading them had been harder at Ninestiles because it was a new approach. But the success of Ninestiles encouraged many parents at Waverley to move quickly from a natural scepticism to adopting higher expectations for their own children and the school. It also encouraged Sir Dexter to turn his attention, with considerable success, to a third local school, the International School.

Fir Vale – the Fresh Start approach

The formula introduced at Waverley exemplifies practices which others have found helped turn around their own schools. Fir Vale, in Sheffield, may in one sense have been fortunate to have been designated as part of the Government's 'Fresh Start' initiative and thereby receive extra money and support. Another part of the package in this case was a new name and a new head teacher. But the programme was not always so successful. Some of the 16 secondary schools to be given a fresh start did not last the course; they were closed. Across the Fresh Start programme as a whole, progress ranged from 'limited to very good', according to the inspectors. Fresh Start was damned almost as soon at it had started when the first of such schools failed to show substantial immediate improvement in their exam results, though it has had some quiet successes since.

Fir Vale seemed better chosen than other candidates for the programme.

Islington Arts and Media College, in North London, seemed to slip further into decline after its head teacher invited the television cameras to record progress: inevitably the pupils played up to the cameras and the TV programme focused on confrontation rather than progress. Happily, after a period of calm and a new head teacher, that school is now making good progress. A Newcastle Fresh Start School, which had also subjected itself to the glare of publicity, was forced to close and, despite attracting a successful and high profile independent-school head teacher, a similar fate befell a Brighton Fresh Start college. A spying TV crew is, of course, not the only reason why some failing schools do not improve. Government officials who work with many schools in special measures cite several reasons why some such schools continue to fail. Sometimes the 'hero head' or 'superhead' parachuted in to rescue the school lacks any support within his or her new school. There are no middle managers to provide the right back up. The teachers are hostile, sometimes supported by union activists determined to capitalise on any ill will towards the inspectors who 'failed' the school and the newcomer invited to rescue the school. A school will not succeed either unless discipline is quickly restored, and parents are engaged and persuaded that things can get better. And, though this aspect is often less emphasised, a school with a much larger than average number of underachieving pupils will not see a rapid recovery either: the new head teacher must quickly start making the school more truly comprehensive by attracting a broader range of students. Also the school must see a fresh and enthusiastic intake of new staff to help lift the spirits and morale of those who have stayed, and who may often feel jaded about the prospects for recovery. Money helps too, but by itself will not make the difference. None of this is easy: the Ridings in Calderdale only started to see real exam improvement in 2003, seven years after it first attracted national notoriety. Other schools would not have lasted that long with results hovering below 15 per cent of pupils gaining five good GCSE grades.

Fir Vale may have been in the 'back yard' of David Blunkett, who was not only Education Secretary from 1997 until 2001 but also a local MP. Though Fir Vale suffered the same media attention as some other schools, it handled it differently and also it seems to have taken the right mix of steps from the start. The result has been that while only 8 per cent of pupils gained five good GCSE grades in 1998 that number rose steadily to 34 per cent in 2003. Of course, 34 per cent remains significantly below the national average, now over 50 per cent in state schools. And it would be foolish to underestimate the challenges this school still faces. Many pupils still have insufficient English to understand their lessons, a large number of the pupils being refugees or asylum seekers. More than half of all pupils are eligible for free school meals, the most commonly accepted indicator of poverty. The pupils who join the school have performed significantly below

average in their Key Stage 2 tests at age 11. Two in five pupils have a special educational need, mainly moderate learning or emotional and behavioural difficulties,
though the proportion of pupils with statements of special needs is relatively low.
Three-quarters of the pupils are Muslim, and for some Muslim girls there is a
tension between family and further education. But the school is now on a cycle of
continuous improvement, as it puts its motto of 'making dreams a reality' into
practice. From being the school which people crossed Sheffield to avoid, it has
become one with more applications than places. The school achieved its ambition
to become a business and enterprise specialist college in September 2004.

In its 2001 inspection report, Ofsted described Fir Vale as 'a good school with
many outstanding characteristics'. The report went on to say:

> The excellent leadership by the senior management leadership team inspires pupils and
> staff to do well. The achievement of pupils in relation to their starting point on entry at
> age 11 is good. The outstanding leadership of the head teacher gives the school a clear
> sense of purpose and direction, not least in ensuring that all pupils are valued and
> encouraged to meet their aspirations. Teaching is good and often very good.[4]

That judgement came ahead of substantial exam improvements in the years
that followed.

Hugh Howe expects his school's results to continue improving. He sees four
main factors in the school's success: leadership and vision; raising expectations;
better teaching; and improved discipline. 'There's no quick or easy answer for
failing schools,' he says, 'and I'm always loathe to say that there is any one factor
or magic formula. But the absolute priority is leadership and vision. A vision
was needed for what was a problematic school. There were challenges and local
difficulties to be resolved. We had to communicate a simple but clear vision to
all our stakeholders. In practical terms, that had two central pillars. We talked
up attainment – children coming to Fir Vale should leave with more than they
arrived with. We also aspired for young people and staff to do the very best they
could – this is not an arrogance, but a striving for excellence. There was a
five-year strategic plan agreed with governors, which set out the practical ways in
which we were going to achieve our goals.'

As a 'new' school, any staff from Earl Marshal wishing to join Fir Vale had to
apply for a job: the result was that half the staff at Fir Vale were from Earl
Marshal and half were new. Though some started out unconvinced that change
could happen, early signs that things were really improving helped convince the
older teachers to overcome a weary sense of having 'seen it all before'. They
started to embrace the new vision for the school. Teachers were then expected to

---

[4] *Fir Vale School Inspection Report* (London, Ofsted, 2001). Available at www.ofsted.gov.uk.

set realistic targets, based on clear data rather than 'gut reaction'. This allowed for a systematic approach that enabled all pupils to strive for their best.

Parents had to play their part too. Many had felt let down in the past by the previous school. Many others had simply chosen other schools across Sheffield. It was vital that they were part of the new vision for the school from the start, because their support was not only essential to raise the aspirations of their own children, but to persuade others that Fir Vale was changing. They were asked what they wanted from the school, but were also challenged to ensure that students were regular and punctual in their attendance. A result of this was that average attendance now exceeds 90 per cent whereas before it had hovered between 70–80 per cent. Parents also were encouraged to see that they needed to make time and space for their children to do regular homework, not always easy in a noisy, busy household. 'There was a mixture of optimism and scepticism,' recalls Mr Howe, 'but once they started to see that our methods were working, they began to accelerate their support. They appreciated that they could make a difference.' As the results at Fir Vale improved, so did parental confidence. The school is now over-subscribed. From just 340 pupils in 1998, its rolls have expanded to 742 pupils in September 2004, and over 55 potential pupils are disappointed each year.

Mr Howe says that his staff know 'there are times when I will be very autocratic and there are other times when I will be very consultative. It depends what is appropriate for a particular type of intervention.' He believes in leading by example, continuing to teach a couple of history lessons each week to see things at the sharp end. 'High expectations are about helping our pupils to focus on who they are and what they are, academically, socially and culturally,' he says. Aspiration can be a difficult issue for Muslim girls, where their parents are worried about the influences they may face in further and higher education. It is hard for parents to accept that their daughters may acquire a degree of independence in such settings. Two programmes at Fir Vale proved particularly valuable. A link with the University of Sheffield, called 'early outreach', started to engage youngsters from Year 9 through visiting lecturers, campus visits and residential stays to introduce them to university life. Crucially, parents were fully involved, which reassured many that the university could be a safe, stimulating and culturally respectful environment. Fir Vale has no sixth form, making it vital that the school develops strong links with Sheffield College, the local further education college, and secondary schools with their own sixth forms. The Excellence in Cities programme has been important here, bringing Fir Vale together with such schools through formal clusters. Mr Howe and other head teachers in the North East of Sheffield has been pressing hard for more coherent sixth-form provision in the area, and a new dedicated sixth-form centre is due to open at Longley Park in 2004. One innovation which has been particularly valuable has been the appointment of 'transition tutors' who not only help young people make the right choices, but as importantly, help them to settle in to their new environment and access whatever support may be available, such as education maintenance allowances and help with travel costs. The tutors are funded by the local Learning and Skills Council. The result of these efforts has not only been seen in the better GCSE results, but in improved staying-on rates after GCSE – over 75 per cent compared with around 60 per cent in the past.

Teaching was improved with more structured lessons and a new system of monitoring their success. 'We knew what a successful lesson looked like, and if we were to be an effective school, we shouldn't need somebody outside to tell us what was a good lesson,' says Mr Howe. 'We should do to ourselves what others would do to us.' His own views of an effective lesson are not much different from those of other effective head teachers – it has a good structure, with a beginning, a middle, and a summing up at the end; it has pace; it gives pupils the confidence to be active learners rather than passive recipients of knowledge; and it addresses the needs of individual pupils, identifying able students who could benefit from the school's gifted and talented programme as well as those who might require extra tuition. But he goes much further than this. There is a rigorous programme of self-review at Fir Vale, which initially involved the head teacher observing at least one lesson taken by every staff member once a term; now such observation continues with a department head or member of the school's leadership team doing the observation. They are clear what they are looking for in such observations, and from time to time they are joined by others to ensure a consistency across the school. In effect, Mr Howe is keen to ensure that the demands Ofsted would make in one of its routine visits are being applied as a matter of course every term.

But keeping good teachers is a challenge. Where schools fail to improve or slip back, Ofsted identifies high staff turnover and recruitment difficulties as two of the most important factors. Mr Howe's solution was to be flexible: he paid those who stayed for two critical years five per cent loyalty bonuses. As a result, the school has not only kept good staff, but it has also managed to attract others. 'We've been able not only to keep successful teachers, but to encourage new teachers to a challenging inner city school.'

As at Ninestiles and Waverley, a codified approach to rewards and sanctions brought order to the school. 'There was a lack of control when I started,' says Mr Howe. 'It's not that there wasn't any discipline or sanctions, but there was no effort to engage youngsters or gain their support.' Children are expected to be punctual and attend regularly, and to come to school in the right frame of mind. They must wear a uniform too. Fir Vale uses the Assertive Discipline programme as a model which all teachers and all pupils learn. It is a combination of rewarding youngsters with praise and kudos for good behaviour and achievement with a codified set of sanctions when they misbehave. The system is taught to all staff when they join the school. Sanctions depend on the level of misbehaviour. In addition, fixed-term exclusions of anything from 2 to 45 days are automatically used for physical attacks or fighting and for verbal abuse, including swearing at a teacher. But for other incidents, the code specifies a quiet word, followed by a formal warning, then being moved elsewhere in the classroom, followed by detention, and then being referred to the school's learning support unit, a separate base with its own staff, where they can go for anything from a day to several weeks. There is an effective mix of the traditional and the modern here: tough on indiscipline and tough on its causes. Permanent exclusions are also used but sparingly – six pupils were permanently excluded in 1998–9, but three in 2002–3.

If these are the main factors in Fir Vale's improvement, the school also has an effective team working with children with statements, others with special needs and those with specific emotional or behavioural difficulties. There are staff too to support those who speak a language other than English at home. Around 20 parents and other local volunteers a year act as volunteer mentors for ten hours a week, working with difficult pupils: some have gained accreditation and become professional learning mentors. For some pupils, extra arts and music lessons have helped them regain an interest in learning and have had an almost therapeutic effect. The school also benefited from wider programmes and significant capital improvements. And the design of the building supports discipline by giving teachers a full view of what pupils are up to. While the school's turnaround started before their move into a new building, Mr Howe says the new structures have improved staff and pupil morale. 'Our reception area is light and open,' he says. 'The corridors are big, wide social spaces, so that children can socialise inside or outside during break times. The new school building has contributed to our success.'

In recent years, there has been a lot more money than before available to help failing schools to recover. And while schools in some parts of the country lost out in 2003 with a new national distribution formula, many others continued to see relatively large increases in their budgets. Those linked with special initiatives gained help from that, and a new Leadership Incentive Grant, worth £125,000 a year, is being provided to 1,400 secondary schools with weaker results in 'Excellence in Cities' areas, in special measures or with a high take up of free school meals. Fir Vale benefited from a number of such initiatives as it was on the road to recovery. As well as being part of an Education Action Zone and the Government's inner city improvement initiative, Excellence in Cities, Fir Vale received extra support (both financial and practical) from the DfES and Sheffield City Council to help fund its programme of improvement. The most ambitious and expensive programme was building a new school, for that brought with it a new sense of belief in the pupils and teachers, and their capabilities. The school has a brand new building with computer whiteboards replacing traditional blackboards, and a modern design which allows teachers to see everything that is happening throughout the school.

King's College for the Arts and Technology – the private-sector approach

One hundred and eighty-six miles south of Fir Vale, the King's College for the Arts and Technology in Guildford, Surrey tried an even more controversial approach. The newspapers said it was being 'privatised'. But the former King's Manor School had in reality been put under the management of a not-for-profit company formed by the successful Kingshurst City Technology College. And away from the glare of national publicity, this school has been seeing its exam results improve at a rate far faster than the national average. In 2003, 28 per cent of students gained five good GCSE grades compared with just 10 per cent in its last year as the King's Manor School. The proportion of pupils gaining five A–G passes rose substantially from 70 per cent to 89 per cent at the same time, higher than the national average.

King's College was one of three secondary schools in Surrey where private management was introduced by the county council in the early years of this century to help lever up results. Abbeylands in Addlestone, drawing pupils from Runnymede, was taken over by Nord Anglia, a company listed on the stock exchange, and has improved under its new name, Jubilee High School. The company running King's College is different. 3Es enterprises was set up by Kingshurst City Technology College in Birmingham. The not-for-profit company believes its regeneration work is helped by an ethos which focuses on the development and dissemination of innovative practice to raise standards, building partnerships with business and other institutions to provide high quality teaching and learning experiences and exchanging ideas in both curriculum and management. It also runs a business and arts designated school in Camberley, Surrey, itself another former failing school and the new Business Academy in Bexley.

King's College had 750 students in 2003–4, compared with 280 in 1999–2000. When it is full, it will have over 1,100 students. But its head teacher, until 2004, David Crossley was particularly pleased when 200 parents made the college their first choice of school for September 2003, suggesting growing confidence in the local community about the school's strengths. In the old school, just 40 a year used to do so. When Ofsted visited the once failing school in March 2003, it saw a 'good and improving school, with many excellent features'. The proportion of pupils with five high GCSE grades rose from 10 per cent in 2000 to 27 per cent in two years. The results are still below average nationally and for Surrey, but seem to be heading in the right direction. Ofsted in 2003 confirmed that both new and existing students were making good progress. Mr Crossley confidently expects results to exceed national norms from 2005 once the newer students reach Year 11. Key Stage 3 results in 2003 and 2004 are very encouraging. In addition imaginative early entry policies have resulted in almost half of the current Year 10 cohort gaining three or more high grades already. The reason is an important one for any failing school hoping to recover: the school has now got a more comprehensive intake. It has more high fliers, whereas during its decline in the past, it had become disproportionately a school for those who had special needs or had started with a below average primary school performance. The school still takes pride in its work for children of all abilities, but it recognises the need for balance. Many students are in a position to take some of their GCSEs a year or two earlier than usual, a sure sign that efforts are being made to stretch the most able students.

But where Fir Vale enjoyed the support of the LEA and the Government, King's College had an extra hand from the private sector, if that is the right term for the commercial arm of a city technology college. 'The 3Es convinced people that something significant was going to happen,' says Mr Crossley. 'It also brought a range of expertise which allowed us to do things differently. There has been a marked change in students' attitude to learning.' The company also provided high-profile governors, including celebrity chef Prue Leith, who chairs the governing body, and Professor Patrick Dowling, the Vice-chancellor of Surrey University, which runs a number of projects with the school designed to raise student aspirations. There remains a strong partnership with Surrey County Council, too. All these external partnerships are important in showing public confidence in the school, but the most important change has happened within the school. And some of the change at King's College has been cultural.

Restoring discipline and order, which has included the introduction of a new school uniform, was a crucial factor in the battle to win back parents. As Mr Crossley puts it: 'Parents have been impressed by the calm and orderly way in which pupils are willing to learn.' Certainly the restoration of order is a common first step in the road to recovery. Without it, there can be little prospect of developing a culture of learning in the school, or of seeing better outcomes.

The school has also won specialist status in technology. And like Ninestiles School it sees ICT as a vital part of its new approach. ICT is said by the head teacher to be all pervading. The school has a relatively good ratio of one computer for every four students, which enables around a quarter of lessons to be taught using new technology. But the classroom is different from the norm in one other vital respect: on every teacher's desk there is also a desktop computer. 'It's a bit like the old notion of the eyes on the back of the teacher's head,' says Mr Crossley. With that computer, teachers can set and mark homework. They can send pupils worksheets. Where a query needs a quick answer, they can consult reference libraries. And perhaps just as importantly, they can also file reports to the school's database, enabling the vital tracking of pupil progress to take place.

Another factor that is vital to keeping and building the trust of parents is the extent to which the school's development is a shared with parents. In some schools, the report to parents is an annual duty. For schools recovering from special measures, a report home every term is deemed an essential information-sharing exercise, so that parents are kept informed not only of their child's progress but also know what's happening in the school. However, King's College has gone one step further. 'Unlike other schools, we report to parents every six weeks rather than once a year,' says Mr Crossley.

King's College also has a different philosophy. It may be the influence of the 3Es or it may be the inspiration of its head teacher, a man with a strong track record in teaching and school leadership here and abroad. 'We try to capture the fact that each young person desires to be an adult while having the inquisitiveness of a child,' is how he sees it. And that affects how the school is run. The school's pupils do not charge out of their classrooms to create an unmanageably large and undignified queue in the school canteen. Instead they go in small groups at different times. Lunch is staggered and the pupils are treated with respect. The same sort of respect which allows those who are ready to do so to take their GCSEs early. And this respect has seen the proportion of pupils continuing in education after 16 rising from 42 to 75 per cent.

However, there is also a rigorous side to this approach. One official who has worked with many failing schools said that the greatest mistake a school can make is to try to introduce a lot of nice-sounding initiatives, which gain headlines but are disconnected from the main task in hand. King's College does not make that mistake. So, when pupils join the school in Year 7, those with weak literacy or numeracy skills receive extra help. At the other end of the school, where the school has a small but growing sixth form, students study for the challenging International Baccalaureate (IB) rather than A Levels. It is one of only 50 schools in the country to offer the IB, and one of an even smaller group where no fees are charged. Unsurprisingly the sixth form has started to attract students from beyond the Guildford catchment area – some come from London and Portsmouth.

The issue with King's College is whether or not the private sector's involvement was the agent for change, or simply its catalyst. Abbeylands School 14 miles away had a similarly bleak outlook until it was taken over by Nord Anglia, an education company which also runs several independent schools. Unlike the 3Es, Nord Anglia is listed on the stock exchange and delivers a profit to its shareholders. In the late nineties, it had hopes of taking over a significant number of failing schools. Instead, its education arm has focused on LEAs. The talk now is of partnerships rather than take-overs. And Jubilee High School, as Abbeylands is now called, is run by a foundation which is a partnership between Nord Anglia and Surrey County Council. That foundation nominates governors to the governing body, but like other foundation schools, it has a greater number of elected parents than foundation governors. In its first year as Jubilee High School GCSE results improved dramatically: 37 per cent of students gained at least five good GCSEs in 2003, up from 25 per cent in the old school the previous year. And student numbers rose too, with 138 new pupils this term, compared with 90 two years ago, though a full form entry would have 160 pupils, something the head teacher Paul Suchley expects as parental confidence grows.

Conclusions

There seems to be some consensus about the sort of techniques that must be at the heart of a school's recovery, whether it is a failing school trying to recover from special measures or a school that is coasting with an average performance when it should be doing much better. In some schools, this means having a particular style to the lesson that is the school's style. This usually means adapting the 'three-part lesson', which has been promoted by the Government's Key Stage 3 strategy, where there is an introduction at the beginning and a summing up at the end of every lesson. Whatever happens, it is vital that teachers are a part of the recovery project. This does not mean that an old school's staff must all go. Indeed when that happens, there can be a real loss of stability. But at both the Surrey schools we have examined, there has been a significant injection of new blood and the enthusiasm of the new staff members has helped rejuvenate the remaining staff from the old schools. New teachers make up over 60 per cent of their staff now, while those teachers who stayed from the old schools have become much keener on their jobs, say the schools' head teachers.

Of course, there is no panacea, whether it be a federation, a Fresh Start or the private-sector route. Certainly Fresh Start and semi-privatisation have had their failures, and often these have been very high profile ones. And it is perhaps too early to judge whether the federation approach would work without the dynamic drive of a Dexter Hutt. Yet it is worth remembering also just how many failing schools have recovered quietly through the tenacious hard work of heads and teachers, helped by outside agencies and perhaps some extra resources. And it seems increasingly to be accepted that schools can't do it on their own. And while it is crucial to have the support of teachers, governors and parents as well as the willingness by pupils to learn, that added ingredient can make the difference.

How then, do we summarise the wisdom of those who have succeeded? There are perhaps six steps that make the difference – and these are the steps that those in the Government who work with failing schools believe to be of crucial importance, too.

1 **Change the leadership team.** It is not enough just to change the head teacher, though this is usually essential. The 'hero head' cannot do it alone. He or she needs a number of senior people to whom they can turn for support and solidarity in what will be a very challenging time for the school.

2 **Get a grip on discipline.** Without a sense of order, there is little chance of turning other aspects of the school around. It means being tougher on attendance. It means establishing a set of rules around the school which are understood by every staff member and pupil (and parents), and which are evenly and fully enforced. Moreover, it means a sense of discipline among teachers, too. As one seasoned observer put it: 'You can't have the wacky English department doing its own thing, while everybody else is signed up to the new approach.'

3 **You must have clear, high expectations.** Very often in failing schools, teachers have either given up on many students or have simply written them off. This is sometimes presented as a 'caring' attitude, whereas the really caring approach would be to set goals for each pupil which would stretch them, and which they could achieve with good teaching and a degree of application. Parents, children and teachers must all 'own' this approach. 'The school must be very tight on systems,' is how one policymaker put it. This means that there must be regular internal assessment. Youngsters must be talked to in a consistent way about their own expectations. Each department's reviews of their students' individual progress should be discussed and used to assess and drive teachers' expectations.

4 **Teaching must be of a consistently high standard.** Teaching unions often adopt a defensive approach when a school is failed because they believe it will inevitably mean mass redundancies. In reality, there is often a haemorrhaging of staff from failing schools, and the challenge for the new leadership team is to lift a sense of 'corporate depression' from the staffroom. But there must be a rigorous approach to teaching practice. This typically means pairing weak and effective teachers, enabling teachers to observe effective lessons or introducing expert teachers from neighbouring schools. Lessons should be well paced and well structured. Some schools have gone for a 'branded' lesson, where there is a common form to lessons in each year group, which includes insisting that pupils stand respectfully when a teacher enters or leaves the classroom, and raise their hands to ask a question or make a point.

5 **Invest in the future.** There are those who still believe that money can buy improvement. But their numbers have dwindled in recent years. The unpalatable truth is that schools can fail even if they have far more spent on them than on more successful schools. Equally, some investment can make a difference.

An extra £20,000 to £100,000 spent on improving teaching, with external help, is often a good investment and the amount needed depends on the resources already available within the school. New facilities tell outsiders that government, nationally and locally, are prepared to invest in the school's future, and this can improve the confidence of parents thinking about sending their offspring there. But without the other factors in place, the money can be wasted – and some failing schools that have closed have done so after having substantial resources spent on them.

6 Collaboration makes a difference. This last factor is the one for which there is increasing evidence that it can make all the difference. It is about a strong partnership between a successful school and a struggling school, whether as a federation or not. In Government circles, this programme is being dubbed the 'collaborative fresh start', though without the fanfare that accompanied the earlier programme and without the distracting attention of fly-on-the-wall documentary makers. The partnership cannot be a woolly one: there must be clearly defined goals and areas where the schools work together. Local primary schools can be part of the partnership. Together they work on issues like leadership and teaching (perhaps the successful school offers expert teachers).

And what doesn't work? What Professor Michael Barber, who ran the Government's Standards and Effectiveness Unit in Labour's first term in office and who now heads the Prime Minister's Public Service Delivery Unit, has dubbed the 'boutique initiative' seems to be a non-starter. This involves glitzy programmes that are peripheral to sorting out discipline and improving teaching standards. Sometimes these are introduced as part of other 'neighbourhood renewal' programmes or 'healthy schools' schemes. While they may be worthy in their own right, and worth adopting by schools that have the time and energy to devote to their implementation, they are a distraction from the main business in hand. What also seems not to work is the solo head teacher 'knocking heads together' without having the support of at least two or three key leadership staff. And simply merging a failing school with another school without addressing the underlying problems of teaching and discipline will not lead to any miracles either. There is simply no substitute for addressing the basics. And when a school gets those right, there is an excellent chance that it will recover.

5

Accountability, transparency and choice: the value of specialism

The first specialist school in England was the City Technology College in Kingshurst, which opened in September 1988 on the site of a failed comprehensive school in Chelmsley Wood, a socially deprived area to the east of Birmingham. It had close links with business, and with sponsorship from the Hanson Trust and Lucas Aerospace, went on to pioneer techniques which many of the nearly 2,000 specialist schools in operation today now use. Under the able leadership of its principal from 1988 to 2001, Valerie Bragg, the first specialist school focused on teaching the skills in mathematics, science and technology which local employers required.

Improvement was not automatic. Indeed, progress was initially slow as new learning techniques were developed. This was a time when ICT was in its infancy as an educational tool. Kingshurst was a pioneer in this regard. Vocational education was also relatively underdeveloped in secondary schools. Kingshurst became the first secondary school to use the highly respected BTEC National Diploma. As a CTC, the school also enjoyed a greater degree of independence than other schools at the time. These were, after all, the days before head teachers and governors enjoyed the budgetary control they now have through local management of schools. Along the way, Kingshurst came to pioneer other ways to motivate its students. These may seem more common today, but they were often unheard of in English schools in the eighties. So, children had an early start to the day with breakfast being served at 7.30 a.m. There was no 9 a.m. to 4 p.m. culture here, and the school remained open until 6 p.m., offering students the chance to do their homework or enjoy extra-curricular activities. There was an emphasis on improving literacy and numeracy, particularly for those who needed remedial support. Close links with parents were nurtured.

The results were dramatic. By the mid-nineties more than half of the pupils were achieving five good grades at GCSE/GNVQ compared to less than ten per cent for the school which formerly occupied the site. In 2003, 95 per cent of its pupils achieved 5+ A*–C grades at GCSE/GNVQ. The Kingshurst experience was shared by the 15 CTCs created in the period between 1988 and 1993. All except the BRIT School of Performing Arts, specialise in mathematics, science and technology. CTCs were criticised in their early days because of their independence from LEAs. Yet they were all-ability comprehensives, with active policies to ensure that their intake reflected the full range of academic abilities. They were well supported by parents and students, who welcomed their innovation and high standards. In 2003, the 15 CTCs averaged 86 per cent of pupils gaining five good grades at GCSE/GNVQ, compared to an average of 50 per cent for comprehensive schools generally. Their model has more recently been used by the Labour Government as the basis for new Academies[1], though the Academies will offer a number of different specialisms, including business and enterprise.

In 1994, the first 50 technology colleges were opened. They applied many of the lessons learned from the CTCs to existing comprehensive schools, and they kept the same pupils and staff. The schools taught all the subjects of the National Curriculum but specialised like CTCs in mathematics, science and technology. To allow many more schools to specialise, they were required to raise £100,000 sponsorship, whereas the CTCs required a significantly larger commitment. But there were rigorous requirements to ensure that their acquisition of a specialism would help them to raise standards. They applied for designation as a specialist school to the Secretary of State by submitting a plan showing how, if designated, they would raise standards in both their specialist subjects and overall. If designated they received a one-time capital grant of £100,000 plus top-up recurrent funding of £100 per pupil for three years, later for four years.

Their improvement has been twice as fast as that of non-specialist schools over the same period. Since 1994, these 50 schools have improved their results from just 40 per cent of their pupils gaining at least five good grades at GCSE to 69 per cent in 2003, while schools generally have recorded more modest improvements – from 42 per cent to 51 per cent. Over the next ten years, new specialisms have been added in languages, sports, performing and visual arts, science, mathematics, engineering, business and enterprise, humanities and music.

From September 2004, there will be around 2,000 specialist schools, representing almost two-thirds of all English secondary schools, with 1,000 new specialist schools having been designated in the last two years. There have been changes along the way. Initially specialist status was only available to grant-maintained and voluntary-aided schools. Interest in the programme quickly expanded when it was opened to all English secondary schools to apply. In 1997 David Blunkett, the new Secretary

---

[1] Formerly 'city academies' these are independent non-fee paying schools funded directly by the Department for Education and Skills.

of State for Education, changed the requirements for designation to include a community plan under which specialist schools spend a third of their top-up recurrent funding on helping other schools in their area. This helped to answer those critics who tried to suggest that specialism was divisive. Top-up funding was increased from £100 to £120 per pupil. From September 2005 it will be £129 per pupil. Charles Clarke, the Education Secretary since 2002, lifted the cap on funding for specialist schools shortly after his appointment, making sufficient funds available to designate every qualified bid for specialist status. This further encouraged a spirit of collaboration between schools.

Why has the specialist school initiative become so important?

Specialism has become central to the Government's programme for reforming secondary schools. An initiative which was pioneered by the Conservatives has been adopted with enthusiasm by Labour. Yet it is important to understand why this initiative has become so valued. The first and most important reason is that the specialist schools have been remarkably successful in raising educational standards. In 2003, specialist schools averaged 56 per cent of pupils achieving 5+ A*–C grades at GCSE compared to 47 per cent for the non-specialist schools. This nine-point positive performance gap was not a matter of a more selective intake, as closer scrutiny of the results revealed. In fact, the intake of pupils in 1998, when the 2003 GCSE pupils entered secondary school at age 11, was broadly similar to that of other comprehensive schools, when the results of pupils' Key Stage 2 tests were examined. The average Key Stage 2 point scores per pupil in 1998 of 25·7 for pupils entering non-selective specialist schools compared with the 25·3 score achieved by those entering the other comprehensive schools. The better performance at GCSE by specialist schools is not therefore dependent upon their selecting more able cohorts.

Research by Professor David Jesson of York University shows that this has another more significant explanation. It is that specialist schools add more value than other comprehensive schools. Using average Key Stage 2 results at age 11 to predict the proportion of good grades a school should achieve at GCSE, Professor Jesson's study shows that in 2003 the 938 specialist schools could have been expected to achieve 53.3 per cent 5+ A*–C grades at GCSE but actually achieved 56.0 per cent. By contrast the other 1989 schools could have been expected to achieve 48.6 per cent but only achieved 47.1 per cent. On a net basis specialist schools had a value added of plus 4·2 good grades.[2]

---

[2] D. Jesson, *Educational Outcomes and Value Added by Specialist Schools: 2003 Analysis* (London, Specialist Schools Trust, 2004).

The second factor is the gain in self-esteem and confidence experienced especially in inner city schools by those creating a centre of excellence in a particular subject. The ten different types of 2,000 specialist schools operating in 2004 provide a wide range of choice of specialist subjects:

- Technology colleges specialise in teaching mathematics, science, design technology and ICT.
- Language colleges specialise in teaching modern foreign languages and promote an international ethos across the whole curriculum.
- Arts colleges specialise in teaching the performing arts including music, dance and drama; or specialise in visual or media arts.
- Music colleges (the first will open in September 2004) specialise in teaching music but also have a secondary focus on mathematics or ICT.
- Sports colleges specialise in teaching physical education and sport, and also serve as centres of sporting excellence for neighbouring schools.
- Science colleges emphasise the study of physics, chemistry and biology, working with leading university science departments, industry and major UK science bodies to create innovative centres of excellence.
- Engineering colleges focus on mathematics and design technology, providing opportunities to study a wide range of engineering disciplines from civil and electrical engineering to telecom. Their aim is to increase the number of good applicants for engineering degrees.
- Mathematics and computing colleges emphasise these two essential prerequisites for further studies in the sciences and technology and for jobs requiring numerical analysis.
- Business and enterprise colleges specialise in business studies and foster an enterprise culture in schools. They teach business studies, financial literacy, enterprise-related vocational studies and marketing skills.
- Humanities colleges (the first were due to open in September 2004) specialise in either English (both language and literature), history or geography.
- There are also schools with combined specialisms. Additionally schools in rural areas may add a rural dimension in any of the above specialisms.

Most specialist schools not only perform exceptionally well in their specialist subjects, they also perform well overall. Usually the raising of standards in the specialist subject precedes an overall improvement in standards. Many educationalists believe that if a school develops a centre of excellence in one subject, this will, in time, pull up performance in all subjects – this is called the 'locomotive' effect.

Professor David Jesson's research gives strong evidence to this view. In 2003, all nine types of specialist school then in existence (the first Humanities Colleges and

Table 5.1 Performance of specialist schools by category in 2003 (*Source:* Compiled by the Specialist Schools Trust 2004)

Specialism	Number of schools	Pupils achieving 5+ A*–C grades at GCSE (%)
CTC	15	86·3
Science	22	67·4
Mathematics and Computing	9	63·1
Language	135	60·4
Business and Enterprise	18	57·4
Technology	415	56·6
Arts	167	53·6
Engineering	3	51·8
Sports	154	48·4
Average specialist	**938**	**56·0**
Average non-specialist	1,993	47·1

music colleges (which were due to open in September 2004) performed better overall than non-specialist comprehensive schools (Table 5.1).

But, significantly, the performance of specialist schools compared to non-specialist schools is even greater in their specialist subject, thus supporting the 'locomotive' principle. Technology college pupils gain better grades in design and technology, mathematics and science, while language college pupils do better in modern foreign languages and arts colleges do better in performing and visual arts.

In technology colleges, for example, in 2003:

- 59% of pupils gained an A*–C grade in design technology compared with 46% in other schools.
- 51% of pupils achieved an A*–C in science compared with 44% in other schools.
- 49% of pupils achieved an A*–C in mathematics compared with 43% in other schools.

The results in French, German and Spanish are considerably higher in language colleges compared to all other schools. Not only do language colleges enhance entry rates to GCSE language courses but they also receive higher success rates (Table 5.2).

A similar relationship exists for arts colleges. Again, apart from an almost equal percentage entry in GCSE art/design, specialist schools have higher entry

Table 5.2 Comparative performance at GCSE in language colleges in 2003 (*Source:* compiled by the Specialist Schools Trust 2004)

School	French Percentage of pupils		German Percentage of pupils		Spanish Percentage of pupils	
	entered	gaining grade A*–C	entered	gaining grade A*–C	entered	gaining grade A*–C
Language Colleges	64·9	54·1	26·2	53·9	27·2	58·5
Other schools	54·1	40·3	17·2	47·5	11·8	43·3

rates for other arts GCSEs (drama, performing arts etc.) than other schools; and their success rate is substantially higher in each of the relevant subject areas (Table 5.3).

The third – and perhaps most controversial – reason for the specialist school initiative being so valued is that specialist schools have shown the importance of accountability, transparency and choice in raising standards. The Koret Taskforce on American Public Schools published a study in 2003 on how to improve standards in schools.[3] This remarkable document authored by some of the leading thinkers in education in the USA including Diane Ravitch, Terry Moe, John Chubb and Checker Finn concludes that:

> Accountability, choice, and transparency are the essential trinity of principles by which to improve standards in schools. Each must be in place for the others to work. In combination, they transform the education system's priorities, power relationships, and incentive structures.

The Koret group defines accountability as meaning that all of those in the education system – the child, the teacher, the school and district leaders – know what they must produce in the way of results, how they will be measured, and what will happen If they do or do not attain the desired results. Their study gives strong support to the principle of choice which thus brings freedom, diversity and innovation to how education is provided, who provides it, and what options are available to families. They define transparency as the information needed to

---

[3] P. E. Peterson (ed.), *Our Schools and our Future . . . Are We Still at Risk?* (Stanford University, Hoover Institution Press, 2003). More information at www.koretfoundation.org.

Table 5.3 Comparative performance at GCSE in arts colleges in 2003 (*Source:* compiled by the Specialist Schools Trust 2004)

| | Art/design | | Drama | | Performing arts | | Media | | Music | |
| | Percentage of pupils | | Percentage of pupils | | Percentage of pupils | | Percentage of pupils | | Percentage of pupils | |
	entered	gaining grade A*–C	entered	gaining grade A*–C	entered	gaining grade A*–C	entered	gaining grade A*–C	entered	gaining grade A*–C
Arts colleges	26·2	64·3	27·1	65·4	6·4	53·7	14·2	56·2	12·8	65·0
Other schools	26·7	60·0	19·3	62·3	3·2	44·9	8·6	50·9	9·5	58·5

assure both top-down accountability and a viable marketplace of methods and ideas. They conclude that:

> taken together, the result of these three will be a reinvigorated yet very different public education system, a new constitutional arrangement with power distributed where it belongs, checks and balances among those who wield that power, and incentives that pull toward – rather than away from – achievement, productivity, freedom, and accountability.

The specialist schools movement founded in 1988 when the first CTC opened with the support of Kenneth Baker, the then Secretary of State for Education, incorporates all three of these principles. The process starts with the bid for specialist status, something which requires considerable effort and clear thinking. Schools must produce a convincing plan of how, if designated, they will use the extra funding to raise standards not only in their specialist subject but overall. This entails a realistic analysis of a school's strong and weak points. The school improvement plan must have the support the staff. Without this it will not work and the school is unlikely to be designated.

Schools suitable for designation are shortlisted before being designated by the DfES. Ofsted registered inspectors visit shortlisted schools to determine if the bid has the commitment of the staff. It is often easy to spot those schools which rely on a consultant to write their bid in isolation from the real picture: the best bids are those which reflect what is really happening at the school, and do not attempt to regurgitate jargon in a bid to impress the DfES. Designation is not an automatic process. It is awarded where a school can demonstrate why it should become a specialist school and how that status will improve its mission and standards. Not surprisingly, only around 60 per cent of specialist school bids in any one bidding round are successful. Many schools have had to bid three or more times first.

Accountability and transparency

Specialist schools are accountable for the extra funding they receive. And to retain their status (and the extra funding that goes with specialist status) they must rebid every four years. If they have not delivered the targets which they set for themselves in their original bid they may have their specialist status withdrawn – this happens to about five per cent of specialist schools bidding for redesignation each year. Some commentators have suggested that the fact that one in ten of the original specialist schools have had their status withdrawn is a sign of the weaknesses of the programme. In fact, it is one of its great strengths: as more schools become specialist, it is essential that there are both rewards for success and sanctions where promised progress has not been achieved. This process is particularly important as it ensures that specialism brings with it an ongoing commitment. It is not simply about a burst of enthusiasm before initial application, but about a change to the culture and ethos of schools.

The spirit of accountability permeates the whole movement. Every year the Specialist Schools Trust publishes a detailed study analysing the educational outcomes of each school. Not all schools are successful in raising their standards and their results are published too, providing accountability not only to parents and the local community but, perhaps even more importantly, to fellow specialist schools. This rigorous accountability has been largely accepted because as described in Chapter 1, the Specialist Schools Trust has pioneered the development of a fair and transparent value-added system of judging a school's performance.

Professor David Jesson of the University of York, in partnership with the Fischer Family Trust[4] and the DfES, has been able to compare the attainment of pupils when they begin secondary school at age 11 with those same pupils' GCSE results five years later. Professor Jesson has been able to match the results of 96 per cent of all state secondary school pupils who took their GCSEs in 2003 with their 1998 Key Stage 2 point score five years earlier. By using a simple yet powerful regression formula, he was also able to predict what each school might be expected to achieve at GCSE and compare this with its actual results. This is how the Specialist Schools Trust derives a 'value-added' indicator of each school's performance.

Since this approach allows for a fair comparison of the performance of schools with widely differing intakes of ability, schools accept the conclusions reached. Compared to comparisons based on raw examination results this is clearly a much fairer and better approach. As shown in Table 1.1, Chapter 1, the ten leading specialist schools in 2003 on this basis are not necessarily the schools which have the highest percentage of pupils achieving 5+ A*–C grades at GCSE but those who add the most value.

Choice

Choice is an emotive word in English educational circles. To many supporters of equal opportunities, choice often means privilege and the ability to pay for a private school education for one's children, or to attend a good school because you live in a socially advantaged, leafy suburb where the cost of housing is higher.

---

[4] An independent, non-profit organisation which is mainly involved in undertaking and supporting projects addressing the development of education in the UK, the Trust has pioneered benchmarking data that allows schools to compare their performance with similar schools. See www.fischertrust.org.

But, as David Blunkett, Education Secretary from 1997 to 2001, said in a landmark speech to the Specialist Schools Trust in 1997, 'Sameness is the enemy of raising standards.' Sadly the creation of an almost entirely comprehensive system (and the consequent closure of hundreds of grammar schools) in the 1960s and 1970s did not lead to an automatic raising of educational standards for all pupils as was the intention, but often led to a wide gap in attainment between schools in different areas. In many cases, the schools still reflect their grammar or secondary modern origins. The fundamental flaw in the creation of the neighbourhood comprehensive school was the expectation that every child should attend their local school whether or not it is a good school, thus ignoring the benefits of choice and diversity. Ironically, it has also meant that in urban areas, few schools are truly comprehensive. They often have a disproportionate number of low achievers, and this can be self-perpetuating. Many popular schools as a result often have very narrow catchment areas and the quality of education a child receives frequently depends upon the size of the parents' mortgage.

For an inner city child, this often means attending a poor school while children of parents in socially advantaged areas usually attend good schools. Moreover, middle-class parents are often able to use their ability to manipulate the system to get their child into a good school. As Anthony Seldon, the distinguished headmaster of Brighton College, has said, they think nothing of moving into the catchment areas of leading comprehensives to secure educational advantage for their children.[5] The advent of specialist schools, many of which are foundation or voluntary-aided schools responsible for their own admissions, has fundamentally changed this. CTCs pioneered the use of fair banding and the use of wide catchment areas thus increasing choice. Many specialist schools have followed this model.

Nearly all specialist schools are comprehensive schools, admitting a wide range of ability, but because many of them are high-performing schools, they are also popular schools, frequently being oversubscribed by a factor of more than two to one. This means they are often able to attract applications from a socially diverse group of pupils with a wide range of ability even if they are located in the inner city. Specialist schools will bring about the end to poor performance in comprehensive education, not because they select more able pupils, but because they attract pupils from all ability levels and provide choice and diversity in the provision of free state-funded education. They are indeed genuinely comprehensive schools as their average Key Stage 2 results for incoming Year 7 pupils at age 11 confirm.

The biggest problem facing English education is what to do about the 250 or so underperforming schools largely in the inner city areas which are deeply unpopular with parents. These schools are frequently undersubscribed and have an unfairly

---

[5] See T. Halpin, 'Parents "should pay for state schools" ' (*The Times*, 4 February 2004).

high proportion of children with learning difficulties, including those excluded from other schools for emotional or behavioural difficulties and many refugee children whose knowledge of English is weak.

With changes of leadership, some of these schools can be turned around. With inspiring leaders of the calibre of Sir Dexter Hutt at Ninestiles School and Hugh Howe at Fir Vale (described in greater detail in Chapter 4) or Ken Nimmo of Turves Green Boys' School (where the proportion of pupils gaining five or more good GCSEs has improved from 21 per cent to 59 per cent) outstanding improvement can take place.

How specialism helped transform Walker Technology College

One such example is that of Tony Broady of Walker Technology College in Newcastle. In this 1,300-strong comprehensive, the proportion of pupils gaining good GCSE passes has improved from a situation where hardly any pupils gained five good GCSEs to one where 58 per cent did so in 2003, and the school's sights have been set even higher for subsequent years. Located in an area of Newcastle with very high levels of social deprivation, the school's four key feeder primary schools are based in wards which are among the 30 most deprived in the UK, based on multiple deprivation indices. They have greater levels of deprivation than any ward in Greater London. Ninety per cent of local people live in council housing, of which there is a surplus in the area, leaving a lot of properties empty and very few bought through 'right to buy'. Unemployment is high, leaving 43 per cent of Walker's pupils eligible for free school meals. School attendance has historically been a major concern and although it is improving, this is still the case.

But the population is a stable one – 56 per cent of pupils have a sibling who attends or has attended the school and many have parents and grandparents who went there. It is also largely white (only two per cent of Walker's pupils have English as a second language).

When Dr Broady joined Walker School as head teacher in 1984, the school had a very poor reputation. So much so that the head teacher's post had been vacant for a year. His challenge was to get out of 'failure mode' and start an improvement process. But Dr Broady was determined to do so with an unchanged catchment area, believing as he does that deprivation should not be an excuse for low achievement, but that it is a reason for the school to accept greater responsibility for improving results. Initially progress was slow, but in recent years it has been much more marked, as Table 5.4 demonstrates.

Table 5.4 GCSE progress at Walker Technology College 1991–2004

Year	Pupils achieving 5+ A*–C grades (%)
1991	1 (bottom in Newcastle)
1993	9
1996	21
1997	14 (drop due to change in science curriculum)
2001	25 (9th in Newcastle)
2002	42 (5th in Newcastle)
2003	58 (2nd in Newcastle, 9th most improved specialist school, +29 value added in the Jesson research)
2004	Projection: 70? (1st in Newcastle?)

Strategies for improvement at Walker

The gaining of technology college status in 1999, at the third attempt, was a crucial milestone for Walker. The additional money, flexibility and the target setting all helped the school accelerate progress. The school was already investing in ICT, but this marked a further investment and the introduction of a much wider range of vocational courses. The school changed its name to Walker Technology College to give a signal that this new status was permanent and not going to be lost.

Tony Broady is a strong advocate of learning from other schools' experience. He says that when just one per cent of your pupils gain five or more GCSE passes you keep going to conferences looking for the 'magic answer'. It does not exist, but you can get your best 'INSET' from other schools. He quotes several examples of others' good practice which he has introduced at Walker. Like many specialist school head teachers, he is a strong believer in building on tried and tested good practice from other schools.

So, when, on a visit to meet Sir Dexter at Ninestiles School in Birmingham, Dr Broady was struck by the school's 'good order', he decided to adopt their programme of Discipline for Learning. As we have seen in Chapter 4, this system of consequences for disruptive behaviour ranging from a first verbal warning to a day in isolation, helps to ensure consistency for teachers and pupils and involves all staff who manage hour-long detention periods on a rota basis. Having a clear strategy for discipline is one of the first steps towards real improvement.

It was on a visit to Middleton Technology College in Rochdale that Dr Broady began to consider the issue of Year 11 study leave. Typically secondary schools allow their GCSE students several weeks off in the summer term to study at home.

But there are suspicions that the time is not always used to good effect. So, Middleton had cancelled this process. Walker followed suit and cancelled study leave from 2002. Pupils later admitted that they would have been unlikely to revise during this time off school. Revision lessons now continue in school right up until the last examination, sometimes as late as 30 June.

Visiting the Specialist Schools Conference in 2002 gave Dr Broady the idea of extending school-based revision in the immediate run up to an exam. Students can benefit from a last minute refresher session to concentrate their minds. So, a last minute revision session lasting half an hour in the form of a PowerPoint presentation by a member of staff, takes place in the examination room before the exam itself. Bringing the pupils in half an hour early helps boost confidence and also gives the school the opportunity to chase up any non-attendees.

Tony Broady is keen to emphasise that many of these good ideas come at zero cost. Despite money from the Leadership Incentive Grant and the Education Action Zone, he finds balancing his school's budget a continuing challenge and he is carrying a modest deficit. Nevertheless, as with specialist schools more generally, he is keen to share his successes with other schools. So he has put his half hour pre-exam revision sessions on disc for other Newcastle schools. And Walker is happy to receive an increasing number of visitors keen to share the secrets of its success, including groups from the school (Southfields in Cumbria) which his Deputy will join shortly as head teacher.

Specialism helps towards a more appropriate curriculum

Many specialist schools are innovative in their approach to the curriculum, not just in their attitude to their specialist subjects, but more widely. Bold decisions have been taken at Walker over recent years to introduce a more appropriate curriculum for individual students, including a more work-related curriculum for some. GNVQ in ICT is compulsory from Year 9 onwards and it has made a huge impact as has GNVQ Science where the top half of the year group increased the number of passes from 33 students with dual award at Grade C or better in 2002 to 95 students with the equivalent of four Grade Cs or better in 2003. To the critics who say that examination success is simply down to 'skewed' results from the introduction of GNVQ courses, Dr Broady responds that these courses are appropriate for his students. They are convinced they are going to achieve in GNVQs and they are good courses which give good employment skills. He also points out that even without GNVQ success his 5+ A*–C pass rate of 58 per cent would be 42 per cent, still a huge improvement. Possible new courses to be introduced in the future include graphics and media studies, which overlap in content with the GNVQ ICT course.

Another innovation, which has also been a feature of many specialist schools and some other comprehensives, has been the fast tracking of English in Year 11. All Year 11 pupils now take GCSE English Language in November, allowing more time for English literature in the remainder of the year. The percentage of pupils gaining at least one GCSE pass at grades A–G has risen from 83 per cent in 2002 to 96 per cent in 2003 and English has had a significant impact on this.

Walker focuses on success and staffing

Walker Technology College makes no apologies for its focus on examination success. Target-setting has always been an important feature of specialism, though it has, of course, been much more widely adopted in recent years. Dr Broady points out that the school has always worked hard, but that the key was to get a critical mass of pupils succeeding. He employs a variety of strategies to ensure this. For example, 73 Year 10 pupils have given up three periods of science to focus on GNVQ ICT. Work with this group has included periods at the City Learning Centre where they have been given a great deal of individual attention.

A major strength of the school is the stability of its staffing complement. Nineteen teachers have been on the staff for over 20 years. Dr Broady gives high priority to staff development. For example heads of department have five formal reviews each year with their line manager and the head teacher. Promotions are often internal and recruitment often local. The improving reputation of the school certainly aids recruitment. Of eight new staff at the school, six had completed their teaching practice there. Staff are actively encouraged to contribute ideas for the school's development and are involved in its planning.

Improving attendance and out-of-hours provision

Attendance has always been an issue at Walker. Many pupils already have a poor attendance record when they arrive in Year 7 and some have a reading age off any measurable scale. Strategies include a 'first-day response' to absence, attendance rewards, a Governors' Attendance Sub-group and mentoring. Specific pupils and families are targeted with follow-up visits. However, there is still an issue with a 'hard core' of non-attenders.

Like many specialist schools, Walker Technology College is not just an 'examination factory'. It owns an outdoor pursuits centre in the Lake District and is heavily involved in the Duke of Edinburgh's Award Scheme. There are extensive overseas links, including France, Germany, Ukraine, China, Australia, the USA and Norway. Other activities relate more to study support – breakfast clubs, lunchtime and after-school clubs as well as a Saturday morning school and holiday schools.

Setting targets for continuous improvement

The improvements achieved in Walker in recent years are not seen as a cause for complacency. Rather they are the spur for further improvement. Short-term targets for Walker include 70 per cent 5+ A*–C grades in 2004 and first place in the Newcastle League Table. Dr Broady talks about a target of 90 per cent (and retirement) in 2005. The school is considering renewing its buildings under Newcastle's 'Going for Growth' strategy, although the head teacher is keen to avoid the possibility of moving the school site to the centre of the local council estate. He would rather remain on the edge of the estate near a small amount of private housing to keep some element of mix in the school. In his view location is more important than school buildings.

Walker Technology College is an example of a specialist school led with a confidence which has been bred by success. Dr Broady personally has the confidence to disregard agendas he does not share and to focus his efforts on things which make a difference. He loves the fact that when he walks around the local area people comment on the school's success and tell him that it is the talk of the bingo hall. Most of all he appreciates the sharing of ideas with other schools – a key part of the specialism agenda – and he is keen to play a full part in this.

How specialism helped transform Hockerill College

When you walk into the reception area of Hockerill Anglo-European Language College, in Bishop's Stortford, Hertfordshire, among the first things to catch your eye are framed certificates awarded by the Specialist Schools Trust. The school has achieved membership of the Trust's '70 per cent', 'value added' and 'most improved' clubs, reflecting not only its improvement and value added, but the fact that more than 70 per cent of pupils gain at least five good GCSEs. You might well see similar certificates in other successful specialist schools, but as you look further you realise what lies behind an institution with a very distinctive ethos and curriculum.

Hockerill is a good example. To start with it feels more like an independent school. It is one of 30 state boarding schools in England and the buildings have a sense of history. This is reflected in the terminology used – 'cloisters' and 'refectory' – and in the notices about meetings of the cadet corps. But there is something more here, which might be less common in the independent sector. There is a culture of internationalism which permeates the school. Every student studies at least two modern foreign languages. There is a bilingual section for the most able linguists. The International Baccalaureate (IB) is taught post-16. There is an extensive programme of international exchanges. Some of this ethos reflects the background of the current Principal, Dr Robert Guthrie who has taught in independent schools, at an international school and who has an MBA, not to mention being a capped England rugby player. However, the changes which led to the school's current character pre-date his arrival. But above all, this is a very successful school with 80 per cent of pupils gaining five or more good GCSE grades and a value-added score of +20 in the Jesson research for the Specialist Schools Trust.

So, how has this school, described by Ofsted in 2003 as 'excellent' and 'exceptional', developed over time – and how has its specialist status helped it to do so? The truth is that despite being housed in some old and venerable buildings, Hockerill is a relatively new school. The buildings used to house a teacher training college back in the 1850s when the buildings were first constructed. And the Hockerill school was opened in 1980, initially as a boarding school used by Essex LEA. Places were purchased by LEAs, often for pupils with problems. Over time numbers fell, reflecting a decline in state boarding schools generally. In 1994, the school opted for grant-maintained status. This gave the governors a new degree of autonomy. They had the freedom to turn the school into something more successful. Clearly the first and most important measure had to be the introduction of day places. As they expanded beyond being a boarding school, they also decided to adopt an international dimension, incorporating 'Anglo-European' into the name.

The context in which they did this was inauspicious. There were just 300 pupils on the roll. The roll was falling and there were all too many spare places. The school was in debt to the tune of £370,000. Not surprisingly, the buildings were neglected. It had another big problem which related to its history. Local parents did not know Hockerill as a day school; in any case Bishop Stortford already had several good secondary schools with sixth forms.

Sowing the seeds of current success

However, the seeds of current success were then being sown. Around 40 per cent of pupils were achieving at least 5+ A*–C grades at GCSE, broadly in line with the national average at that time; a respectable, but unremarkable result. Specialism in languages was to be the vehicle for real improvement. Although the school had not previously seen the teaching of modern foreign languages as a strength, the head teacher and governors decided to introduce a bilingual section. Internationalism became a major feature and partnerships were established with French and German schools. In 1998 the school applied to establish a sixth form, which it regarded as being important if it were to be attractive to local parents. Though their application was rejected, the school found a way around this, by establishing a partnership with another local school. The route they chose was that of the International Baccalaureate (IB) because this reflected their internationalism and also offered something distinctive which no other school in the area, and indeed no other state boarding school, was offering. The move to 11–18 was absolutely crucial because it attracted more pupils and staff to the school and provided continuity, especially for the boarders. In 2000, the school became one of the first training schools in the country (see Chapter 7 for more on training schools) in partnership with the University of Nottingham. They train bilingual teachers and use 'teaching observatories' which have video and audio links to the university. They are involved in research into the teaching of languages.

A school transformed

Hockerill today is a school transformed. There is no longer any fear of falling rolls. Every place could be taken six times over if parents had their way. Because it remains one of the few state boarding schools in the country, it still has 220 boarders. Now there are also 480 day pupils, with a further 135 students in the sixth form. Internationalism pervades the school, and there is a particularly strong link with France. The annual French trip for students in Year 7 is one of the highlights for students new to Hockerill. The most able linguists join the bilingual section, where they are taught in both English and French. In Year 8 they have a two-and-a-half week 'total immersion' in France. In Year 10 they do their work experience in France. Humanities subjects are delivered in French. As a result of this immersion, many students are able to fast track their GCSE exams in French, taking it in Year 9 or 10. They can then go on to take an A/S and A2 Levels in Years 10 and 11. There is now also a German bilingual section and the pupils demonstrate tremendous confidence in the use of languages. The bilingual section has developed over time and is set to develop further.

Internationalism is not restricted to partnerships with schools in France and Germany. Partner schools have now been established in Belgium, Italy, Romania, Spain and Japan. It is also reflected in the nature of the students, many of whom have parents of different nationalities, and the staff. Empathy with the school's ethos, work experience in another country and the ability to speak another language are all important recruitment criteria. The college makes extensive use of language assistants and gap-year students.

All students take two modern foreign languages at GCSE, some take three. Pupils can study Japanese as well as the major European languages. Overall they now achieve 80 per cent 5+ A*–C grades at GCSE, twice the proportion of students who used to achieve the benchmark. It is true that the intake at Year 7 is slightly above average and that 11 students gain places on the basis of aptitude in languages, but even allowing for this advantage, the school still achieves significantly better than predicted results, with the proportion of students gaining five good GCSEs 20 percentage points higher than expected, according to the Jesson research. Ninety-five per cent of those in the sixth form gain their IB certificate – a figure well above the average – and 55 per cent gain the bilingual certificate. All students progress to higher education with some students winning places at Oxford and Cambridge.

There is a successful mix of the old and the modern at Hockerill, which owes much to the traditional boarding school ethos which still pervades the school. Classes are held on Saturday mornings in addition to those during the week. There are extensive extra-curricular activities, including the cadet corps. The aim is to produce well-rounded individuals with the confidence to operate across national boundaries.

The school does not try to keep its success to itself. Like other specialist schools, it places an important emphasis on working with the wider community. A partnership has been developed with six primary schools in the Bishop Stortford area. Their work includes training primary teachers in delivering modern foreign languages and running masterclasses for some pupils. Free language classes, at 4 p.m., are also offered to primary pupils in French, German, Italian and Japanese. The school is also involved in adult language classes and mixed classes of parents and students. However, unlike many other specialist schools, Hockerill has had difficulties in developing successful links with local business, despite the proximity of Stansted Airport. The school has just produced a CD-ROM about its work to try and address this.

Finally, the school has in recent years begun to evangelise about its ethos and approach. It doesn't believe in keeping the secrets of its success to itself. Newspaper articles, for example in the *Daily Telegraph*, appearances on national radio and television and involvement in the European Day of Languages have all helped to spread the word, as have advertisements in in-flight magazines aimed at attracting more overseas students.

Behind this success, there were two crucial factors. The first, most obviously, was the decision to take day pupils and sixth formers. But the second was the acquisition of language college status in 1998. Dr Guthrie regards this achievement as a crucial milestone in his school's journey. But it was not all plain sailing. At the time he was upset that it took three attempts to make a successful bid, but now he recognises that then the school was very small, had an enormous debt, was stuck in the mid-40 per cent good GCSE grades and had no sixth form. These factors must have affected the quality of the school's initial bids. What language college status finally conferred was external recognition, a new status and a complete change in local perceptions of the school, vital given the drive to recruit more day pupils at that time. Also it brought tangible benefits such as the use of ICT in languages. The subsequent excellence achieved in languages has spread throughout the college, bringing a culture of confidence, risk taking and cross-curricular co-operation.

Hockerill Anglo-European Language College is now an excellent school, exhibiting a 'creative mix' of risk taking alongside a traditional English school with a fairly standard comprehensive intake. The Principal will continue to bring new projects on board, for example a new £6 million centre for languages, humanities and the performing arts. He will not rest on his laurels because, as the new CD-ROM says, 'standing still is the new walking backwards'. Above all the success of the school is a tribute to a clearly articulated, consistent vision. Its principle is to teach language to the highest possible standard. This is a school which has dared to be different and it works.

The challenge of greater change – Academies

Some underperforming schools require drastic measures. Some will be closed and re-established as Academies; others where there is a surplus of places will simply be closed. Ultimately real choice for all parents will come about when parents, even in the most socially challenged areas, will be able to apply to a number of good state schools each with a different centre of excellence in a particular subject. In areas like Brent and Hackney, this dream is already being realised through the creation of a number of rapidly improving specialist schools and Academies which not only give parents the opportunity to choose from a number of good schools, but also to choose a specialism which best fits their child's aptitudes and interests.

Academies start with support of £2 million from sponsors, which is backed up by building grants of up to £30 million from the Government. The sponsors range from successful entrepreneurs wishing to put something back into their community to educational trusts, churches and other schools (including CTCs and independent schools). Seventeen Academies had opened by September 2004, including the innovative Business Academy in Bexley, sponsored by Sir David Garrard, where students spend every Friday on business-related studies, with a model of a city trading floor in the school. Even in the first year, the Academy saw results improving three-fold. There are expected to be at least 200 Academies by 2010, serving at least 200,000 pupils, many of them in London. Many are likely to emulate CTCs in their use of banding to improve choice and achieve a balanced comprehensive intake. Like CTCs, they are independent of their LEA and are funded from Whitehall. But unlike CTCs initially, they have often enjoyed strong support and advocacy from their LEAs. The hope must be that this combination, together with their strong specialist focus, is as successful with Academies as it has been with CTCs.

Conclusions

Specialist school status can be a crucial driver of school improvement. There are those who suggest that it is all about the money or the intake of pupils. In truth, the money, though welcome, is a marginal if important additional sum for schools, many of which have far greater differentials with neighbouring schools in other LEAs. And there is now considerable research to show that once the marginally better intake to specialist schools is allowed for, specialist comprehensives still significantly outperform other comprehensives. The secrets of success lie in the drive which bidding for and keeping specialist status requires – the new partnerships with business and the wider community; the targets in both the specialist subject and the rest of the curriculum; and the leadership and vision which lie behind a successful bid. With many more schools acquiring specialist status, the movement is now central to school reform.

6

Using data to improve performance

If one change has characterised education reform in recent years, it has been an explosion of information about school performance. Each year, school and college performance tables – now renamed School and College Attainment and Achievement Tables – are published by the DfES in England for the national tests at Key Stages 2 and 3, as well as for GCSEs, A Levels and their vocational equivalents. While education ministers in Edinburgh, Belfast and Cardiff bowed to teaching union demands to scrap what they call league tables (and some testing) altogether, English ministers doggedly insist that they are here to stay. More importantly, a raft of information is now provided to every school each autumn by the Government and Ofsted. This enables each school to evaluate its own performance and the performance of individual pupils, to identify where improvements can be made and to benchmark that achievement against that of schools with similar characteristics, such as social mix or the proportion of students whose first language is not English. And, together with Ofsted's new shorter inspections, the Government is planning to introduce new school profiles to bring together key material about schools for parents (see Chapter 11).

The annual feast of information produces mixed reactions. Even if the DfES no longer produces the data on 93 tonnes of paper, preferring to publish them electronically instead, national and local newspapers certainly fell a few trees in their publication. But a fiercer debate has raged in the education world. Teaching unions routinely call for them to be abandoned. Yet parents inevitably consult them to gain an ostensibly objective measure of local schools' achievement, although many educationists warn them that without additional information such as the social class of pupils or the value added by schools, they lack any great meaning. The anti-league table brigade may have been right to demand context, yet even when this context has been provided, their calls for abolition ring no less loud. But how much more objectionable would it be to say that parents should not know how well schools perform in national tests and exams, because they are too ignorant to understand their meaning. For all the fuss about league tables, the real revolution has not been in the availability of newspaper supplements full of dense data. It lies in the development of value-added measures that allow schools to see how well they are doing given the performance of their intake at age 11, or in high schools, 13. Or, in the jargon favoured by some in government, this is assessment *for* learning, not just assessment *of* learning.

And just as the publication of value-added data allows for a more sophisticated analysis of the results, it has also spawned what is sometimes derogatively described as a 'culture of targets'. Nationally, the Government, prodded by a Treasury keen to ensure that taxpayers' money is not falling into some bottomless pit, has demanded proof that extra money produces results. Schools and LEAs have been set goals on everything from exam scores to teacher absence. But while the national targets may arguably have had a galvanising effect when they were first introduced in 1997, their power wore off, at least in primary schools by 2000 (though there was some improvement in 2004). Inspectors suggest that quality of teaching is the reason. An Ofsted report in 2003 found that one in eight literacy lessons was unsatisfactorily taught, with only half deemed to be 'good' or 'very good'.[1] As a result, most years the national scores have been published since then have served to present the targets – that 80 per cent of pupils reach level 4 in English at age 11 and 75 per cent do so in mathematics – as elusive. In 2004, 77 per cent made the grade in English, while 74 per cent did so in mathematics. Encouragingly, there have also been signs of improvement at Key Stage 3 since a new strategy was introduced to improve teaching for 11–14-year-olds. Nevertheless, the use of clear, challenging and realistic targets can be far more effective, where the school has developed them for individual pupils with the support of the leadership team and staff in each subject department. Achievements towards such targets are something the whole school takes pride in. And they are undoubtedly a key element of achievement and continuing improvement in successful schools.

Measuring how much value is added

Professor David Jesson, whose research on specialist schools we have already discussed, is one of the foremost proponents of the use of data to help improvement.

---

[1] Ofsted, *The National Literacy and Numeracy Strategies and the Primary Curriculum* (London, DfES, 2003).

He has worked with many schools to help them use information to improve their results. 'If you aim at nothing, you're likely to succeed,' he says. 'The schools that are most successful are those that are committed to self-evaluation, where they look at their past performance and set their targets focused on improvements in specific subjects rather than a broad brush approach.' By that he means that where a school finds that its achievements in French and geography are particularly poor, by comparison with other subjects, a strong effort to improve the languages and geography departments is more likely to produce results than a general exhortation to improve overall GCSE grades. Since the introduction of the first specialist schools in 1994, a key feature of their development has been the requirement that they set themselves ambitious targets. This has proved particularly helpful for those whose results have been significantly below the national average, and many have delivered substantial improvements partly as a result of such ambition. However, such targets seem only to work effectively when they are both challenging and are owned by the school. Each teacher and pupil should feel that they are *their* targets, not those of the local council or Whitehall, although their success in meeting them will also contribute to local or national improvements. 'The experience of some education authorities of deciding targets for schools and then trying to get schools to agree to them afterwards has rarely been a happy one,' adds Prof. Jesson. 'Schools will know what is possible. And the targets need to be owned by each school.' There is one awkward but interesting point in all this. The Government now publishes level 5 results for 11-year-olds as well as level 4, by school. For some schools, the expected standard is no longer a challenge, whether that be level 5 at Key Stage 3 or the five good GCSE benchmark. In such circumstances, more challenging targets are appropriate: levels 6 and 7 at Key Stage 3 and an average point score at GCSE. Prof. Jesson has found that many grammar schools, for example, record all their pupils as having achieved five or more A*–C grades at GCSE. But not every grammar school performs the same, so something further is needed. Differences only become apparent when either their average point score is compared or their value-added achievement is examined. This then means that different goals need to be set which may be more challenging than those for a school with an average comprehensive intake. 'Unless you have more challenging goals, such schools are less inclined to take targets seriously,' says Prof. Jesson.

Whose value-added measurement do you use?

But here is where it gets complicated. For there is a real difference of opinion between statisticians on how best to measure the value added, or on what basis to award the average point score. The Government has created a sophisticated model, which compares the results of the same pupils at ages seven and 11; at 11 and 14; and at 14 and 16. It then turns this data in to a school level score, where the average is 100. Those significantly below 99 are underachieving; those significantly above 101 are doing well. The problem is that the measure has bunched well over 90 per cent of schools so close to 100 that it renders the measure virtually useless to parents. Professor Jesson has developed an alternative approach, based on predicted scores. So, for example, he would look at the attainment of each GCSE candidate at the age of 11 in a school and compare the results they achieved in their GCSEs with a predicted score based on their prior attainment. In that way, a school can quickly see whether it has added more or less value compared with other schools.

Similarly, while there is agreement that providing an average point score is a more useful indicator of achievement than the 5+ A*–C grade score, there is disagreement about how to calculate it. All agree that using a score which gives more points for an A than a C, and which gives some recognition to Ds and Es, is useful for crediting high fliers and recognising the achievements of those who won't get the five or more A* to C grades that have become the benchmark of success. There is evidence that many schools focus on pushing their D-candidates to gain Cs, which is no bad thing in itself, but similar effort does not go into raising Es to Ds or Bs to As, because there is little extra school kudos to be gained for such achievements. Yet the failure to push those students may be denying them the chance to fulfil their true potential. But though there is agreement that an average point score is useful, there is less agreement on how to calculate it. The Government takes the top eight GCSE exams of each candidate and averages their score to calculate its 'Average Capped Point Score' for each candidate. Others, including Prof. Jesson, say a better way to do it would be to include the results of every GCSE taken, so that a pupil taking 12 or 13 GCSEs had their achievements recognised too. Whatever method is used, there is a general recognition that such data can be useful. 'A school which had most of its pupils gaining five or more good GCSEs but achieved a relatively low average point score would not be serving its pupils well,' adds Prof. Jesson.[2]

But neither of these measures takes account of the social make-up of a school. There are those who believe that in addition to looking at how well a school has brought on its pupils, there should also be measures showing how many pupils are in receipt of free school meals, how many have special educational needs and how many come from an ethnic minority. Those who oppose

---

[2] Professor Jesson sets out his formula in greater detail in Appendix 1.

such views say that this simply lowers expectations; that those from poorer backgrounds aren't born stupid and to label them as such will hardly help them to gain a decent education. And it is fair to say that with a robust value-added measure and an average point score, the arguments for comparing GCSE or Key Stage 3 results with the social make-up of a school seem redundant. If pupils are underachieving when they come to the school, then the score will measure the progress that has been made from that starting point. Similarly, if pupils have many advantages at home and the benefit of a more stimulating environment, the extent to which the school has stretched them will be measured. Labelling such pupils according to their background could harm the chances of weak schools raising their game, though it can be useful for schools with similar intakes to compare their performance.

Targets at work in Staffordshire

One school, which has made real gains through using targets and information about results effectively with parents, students and teachers, is De Ferrers Technology College, an 11–18 specialist school with 1,893 students, in Burton-on-Trent, Staffordshire. When a new head teacher, Michael York, was appointed in 1997, targets were introduced to the school for the first time. John Slusar became Assistant Principal with specific responsibility for developing those targets and making much better use of pupil achievement data. 'We now have a very powerful database,' says Mr Slusar. 'We have information on every student's achievement and their targets in every subject.' The school uses standard SIMS[3] technology, which is widely available, but benefits from having one person in charge of collecting and collating the data. In 1997, 39 per cent of pupils achieved five or more good GCSE passes; by 2003, the total had risen to 59 per cent. But progress wasn't always rapid. Between 1999 and 2001, the proportion gaining five good passes hovered between 51 and 53 per cent, even dipping between 1999 and 2000, something which many schools experience where a cohort in one year may be less able than that in an earlier year. De Ferrers didn't rest on its laurels: it wanted to do better, though its results were already slightly above the national average.

'We gained specialist school status in 2001, when we became a technology college,' recalls Mr Slusar. 'That has provided us with extra money: £1 million over four years, and it has given us an added focus on mathematics, science, technology and IT. But it has also meant we needed to develop stronger individual

---

[3] SIMS is the management information system used by most schools in England. More information is available at home.capitaes.co.uk/sims/index.asp.

targets for each student. Prior to 2001, we used to give teachers the information about each student. To be honest, not everyone acted on them, maybe only a third of staff used the information. Students were not set their own targets in each subject. All that has changed. Now, every student knows what's expected of them. And their parents do too. From mid-October each year, students discuss with their teachers what they can achieve. Then early in the New Year, parents sit down for 15 minutes with their child's tutors to discuss the individual targets and how they can help meet them. Some targets may be more ambitious than those the Government sets: so, we might set a student's sights on a level 6 in the Key Stage 3 English or mathematics test rather than a level 5, which is the expected average grade. The result of this individual focus is that students put in more effort and get better grades. They also are more aware of their own strengths and weaknesses. A few years ago, they might know whether they enjoyed a subject or not, and whether they liked the teacher, but they wouldn't have the same concrete evidence of their own abilities. And because of the meetings with parents and students, every member of staff has to be on top of the information about each student. It has forced them to treat the data more seriously.'

An additional feature of the De Ferrers' approach has been to provide parents and teachers with a simple illustration of each child's performance. Marks are standardised to allow an accurate comparison of performance in each subject. 'This allows the student to ascertain their strengths and areas for development,' explains Mr Slusar. 'By Year 9 it may influence their option choices. It also enables the college to provide an Order of Merit in each subject – and across all subjects. We are therefore in a position to reward excellence and those making most progress from one year to the next.' The scheme also benefits heads of department (or Directors of Faculties, as they are called at De Ferrers). Mr Slusar offers as an example the Science Faculty, with 12 staff and 360 students in one year group. There are four things the Director would do to use the scheme. First, he ensures there are common schemes of learning. Second, he ensures there is a common examination. Third, Mr Slusar provides him with a standardised mark for each student in each subject. And fourth, he takes the Order of Merit and proposes a National Curriculum level (related to the levels in national tests). His staff member can accept that level, or propose reasons to lower or raise it. The calculation of the standardised mark uses some basic statistics, but Mr Slusar says that the calculation can be made on the computer in 30 seconds, and it would take 'even the least mathematical teacher less than ten minutes to master the process'.

To make this calculation, Mr Slusar starts by putting the raw exam marks for each student onto an EXCEL worksheet. He uses the computer to calculate the standard deviation between the different marks – in other words, the extent to which marks differ from the average.[4] In order to get a simple comparable figure for parents and students, these scores in individual subjects are related to the mean or average for the college (say, 50) and the standard deviation in the college (say, 20). The marks are adjusted so that 50 becomes the mean and 20 the standard deviation in each subject to make them easier to compare.[5] This formula can easily be stored in the computer. Once the marks have been calculated, candidates are put in order and assigned part levels based on those marks. In discussion with the teachers, a whole level (such as 3, 4, 5 or 6) is then determined. The part level is used to monitor progress during the year, though for simplicity the whole level is the one reported to parents. Though the formula may seem complex, it is relatively easy to use with an EXCEL or SIMS worksheet, and can be invaluable in monitoring the progress of individual students. Moreover, because progress in each subject is being compared on a like-for-like basis, it gives students a realistic sense of their best and weakest subjects.

A useful management tool

The information not only helps pupils to fulfil their potential, it has become an important management tool as well. As Mr Sulsar remarks, 'Our performance management system is such that every member of staff knows which of their students is achieving above or below their potential in each subject. They have enough data to know whether this means their own overall performance will come out as positive or negative.'

A criticism of the addition of value-added information to performance tables has been its complexity. Although the Government data uses figures above and below 100 to decide whether schools are adding value reasonably, they discount the vast majority of schools which fall in the 98–102. The early tables also broke the value added down from ages 11–14 and from 14–16, a limited construct which allowed schools which did little in the first three years of secondary school to gain kudos for catching up in the GCSE years, but penalised those schools

---

[4] The standard deviation is the most common way to measure dispersion in statistics. You will probably find is easier simply to use your computer to calculate the standard deviation. But to calculate it yourself for a group of 30 pupils, you would first obtain the average mark (add together the marks of each pupil in the class and divide the total by 30). You would then calculate the difference between each mark and the average. This is the mark's deviation from the mean. The standard deviation is the square root of the mean of the squares of these values.

[5] Where the college mean is 50 and the subject mean is 59.9; and the college standard deviation is 20 and the subject standard deviation is 17.3, you would do the following: $20/17.3 = m$ and $(59.9 \times m) - 50 = C$. The formula to produce the standardised mark is then $m \times$ raw mark $+ C$.

which had a more consistent record. Mr Slusar believes it makes far more sense to measure progress from 11–16. At least, now that pupil level data are available for five year comparisons, the Government's tables will do this. De Ferrers moved its students from the 58th percentile of achievement to the 77th percentile between Years 7 and 9, and though it fell back to the 73rd percentile by GCSE standard, this was still a considerable advance on their performance at the age of 11. Yet on the 14–16 data provided by the DFES in 2002, the school had a relatively low 95.6 value-added score. All this illustrates the importance of data being properly constructed, and of it not providing perverse incentives to reward past failure.

Involving parents in the process, in Oldham

A feature of the successful use of data appears to be finding ways successfully to communicate its meaning to parents and students, rather than simply seeing it as a tool for teachers and the school leadership team. Another school that has made this transition, with some considerable success, has been The Hathershaw Technology College, a 1,000-student technology college in Oldham. Serving some of the most deprived wards in Greater Manchester, the community has had its fair share of community troubles over the years. The racial disturbances of 2001 brought the area to national attention, though the fallout proved to be positive, as the school worked hard to bring communities together. Forty-three per cent of students are from either Bangladeshi or Pakistani heritage families, but Her Majesty's Inspectorate has been impressed by how many exceed the standards achieved nationally by these ethnic minority communities.

The school is popular with parents, and is oversubscribed. One reason is the level of engagement it has with them. After taking over as head teacher in late 2002, David Ashley organised a special day for parents. He used this occasion to share with them the school's expectations for their students and to give them practical ideas on how they could help their own sons and daughters to succeed, including supporting them in their homework and coursework projects. The parents' day was not going to be like the stereotypical parents' evening, as Mr Ashley explained. 'We called it a "Preparing for Success" day,' 'because we didn't want parents to see at as being like their traditional image of a parents' evening, where they go to find out how their child is doing, and where they are falling behind. We thought they would be more likely to come to a day with a positive title, where they could find out a lot more as well. We used a normal school day for the event, and replaced the normal timetable with activities around the theme. Ours was a school where there had been a tradition of low aspirations among parents and pupils, and this was one way of trying to overcome this.'

Like De Ferrers, Hathershaw has developed a progress chart for individual students, which does not just show what they would be expected to achieve if they simply reflected their prior attainment at 11. For the school as a whole, Prof. Jesson has calculated this would mean just 22 per cent of students gaining five good GCSE grades in 2003, but students are shown what the best students with their prior attainment can achieve. 'Most students and their parents were surprised when teachers had the conversation with them about this data,' reflects Mr Ashley, 'but it showed them what could be achieved when students work hard and do well. We say that there is no reason why most should not gain five grades at C or higher and go on to college.' Using a graph parents are shown the point score achieved by their child at Key Stage 3, along with what the child should get as a minimum and if they work hard. So, for example, a pupil with 33 points at Key Stage 3 could expect to gain at least two grade Cs and six Ds, but with extra effort could get one B and seven Cs. Such data shows the parents the difference which hard work can make to results, and in this case, subsequent opportunities for further education. The chart also grades students' effort, behaviour and homework in each subject on a scale of 1 to 3, where 1 is 'good', 2 'satisfactory' and 3 'cause for concern'. Parents are encouraged to discuss the table with their child, and perhaps establish why behaviour is good in most subjects, but a cause for concern in some. They are encouraged to remind children what they can achieve, and to use the individual targets to help them to do this, and to praise and reward their child for effort and achievement.

The tactics seem to be working. The proportion of students achieving five or more good GCSE grades increased from 32 per cent in 2002 to 53 per cent in 2003, having hovered around the high twenties and low thirties for some years previously. According to the value-added tables prepared by Prof. Jesson, the school ranks eighth in the country among specialist schools for the value it has added for students between Key Stage 2 and Key Stage 4.

Not only do parents have more access to how their children are doing, they are given the opportunity to rate different aspects of the school's performance through a questionnaire. One hundred and six parents of Year 7 pupils were asked whether or not they were satisfied with the care of their child in the school – 42 per cent were very satisfied; 54 per cent satisfied; and only 2 per cent were unhappy. Other issues included behaviour and homework, where there was slightly more concern, but more than three-quarters of parents were satisfied. Such surveys are valuable in helping schools to identify parents' concerns early and to address them. The 'success' day was a good opportunity to hear such concerns on a one-to-one basis. The form also gave parents the chance to suggest improvements, and to comment anonymously if they wished, though an offer to follow up issues individually was made. Almost 90 per cent of parents would recommend Hathershaw to their friends, a strong overall vote of confidence.

But Mr Ashley realised that there would be no point in raising expectations unless there was a reasonable prospect that students could achieve. Futhermore, if any school starts with a built in disadvantage in terms of its pupils' prior attainment, Hathershaw is that school. Its students are in the bottom five per cent nationally, judging by their Key Stage 2 results, at age 11. Even by Key Stage 3, an area the school is now striving to improve, pupils are in the bottom 15 per cent nationally. One tactic employed by the school to raise results was to enter many students for a GNVQ exam, which is worth four A–C grades where pupils are successful. This is a move Mr Ashley vigorously defends, despite some controversy elsewhere about its growing use. 'We made use of GNVQs,' he says. 'We saw them as a vehicle for engaging students who would otherwise not be engaged at all. But it boosted all the other subject areas, including English and mathematics, because we achieved that engagement. Even without the GNVQs we would have seen a substantial improvement in 2003. So because this was the first year group to be taking the GNVQs we had some confidence when we organised our "success" day that results would improve. By engaging parents we wanted to ensure that students were motivated to do as well as they could.'

While the data clearly made a big difference to parents' and students' expectations at Hathershaw, it has also begun to transform teacher practice. Teaching staff have had faculty targets and student progress charts available to them for some years. More recently, they have had access to a comprehensive centrally compiled database where they can quickly access information not just on students' academic progress, but also on their behaviour and attendance. Each term, every member of staff reports on the current levels of achievement of each student in their classes.

'It is now much easier for teachers to see how pupils are progressing and behaving around the school,' Mr Ashley explains. Attendance has been pushed up to 90 per cent from the mid-80s. But crucially there has been far less 'casual truancy' where students skip school from time to time, although there remains a problem with a hard core of truants who could be regarded as technically on the roll though they are rarely seen in the school. Hathershaw uses the Discipline for Learning programme, developed by Ninestiles School (see Chapter 4). Any students who are deemed to be involved in constant misbehaviour or more serious incidents can have their behaviour tracked by every teacher, allowing problems to be nipped in the bud, and it enables the school to develop individual plans to improve the behaviour of target students. As a result, while short-term exclusions are still used, permanent exclusions are rare.

The data is also invaluable for performance management and staff review. 'Staff can easily use the data in their applications to cross the performance pay threshold, showing where pupils have exceeded expectations, for example,' adds Mr Ashley. 'And for what we call staff review, every head of faculty analyses the exam results on a class by class basis with each teacher. This allows us to identify good practice, which can be shared. It allows us, for example, to examine how well our policy of setting by subject ability is working, not least for those students of below or above average ability. It helps to encourage students who might expect a B to strive for A, as much as pushing those who might get Ds to get Cs in their GCSEs. We can also see where setting in one subject impacts on other subjects. And it allows us to evaluate evidence quickly. There has been a lot of debate about whether putting girls and boys in separate classes might be a good way of improving results. But when we tried single gender classes in English, we could very quickly see that it did not raise overall achievement. Overall, it has led to a staff culture where we work on the basis of evidence rather than hunches.'

There is an additional, and perhaps potentially more controversial benefit for students, too, in that they can now know more readily in which subjects they are most likely to succeed in their GCSEs, long before they sit any mock papers. 'We could tell a Year 9 student their percentage probability of achieving a grade C in French compared to gaining the same grade in say, art,' explains Mr Ashley. Of course, the difficulty here becomes obvious: students might be dissuaded from doing foreign languages, for example, if they thought a C unlikely, and this might be to their detriment in later life. But this is a problem Hathershaw has recognised. 'We start from the principle we've always had about data, which is that people must be educated in how to use the data. So we would sit down and chat through the options with each student. Even if they might find it easier to get a C in art than French, the latter might be important in their career or college choices, and would be worth the extra effort. However, it would be morally wrong not to share information like this with students when we have it. The main thing is that they have all the information they need to make meaningful choices.'

The Autumn Package and PANDAs

An important element of the panoply of information now available to schools is the Autumn Package, issued by the DfES, and produced jointly with the QCA and Ofsted.[6] The package gives teachers a summary of national exam results, a comparison of their pupils' progress with that made by other pupils who had achieved similar results in their Key Stage test results, and a comparison of a school's performance with similar schools. A new computer software package, the PUPIL ACHIEVEMENT TRACKER, allows schools to import and analyse their own pupil performance data against national performance data.

---

[6] To see more of what the Autumn Package involves, visit http://www.standards.dfes.gov.uk/performance/.

The DfES says that the Autumn Package can allow schools to analyse their performance, to ask themselves how well they have done, what they could have done differently, how well they can expect to do in future years and what more they need to do to achieve good results. For many schools, the most useful information available is contained in the Performance and Assessment reports (PANDAs) provided by Ofsted[7], which offer them comparisons with similar schools. Schools are shown how different schools with similar proportions of pupils eligible for free school meals perform, for example. And while some have argued that using free school meals should not be a substitute for good results, the effect is to show the spread of schools with similar characteristics, something which can be very persuasive in the staffroom.

Using PANDAs at Spen Valley High School

Angela Cross, head teacher of Spen Valley High School, an 818-pupil mixed comprehensive in Kirklees, believes that by using benchmarking data schools can be motivated to improve their performance. The school was in serious weaknesses until 2002, when Ofsted called it a 'satisfactory and rapidly improving school'. Ms Cross has seen the proportion of her students gaining five or more good GCSEs rising from 18 per cent in 2000 to 28 per cent in 2003. 'The PANDAs were particularly useful in helping us to set targets for each subject and each individual student,' she says. 'We reported how well they were doing to their parents, every term, and having the targets meant that pupils could see clearly when their improved performance was leading to them attaining a higher [National Curriculum] level. At a school level, it was useful to benchmark our results against schools with a similar proportion of pupils being eligible for free school meals.'

Like an increasing number of schools and LEAs, Ms Cross used the PANDAs along with data from the Fischer Family Trust, which allows schools to see the spread of achievement among similar schools that much more clearly. Before she came to the school early in 2001, PANDAs often stayed in the cupboard. They are hefty documents, extending to around 100 pages of detailed data, and schools need to be somewhat selective in using them well. 'We had to use elements of our PANDA,' recalls Ms Cross. 'It was particularly important to show subject leaders how to use the parts of it that could be most productive for them. We set school and individual student targets based on triangulated data from PANDA, Fischer Family Trust and NFER. I think since we started setting these targets, there has

---

[7] To see what a PANDA looks like for an anonymous secondary school, go to the Ofsted website at http://www.ofsted.gov.uk/publications/index.cfm?fuseaction=pubs.summary&id=3123.

been a lot of buzz around the school. We now have a review of how we are doing, which the whole school takes part in. Students spend time discussing their performance with their form tutors or other teachers. Parents no longer have to wait a year to find out if something is wrong. We send reports to them three times a year which are a nice quick easy way to get information to parents. We also have year group parents' evenings and at least two review days which parents may attend.'

As elsewhere, ICT is essential in making the information more manageable and useful. 'We use an ICT management system with a school-wide network. Teachers put their marks into the system, and we collate all the information centrally, automatically generating reports about individual students and subjects.' An associate head teacher leads this work, with administrative support. Spen Valley ensures that every subject area has access to part-time administrative support. 'Staff have taken to the new systems well. Once they have inputted their original mark books, it's relatively straightforward after that. They can access the system whenever they like. And we can generate paper reports for parents.'

A complaint, which many schools have made about targets, is that LEAs, driven by national goals, try to set unrealistic targets for some schools, which fail to take account of their intake. 'Our targets were LEA driven, and were initially too difficult to achieve. Because we could provide them with information on the ability of our students, as well as figures on free school meals and special needs, we were able to persuade them to be more realistic. Having the information allows us to be more in control.'

Like Ofsted reports, the PANDAs offer schools grades ranging from A to E on how their performance compares with other similar schools. These grades were particularly interesting to Ms Cross and her staff who have seen what were Es last year move up to Cs. The school has a secondary modern intake, due to a selective school in the catchment, so she was particularly pleased to be awarded 'A' for the proportion of students gaining at least five A–G grades, including English and mathematics. Having such a good information system had other benefits, too. It saved a lot of time preparing for the school's Ofsted report in November 2002, a particularly crucial inspection given the school's previous designation as having serious weaknesses. Ofsted said: 'The leadership and management of the headteacher are first rate; she is calmly turning the school around,' though it urged more improvements in teaching and further information for parents.

Using PANDAs to compare like with like at John Kelly Girls'

Another head teacher who is a great believer in PANDAs is Kathy Heaps, principal of John Kelly Girls' Technology College, whose ideas for improving the transition from primary to secondary school we saw in Chapter 2. A statistician by training, Ms Heaps has always been fascinated by the potential offered by statistics to improve educational standards. 'Before SATs [Standard Assessment Tests] came along, we used to do the London Reading Test in the school,' she says. 'Then we would compare the results of the girls five years later and see how many got five or more good GCSE grades. I have to say it was a fantastic predictor of results. We then used a package called YELLIS, which allowed us to predict GCSE results from Year 10 performance. But with PANDAs and the Autumn Package, we no longer need to do so.'

For Ms Heaps, the most important measurement is the extent to which individual pupils improve between the age of 11 and 16. 'I was anti-league tables when they were first introduced, because they didn't measure the movement that pupils made at a school. What matters to me is not the raw data but what you can do with that information. I particularly like the PANDAs because they set our performance in context. It is very important to see where I am nationally, to see measures like the proportion of students gaining at least one pass and to compare like with like when it comes to intake of special needs. The benchmarks, especially when you get [grade] As are very good for staff and parents morale.' John Kelly's overall performance might be average on a raw league table, in a borough where competition is stiff between schools, so, being able to show As and Bs for Key Stage 3 and GCSE performance, when the proportion of pupils eligible for free school meal is taken into account is particularly valuable. It also helps to show that the extra money the school receives because of its large number of underprivileged students is making a difference. The only complaint which she makes is that the PANDAs base some of their information on the previous school inspection, which becomes increasingly outdated in a six-year inspection cycle.

Kathy Heaps is proud to give presentations to parents and governors to show them these figures, but this does not mean she is complacent about her school's results. 'The subject work is particularly important. The PANDAs allow us to make comparisons in each subject,' she adds, and like Angela Cross, she also uses the Fischer Family Trust data to see how well they are doing by subject. The Fischer spread includes figures for the 25 per cent of top performing schools which share similar characteristics. 'To know that you're in the upper quartile is valuable and it is something which schools can strive to achieve.' As in the other schools we have seen, the data's most important function is in helping to set individual student targets. Each girl meets with her form tutor twice a year to review progress against National Curriculum levels.

But crucially this data is valuable as a management tool, as Ms Heaps remarks: 'Being able to show a member of staff what they are achieving does spur them on. We use the data also for their threshold assessment [for performance related pay eligibility] and for performance management, particularly in helping them to develop teaching and learning strategies and formulating the most appropriate lesson objectives.'

Like other London schools, John Kelly Girls' has been grouped with other similar schools across the capital, as part of an initiative developed by the London Schools Commissioner, Professor Tim Brighouse. There are 27 different such 'families' in the capital. And Ms Heaps thinks such groupings would be a useful spur for schools like her own: 'We are not in competition with these schools, as is so often the case when partnerships are developed. Too often we are expected to work in families of schools which are determined by their geographic location, but in places like London, there is a lot of local competition. Linking schools with similar intakes is more likely to make a difference. If *they're* doing better than me, I certainly want to know why.'

The level of information available to schools seems to grow all the time. With computers, instant analyses can be calculated, and exciting graphs produced. League tables are likely to continue to appear in England, even if the data expands to offer more contextualised information. But as the Government starts to place more ownership of targets with schools, the challenge is to use that responsibility to advance the achievement of individual pupils. That is what each of the schools we have seen in this chapter has been able to do. And there would seem to be a number of common features to how they use information, and how others could do so as well.

Key points in this chapter

Make full use of the data now available, particularly value-added information: The sophistication of the information now available is such that schools can no longer complain that it fails to take account of their context, or the point from which their pupils started. There is a debate about the value-added information used by the Government, but it is relatively easy to calculate how much has been achieved using alternative calculations, such as those developed by the Specialist School Trust. Moreover, the profiles provided by Ofsted and the Fischer Family Trust can be a great spur for improvement in every school department.

Compare your pupils' performance with similar schools: It has never been easier to benchmark data with other schools. The excellent information, provided by the Fischer Family Trust, allows schools to see how well they should do, when compared to other schools in a similar context. Factors considered include gender (girls normally outperform boys), social background (measured through take up of free school meal), special needs, and the proportion of students speaking

English as an additional language. An ambitious school will seek to achieve in the upper quartile of schools exhibiting similar characteristics, in both its Key Stage 3 and GCSE results.

Set challenging but realistic targets for the school: By using the information about pupils' achievement at the age of 11, most schools can now project the likely results for any year group in their Key Stage 3 and GCSE exams. With the help of Fischer Family Trust and Ofsted data, it is possible to benchmark targets more precisely. A good school will constantly be challenging itself not just in its overall performance, but in particular subjects, not least those where performance is below par.

Use the data on a subject by subject basis with teachers: Most schools have some subject departments that are stronger than others. There may be various reasons, ranging from difficulties in specialist staff recruitment to weakness in subject leadership. There may even be particular challenges interesting students in some subjects. In the past, concerns were often based on intuition, but this made it more difficult to foster improvements. With benchmarked and value-added data, on a subject by subject basis, it is much easier for school leaders to point to evidence where concerns exist. By contrast, plaudits can equally be awarded based on the evidence, where they are deserved.

Develop individual pupil targets, and regularly monitor them: The most important targets are those set by teachers and form tutors with individual pupils, helping them to realise their potential in each aspect of the curriculum. Good schools will find time to monitor progress each term, identifying where progress is weak, so students can be helped to catch up, where necessary. Having such information can help pupils to make an informed choice about their likely results at GCSE, too.

Involve parents fully in the process: The days of the annual, intimidating parents' evening, as being the only proper contact between teachers and parents are disappearing. Parents should expect termly reports on their children's progress so that problems are not allowed to fester before they hear about them. There are various ways in which the information can be presented, from the sophistication of De Ferrers' or Hathershaw's formula to straightforward explanations of where pupils are in National Curriculum levels, and how they are behaving, and where they could reach with motivation and support. By involving parents and treating them as partners in the learning process, schools will get more co-operation and understanding about their goals.

Make good use of ICT and administrative support: ICT should liberate teachers, not make them its slave. Schools should ensure that one senior teacher takes responsibility for ensuring that the technology is used to its full potential to provide

easy access for teachers to data about every pupil, and readable information for students and teachers. This is where a good administrative officer can be invaluable. He or she can collate the data, keep the systems up to date and resolve practical difficulties with access. Teachers should be able to input information with more ease than the traditional marking of books.

Share ownership of the data: Above all, good schools say that targets and data belong to everybody in the school, not just a few people in the know. So, pupils should know how well they are doing. Teachers should be able to detect patterns and changes quickly. And parents should be kept fully informed about their child's progress. Doing otherwise makes the data seem irrelevant to everyday school life, when it has a central role to play in fostering improvement.

7

Teamwork: teachers, trainees and teaching assistants

A good school is one where all its staff feel they are part of a team, with shared goals and a chance for everyone to help influence their school's future development. But the nature of that team has already started to change to reflect a different type of school organisation that is emerging in the first years of the twenty-first century. It was a model foreseen by Professor Michael Barber, who in 1996 was among the first to spell out what a typical secondary school might start to look like.

> There would, of course, be traditionally taught classes . . . not least because the evidence shows that direct teaching can be remarkably effective. However, one might imagine a range of adults in the school, assisting with the learning process: a businessperson contributing to a small group undertaking a cost-benefit analysis; a chemistry PhD student, under a teacher's supervision, contributing to a science lesson on the structure of atoms . . . or business and community mentors spending time counselling individual students. Students might be in formal lessons, in small groups or in the large extended library or learning resources centre, drawing on a range of resources through both traditional and technological means . . . . Elsewhere, a group of over a hundred students might be in a traditional lecture relevant to many of them.[1]

Professor Barber now heads the Prime Minister's Delivery Unit, and was the first head of the Standards and Effectiveness Unit at the Department for Education and Employment, in 1997. And the nature of the school team has been changing in the direction which he foresaw. Just as the role of management has expanded, with more deputies and assistant head teachers being employed to take responsibility for anything from finance to computerisation, so has the nature of the staff employed

---

[1] M. Barber, *The Learning Game* (London, Gollancz, 1996).

by the typical school. Teachers' time has become more circumscribed, and with it there has been a growth in teaching assistants and other support staff. It is increasingly accepted, for example, that subject departments in secondary schools should have some dedicated secretarial support, something that seems innovative in education, yet would be unremarkable in most walks of life. The teacher's career structure has changed too: after a slow start, the advanced skills teacher, initially dubbed 'the super teacher' is proving a valuable part of the team in a growing number of schools. Performance related pay, at least at the top of the teachers' pay scale, seemed in 2004 finally to be moving towards becoming a reward for excellence, rather than simply an incremental entitlement, awarded to all but the very poorest teachers. The changes have helped to make teaching better paid, though as a graduate career, its attractions still depend as much on a combination of public service, longer holidays and decent pensions, as on the annual salary.

But despite these changes, there remain cultural features of the school team which haven't changed. Teamwork is seen as essential in every school. This can have many positive benefits – and should play an important part in the management culture of the school. But it can have its downsides, too. Removing a weak member of staff remains a controversial and long-winded process: not because the law doesn't permit fast tracking the procedures, but because head teachers often want to avoid the wrath of their staff and their unions by doing so. Yet the clock-watchers and poor teachers add to the workload of their more capable and hardworking colleagues, who waste no time in groaning about them among themselves. As we have noted, it can still take up to two years of informal procedures before formal dismissal procedures are invoked against incompetent teachers.[2]

In this chapter, we will consider the changing nature of personnel in schools, looking at how schools have employed many more support staff than before, how relevant expertise does not always mean having Qualified Teacher Status, the growing role of schools in training their own teachers, and the ways in which schools can make continuous professional development a valuable and integral part of their programme.

Teachers: use of time and numbers

The teaching workforce has been growing. There were 427,800 teachers (apart from supply staff) employed in England's schools in 2004, some 28,600 more than

---

[2] J. Earnshaw, E. Ritchie, L. Marchington, D. Torrington and S. Hardie, *Best Practice in Undertaking Teacher Capability Procedures* (London, DfES, 2002).

seven years before.[3] Critics say that these full-time equivalent figures hide some trends they regard as more worrying. They charge that most of the new recruits are part-time or poorly qualified overseas staff. In secondary schools, the number of 'qualified regular teachers' has increased from 187,660 to 200,700. Most of that increase is made up of full-timers, just 3,300 are figures based on adding together the hours worked by part-timers. But there has also been a four-fold increase in overseas trained teachers, many from the Commonwealth, and 'instructors without qualified teacher status', from 1,500 to 6,900. Not all head teachers think this is necessarily a bad thing. These teachers are often a response to changing times. Some schools find it more valuable to employ a team of computer experts who know their stuff rather than rely on well-meaning amateur volunteers from the staffroom. There has also been a big increase in graduates training to be teachers on one-year Graduate Teaching Programme (GTP) courses, where they are moulded in schools rather than teacher training colleges, though most GTP programmes are linked to such colleges. Their numbers rose from 250 in 1997 (mainly the School Centred Initial Teacher Training programme) to 4,750 in January 2004.

Behind these figures lie some potential problems. Despite improvements in the recruitment of mathematics, science and languages graduates to teaching since 1999, a significant number of lessons in these subjects are still taught by people without a post-A Level qualification in their subject. One in eight mathematics lessons is taught by a non-specialist, though some may be taken with those holding physics or economics degrees. Eighteen per cent of Spanish lessons and 15 per cent of French lessons were taught by non-specialists, though it is likely that many of these lessons were being given by Spanish and French nationals with fluency in their native tongues. Overall, 17 per cent of secondary school classes were taken by non-specialists. The Chief Inspector of Schools, David Bell, has said that the absence of specialist teachers can be a particular problem for schools, and is having 'an adverse impact on achievement'.[4] But his inspectors have also reported that the quality of lessons observed in the ten years since Ofsted started its work has steadily improved, reflecting a better quality of teaching overall.

How teachers spend their time has become a source of much controversy. The Government established a taskforce, involving the main teaching unions, though subsequently boycotted by the National Union of Teachers, which made important recommendations designed to re-engineer the teaching day. The 'workload agreement' of 2003 was signed by all the other teaching and head teachers'

---

[3] *Statistics of Education: School workforce in England* (including pupil:teacher ratios and pupil:adult ratios) (Provisional January 2004 census data) (London, DfES Statistical First Release, January 2004).
[4] *Annual Report of the Chief Inspector of Schools 2001/2* (London, Ofsted, 2003).

associations and pledged to reduce teachers' overall hours by 2007, by changing teachers contracts so they did not routinely undertake administrative and clerical tasks; they covered for absent colleagues less; and that they had guaranteed planning, preparation and assessment time within the school day. The agreement also promised to reform support staff roles to help teachers and support pupils. Personal administrative assistants for teachers, cover supervisors and high level teaching assistants would be introduced. And new managers, including business and personnel managers would be recruited.[5] By January 2004, the agreement's signatories were reporting that, despite some resource difficulties caused by funding changes in some education authorities, 87 per cent of LEAs had started to implement the first changes.

Teaching assistants and support staff

Teaching assistants have long played an important role supporting children with special educational needs, but their supportive role in the classroom has greatly increased more recently, not least in helping teachers with core subjects such as literacy and numeracy, or organising remedial classes for those falling behind. More controversially, the Government has promoted the idea that teaching assistants might take whole classes to free teachers for lesson preparation – increasing their 'non-contact time' – though this is more relevant in primary schools, where it is often difficult for single-class teachers to find this time during the normal school day. There were 132,600 teaching assistants in English schools when the 2004 school census was conducted, the majority of them in primary schools.[6] Nevertheless, on the more detailed data available for 2003, secondary schools reported 22,260 assistants, a threefold increase since 1997. And while 430 were helping ethnic minority pupils and 14,920 were working with children with special needs, nearly 7,000 were helping with other lessons. Moreover, secondary schools reported an array of other staff, some 50,000 in total, including secretaries, bursars, clerical staff, librarians, welfare assistants and learning mentors. This group had expanded by 50 per cent since 1997, far faster than the growth in teachers.

As schools have employed more classroom assistants, their role and recognition has changed far beyond the notion of a 'mums' army' advanced in the early nineties by John Patten, when he was a Conservative Secretary of State for Education, something for which he suffered much criticism and derision from the teaching unions at the time. Many of the teaching assistants are mothers (or

---

[5] *Raising Standards and Tackling Workload: A national agreement* (London, DfES, 2003).
[6] *Statistics of Education: School workforce in England* (Provisional January 2004 census data) (London, DfES Statistical First Release, January 2004).

fathers) of those in the schools where they work. But teaching assistants are largely being treated as professionals, with a proper salary scale, and a career structure which offers a senior assistant a higher salary than a newly qualified teacher. There are foundation degree courses available to improve pedagogic skills, and for those who wish to, increased opportunities to train as a teacher. With growing numbers has come growing status.

Teaching pupils to learn

The buzz-words of education are an ever-changing feast. And anybody who had stayed out of the education world for the last decade might be puzzled to find that the talk today is no longer just of good teaching, but of 'teaching and learning'. Pupils are expected to be 'active learners'. Part of the job of teachers is now to help them become more enquiring. In the wrong hands, such jargon might seem like an excuse for teachers to do less. After all, it is certainly true that in primary schools, a big factor in the appalling standards of literacy and numeracy was a trend towards leaving younger children to find out how to read and write for themselves, absorbing rather than learning how to read. But, in fact, there is growing evidence that in the right circumstances a focus on improving pupils' ability to learn and discover information for themselves does help to improve achievement.

George Spencer Foundation School in Nottingham was one of the country's first technology colleges in 1994. The 1,300-pupil comprehensive is popular with parents and prides itself at being at the forefront of innovation. Not only does it now call itself a 24-hour school (a concept developed with cable providers NTL), it has pioneered new approaches to teaching 12-year-olds, all part of a 're-engineering' of Key Stage 3 initially called 'Curriculum 2001'. Tom Clark, who led the changes as head teacher from 1983 to 2003 explains: 'We switched the emphasis from teaching to learning. Pupils continued to have all the traditional lessons, but they also spent time learning how to learn, particularly looking at different styles of learning.'

What this means is that as well as being taught through formal lessons, students learn to research information, to marshal that information to make an argument or to test a theory. Homework and study time is used more effectively, and students are better prepared for more independent study in later life and for the demands of the workplace. At George Spencer, each student has a 'learning manager' to help guide them. This is not an uncontroversial notion. When Chris Woodhead resigned as Chief Inspector of Schools, his most trenchant criticism of the Government was reserved for the idea that teachers should become learning managers. He sought to present it as a bureaucratic caricature of what teachers should do.

But as Tom Clark sees it, there are different types of teacher, and their different roles will become increasingly apparent as technology advances and pupils are expected to become more than passive recipients of knowledge. He explains: 'The learning manager is somebody who understands how children learn, and manages their learning. They may or may not have Qualified Teacher Status. I think the highest moral imperative in education is to enable students to learn how to learn, to become lifelong learners. If you're going to help young people to learn how to learn, you have to consider learning styles, multiple intelligences and cognitive development, recognising that students have their own preferred ways of learning, and that they will change and are different at different times. The good pedagogue or learning manager understands that and manages student learning. What this also does is it takes away notions of chronology. Students progress when they are ready not in the first week of May in Year 9. Some of the press – and some powerful figures – may caricature this as undermining traditional teaching. But those criticisms often trivialise the argument and then criticise the "trivialisation" which they have brought to it. At George Spencer School, we tried to make a switch from highly effective teaching to highly effective learning. To do that we had to re-emphasise our understanding of how and when students learn. It was a calculated risk. But we believe it will pay dividends not just in terms of attainment and targets, but also in empowering and growing our students as informed learners.' The programme started with the Year 7 intake in 2001, and those students had reached Year 9 when we spoke in early 2004. He continues: 'If an institution, with the agreement of its whole staff, focuses on any project, then it can make a difference. In this case, the project caught the moment, it caught the enthusiasm of young staff who saw it as very much a part of their own training and development. They feel good about it, but we won't know really until these students come to take their GCSEs what difference it makes to their results. But a lot of people who are experienced and not necessarily enthusiastic for the concept have visited and formed the view that it is effective. The Ofsted team which visited in late 2002 did and put a note in their report saying that this was exciting and likely to be successful. School Standards Minister David Miliband came and instead of the sanitised carefully managed walk round the school, he actually spent time talking to 12- and 13-year-old children about these concepts. But in any case we're careful not to let the effective teaching drop. Instead, we're adding another dimension.'

Ofsted was indeed unstinting in its praise for teaching at George Spencer, saying that 'teaching is excellent and pupils' learning is very good'. Ofsted described the school as 'an exemplary specialist technology college', noting how it had used its specialist status to make a difference. The inspectors summed up teaching at the school as follows:

Teaching is excellent overall. The proportions of lessons that are good, very good and excellent are well above what is usually seen. The teaching of English is very good, and the teaching of mathematics and science is good. The strategic decision taken by the school to focus on teaching and learning is having a significant effect upon practice, particularly in Years 7 and 8, through the 'learning to learn' initiative. Most pupils start the school with good levels of basic literacy and numeracy skills, and teaching builds on this effectively. Learning proceeds at a very good pace and pupils apply themselves very well. The main strengths in teaching are the high standards of knowledge teachers have of their subjects, careful planning for what students are to learn, the wide range of effective teaching methods and the high levels of challenge built into lessons. Teachers are aware of pupils' differing stages of learning and adapt lessons appropriately.[7]

The inspectors' judgement is a fairly comprehensive rebuttal to the critics of active learning and learning managers. But George Spencer's success means that it is constantly being refreshed by young enthusiastic new staff, and many of them bring their expertise to other schools, where they are greatly in demand. As Mr Clark puts it: 'Over time, you recruit to the mission. If you pretty straightforwardly lay out what you're trying to do when people apply for the job, then they're clear what to expect. And it is a young staff. Part of the paradox of successful schools is that being successful can increase turnover because your staff become attractive to other schools.'

When Mr Clark and his staff embarked on their new approach to learning, the school set aside five days, five times a year which would be devoted to helping students learn how to learn, while the remaining 35 weeks of the year would be devoted to more traditional curriculum delivery. This has now been reduced to three days, three times a year. 'Very often in your initial enthusiasm to get it right, you can end up doing too much and making things too complicated,' he adds. 'With our learning style weeks, the focus was on applied situations where pupils could experiment in developing their understanding on different ways of learning. So, some time might be spent learning how to use the Internet as an effective research tool, rather than being distracted by its many other functions. At other times, students might explore emotional intelligence. These were challenge weeks where students were challenged to use different learning styles, with specific tasks or projects. Some of these activities might have been ones that the school did anyway, for example preparing a newspaper in German in Year 8. But we repackaged them as part of the challenge weeks.

'As students learn how to learn, some purists say they should also be able to decide what they learn. We've not done that, nor do we feel that it would be right

---

[7] *George Spencer Foundation School and Technology College Inspection Report* (London, Ofsted, 2002). The full report can be read at http://www.ofsted.gov.uk/reports/122/122903.pdf.

to do so. And when these students move into Key Stage 4, we would hope that they won't need discrete lessons in how to learn. It should have become second nature by then.' So confident is George Spencer about the impact of the new learning styles that is expecting between 70 to 80 per cent of its students to sit the Key Stage 3 tests a year earlier than would normally be the case. 'There isn't a one size fits all approach here either. It would be as wrong to say that all students should sit Key Stage 3 after two years as it is to say that they should all sit it after three years.'

Will computers take over from teachers?

The changing nature of the school workforce has implications for the working of schools, something that many head teachers increasingly recognise. It is not just a matter of pay, though the assistants' main union, Unison, has negotiated more formal structures in that regard. It also affects the nature of teaching and those we define as teachers. ICT is encouraging more independent learning. It also allows classes in different parts of the world to join together for a masterclass, to pay a virtual visit to a zoo or museum. When such experiments are talked about, they are often accompanied by excitable headlines about 'classes of 90', yet there is no reason why a group of classes shouldn't join together in the school hall to experience first-class teaching than that they should share the same space for an assembly or a movie. And should we worry if confident and competent French nationals are teaching French alongside graduates from a British university? Is it not better to have someone who is a native speaker? The question should surely be how we combine their fluency with the right pedagogic skills, rather than complaining that the French speaker has not gained a degree in French followed by a PGCE. In some ways, the rapid growth of ICT in schools has forced head teachers to confront such realities.

Mike Griffith, Assistant head teacher at Arbour Vale School, a specialist sports college catering for pupils with special needs in Slough, Berkshire has been seconded to run the DfES's 'video-conferencing in the classroom programme' since 2002, having developed some of the more advanced uses of the technology, which he initially shared with other schools through his 'Global Leap' website (www.global-leap.com). Mr Griffith used the technique in many of his lessons from 1999, and found that they could bring lessons to life: 'We had a group doing a project on the Arctic. They had done all the usual research, even using the Internet and CD-ROMs. But it really came to life when they were able to speak directly to pupils in a school in Northern Canada, within the Arctic Circle. And when we did a lesson on earthquakes a teacher living on the San Andreas Fault in California took the class.' His pupils regularly joined forces with their counterparts in other schools – and recent classes have been shared with teachers in Birmingham and further afield in Finland and Uganda.

The rapid spread of broadband has extended the capacity of schools to make full use of video-conferencing. There has also been some improvement in the number of British public bodies enabling students to interact with them, without having to go on day-trips. The Public Record Office, holder of the national archives, offer schools courses on subjects like the Domesday Book and the Battle of the Somme through its award-winner 'Learning Curve' (http://learningcurve.pro.gov.uk) while the Science Museum will arrange question and answer sessions with its curators. Through the DfES project, equipment is being lent to museums and galleries to allow them to present live interactive video-conference lessons to schools. Each month, the project makes available over 50 lessons directly to classrooms. In other cases, schools such as Coloma Convent Girls High School in Croydon, South London, have used the technology to deliver A/S Level lessons in law to 18 girls through video-conferencing, when a specialist teacher was not available. Instead they used a tutor based in Somerset who taught them online, set them assignments, responded to their e-mail queries and paid a termly visit to the school.

Another programme which has been enjoyed by schools in London, through a partnership with the Goldman Sachs Foundation and John Kelly Girls' Technology College is the Motivate programme, developed by Cambridge University (http://motivate.maths.org). Motivate uses video-conferencing to enable primary and secondary school students to work with professional mathematicians to learn about subjects like geometry, fractals, gyroscopes and chaos theory, and their real-world application. Jenny Gage, the scheme's co-ordinator says that students taking part in the video-classes see how mathematics is used outside the classroom. 'They see mathematical applications in everything from avalanches to robots. What they learn in ordinary lessons sometimes seems divorced from real life. In our classes, they can see why mathematics is important.'

ICT has also played a major part in George Spencer's approach since 1994, when the school became an early investor in the new technology and gained technology college status. It now has over 400 terminals available to students and information technology is practised across all parts of the curriculum. There is a wireless and industry-standard IT network. There are electronic whiteboards in every faculty, with a suite of computers. Terminals are also dotted across the school. But ICT is embedded throughout the curriculum, as a tool for teaching and learning rather than a separate subject, except where students might be taking an exam, such as a GNVQ ICT. Mr Clark says: 'You don't have lessons in how to use your pen, and apart from learning to use software packages, after proper induction, you shouldn't need lessons in how to use ICT. That would make it for its own sake, rather than simply serving the purpose of helping wider learning.' Pupils regularly come in during the holidays to use ICT – and the facilities are open to them in the school ten hours a day. A Graphics Design Centre for Technology has enabled students to learn practical applications of the latest ICT. There is also a multimedia languages centre and a fully computerised library system.

But Mr Clark regards ICT as an integral part of the curriculum, not something that has its own subject department. And this influences how he staffs the subject. He explains: 'We tend to be a bit hung up on Qualified Teacher Status (QTS). The presumption is that qualified teachers are good at everything. That might include health education, ICT, counselling, mentoring, knowing their subject and knowing about pedagogy. I don't think there is a "one size fits all" teacher. Some people who support students in their learning don't necessarily have QTS. We can be patronising about these professionals. We're prepared to call them classroom assistants or assistant teachers, and if they're any good, we offer to train them to gain QTS, but we don't necessarily value them in their own right.'

'You wouldn't have a department of writing or pens, then why would you have an ICT department?,' he says. 'The model we developed was that every teacher who came to the school was required to reach a particular level of ICT competence within three years. When people joined the school, we made it a condition of their employment. If they didn't meet the standard, they could technically be dismissed. But we provided plenty of training in Cisco, Intel and through the New Opportunities Fund [supported by the National Lottery]. If they had the right attitude professionally they would develop these skills. And we never lost anybody through this condition. But we sent out quite an important message. ICT is not separately timetabled at Key Stage 3, though there are specialist courses in the sixth form. We hadn't had separate classes at Key Stage 4, but there is a little bit of examination provision now.' The absence of formal ICT teaching causes no problems passing the ICT Key Stage 3 tests. 'We just soared way above the targets that were set. As far as we were concerned, they were set too low. ICT is a way of life in the school.'

The school uses a mix of trained teachers and staff from other backgrounds to manage its ICT resources. Four full-time technical staff are employed, who also manage computer networks for six other schools, and have worked with a hotel chain and a local charity. There is also a five-strong team of information managers, who support other staff in developing ICT examination materials; help students access ICT programmes; and keep the school's website up to date. They also liaise with the school's own ICT training company. These are not formally trained teachers, at least when they first joined, as Mr Clark explains. 'Some started out working in the school library, and developed their skills as the importance of ICT grew in the school. They had the opportunity to gain Qualified Teacher Status if they wished, since it might help their later careers, but not everyone felt they needed QTS. They have come to us from relatively low paid jobs in public service, where they have been using ICT. Here they feel they have more of an opportunity to use their expertise and their interest to make a difference.'

ICT has important implications for how the curriculum is taught, offering important opportunities for interactivity through whiteboards and for teachers to consult references quickly. There are two strong implications for the staffing structures of schools. The first is the potential for remote teaching, through masterclasses and specialist lessons with great museums, galleries and other resources. For some schools, especially those in remote areas, shared lessons can reduce the sense of isolation. The technology also allows classes to be shared with those in other countries, a potentially valuable addition to many language and geography lessons. But it would be foolish to imagine that these opportunities will require less staffing. To be effective, a video-lesson will have the same sense of purpose that any regularly taught lesson would have, and will normally be linked to the school's curriculum (though advanced university-led classes can help stimulate the more able students). The teacher will normally need to plan their use wisely and carefully in that context. There may, of course, be cases where a specialist course, especially in the sixth form, can be provided using video-conferencing that might not otherwise be available. And this can improve student choice. But in these circumstances the work that teachers should already have done to improve student learning techniques will be particularly valuable. The second change is one that can affect many subjects, but is most noticeable in ICT. That is the use of people other than those with Qualified Teacher Status in schools to facilitate and train others in ICT use. That implies an integrated approach to ICT, which is not yet the reality in most schools. But in time, the idea that ICT should be taught separately in secondary schools, beyond any initial orientation, will seem as fanciful as the notion that secondary pupils need to learn how to use a pen. ICT will not be the only subject where non-teachers will play a growing contribution: the growth of business and enterprise will see those with real-world experience helping teach lessons; linguists are increasingly in demand, even where they do not have QTS; and the Government's 2004 mathematics inquiry recognised that the system could no longer rely solely on mathematics graduates to teach pupils in the future.

Flatter management structures; better staff development

Most schools have expanded their number of posts for deputies and assistant head teachers to meet the challenges presented by local management of schools and other added responsibilities over the last 15 years. But there is something to be said for a flatter management structure, where many staff have extras responsibilities. All staff at George Spencer have personal development targets agreed with them in their annual review. They also have more opportunities to gain experience and responsibility from an early stage. The school has just one deputy, but many other staff taking specific responsibilities. It has replaced the traditional hierarchies associated with senior management teams with a new type of strategic leadership. 'We wanted to energise our middle managers, giving them time, autonomy and status,' Mr Clark says. 'One way we seek to retain good staff is by what has been called "distributed leadership" which involves flattening the management structures, then energising the staff by giving them significant responsibilities, accelerating their professional development in the process.

'It is the middle managers – curriculum and pastoral leaders and heads of subject faculties – that should energise the school. Indeed, one study by the Teacher Training Agency showed that one reason staff wished to leave schools, was more often because of poor middle management rather than poor senior management. To recognise this fact, our school decision-making team is formed differently from other schools. Some people were on that team by virtue of their post. For instance, if you are a key stage manager, it goes with the territory. But the curriculum leaders nominate one of their own team, who serves for two years. Similarly, the heads of year nominate somebody for two years. And at George Spencer, we have a staff development officer to look after our staff's training and professional development, and she was on the team too. I wasn't on the team – it was chaired by the deputy. Others might be invited to talk about particular issues. The people there weren't the oldest, or those who had been there the longest, or even necessarily the best paid, though they were of course paid appropriately for their jobs.'

Advanced skills teachers and performance related pay

They were dubbed super teachers when the concept was first imported from the United States in 1997, where the 'Master Teacher' idea had been developed, but advanced skills teachers (ASTs) have become an important part of the workings of a significant number of schools. Selected through external assessment for their excellent classroom practice, the ASTs can earn salaries of up to £50,000 a year to share their skills and experience with other teachers, both within their own school and in other schools. Typically, they have an extra day a week when they are not teaching classes to allow them to pursue these activities. There were 1,420 ASTs in English Secondary Schools, according to the 2003 DfES census[8], and those schools

---

[8] *Statistics of Education: School workforce in England* (including teachers' pay for England and Wales) 2003 edition (London, DfES, 2004).

that employ them often employ several. Their role has evolved over the years, and they may produce teaching materials, provide model lessons, particularly to gifted pupils, give extra support to subject leaders or help teachers with difficulties.

George Spencer School was one of the first in the country to employ ASTs, and did so when they were a relatively new innovation heavily criticised by some of the teaching unions and shunned by some LEAs, which declined even to collect the government money available to support the initiative. There are five ASTs at the school, and they have been invaluable in developing the pedagogy behind the school's new approach to learning, as Mr Clark explains: 'When we had one of the first advanced skills teachers in the country, it was a political hostage to fortune. In our area, we had already been criticised for being one of the first technology colleges in the country. Now we were employing ASTs. This was seen to be elitist and politically incorrect. But for us, it was precisely the right territory because our learning styles initiative was led by one of the ASTs, who made it her business to become expert in the pedagogy.'

Moreover, for Mr Clark, having the ASTs also allowed the school to play to the strengths of individual staff members. 'I believe there are teachers who are terrifically expert in their subject, and really good at writing content. And there are teachers who are expert in learning and pedagogy. There are some that are both.' Yet both sets of expertise are necessary. And in the future, ten or 15 years down the line, with the development of ICT, the teachers who are expert in content will be able to write content not just for their own school, but for schools across the country and perhaps the world. Those who are expert in pedagogy become the real managers of pupils' learning. They will help students manage this content and their learning development. ASTs are expected to work with other schools, and as George Spencer is a training school and a 'leading edge' school, it is working with other Nottingham schools to share its insights. This learning to learn project has been adopted by Nottingham LEA, with George Spencer as a resource. The ASTs are at the heart of this work.

Performance related pay was first introduced by the Labour government in its first term, after considerable controversy with the teaching unions. Its introduction was a big change in the culture of education. The system that emerged changed the teachers' pay structure to enable a majority of classroom teachers to earn more than previously. If they passed a performance threshold, they could gain an initial salary boost of around £2,000 a year, and access other incremental increases based on performance. The unions said the whole scheme would be divisive. But they need not have worried too much about the scheme as it first developed. Many schools went through the motions and decided for the sake of staffroom peace to upgrade all those who applied: true, some declined to apply, and a small number failed on application. But the system that emerged was not that initially envisaged by ministers. The Government tried capping the money available to schools for uplifts above the threshold, but they simply faced criticism about underfunding. As a result, a new scale was announced in 2004, after discussion with most unions. The Government said that good teachers could continue to access three grades beyond the threshold, but a new 'excellent teacher' scheme with higher salaries was expected to start to develop a genuine system of performance related pay in 2005. At the same time, it is planned to align pay for ASTs more closely to that of other school leaders.

Initial teacher training in school

The notion that schools should take greater responsibility for training teachers has grown in recent years. Thirty-five thousand people train to be teachers every year, but an increasing number are now being trained by schools themselves. The Graduate Teacher Programme (GTP), allows 'mature trainees' (which have been defined as those aged 24 or more) to train in schools, and receive up to £13,000 a year salary while doing so with the school receiving a training grant of £4,000 per trainee. By 2003–4, there were 4,750 trainees on the programme. Many head teachers have seen the scheme as an ideal way to gain suitable candidates for vacancies in their schools. They have seen great advantages in training teacher apprentices within their schools, where they can emphasise the practical rather than the theoretical. Because the scheme has been focused on those who have already worked in other jobs, it has also brought many with outside experience into school, a valuable commodity in an environment where most teachers have followed a path from school to university to school. In fairness, it is worth adding that there has been an improvement in the quality of teacher training colleges, too, in recent years, particularly in courses for primary teachers. The Chief Inspector of Schools reports that 'most providers of primary and secondary initial teacher training (ITT) are well managed and ensure that good-quality training is maintained'.[9] But the extent of experience offered by training in school is something that many trainees and head teachers see as very valuable. Lesley McRobert, a former independent school science technician, trained at Notre Dame High School, a Catholic comprehensive in Norwich. She says: 'I think it gives you a lot more classroom experience than training college. It is also a great advantage if you get offered a job at the school because you already know the staff and pupils.' Mrs McRobert was later offered a full-time job at the school. As Richard Cranmer, the school's head of training, put it: 'They bring fresh ideas and enthusiasm. They are better at applying subjects because

---

[9] *Standards and Quality 2003: The annual report of Her Majesty's Chief Inspector of Schools* (London, Ofsted, 2004).

they have experience of the world outside.' He added that being able to recruit teachers through the GTP also helps schools to recruit the teachers they need, particularly in shortage subjects. 'You know them already – their strengths and their weaknesses – after a year training in the school,' he said.[10]

George Spencer School has also been enthusiastic about the GTP programme, as Tom Clark explains, 'We had already developed the capacity to receive trainee teachers on the Graduate Teacher Programme. A lot of people coming this route have so much to offer. The concept of the school being a bit like a teaching hospital, where teachers learn through internships, is something that appealed to us.' But George Spencer has gone one step further and has been designated by the DfES as a Training School. Training Schools are intended to show initial teacher training students what the DfES calls 'excellent practice across the range of teacher training activities, especially in initial teacher training and the continuing training of the whole school workforce'. They are also expected to work collaboratively with other schools and with teacher training colleges towards these goals. By early 2004, the Government was funding 130 secondary schools and 38 primary schools with up to £65,000 a year, which it had designated as Training Schools. Ofsted was particularly impressed by the programme, with the Chief Inspector commenting in his 2003 report:

> All of the Training Schools have contributed to improvements in the quality of ITT and, in the majority, the effect has been strong. The number of trainee placements has also increased significantly with schools' involvement in a range of training programmes, including the Graduate Teacher Programme and flexible routes. Most schools focus strongly on collaboration with other schools to offer initial teacher training; extending the number of trained mentors; [and] introducing secure internal procedures for monitoring and assuring the quality of school-based training.[11]

Other Training Schools believe that their role has helped them to become better schools, as well as supporting the trainees. Birkdale High School in Southport runs courses for trainee English teachers at Edge Hill University College. 'It gives us a much bigger input into the teachers of the future. We also get a good view of potential teachers and can better assess what they are like in the classroom,' was how Graham Fletcher, the school's head of English who also manages the programme saw it.[12] In Birkdale, the school lays on something extra. Its best teachers are on hand from 4 'til 6 p.m. three evenings a week to help students

---

[10] Interviewed in June 2003 by Conor Ryan for 'Education Notebook' (*Daily Mail*, 19 August 2003).

[11] *Standards and Quality 2003: The annual report of Her Majesty's Chief Inspector of Schools* (London, Ofsted, 2004).

[12] Interviewed in June 2003 by Conor Ryan for 'Education Notebook' (*Daily Mail*, 19 August 2003).

through an online chat room after college tutors have gone home. And some worrying signs of the lack of knowledge of some trainees were quickly uncovered. 'When we started the chat room, one trainee asked for help preparing a lesson for the next day on the iambic pentameter in Shakespeare's *The Tempest*. We knew we were in for a long session when she said she didn't know what an iambic pentameter was.' Birkdale also allows trainees to hear live video-lectures from leading examiners in other parts of the country, making full use of new technologies which clearly have the potential to revolutionise teacher training and continuous professional development for the future. 'We hope to set up a system where trainees can watch classes from their lecture halls, and where they can watch each other teaching without having to crowd into the classroom,' Mr Fletcher adds. Tom Clark points out the advantages to George Spencer: 'Being a training school helps us in different ways. First, it is stimulating to be working with other schools in a Midlands consortium. Second, it helps us to develop an understanding about how teachers are trained. And certainly there are recruitment opportunities.' George Spencer itself takes about nine trainees each year, and 70 trainees have been through the school since 1997.

A new school-centred initial teacher training programme is the Teach First programme, developed by Rona Kiley and modelled on the Teach America programme. This programme is aimed at recent graduates with good degrees who are encouraged to try teaching before making a career decision. This has proved to be very successful in its first year.

The new pedagogy

The role of schools has changed a lot with regard to teaching. So has the role of the teacher. There are more people to offer support, and they have new career structures. Some schools are becoming more adventurous not only in whom they employ to teach, but in how they offer lessons. There is a growing role for schools in shaping tomorrow's teachers as trainers. And new technologies have still barely scratched the surface of the possibilities for changing the Victorian model that still informs many classrooms today. But above all, there is a new emphasis on the pupil as actively acquiring knowledge rather than simply being its passive recipient. And that is changing the nature of what schools want teachers to do and become perhaps more than any other single development.

Key points in this chapter

The changing team: Teacher numbers have grown in recent years. But the number of support staff has risen faster. There are more teaching assistants working with classroom teachers, in both secondary and primary schools. Good schools now provide secretarial support to those leading subject departments. There are also opportunities for those with specialist expertise in subjects like ICT to contribute to schools.

Teaching and learning: Schools increasingly see the importance of teaching students how to learn, to research and to acquire knowledge, so that they are active learners, rather than simply passive recipients of knowledge. Good schools recognise that there can be two types of teacher: the one who can help students to manage this process and the one who can develop content. Both are important to the teaching and learning process.

Flatter management structure: Some good schools find that an important way of motivating good teachers is to give them greater responsibility at an early stage. A flatter management structure, with fewer deputies and assistant heads, and giving teachers more specific areas of responsibility, can help in this task.

Rewarding the best: Good schools often make the most of their best classroom teachers through awarding them advanced skills teacher status. ASTs can help develop areas of the curriculum and build links with other schools, including feeder primaries. Changes in 2004 may mean that performance related pay becomes much more aligned to performance in the future.

Teacher training: A greater proportion of teacher training is now taking place in schools, either through the Graduate Teacher Programme or with schools becoming Training Schools or on the new Teach First programme, where they build links with higher education to improve the quality of initial teacher training. Good schools recognise the need for teachers to be lifelong learners, extending and building their knowledge during their school career.

8

Broad and balanced learning

In James Callaghan's famous Ruskin lecture of 1976, the then Labour Prime Minister signalled his support for 'a basic curriculum with universal standards'.[1] But it is was to be a Conservative Education Secretary, Kenneth Baker who would start to turn the Callaghan vision into reality, with the introduction of the National Curriculum for English and Welsh schools. The process was a fraught one, with Margaret Thatcher apparently wanting a curriculum focusing on the basics while her Education Secretary preferred something more 'broad and balanced' which covered the humanities and the sciences. But lying behind the discussion about the curriculum was a worry among traditional educationists that something in education had been lost: that the traditions of the old grammar school and learning by rote had been replaced by something less rigorous and certainly less satisfactory. As Callaghan had noted, this was a concern felt by many parents too. 'There is the unease felt by parents and others about the new informal methods of teaching which seem to produce excellent results when they are in well-qualified hands but are much more dubious when they are not,' he told his Oxford audience. 'There is little wrong with the range and diversity of our courses. But is there sufficient thoroughness and depth in those required in after life to make a living?' This concern persisted and after Baker's curriculum came National Curriculum tests finally introduced in 1995, at ages seven, 11 and 14 in English, mathematics and science (though some of these have subsequently been downgraded in Wales and the tests for seven-year-olds are being made more flexible in England).

---

[1] From a text on the *Guardian* website at http://education.guardian.co.uk/thegreatdebate/story/0,9860,574645,00.html.

Mrs Thatcher had been right to worry. By prescribing so much of what was taught in schools, the basics were left behind. The results of the first National Curriculum tests shocked the nation when fewer than half of 11-year-olds achieved the level expected for their age. The new Labour Government was determined to improve primary school standards, so the Education and Employment secretary David Blunkett ensured that primary schools had a daily literacy hour from 1998 and a National Numeracy Strategy from 1999, which ensured that more time was given over to English and mathematics. The changes prompted some significant improvement in the results, though they stalled between 2000 and 2004. Nevertheless, many secondary teachers found that as a result of the more structured approach to reading, spelling and grammar, pupils were better equipped than they had been previously. Moreover, Ofsted reported substantial improvements in the quality of teaching and of teacher training. This was not enough to prevent the national mood swinging from prescription back towards a more *laissez-faire* attitude once again. Charles Clarke published a primary strategy in 2003, which, though it insisted it was not downgrading the basics, gave renewed emphasis to other subjects which some had felt were neglected by the literacy and numeracy drives. However, the daily structured lessons still survive. In secondary schools, a relatively prescriptive 'Key Stage 3 strategy' to improve lessons for 11–14-year-olds has been in place since 2001, with the 2003 and 2004 results showing some improvements in English and mathematics.

Reform of the curriculum has often taken place in isolation from the qualifications needed to measure them. When A Levels were introduced in 1951, they were intended to ensure that universities had students better prepared in their specialist subjects. The switch from O Levels and CSEs to GCSEs in 1988 was supposed to produce a more inclusive approach, where students deemed worthy only of a CSE were not able to strive for an O Level. Changes first promoted by the Conservatives in 1996 and adopted by Labour in 2000 saw the elevation of A/S Levels so that students would sit more subjects in the lower sixth form, before specialisation in the upper sixth. This would reintroduce greater breadth to the system. But the 2000 reforms were only moderately successful: four subjects became the norm (plus general studies in many cases) in the lower sixth form, but the fourth subject tended to complement rather than contrast with the other three studies. Moreover, an attempt to introduce key skills such as number, communication and ICT faltered on the combined apathy of many schools and lack of interest from universities in students' scores in their tests. Meanwhile, various half-hearted efforts were made to introduce vocational education. By 2004, a new solution was on the table. A working group headed by the former Chief Inspector of Schools, Mike Tomlinson proposed that A Levels and GCSEs should become part of a wider 14 to 19 framework.

The core curriculum

Kenneth Baker's National Curriculum is not quite the same as the curriculum studied by 11–16-year-olds today. It covers the same subjects, but is less prescriptive, notably as a result of changes made in 2000. Not every student has to study all its subjects. Ron Dearing[2] reduced many of the requirements after initial complaints from teachers. David Blunkett and Charles Clarke, the Education Secretary since 2002, have overseen a number of other changes. Modern foreign languages have become optional after 14 though pupils still retain an entitlement to request lessons, as efforts are concentrated on introducing the subject in primary schools at Key Stage 2. Other subjects can be dropped where students want to pursue a more vocational route. The Association of Colleges estimates that around one in 12 14- and 15-year-olds is currently spending at least a day a week in a further education college, often linked to time in the workplace. Plans for junior apprenticeships are likely to increase those numbers. Citizenship has become a compulsory subject in secondary schools, and there has been more attention given to subjects like health and sex education, through personal social and health education, on which guidance has been issued by the QCA.

Nevertheless, there has still been quite a bit of prescription, though current proposals are likely to reduce it post-14, as pupils are encouraged to pursue different 'pathways' towards achieving qualifications. These may be vocational or academic, or a mix of the two, and the combinations available will depend both on school timetabling and co-operation between different schools and colleges. Some schools, which are free of most curriculum restrictions, believe that the greater flexibility they enjoy is part of the reason they achieve higher standards. The Leigh City Technology College, an 11–19 mixed comprehensive in Dartford, Kent, has achieved a remarkable increase in its GCSE results in the 14 years since in started operating in 1990. The proportion of students gaining five or more good GCSEs has risen from 13 per cent to 77 per cent in 2003. This is all the more remarkable because it is situated amid the grammar schools of North West Kent, which cream off the brightest local students. On a value-added basis, it scores among the best in the country, according to the analysis by Professor David Jesson which looks at schools' Key Stage 2 results and their projected GCSE scores. The college focuses on science, mathematics, technology and information technology. And it has a strong record for its vocational education, something which is not just for the least able students, but is taught to everyone. Frank

---

[2] Ron, now Lord Dearing, was given the task of streamlining the Curriculum by the Conservative Government. He subsequently became an invaluable aide to successive ministers, reporting on higher education reform and helping establish the University for Industry through learndirect.

Green, The Leigh's Principal, explains: 'We do always look at what's in the best interests of the student. And most CTCs went down the vocational pathway to a greater or lesser extent in the mid-nineties. We did that and have been cited by [the exam board] Edexcel as possibly the best example of vocational learning in pre- and post-16 education offered by schools.' The Leigh also has a special unit for hearing-impaired children, and alongside more traditional languages such as French, German and Spanish, students also have the option of learning British sign language through a deaf studies course. Around 30–40 students in each GCSE year group take this option, an alternative for which they receive accreditation.

Recent years have seen the controversial growth of modular courses, where students have their studies assessed each term, and they can then bank their grades towards the final total. There has also been a substantial growth in coursework – around a quarter of the marks in GCSEs in most subjects (and 60 per cent in some) are awarded for project work completed before the final exams. The growth of modularity at A Level, after the exam was split between an A/S and an A2 year in 2000 led to many complaints of over-examination, while ministers stressed that traditional end-of-course examinations remained an option. But The Leigh sees value in both modularity and coursework, provided a substantial proportion of it is developed and assessed within the school. 'We divide our school year into six terms,' explains Frank Green. 'In every year group, in every subject, the curriculum is divided into modules of six units a year. Students are assessed every six weeks and their teachers report on their progress every six weeks. Each department decides how that assessment is done: sometimes there are formal tests, sometimes it might be a project, a poster or newspaper design, or another piece of work that is assessed. It could be an average of the marks awarded for the student's homework. Whatever method is used should encourage the publication of "end product", rather than simply awarding students a mark out of ten. At the beginning of each module the teacher should have a discussion with the student about what they will learn in that module and how far they should progress. With the assessment, there can be movement of students up and down ability sets, for example. But the reporting process at the end of the module should be a negotiated grade with the student – and students are encouraged to challenge teachers if they think the grades are unfair. So, if a student getting a B thinks he should have had an A, the teacher can show him the work of a student with an A grade, and explain why his work is not as good. After this process, it is far easier to discuss the targets for the following term, and the potential for improvement. For the children, six weeks is a time frame that they can easily comprehend, whereas a year is not.'

Ofsted seems to agree with Mr Green's assessment. When inspectors visited the college in 2001, they reported that the modular system supported good teacher assessment:

All work is properly marked and end of module test results recorded electronically. Teachers are able to identify students whose standards of attainment are on a downward slide and are able to intervene quickly to ensure limited damage is done to the overall performance of such students. Each student can be tracked very effectively. Students have a good knowledge of their own learning. They are involved in their own reporting system . . . The modular system gives them a new start every six weeks so that if they find a particular unit of work too hard they have every opportunity to improve on their scores next time.[3]

11–14 education or 11–13 education?

Until recently, the first three years of secondary education were often overlooked by schools. They were seen by some as wasted years. GCSE studies from the age of 14 and the results achieved made or broke a school's reputation. Yet student attitudes developed in the first three years of secondary school have a strong impact on later performance, as well as on truancy and behaviour. Students who are bored early on are unlikely to regain that interest in time for their GCSEs. It would be an exaggeration to suggest that 'Key Stage 3' – Years 7 to 9 – has acquired greater or even equal importance in most schools to those GCSE studies. But since the introduction of the Key Stage 3 strategy in 2001, there have been important changes. Lessons are more formally structured than they were before, in 'three-part lessons', with teachers expected to introduce their topics and sum up what has been learned. There is also a greater emphasis on reinforcing studies through other subjects, so that mathematics might be reinforced in geography or science lessons, for example. Results and teaching are slowly starting to improve; a fact that has been reflected in national test results and inspection reports. But some schools believe that Key Stage 3 doesn't need three years to deliver.

A growing number of schools believe that some or all of their students should be able to sit their Key Stage 3 tests early, so long as they are ready to do so. The Leigh CTC has introduced a two-year teaching programme allowing students to take their Key Stage 3 tests in Year 8, which would give students more flexibility in their GCSE studies. Frank Green explains: 'The advantage of splitting the curriculum that way is that the tests are a useful diagnostic tool for the students who are not yet achieving well and have difficulties in their learning. It is possible that it will be too challenging for some youngsters, but I'm not sure it would be any less challenging had they waited until Year 9. If they haven't got to level 5 in Year 8 – or at least to level 4 – then we've got significant issues.' Students

---

[3] *The Leigh City Technology College Inspection Report* (London, Ofsted, 2001). Available at www.ofsted.gov.uk.

who miss this target get other help and support, but they are also much more likely to go on to other more work-related programmes in Year 10 and 11, which will be suited to their interests and aptitude. But there is also a big advantage for the majority of the year group – more than 80 per cent of them – in that they have three years to tackle Key Stage 4. Mr Green thinks the pressure that has been built through a constant examination system from half way through Year 10 right the way through to the end of Year 13 is too much, and that doing the tests a year early helps to ease that pressure. 'It is not necessary for children to take so many examinations to ensure that they are ready for the workplace or to cope with a university standard of work,' he adds. 'We want to spread it out, and make it easier for the children to be in control of when they take their examinations.' Between 50 and 60 per cent of students are expected to choose to do their GCSEs – some or all of them – in Year 10; the other 40 per cent will probably elect to take their GCSEs in Year 11. Other schools have opted to let most or all of their students sit Key Stage 3 tests in Year 8, and this trend may accelerate in the future.

14–19 education

There has been a significant shift in thinking about how education should be divided. With considerable concern about the numbers of young people leaving education at age 16, when school is no longer compulsory in law, the Government has sought to develop a continuum from age 14 to 19. The former Chief Inspector of Schools, Mike Tomlinson, was tasked with developing a new qualifications and assessment framework which reflected this shift.[4] With his working group on 14–19 reform, Mr Tomlinson has proposed replacing the existing GCSEs (which themselves were introduced because of concerns about a divide between those taking CSEs and O Levels) and A Levels (which had been reformed in 2000 to give them greater breadth) with a new four-part diploma that would enable students to progress from entry-level studies to advanced studies, and achieve recognition for each stage of their development. The GCSE stage is broken in two again, with a foundation stage (equivalent to grades D–G) and an intermediate stage (grades A–C). Under the proposals published in February 2004, students would be required to take core subjects including English, mathematics and ICT, within which there would be a more applied focus. But they could then opt for an academic or a vocational pathway, depending on their aptitude, or they could mix different subjects. To enable universities to differentiate between high fliers who

---

[4] Mr Tomlinson's proposals can be read in full at www.14–19reform.gov.uk.

may all have achieved a similar number of grade As, A and B grades would be split into A1, A2, B1 and B2. Coursework would be replaced by a single project or essay. There would also be credits for extra-curricular activities, such as community work or sports. At advanced level (or for students aged over 16 taking intermediate or foundation diplomas) there would be a choice between a specialist diploma akin to the current A Levels, or an open diploma, which would be more like a baccalaureate, though there would be no attempt to compel a particular mix of subjects.

Tomlinson's report followed controversy about A Levels, after complaints about the quality of marking of some papers in 2001. Since 2000, the A Level has been split into an A2 and A/S exam. Those in the lower sixth form have been expected to take one or two extra A/S Levels in addition to their specialist subjects. While most students have taken at least one extra A/S Level, few have used this as an opportunity to broaden their studies. And since the introduction of the exam coincided with significant modularisation of courses, many students have faced more exams, though some schools have opted to continue to assess students only at the end of the course. An attempt to encourage 'key skills' including communication and number was largely dropped after resistance from schools and indifference from universities, though many further education (FE) and sixth form colleges were more willing to provide such courses.

Already, schools like The Leigh CTC are embracing a more flexible approach to GCSEs. By shifting their Key Stage 3 tests to Year 8, they are giving students much more flexibility than they would have in the more typical study pattern. Mr Green says: 'One of the discussions we had in introducing the new model is that when you get into Year 10, and you've got a student who is doing pretty well and is going to get a grade C, come what may, and he is not keen on doing French or whatever, they have the chance to focus on their real interest, which might be IT or engineering. So that student has freed up the time to take an extra course in IT in Year 11 instead, while having got a C in French already under his belt. Another student might equally say she'll get a GCSE in English out of the way, because she might want to be a vet and wants to get all her sciences sorted out, so she can get A grades at A Level for veterinary college. But you've got three years to do all that, not just two.'

But there is another alternative to A Levels, which both state and independent schools have embraced. The International Baccalaureate (IB) is offered in over 50 English and Welsh schools and colleges, including a number of specialist schools, CTCs and Academies. Others, including The Leigh are planning to offer it. Unlike A Levels, the IB expects students to continue with broader studies before they go to university, and is much closer to the model adopted by continental countries and the Republic of Ireland. There are four elements to the IB programme.

Students normally take six subjects, at least three of which must be at higher level. Their subjects must include English and mathematics, and they must learn a second language. They study a social science and physical science. Students can take an arts subject or one subject from one of the other blocks – an additional language, humanities, further mathematics or science. Sometimes students take a seventh subject outside the diploma. They study an interdisciplinary course in the theory of knowledge and are expected to write an extended essay of up to 4,000 words, which allows them to prepare for the independent research and writing skills needed at university. They are also expected to take part in what is called 'Creativity, Action and Service' which involves participation in community service, a creative activity, such as theatre production, or sports.

Impington Village College, in Cambridgeshire, a specialist language college catering for over 1,300 students, has offered the IB alongside A Levels since 1991. Its Warden, or head teacher, Jacqueline Kearns explains that the IB does require greater effort by both teachers and students, but the latter have started to vote with their feet.[5] 'The proportion of students choosing the IB in 2003–4 was 67 per cent. In 2002, we saw an increase for the first time in years from about half of students to about 59 per cent, and the numbers rose again in 2003. In part this was a sustained response to the A Levels crisis. But students also choose the IB because of the breadth and challenge, which, with the extended essay, they see as a good preparation for university.' Mrs Kearns says that higher and standard level courses take 240 and 150 teaching hours respectively, but at Impington, some teachers have to run classes after school to provide the full complement of hours. Science and mathematics courses, in particular, have a very high volume of content, but results are still good. 'We gain outstanding results at IB, even compared with international schools that enjoy luxurious levels of staffing and resources. Indeed, a greater proportion of students at Impington takes a bilingual IB Diploma than in other schools worldwide. In 2001, 60 per cent of our students gained bilingual diplomas, nearly twice the world average of 32.4 per cent.'

While rejecting compulsory breadth, several elements of the IB have been attractive to the Tomlinson working group, particularly the extended essay and community service. Mrs Kearns says: 'Participation in service projects enables students to become socially responsible and compassionate members of society. The programme promotes collaboration and leadership skills. It is also a good

---

[5] For a more detailed explanation of how the IB operates at Impington, see J. Kearns, 'Challenges at the chalkface' in *Bac or Basics: Challenges for the 14–19 curriculum*, ed. C. Ryan (London, Social Market Foundation, 2004). To read the requirements of the International Baccalaureate, visit www.ibo.org.

way to provide education for citizenship in the sixth form. At Impington, all sixth form students devote an afternoon a week to these activities. The IB requirement is that students must spend at least 50 hours on each of the elements of this pro-gramme.' Students are assessed for the IB through moderated internal marking, assessed public presentations, and a record of their creative, action and service activities and examinations taken at the end of May in the final year. They must meet all the course requirements for the Diploma to be awarded. Subject courses are graded from 1 to 7, with three additional points from the Extended Essay and the Theory of Knowledge. Students must get 24 points, including 12 points in their higher subjects to be awarded a Diploma.

Unusually, The Leigh CTC is considering shifting not only to the IB for sixth formers, but to join with two other Dartford schools to offer the International Baccalaureate Organisation (IBO) 'middle years programme' as an option for GCSE-age students. According to the IBO, this course:

> provides a framework of academic challenge and life skills for students aged 11–16 years. The five-year programme offers an educational approach that embraces yet transcends traditional school subjects. It follows naturally the Primary Years Programme and serves as excellent preparation for the Diploma Programme.[6]

In addition to traditional curriculum subjects, the programme encourages students to study different approaches to learning (or learning styles). They start to under-take some community service, learn health and social education and about the environment. They also study an area called 'homo faber' which is about the impact of individuals on society. These 'areas of interaction' pervade eight subject areas and interdisciplinary teaching and projects. There is also a personal project – an essay or an artistic production – chosen with teachers. A portfolio of achieve-ment will record these accomplishments as well as marks awarded in GCSEs or other national tests. There may be opportunities here for other schools to consider, too.

The IB was rejected by the Tomlinson group, because it was felt not be suffi-ciently inclusive. Certainly many sixth form teachers expect five grade Bs as a minimum GCSE score before students take the course. But for those schools which offer the course there is a sense that students are gaining a much broader and richer curriculum than that offered in more traditional sixth form studies. Chapter 15 describes the French system under which three quarters of children take the baccalaureate examination which requires study of six subjects.

---

[6] International Baccalaureate Organisation website www.ibo.org.

Vocational education applied and technical challenges

The debate over vocational education has raged since the 1944 Education Act which introduced three different types of school in England: Grammar schools, secondary modern and technical schools. Largely forgotten now amid memories about grammar schools and secondary moderns is the fact that the legislation was also supposed to create a third type of secondary school: the technical school. Had that happened to any significant extent, perhaps vocational education would not be seen today as a poor relation of academic studies. But the last 20 years have been marked by considerable activity in this area by successive governments. The Conservatives had their Technical and Vocational Education Initiative. Labour has sought to allow students to spend part of their week studying in college and in the workplace, as well as in school. The likelihood is that this option, which the Association of Colleges estimates is being taken up by around 100,000 14- and 15-year-olds, will become more integrated into the Apprenticeships scheme in future. Students who are not academically minded would continue to study English, mathematics and ICT in their school. But they would then spend the rest of the week in an FE college and the workplace. This raises important issues about how courses are provided in schools, and by consortia of schools and colleges. But it also raises questions about how well a good school offers vocational education for its students generally.

Clarity of terminology is important in this debate. Applied studies of mathematics and science are increasingly offered by many schools, as a sensible way to engage students in subjects which some find boring. The post-14 Mathematics Inquiry by Professor Adrian Smith, published in 2004, recognised the importance of such courses to re-engaging many young people with the subject.[7] However, vocational education is often used as a shorthand for learning a manual trade, though many apprenticeships are in the service sector or in business studies.

City Technology Colleges have seen vocational education as an important part of their mission. And The Leigh CTC is regarded as one of the most effective in translating the concept into practice for all its students. Frank Green, The Leigh's Principal explains: 'There is an entitlement to vocational education for every student. It forms one of the option blocks from which they choose their subjects for GCSE. All students do an IT vocational course – an applied GCSE – and they will take the digital applications course when it becomes available, as part of the core curriculum, along with English and mathematics. Every student also does an GNVQ science course, too, though this is something we have only introduced

---

[7] *Making Mathematics Count*, the report of Professor Adrian Smith's Mathematics Inquiry into post-14 mathematics education. Accessible at www.mathsinquiry.org.uk/report.

more recently. Then there's an option block that includes vocational courses: this has got art, design, engineering, business studies, leisure and tourism, and performing arts in it. We also have some subjects which are not accredited in terms of public exam results – in a sense we don't so much mind this since we have established our own credibility independently. So, we use our status as a regional Cisco academy – linked to the global IT firm – and offer a certificated course for 14–16-year-olds through that route. We are considering offering a similar Microsoft course.' Engineering has also proved particularly popular with disaffected boys at The Leigh CTC.

Catering for the brightest

Bright youngsters have not always been encouraged to use their talents and abilities to the full in the state system. They have then switched off from lessons they regard as too easy. Until recently, many schools felt that providing extra provision for their most able students was elitist. But times have changed. Most secondary schools now regard catering for their brightest students as being as important as ensuring that those with learning difficulties are given the chance to succeed. The 'gifted and talented' programme, which was launched five years ago as part of Excellence in Cities, a government-funded scheme for urban schools, now runs in over 2,000 schools. It offers extra classes for bright students, sometimes at 'advanced centres' in mathematics and other subjects, as well as summer schools. Talented young artists, musicians and scientists are no longer seeing their abilities unfulfilled. There is a National Academy for Gifted and Talented Youth based at the University of Warwick, modelled on a similar programme in Johns Hopkins University, in Baltimore, Maryland, which runs successful summer schools and helps schools develop year-round activities. Partnerships abound with some linking independent and state schools, and others marrying universities to inner city schools. Leeds University classics students organise after-school Latin classes for up to 60 gifted pupils at some of their local high schools.

Such programmes may be a part of what's on offer in most secondary schools. But their implications are not always carried through to the classroom. The Chief Inspector of Schools, David Bell warned in late 2003 that everyday lessons are often not made interesting enough for gifted pupils. Those running local schemes believe they are making a difference. They are also an important link between primary and secondary schools. Around 40 ten- and 11-year-olds regularly spend two-and-a-half hours of their Saturday mornings taking extra mathematics classes at the St Thomas More High School, on Tyneside. These are bright primary school pupils spending time learning more mathematics at their local secondary school, and it is clear that they enjoy working with other gifted youngsters, who have a shared interest in mathematics. Places are limited and there is typically one pupil nominated by each local primary school. Claire Johnson, the North Tyneside Education Service Inspector and Programme Co-ordinator, says: 'To take part, children must love mathematics. Their enthusiasm is real. At the end of one recent Saturday session, one child asked for more algebra to take home with him. They work with others of similar ability. They are challenged because they are no longer a big fish in a small pond. Parents say that their children have become much more confident as a result. And they enjoy making new friends, too.'

North Tyneside runs a whole series of such schemes, many for secondary pupils. Those whose talent lies in sports are helped to balance their schoolwork with the need to train through the 'junior athletes programme' for 11–16-year-olds which the LEA runs with John Spence Community High School, a North Shields specialist sports college and the Youth Sport Trust. This programme gives support to 140 local youngsters, who compete regionally, nationally and internationally in sports including football, swimming, gymnastics and netball. It particularly tries to make sure that schools make allowances for their sports stars. 'If you have a boy who has been signed by Newcastle United, there is not a great deal of point teaching him football in school. His time might be far better spent catching up on the coursework he missed out on while at club training sessions,' explains Claire Johnson. In a third popular initiative, nearly 600 14- and 15-year-year olds from across Newcastle, Gateshead and Tyneside attend Saturday masterclasses every March at Newcastle's two universities. Started in 2000, this scheme brings university lecturers and school teachers together to provide advanced classes in 13 subjects for the top students who are expected to gain an A or an A* grade in their GCSEs. Traditional subjects like mathematics and physics are taught alongside specialist courses including medical science, and town and country planning. The students are encouraged to think about A Levels and university after their GCSEs, and they are given a taste of university life. They are taught in lecture theatres and seminar groups, and they have the chance to access specialist facilities and expert lecturers. Crucially, they see there is nothing strange about their level of ability.

An evaluation found that more than half of the students attending said the masterclasses made them more likely to want to go to university and 38 per cent of those taking medical science classes were more likely to consider studying medicine afterwards. North Tyneside also believes that the scheme has focused teachers' minds on the need to stretch their brightest students. Moreover, even in selective areas like Kent, schools like The Leigh CTC find that as their results improve, bright students are opting for them over grammar schools, and they too need to find extra ways to stretch the most able. However, if programmes for gifted and talented pupils are to be meaningful, they must have a real impact on everyday lessons as well as on extra-curricular activities. In other words, it is not enough simply to offer a bright student an hour or two of stimulating lessons once a week, if they do not get that same level of stimulation for the other 25 or more hours per week they are in the classroom.

Catering for the least able

Most comprehensives have a significant proportion of students who have not reached level 4 in the Key Stage 2 tests and require extra help with literacy and numeracy if they are to access the secondary curriculum. At The Leigh CTC, Mr Green says that it is important to provide the right support: 'Under the old levels 1–5 scale for special needs, we had 270 children on that register. We currently have 41 pupils with formal statements, which is around twice the national average. Some of those are hearing impaired, so you have a different range of challenges as well as the usual range of learning disabilities. But while we have a significant number of educationally challenged children, we don't run any separate classes. We use our learning assistants to work with classes and help the pupils to fit into our different teaching groups.' At The Leigh, there are 225 pupils in each pre-16 year group, and they are divided into two groups of around 112/115. Each of those groups is split into four or five teaching groups which will generally be split by ability set – but it is up to each subject department to arrange the groups. These groups had been age-related until 2004, but were due to become more stage-related from September 2004, as the new curriculum structure developed. 'The learning assistants tend to work with sets four and five. They will have reading recovery programmes, literacy and numeracy support. In Year 8, when other students are taking German or Spanish, as a second foreign language, there will be additional literacy lessons for these students.' Mr Green judges the success of those students with literacy and numeracy problems by their results at GCSE level. None of the students at The Leigh fails to get any GCSE passes (compared with a national average of just over 5 per cent) and 98 or 99 per cent get at least five A–G passes (the national average is 89 per cent). Few students gained below an E – from 1998–2003, the Principal reckons that only five students have gained below a grade E in English. For such students, an 'individualised' curriculum is particularly important.

Three areas of concern

Languages

The lack of qualified language teachers was one of the reasons which caused the Government to drop the teaching of a foreign language as a requirement for secondary school pupils. The number of pupils opting to take a GCSE language course is dropping as are the number of schools bidding for specialist status in languages. This is a worry which could perhaps be addressed by better co-operation with our European Union partners to encourage the greater exchange of teachers.

Science

Another area of concern is the teaching of physics and chemistry at A Level. The introduction of the double science award may have contributed to a decline in the share of A Level entries by those studying A Level physics and chemistry. The two subjects are perceived as being hard, possibly because of the lack of specialist physics and chemistry teachers at GCSE. Fortunately, the advent of specialist science colleges, which are expected to offer separate sciences at GCSE has proved popular and started to reverse the trend.

The purpose of education

In Chapter 1, we attempted to define the overall purpose of education, quoting the *Concise Oxford Dictionary* which defines education as the giving of intellectual, moral and social instruction. While it is essential that every child learns essential skills such as literacy and numeracy and performs adequately in national examinations, it is just as important that schools inspire the love of good books, develop enquiring minds and teach the appreciation of our history, culture and the duties and responsibilities of a good citizen. The use of a longer day has been used in many schools to meet both the requirements of the National Curriculum and to transmit our culture to our children. Many schools now have an extensive after-hours programme of enhancement activities, teaching languages, drama or sport. For this wider education a good library is just as important, perhaps more so than good computer laboratories.

Some schools are now using the accelerated reading programmes of Renaissance Learning developed in the USA (www.renlearn.com). This encourages children to read books through stimulating online questionnaires on the content of books. Other schools are now renewing the study of the classics. It is hoped that the new humanities specialist schools will lead the way in developing innovative and exciting ways to teach English, history and geography.

Technology changing the curriculum

Secondary schools have seen another important change in the last decade: the relatively rapid expansion of ICT. With broadband access particularly, teachers can access a much wider range of resources to bring the curriculum to life. As Frank Green says: 'ICT is going to be used more and more. We have 400 fixed-point machines and 300 laptops, a wireless and a wired network. I can't believe the time is that far away when students will have some sort of electronic device to replace their exercise books and text books. Business, science, technology and mathematics make particular use of ICT. I have set staff the target of getting all the college's curriculum available electronically to students from September 2004.' Schools vary in the extent to which they are wired up. Some schools try to deliver as much as possible online, using interactive whiteboards as the norm. For others such technology still remains a relative novelty. And it is also fair to say that the Government devoted more effort initially to wiring schools than to the content available on the Internet. The National Grid for Learning brings many of the available resources together on a single portal. But it is with Curriculum Online (www.curriculumonline.gov.uk), a government-supported digital library of educational resources, and an explosion in resources from other providers, that the true potential of ICT to support and transform the curriculum is beginning to be realised. The Government is providing thousands of pounds in electronic credits to schools, to encourage them to buy materials from the new portal. One of the great advantages of the new portals is that they connect available resources much more clearly to the expectations and requirements of the National Curriculum. With the growth of broadband, video-based resources are also much more accessible online.

But it is still relatively early days when it comes to delivering the curriculum through new technologies. Although teachers are now better trained than before, only a minority of schools genuinely tries to integrate such resources into all their lessons. Yet as we shall see in Chapter 17, there is an inevitability about this progress which may mean that the ways in which most pupils receive their curriculum entitlement by the end of the decade are very different from the ways in which most now do so.

Key points in this chapter

Changing Key Stage 3: The government's Key Stage 3 strategy has heralded some improvements in teaching for 11–14-year-olds. A better structure to lessons and more integration across subjects are two important gains. But some schools argue that the Key Stage 3 tests could be taken by most children in Year 8, thus freeing up time for GCSE preparation and other activities.

What future post-14? The Tomlinson committee's recommendations are likely to see a less age-related structure to post-14 studies, with students increasingly taking exams when they are ready to do so. In the sixth form, there will probably be requirements to study key skills and to complete a long essay or project, with the option of taking either a specialised or a more general diploma. A small but growing number of successful schools has opted already for the International Baccalaureate, which combines breadth, specialisation and traditional extra-curricular activities.

Vocational education: For students without an academic leaning, vocational courses combined with key skills can be a more valuable use of their time. Courses have been developed which combine school, college and work, and these will probably move towards becoming early apprenticeships in the years ahead. But some schools believe it is important that vocational (applied and technical) studies are seen as an integral part of every student's education. And even where they are not, it is important they are seen as an option no less valuable than the academic route.

Catering for the brightest: Schools which once shunned special lessons for their brightest students are now much keener on providing extra lessons to stretch their ablest students. There are a growing number of masterclasses and advanced learning centres to cater for their needs. But it is important that bright students are properly catered for throughout the school curriculum, and not just in extra tuition. One way to ensure this is to identify the gifted and talented at an early age.

Supporting the least able: Despite improvements in primary school, many students still start secondary education without the basics of literacy and numeracy. Schools should cater for such students by offering extra support from teaching assistants and through extra classes. Some schools organise such classes for children post-14 as an alternative to other aspects of the curriculum.

Going online: Increasing resources are available online to help bring the curriculum to life. Every school and subject department needs to think about how such resources can add value to lessons, and what the implications are for future teaching and learning styles.

9

Term times, timetables and changing classrooms

Britain in Victorian times was very different from its twenty-first century incarnation. Agriculture was then a great employer. One in eight people worked on the land in 1901, and many people earned their living through agricultural labour. Hence, many children were expected to help with the annual harvest each year so that none of it was wasted. Times have changed; today, fewer than one in 50 people works on the land. The annual harvest remains an important part of the farming community's timetable, but it has little immediate impact on the lives of 98 per cent of the population who earn their living by other means. The combine harvester has long replaced the scythe, too. Yet today's school timetable largely reflects decisions which were made to accommodate the Victorian pattern of agricultural working. Furthermore, the terms after Christmas are determined by the date for Easter, which can fall between 21 March and 25 April, depending on the timing of the full moon. Schools can therefore end up facing a very long term after Christmas followed by a short burst towards the summer tests and exams. All this is disruptive to the efficient working of a school timetable. Yet, despite growing evidence that change could improve standards and behaviour, and make life less stressful for teachers, those who have sought to reform the school year have found themselves facing formidable and immoveable obstacles.

Modest changes at a national level

The biggest problem with the system which we have inherited is the pattern of irregular terms, caused in large part by the irregularity of Easter. But annual variations make curriculum planning and assessment difficult in other ways, too. Moreover, autumn terms lasting 16 weeks have often been the time when schools face the greatest disruption by their pupils, and the greatest teacher absences through exhaustion. Truancy and exclusions often reach their peak in the weeks before Christmas. Then, the six-week summer break, even though it is shorter than the eight or ten weeks prevalent in some countries, can lead pupils to forget a lot of what they learned during the previous year. Keeping pupils occupied becomes particularly difficult for parents.

Some reform is set to take place. In 2005, many schools are likely to see some change to the school year. Instead of three terms broken by half-term breaks, there will be six. And while schools will continue to be required to teach pupils for 190 days a year, with a further five days set aside for teacher training, there will be a slightly longer break in October and a fixed two-week break each April, regardless of when Easter falls. Indeed, some LEAs were due to adopt this pattern from the autumn of 2004. According to Chris Price, the former Labour MP who chaired a commission established by the Local Government Association to consider radical reform of the school year, the biggest benefit should come from having the same holiday times across different education authorities, though, even here, there may still be some flexibility not least about the dates when teacher training takes place. 'This could cut down on the problem of parent-condoned absence, which sometimes happens when children attend schools in different local authorities and have different holiday times,' says Mr Price, who also believes the longer October break should improve behaviour and cut teacher sickness. 'All the work we've done suggests there is also an enormous psychological advantage in providing a longer break in October. The weeks up to Christmas are those where you get a lot of pupil and teacher absence, as well as more exclusions for bad behaviour.'

But Mr Price was clearly disappointed that intense opposition from some of the teaching unions forced him to abandon plans for a five-term year used by many CTCs, where children would have shorter summer holidays matched by longer breaks during the school year. Because, if he is right that a few extra days off in October can have such beneficial effects, a more even school year with terms of around eight weeks, interspersed with two week breaks, and a four-week summer holiday, could have even more recuperative benefits. This, at least, is what some CTCs have found.

The five-term year in action

Such a timetable has helped make John Cabot City Technology College in Bristol one of the country's most successful comprehensives. The CTC has had a five-term year since it opened in 1993. Eighty-three per cent of pupils at the 1,040 pupil school achieved at least five good GCSEs in 2003, a figure well above the national average. Each day is an hour longer than in most other schools, so that pupils are taught for 30 hours a week rather than 25 and pupils are taught for 40 weeks at the college each year. When Ofsted visited the school in December 2002, it observed that:

> students' achievement in Years 7 to 11 is even higher than the good quality of teaching that they receive in the different subjects. This is because students respond very positively to the extended curriculum . . . . Students' very good attendance during all five of the separate eight-week terms assists the continuity and very good progression of their learning. Students work hard and with enthusiasm.[1]

Acting Principal Nick Jones, who has taught at the school since it first opened, explains some of the benefits: 'There is a fairly regular pattern to the year. Terms typically last eight weeks, broken up by two-week breaks and four weeks off in the summer.' At John Cabot, pupils and teachers enjoy a fixed fortnight off in October, March and May, as well as Christmas. Term starts in mid-August, rather than early September. The timetable for 2003–4 can be seen in Figure 9.1. Shorter summer holidays also mean students don't forget what they've learned, and the longer breaks during the school year help discipline. 'We have very few problems with truancy at John Cabot,' he adds. Others schools have different holiday times, which can be a problem, as Mr Jones admits. 'I had three children at different schools at one stage, while my wife was working at the university, with its own term times. Juggling different timetables can be difficult.' But one recent straw poll at a recent annual governors' meeting for parents found continued widespread support. Only one of the 70 parents present wanted change.

The biggest objection to such a radical alteration to the traditional school timetable is that teachers value their long summer holidays. They see it as a 'perk'

Term	Start	End
Term 1–Y7 & 12	Tuesday 26 August 2003	Friday 17 October 2003
Term 1–Y8, 11, 13, 14	Thursday 28 August 2003	Friday 17 October 2003
Term 2	Monday 3 November 2003	Friday 19 December 2003
Term 3	Monday 5 January 2004	Friday 5 March 2004
Term 4	Monday 22 March 2004	Friday 21 May 2004
Term 5	Monday 7 June 2004	Friday 23 July 2004

Figure 9.1   The John Cabot CTC school timetable 2003–4

---

[1] *John Cabot City Technology College Inspection Report* (London, Ofsted, 2002). Available at www.ofsted.gov.uk.

of the job, and the feeling is that they would be reluctant to trade six weeks off in summer for longer breaks during the year. Certainly, some of the CTCs which have gone for a five-term year have done so while maintaining the six weeks off in the summer. Indeed, the Local Government Association commission had originally been expected to recommend a five-term year. But Mr Price admits that some teaching unions objected to shorter summer holidays, and the commission was warned by the Teacher Training Agency that it could make it far harder to recruit new teachers, who see long holidays as a 'perk'.

And it is also the case that teachers coming to John Cabot know the score when they submit their applications and accept a post, as Nick Jones acknowledges. 'They know when they are coming to the school that this is the pattern of our school year. The shorter holiday in the summer is compensated for by a series of two week breaks during the year. A two week holiday is after all enough to feel like you've had a break. With a one week break, you take a few days to start to relax and before you know it you're preparing to return to school. The longer break is not only good for the students, it gives teachers the chance to recuperate after a busy term. Two week breaks allow teachers to really recharge their batteries.' There is another benefit too, in that the longer holiday in March is ideal when organising a school trip outside Europe. 'The two-week break in March enables us to organise longer school trips – 18 of our 70 teachers joined pupils on a ski-trip to the States in 2003,' says Mr Jones.

However, the biggest argument in favour of the five-term year is educational. A phenomenon long experienced by teachers is the summer memory loss of students, where the enjoyments of summer lead them to forget a lot of what they learned over the previous school year. A lot of time has to be spent recapping information. A shorter summer break can lessen this problem. Mr Jones regrets that other state schools don't copy the more radical John Cabot experiment. 'I definitely feel that the pattern of the year is one of the things that makes us a successful school. I am disappointed that this clearly successful pattern is not being adopted more widely,' he says.

Research backs a five-term year

Research by Professor Brent Davies and Professor Trevor Kerry from the International Educational Leadership Centre based at the University of Lincolnshire and Humberside has shown that there is a very high level of approval for the five-term year in the six CTCs which have adopted this pattern. CTCs have found it easier to experiment because of their independence. And by adopting the five-term year from their inception, CTCs have not had to negotiate changes with staff and parents. Those teaching there know the score, as do those choosing to send their children to the CTC. Davies and Kerry have looked at research from schools in the

United States, as well as CTCs in England for their studies. American schools often have ten-week summer holidays, rather than the six or seven weeks that is the norm in England. And American studies had identified the phenomenon known as 'summer learning loss', where students regress a little during the summer holidays. One study[2] concluded that students forget what they had learned in mathematics more than other subjects; that summer learning loss seems to worsen as students get older; and that that those from low-income families forget most. There is a growing interest in what is called 'year round education' in the USA, with most teachers seeing it as beneficial to learning.

Davies and Kerry asked pupils, teachers and parents in CTCs in Bristol (John Cabot), Northamptonshire, Nottingham and Bradford what they thought of the five-term school year. After all, they had by then had the chance to experience its strengths and weaknesses. Students proved to be the most enthusiastic supporters, with 93 per cent of Year 8 and 98 per cent of Year 10 students preferring it to the three-term year which most schools favoured. Teachers were overwhelmingly in favour too, with 92 per cent support. Parents were less enthusiastic, perhaps because of the problems they faced juggling different school holiday patterns. Nevertheless, 78 per cent of parents preferred the five-term to the three-term year.[3] In a more detailed look at students' attitudes in one of the CTCs, Year 8 students felt they recalled more information, worked better, had improved concentration, got more frequent breaks, were better motivated and learned more. Their Year 10 counterparts had similar responses, but also said the more frequent breaks helped them to manage their work better, reduced their need to revise for GCSEs and enabled them to set better long-term targets. Teachers also believed their students worked harder, worked to better-defined task deadlines and allowed for more effective planning of course content. Parents saw children doing more homework, being more motivated and doing better. They also thought the two-week breaks which replaced mid-term holidays allowed more time for both homework and leisure. Whether this reflected the five-term year or the demanding nature of CTCs in general, there was also a sense that their children's workload was very heavy. Davies and Kerry concluded that 'the five-term year, and other forms of calendar reform, may have distinct advantages over the outmoded agrarian calendar'. They warned, however, that any move towards change needed careful planning and consultation. And as East Sussex council found when it consulted parents and teachers

---

[2] H. Cooper, B. Nye, K. Charlton, J. Lindsay and S. Greathouse (1996, *Review of Educational Research*) cited in B. Davies and T. Kerry, 'Improving student learning through calendar change', *School Leadership and Management*, **19**(3) (1999).

[3] B. Davies and T. Kerry, 'Improving student learning through calendar change', *School Leadership and Management*, **19**(3) (1999).

locally, such support is not always forthcoming. Indeed, it was the fact that 73 per cent of 23,000 respondents to the local council's plans were opposed to the five-term year that led the Local Government Association to water down its plans so drastically, as much as the predictable opposition of the teaching unions. Nevertheless, the CTC experiences suggests that there remains a powerful case for such change. Perhaps after more schools have had the five-term year, there will be further movement towards this model, though there is nothing to stop any education authority or school from adopting its own pattern, so long as it wins the support of its staff and parents first.

Dawn to dusk: a longer school day

The school year is not the only timetabling factor that has sometimes felt as if it were set in stone. The school day has often seemed equally rigid. There has been a welcome trend in recent years away from seeing schools as 9 a.m. to 3.30 p.m. institutions, where life all but stopped after the last bell. Many schools have started to offer breakfast clubs starting at 8 a.m. and after-school activities which lengthen the opportunities for students to engage in extra-curricular work, to do their homework, play sports, learn music or simply enjoy a decent breakfast and to supplement formal classroom teaching. In some schools these activities are complemented by evening and weekend learning activities, often using computer suites, which are open to the wider community. The big increase in 'study support' has been funded in part by the lottery and from government's special grants, and even when these funds start to dry up, most schools wish to continue to run the activities.

But more radical challenges are emerging to the way in which the formal school hours are organised. There is growing evidence that children learn most in the morning, and take in a lot less information after lunch. In that respect their concentration patterns are no different from many adults. Some primary schools have started to run morning-only lessons starting at 8 a.m. similar to the pattern of some continental European schools. In secondary schools, the most interesting new timetabling patterns have involved themed sessions, which go beyond the traditional 40-minute periods and allow proper in-depth study of particular subjects. Thomas Telford School has been perhaps the most forthright exponent of this way of working. But it is not alone. An increasing number of schools recognise that building design can make a big difference to the effective use of time, and the constant movement between classrooms not only wastes teaching time, it can also contribute to disorder in the school corridors.

Telford's Ofsted report in 2001 described how lessons are organised, and how they benefit both teachers and students. There are no bells to disrupt lessons, but an orderly progress takes place among students.

Most subjects have one three-hour lesson a week, with the exception of modern foreign languages and physical education. These two subjects have three hours a week divided into two lessons a week, each lasting one and a half hours. Because teaching is so good teachers are skilful in their planning for these longer lessons and make the most of that learning time by providing a variety of activities. For pupils there are some days when they only have two subjects and they can really get involved in the work in those subjects. Similarly for teachers, there are days when they only teach two classes, which is less demanding in both preparation time and in teaching. The school recognises that teachers and pupils need breaks and these occur once within the three-hour lessons. However, they are not long and, therefore, do not interrupt the learning. The way the breaks are organised is very good. They are staggered so that the whole school is never on the move at the same time. Queuing is kept to an absolute minimum and, therefore, there are very few opportunities for pupils to be distracted from the business of learning.[4]

Telford also operates a longer school day which makes full use of new technology and more traditional teaching methods. Each student has a personal tutor, with whom they agree their own individual goals. After formal lessons finish at 4 p.m., the school opens for what it calls Session 3, when other activities are on offer. The school's head teacher, Sir Kevin Satchwell, explains: 'The longer day and year enable students to take full advantage of the National Curriculum, spend extra time on science, technology and mathematics and develop an understanding of industry, commerce and culture. The extra-curricular programme gives students a choice of opportunities which complement and extend their education. These range from sports and hobbies to community work and form an integral part of the timetable. Learning activities are directed towards self-reliance, confidence and teamwork.'

Study support aids achievement

There is also important research evidence that participation in 'out-of-school-hours learning' or 'study support', which such extra-curricular activities are now called, can make a difference to student attitudes to learning, their attendance and their academic achievement. A study by Professor John MacBeath and colleagues, published in 2001, sought to examine the impact on students on participation in such schemes.[5] The researchers found 'firm evidence in all the schools studied that pupils who participate in study support do better than would have been expected from baseline measures in academic attainment, attitudes to school and attendance at school'. Boys and girls seem to benefit equally from study support, but the researchers discovered that such programmes were of particular benefit to

[4] *Thomas Telford School Inspection Report* (London, Ofsted, 2001). Available at www.ofsted.gov.uk/reports/index.cfm?fuseaction=summary&id=123627&bar=no.
[5] J. MacBeath, T. Kirwan and K. Myers, *The Impact of Study Support* (London, DfES, 2001).

students from ethnic minority backgrounds. Prof. MacBeath and his colleagues were able to draw on the experience not just of extensive programmes funded by the DfES and the national lottery after 1997, but on earlier pioneering initiatives supported by the Prince's Trust and developed by Strathclyde region in Scotland. Strathclyde claims to be the first UK local authority to fund such activities, and had done so since 1991. The MacBeath study also found that student attendance was helped by study support, particularly that which was focused on particular GCSE subjects or on 'drop-in activities'. Sport was also seen to improve attendance in some schools. And the reasons why pupils liked such activities ranged from their valuing of relaxed informal relations with staff, to access to learning resources and the fact that they were being treated more like adults when there.

Homework: helping achievement or stressing families?

The Government not only supports study support financially, it also provides guidelines on what homework might be reasonable for children of different ages. The concern when these guidelines were first issued in 1998 was that an inconsistent amount of homework was being set by different primary schools. This had two potentially harmful effects. First, it made it harder to sustain improvements in children's reading, which needed reinforcement at home. Second, it left some pupils ill-prepared for the demands they would face in secondary schools. The guidance suggested anything from ten minutes reading to 50 minutes reading and exercises for primary pupils, depending on their age. It also suggested a recommended minimum for secondary schools. Between 45 and 90 minutes a day should be set in Years 7 and 8, rising to as much as two-and-a-half-hours for those preparing for their GCSEs.[6] There have been other studies which have questioned the value of homework. A review of the available research on the subject by the National Foundation for Educational Research[7] concluded that 'there is a positive relationship between time spent on homework and achievement at secondary school level (especially for older secondary students)'. But the author of this research also cautioned that 'correlations between time on homework and achievement should not be taken as evidence that more time on homework necessarily leads to better achievement'.

Another more sceptical study by Dr Susan Hallam from the Institute of Education claimed that homework could put 'a strain on family relationships'.[8] According to the Institute's press summary of her findings:

---

[6] The guidelines can be read at http://www.dfes.gov.uk/homework/.

[7] C. Sharp, W. Keys and P. Benefield, *Homework: A review of recent research* (London, NFER, 2001).

[8] S. Hallam, *Homework: The evidence* (London, Institute of Education, 2004).

homework can cause friction between parents and children, especially in middle-class families where concerns about a child's future can lead to a climate of pressure to succeed. The resulting damage to the parent-child relationship may outweigh any educational advantage homework may bring.

As if that were not enough, the Institute's press release added that 'homework can also create anxiety, boredom, fatigue and emotional exhaustion in children, who resent the encroachment on their free time, even though they think homework helps them do well at school'. However, even Dr Hallam was forced to concede that 'homework can also encourage parental involvement in their children's studies, increase children's independence and provide opportunities for practice and skill development. Positive parental involvement in homework has been shown to be the strongest predictor of better grades'. Perhaps most significantly given the apparent sceptical tone of the report towards homework, Dr Hallam says:

> Homework clubs give children the benefits of homework without the rows at home. Children feel they make homework enjoyable and give them a better chance of passing exams. They provide a suitable learning environment with appropriate resources and adult help if necessary, and they take the pressure off the parents. They may assist in raising standards for those who need extra support or who find it difficult to do homework at home. As such, they help to bridge the gap between the haves and the have-nots.[9]

So, despite the scare stories which sometimes follow such reports, there is actually a considerable consensus between many homework sceptics and supporters: out-of-hours study support can not only be good for attainment, it can be particularly helpful to those from disadvantaged circumstances. As the MacBeath report put it 'study support is effective because of its ethos . . . students move towards becoming self-regulated learners' or, in the jargon now used by the Government, it encourages personalised learning, where students do more research for themselves, whether in the traditional school library or more likely these days, using the Internet. Young people's inquisitive natures are fostered and encouraged, and they want to learn more as a result.

The dawn to dusk extended school

To accommodate this new approach, schools can no longer be simply 9 a.m. to 3 p.m. or 9 a.m. to 4 p.m. institutions. The truth is that too many schools remain idle for too many evenings each week and during the holidays. But these are

---

[9] Quoted on Institute of Education press release, February 2004.

community facilities and they should be made more available to their own pupils and local residents. Increasingly, breakfast is provided for those wishing to start early – some of whom might miss out at home. After-school homework and sports clubs have benefited from government and lottery funding. And newer schools are branding themselves for their open access. Bexley Business Academy, a new government-funded Academy in Erith, Kent opens from 7 a.m. to 10 p.m. every day for its 800 students and the local community. The Academy also devotes Friday afternoons to business and enterprise alongside using a purpose-built mini-stock exchange and trading floor where youngsters learn about the markets in the nearby City of London. In the future, the school intends to extend its campus to provide a primary school and a crèche on the site.

The Government has funded 240 primary and secondary schools to become 'extended schools' offering the full range of health and social care services within the school grounds. These schools also provide adult education classes and other community activities. Downham Market High School, a technology college with over 1,560 pupils aged 11 to 18 serving an area covering 100 square miles of West Norfolk, is one such example. Pupils can start the day with breakfast. 'We're a very rural school,' Deputy Head Chris Shaw explains. 'And the first school buses arrive at ten past eight, though classes start at five to nine. Pupils can get sandwiches and rolls and then use the library and computers. In the evening, many pupils stay on to use the library, to learn music or play sports until five or six o'clock. The school is open during the holidays too.' The school has been praised for its wider community activities for parents and local firms, a mission it has started because it recognises the huge value of its assets. 'We've worked out that our buildings and playing fields are a public resource worth £20 million. We should make that available to the local community as much as possible,' says Mr Shaw. This leads the school to operate a business centre, where parents and those running local small firms can use computers, photocopiers and the Internet. There is a sports centre and a swimming pool, which is open throughout the year, on site; these are jointly run with the borough. A mothers and toddlers' group meets regularly in the school and sixth formers from the school help out as part of their studies.

In a sense, this approach changes the whole nature of schools, which is why The Hermitage School, a 1,000-pupil technology college in Chester-le-Street, County Durham has chosen to call itself a 'learning community'. It first adopted that role in 1997, before the Government's more recent drive to encourage 'extended' and 'full service schools'. But, as The Hermitage's head teacher Ian Robertson explains, this is far more than a name change. It represents a philosophical shift in the approach to learning. The school has joined with two neighbouring primary schools, Bullion Lane and Newker. The Hermitage runs lessons from 8.45 a.m. to 3.00 p.m. for Key Stage 3 and GCSE students and until

4.00 p.m. in the sixth form. But also the school is very busy in the evening from 6.00 to 9.00 p.m. with adult learners. There is a popular breakfast club available to youngsters from 8 a.m., as part of the school's 'healthy schools initiative'.

'The reason we call ourselves a learning community is that we're for learners of all ages,' says Mr Robertson. 'Everybody connected with the school is a learner. Of course, we have students on roll aged 11 to 18. We have nearly 100 employees, and they are learning too. And we have an adult education programme with over 1,000 part-time learners coming through the school on a weekly basis, doing everything from traditional recreational keep fit and flower arranging courses to studying for high tech computer qualifications.' But that's not all. The partnership with local primary schools means that 100 8–13-year-olds come to a Saturday morning kid's club. 'They are involved in a variety of activities – there's a pottery club, computer club, dance club, arts club, and plenty of games and sports. They see themselves as part of The Hermitage Learning Community. And for those youngsters, the beauty of it is that they start to recognise that they will be engaged in learning for the rest of their lives. They will become Hermitage students when they finish primary school. But they also see and hear about their grandparents attending the night classes. This builds the whole concept that learning is for life.' Naturally, this early contact with the secondary school also goes a long way towards easing the problem of transition between primary and secondary schools. 'Most of the youngsters who come here know us well in advance, and are therefore quite comfortable coming into school.'

The Hermitage has developed a 'super learning centre' which opens on weekdays from 8.30 a.m. to 4.30 p.m. as a mix of social centre, library, homework and computer club. 'The idea came about in 2003 because we wanted a social centre in the first instance for our Year 10 and 11 students. They needed somewhere to sit, to talk, to watch a bit of telly and to socialise when they weren't in class. And therefore we decided to put that venue where the old school library was, which was looking a little bit dilapidated. We changed some of our classrooms and did some refurbishment, knocking three old classrooms into one large room, and we kitted it out in a high tech way. We put the library stock in there, along with computers with Internet access.' Anne Fine, the award-winning children's author and children's laureate from 2001 to 2003, opened the centre, and used her visit to provide certificates to student librarians. The centre is located right at the front of the school, easing community access too. Students enjoy a variety of activities after the bell goes at three o'clock. 'They can do their homework in the super learning centre, get involved in sports, drama and art clubs. The school is very strong in sports and creative and performing arts.'

The school is oversubscribed, with over 180 applicants for 165 places each year. Parents appreciate the extras offered by The Hermitage being a full service school. 'For some parents, it's crucial. It gives them that bit of community focus in their lives. For many folks, their lives are centred around what goes on at the Hermitage. For instance, on a Sunday morning, there's a church service at the school as well. On a Friday night in the main hall, there's an elderly residents' group that play bowls. Several nights a week, the coronary care group meet there for a fitness session. It all adds to the richness of community education, and the sense of community ethos.' The school also hosts a Parentaid advice centre, which gives mothers and fathers quick access to services like hospitals, libraries, social services and education. While the information is provided online, there is also a personal presence at the school. Business links are developed as a practical way of offering extended work experience and mock interviews. Local businesses also use the school for their IT training.

These activities are all important to the life of the school, but Mr Robertson cautions those who believe that they are a substitute for targets, good teaching and leadership in raising standards. 'Let's be perfectly honest about this. The reality is that full service and extended schooling makes a huge difference to the nature of schools, but much of the work we do is part of a long-term process. I think we'll see the benefits in perhaps five years' time. I don't believe it will have any immediate impact on our GCSE results. But I think long term we are sowing the seed of the value of education, the value of community learning. And if that seed is sown properly, and people embrace that, then we will see whole-school benefits, and we will see benefits in terms of academic results, because it changes cultures and it changes people's perceptions of learning.' The Hermitage had 62 per cent of its pupils gaining five or more good GCSEs in 2003, a figure above the national average, and significantly better than the 40 per cent who reached this standard in 2000. But Mr Robertson says the factors which have delivered those improvements reflect the basics of any good school: 'School leadership, in terms of having a clear focus on what we want to do for the students, the quality of teaching and learning, being at the forefront of what we do all the time, support-ing students by focusing on targets for their academic attainment, involving the parents as much as we can. The whole service school concept is not a substitute for these basics.' The cost of providing a full service school is between £30,000 and £50,000 a year, according to Mr Robertson, and while some of this was ini-tially covered by special government grants, the school plans to continue with this approach in 2005 and beyond, when the grant finishes.

A new approach to school buildings

Changes in the nature of schools have an effect on their design. With new technology, traditional blackboards are increasingly being replaced by interactive whiteboards. But if schools are to become living community centres, and their students are to enjoy a full range of extra-curricular activities, they must become fit for purpose – design matters. Long school corridors are almost an invitation to pupils to run down them, and they make discipline harder. Isolated staff rooms and limited social space for students can create a sense of 'them and us' which makes it harder to create a sense of a school community where pupils take more responsibility for their actions and their learning. Traditional classrooms aren't conducive to using ICT in its most efficient way. And many schools have had to spend thousands of pounds providing disability access because there had been little consideration of the needs of disabled students when the school was first built.

The Government has set itself an ambitious goal of allowing every secondary school pupil to learn in 'state of the art' school buildings within 15 years.[10] Its schools of the future programme has given particular encouragement to architects and others to think creatively as they use an unprecedented investment in new buildings and refurbishment. The most creative head teachers are often frustrated by trying to deliver a twenty-first-century curriculum in buildings which either physically date from the nineteenth century or which reflect design patterns that first emerged then.

Blyth Community College in Northumberland, has sought to embrace this vision, after it benefited from a £15 million new-build programme. The school, which reopened in 2000 after an amalgamation, hopes that the new building will help it to improve standards – just over a quarter of its pupils gained five good GCSEs in 2003. The school's website proclaims 'Public entry [to the school] is through a radiating plaza that is focused on a glazed circular Cyber Café below a feature tower.' In practice, the high school for 13–18-year-olds [the council still has middle schools] combines integrated computer facilities with a food court and cyber café, a 440 seat auditorium and community facilities. The school also has its own gym, tennis courts and football pitches. head teacher Peter Smith says the school's improved information technology and performing arts facilities has been important in encouraging a growing number of students to remain in education post–16 (up from 30% to 52%). He points out that pupils are not the only beneficiaries: 'There is a small staffroom, but every department has its own staff lounge too, dispersing teachers through the building. There are also three large indoor circulation areas for students. All this is having a significant effect on behaviour.' Blyth was built with government and county council funding, through a partnership that involved him in fortnightly meetings with the council,

---

[10] To read more about government plans, visit www.teachernet.gov.uk/schoolbuildings.

architects, landscape designers and builders.[11] In its 2003 report on Blyth, which found a satisfactory but improving school, which still faced challenges after much disruption, Ofsted said:

> The new school building provides very good quality accommodation. Most teaching spaces are large, well laid out, and grouped together in department areas. Enclosing all teaching rooms is a single, large, and interestingly designed building which eases the movement of pupils around the school and gives plenty of indoor social areas. The suites of rooms for history, music and art and design in particular are excellent facilities for teaching. The large library space is a shared community facility. It is spacious and welcoming, and gives access to many modern and more traditional learning routes.[12]

A new building was an important part of the recovery programme for Fir Vale School in Sheffield (see also Chapter 4). A Private Finance Initiative deal is paying for the new school, which is housing the most impressive success story in the Government's Fresh Start initiative to improve failing schools. In a £12 million programme, new classrooms have been designed to reduce delays between lessons – saving an hour a day. And the design supports discipline by giving teachers a full view of what pupils are up to. While the school's turnaround started before their move into a new building, the head teacher Hugh Howe says the new structures have improved staff and pupil morale. There is a bright and open reception area. There are big, wide social spaces rather than narrow corridors. According to Ofsted the new building has made an important contribution to a once-failing Fir Vale becoming a good school:

> The new building represents the fulfilment of a dream, having been planned with a high degree of involvement of key school staff, whose experience has led for example to wide corridors, a natural pattern of circulation, and the strategic location of the offices of senior staff. The building itself is already having an impact on behaviour, on learning and indirectly on the local community, who supported its first open day with keen interest. In relation to subject teaching, accommodation is very good and in some areas excellent, for example the learning support centre, ICT, music, drama and physical education. Access is possible for all.[13]

Frank Green, Principal of The Leigh City Technology College in Kent believes that schools may need to start thinking small again, even if they do so within a single campus: 'I think we need to go back to some of the ideas of the village school. If I were building a new school I would have centres of 150 pupils where

---

[11] Interviewed by Conor Ryan. 'New Schools of Thought' (*Public Finance*, 11 April 2003).

[12] *Blyth Community College Inspection Report* (London, Ofsted, 2003). Available at www.ofsted.gov.uk.

[13] *Fir Vale School Inspection Report* (London, Ofsted, 2001). Available at www.ofsted.gov.uk.

each young person had their own space from five to 16. This would reduce the problems associated with moving from primary to secondary school, and between classes all the time. There would be some large lecture theatres and video-conferencing rooms, but for two-thirds of the time, students would work within their own area, and teachers would come to them. With so much information and knowledge online, teachers would continue to provide inspiration, but pupils could take more responsibility for their own learning.'

These changes are happening in a growing number of schools. But the structure of many schools remains much as it has done for over a century. The challenge for schools is how to adopt the best features of others in ways which enhance rather than distract from the main business of teaching and learning.

Key points in this chapter

Five-term year: There is evidence that the current pattern of the school year is disruptive to curriculum planning and assessment. Schools which adopt a pattern of five terms of even length, interspersed with longer breaks during the year and shorter summer holidays find that this pattern helps standards and behaviour. It can also improve pupil concentration and retention, and be better for teachers, too. Research suggests that where it has been introduced, it enjoys the strong support of the whole school community. However, there are difficulties in switching, except for CTCs and Academies:

- term times are normally decided by education authorities, and it is difficult to move outside that pattern;
- parents may be concerned if they have other children in the system with different holidays; and
- staff may not welcome losing longer summer holidays.

There are variations to the pure five-term year, some of which allow for six-week summer holidays that may help solve these problems.

Length of school day: A longer school day can certainly help with curriculum planning, and has been seen by Ofsted as a positive factor in schools where it has been introduced. But a longer day can also be introduced less formally through providing a range of activities before and after formal lessons, including breakfast clubs, and after-school homework, computer, sports and arts clubs. In moving towards a longer day, it is important to find out what pupils want, and to consult with staff and parents. Staff will be needed to co-ordinate early or late activities, and there will be some additional funding implications. But the evidence is that such activities are socially and academically beneficial.

Length of lessons: The pattern of 50-minute lessons, with pupils constantly moving around the school can not only be a cause of indiscipline in schools; it also wastes a lot of valuable learning time. Some schools are now organising lessons in blocks: perhaps an afternoon devoted to business studies or a series of half-day learning blocks through the week to reduce boredom and promote a better understanding of subjects. It is worth considering how the pattern of lessons can be developed to achieve the maximum educational benefits.

Community involvement: Schools should be a living part of their communities and by fostering a spirit of lifelong learning by becoming an extended or full service school, there can be strong mutual benefits. Adult education and other community activities create a bond between local people and their school. Links with primaries reduce the problems of transition at age 11, and help improve the range of learning activities for junior pupils.

Think about the school design: It is not easy changing the design of an existing school building, but when the opportunity for a major refurbishment or a new build arises, it is important to think carefully about how the school should fit the changing pattern of secondary education, rather than trying to fit everything around the design of the school. Social spaces, computer terminals, staffrooms, community use, minimising long corridors, and visibility are all issues that should be considered. Consult key staff on what they think would work best.

Don't see these changes in isolation: Unless these measures are linked to a more straightforward programme for school improvement, such as those described in other chapters, they will not achieve dramatic improvements. But they can complement such programmes and add to their effectiveness.

10

Discipline and attendance

Considerable anger and frustration are felt by teachers in inner city comprehensives when they read criticism about their schools in the media. Teachers are blamed for not achieving good examination results, yet little attempt is made to understand the problems which face our inner city schools. Not the least of these are the maintenance of discipline and regular attendance. Schools seeking to recover from failure quickly realise that the most important challenge is often a restoration of order and pride in the school. That means having clear sanctions (and rewards) which are fairly applied to all, with a sliding scale of punishments. Programmes such as Assertive Discipline or Discipline for Learning, developed by Sir Dexter Hutt at Ninestiles School (and outlined in Chapter 4), are proving increasingly popular in achieving this. These rules must be clearly understood by every teacher, pupil and parent. Tackling truancy is equally important, as it sets a standard for what is expected. The law has introduced tougher penalties for parents seen to condone their child's absence. But improved attendance and better discipline often go hand in hand with a new sense of order and calm in a school, as much as with legal sanctions. They also depend on children being taught right from wrong in the home, so that the school's efforts are properly reinforced outside the classroom. In this chapter, we shall see some of the ways in which schools have addressed these problems.

There is often a correlation between social disadvantage and poor discipline, though there are a growing number of successful inner city schools which are starting to challenge the notion that the two are invariably interlinked. It is true that many inner city schools have a preponderance of pupils from extremely disadvantaged families, with many such schools having over 50 per cent of these pupils entitled to free school meals. While many single parents do an excellent and unenviable job bringing up children on their own, the absence of a father can exacerbate disciplinary problems, particularly for boys. In households where neither of the parents is in work, and the family depends on welfare, it is that much harder to overcome inter-generational disadvantage, since there is no culture of work or aspiration. These problems can be compounded where there is a high degree of mobility among pupils meaning that most of those sitting their GCSEs in Year 11 did not start in Year 7 at the same school. Schools can face additional challenges where a significant number of their pupils lack English as a first language, particularly in cases where they are recent migrants.

These are the everyday difficulties facing many inner city schools and many schools have devised practical ways to overcome them. After all, it is worth recognising, for example, that many Chinese and South Asian children now achieve higher GCSE results than white British youngsters, according to the Government's pupil census.[1] But while tackling issues such as high mobility and English as an additional language in isolation can be challenging, the job of head teachers is made considerably more difficult when they are accompanied by other factors. This is particularly so when there is a culture of bad or violent behaviour in the community, especially among boys. Such a climate can create bad peer groups, with social pressure not to study hard on those pupils wishing to learn. In some schools it is 'not cool to learn' – breaking through that barrier is tough indeed. Schools may also face serious drug and substance abuse problems, inside or outside the school gates. There may be racial conflicts between different ethnic groups. Many students may have serious literacy problems upon entry to the school. And when parents won't get involved in their child's work, or are actively hostile to the school's mission, it is even harder. Sometimes parents will not get involved because of fear of doing so, or linguistic difficulties, and schools are able to work to break down these barriers. It is essential to do so where truancy is a serious problem or where students are missing valuable lessons through term-time holidays.

Without order and discipline, learning cannot take place. But how can order be created in schools where there is no respect for learning? Some of the problems can seem intractable. Yet an increasing number of inner city schools are achieving excellent academic results, especially on a value-added basis. Such schools as the Phoenix High School in Hammersmith and Sir John Cass in Tower Hamlets have significantly improved their performance – from 6 per cent of pupils gaining at least five good GCSE grades to 25 per cent doing so in 2003, in the case of Phoenix and from 8 per cent to 79 per cent in the case of Sir John Cass.

---

[1] *National Curriculum Assessment and GCSE/GNVQ Attainment by Pupil Characteristics, in England, 2002 (final) and 2003 (provisional)* (London DfES Statistical First Release, 24 February 2004).

The Specialist Schools Trust annually publishes a list of high performing specialist schools in inner city areas which have a high proportion of pupils eligible for free school meals and whose intake of ability is low as measured by the average point score at Key Stage 2 of their Year 7 pupils. Use of a value-added measure ensures that schools are judged fairly on their outcomes taking into account the nature of their intakes. On average, pupils achieve 25.3 points at Key Stage 2, but many inner city schools have Key Stage 2 average point scores as low as 22. Where a school has such a low entry score, it could expect that only 15 per cent of its pupils would gain five or more good grades at GCSE. But a growing number of schools are defying this expectation. In 2003, there were a number of schools that had particularly high value-added scores, based on a comparison of their predicted GCSE results compared with their actual results. These are shown in Table 10.1. How, then, have these schools achieved such excellent results, bearing in mind the high degree of social disadvantage of their pupils? Before describing in some detail the techniques used by one particular school, let us first consider the broad principles of what is required to restore order and discipline to a school.

As we have seen, a good head teacher, backed by a strong leadership team, is essential. If a school has a weak or ineffectual head teacher, there is little hope of instilling an ethos of order and discipline which values high achievement. There are many good examples, a number of which are featured throughout this book. But in terms of speedily restoring discipline to once failing schools, William Atkinson at Phoenix High School, Sir Dexter Hutt at Ninestiles, Haydn Evans at Sir John Cass, Tony Broady at Walker Technology College and Peter Crook at The Academy in Peckham are all exemplars. Of course, leadership styles can differ markedly. Some eschew the role of the head teacher as the Homeric leader in favour of a more consensual style. But all outstanding head teachers have in common one key attribute – total commitment to succeed as well as the willingness to accept personal responsibility for solving problems. But how do good heads restore order to their school? Here are 14 ways in which the best head teachers have sought to turn their schools into calm and orderly centres of learning.

Ways to turn schools into orderly centres of learning

1. Have clear sanctions

It is essential to have clear sanctions that are fairly applied and which are understood by every pupil, teacher and parent. Of course, violent pupils should be excluded to protect the safety both of the other pupils and of the staff. But good head teachers of inner city schools only use permanent exclusion as a last resort, and rely instead on a sliding scale of sanctions, often based on successful

Table 10.1 How high added-value schools performed against their predicted results in 2003 (*Source:* compiled by the Specialist Schools Trust)

School name	Average Key Stage 2 point score (1998)	Pupils eligible for free school meals (%)	Pupils with 5+ A*–C grades at GCSE (2003)		Value-added score
			Predicted (%)	Actual (%)	
Sir John Cass Foundation and Redcoat Church of England Secondary School	23·4	58	30	79	49
Selly Park Technology College for Girls	24·1	55	41	82	41
Loxford School of Science and Technology	23·4	41	30	65	35
Ernest Bevin College	23·8	36	29	60	31
The Hathershaw Technology College	22·6	44	22	52	30
Small Heath School	23·5	55	31	60	29
Walker Technology College	23·3	37	29	58	29
Ninestiles School	25·0	27	46	75	29

programmes like Assertive Discipline or Discipline for Learning. These rely on a tariff of intermediate sanctions which may include:

- asking pupils to leave class to stand in the corridor;
- sending unruly pupils to an isolation unit in the school or a 'learning support unit' – usually another classroom where they are taught separately from their normal class;
- sending pupils to the head teacher;
- removal of privileges such as sports or play time;
- detention after school;
- requiring parents to attend meetings at the school to review their child's behaviour;
- requiring unruly pupils to do community service within school, such as picking up litter in the playground;
- temporary exclusion from the school.

2. Be visible

Good head teachers and their teams are highly visible. They recognise that writing memos will not solve the problem of poor discipline. The Phoenix High School senior management team are frequently to be seen patrolling the corridors. Since it is a large site they keep in touch using walkie-talkie radios. So, woe betide pupils who are found misbehaving in the corridors: they will be asked what they are doing, and given a suitable sanction on the spot. Similarly the playground and lunchtime areas are kept free of trouble by such high profile staff patrols. Some schools find that teaching assistants can play a similar role. Moreover, as the School Standards Minister David Miliband pointed out in a speech in March 2004, it is important that students are kept on site during break times to avoid disruption and afternoon truancy.

3. Bring back the school uniform

Many successful inner city schools have adopted the use of school uniforms. The trend away from uniforms has been reversed. After all, they provide an important sense of identity which is particularly valuable to an improving school. The wearing of an attractive school uniform fosters a sense of community and pride in the school, as well as discouraging competitive dressing and the challenge to the values of the school through outlandish clothing or hairstyles. Providing pupils have a say in what the school uniform will be, there is surprisingly little resistance to the idea by children themselves. So, it is worth giving them a say in the design. And while uniforms are usually blazers or school sweaters, they can be more imaginative. Jo Shuter, head teacher of Quintin Kynaston Technology College in Westminster, consulted her pupils on what kind of uniform they would like to wear and then asked Schott, a fashionable American brand, for advice on fabrics and style for hooded sweatshirts. A local company was then able to produce similar clothes at a more reasonable price. The hooded tops are worn with pride. This builds a sense of community and helps staff to identify pupils who are truanting in shopping malls. Lord Harris, the sponsor of Harris CTC asked his pupils to submit designs. He then arranged to have the winning design produced at low cost. When the failing Sylvan School became the Harris CTC in 1989, all the pupils were required to wear the new school uniform. There is a good social equity reason for uniforms too, in these days of designer teen-wear. The wearing of school uniforms and suitable footwear also prevents 'competitive dressing' which can lead to theft by jealous peers who cannot afford to purchase designer trainers or T shirts. However it is not sufficient just to require the wearing of a school uniform; appropriate shoes are equally important. And good schools extend their dress code to ban outlandish hairdos or the wearing of body jewellery such as tongue bars, nose-rings and earrings.

4. Don't tolerate truancy

Regular attendance at school is essential if pupils are to learn and keep up with lessons. But some underperforming schools have as few as two thirds of their children attending regularly. Sometimes pupils are switched off by the lessons; too often, there is a degree of parental collusion in their absence. The Government estimates that 50,000 pupils truant from school each day of the year, yet despite some individually successful initiatives, this figure has changed little since it was first highlighted by the Social Exclusion Unit in 1998. One problem may be that the data is imprecise. Schools report 'authorised' absence – such as a pupil being off sick or given permission to take a day off for an appointment – and 'unauthorised' absence which should reflect truancy. According to the latest data for 2001/2, published in 2003, the average pupil absence figure is nearly 16 days a year.[2] Despite some high profile truancy problems with ten- and 11-year-olds, the biggest problems are in secondary school, particularly among 13–16-year-olds. It would be far better if schools had to report their average attendance – which would be around 92 per cent in secondary schools.

Many schools now use computer assisted registration. Brooke Weston City Technology College pioneered the use of the smart card to take attendance

---

[2] Derived from a DfES Press Notice, 17 September 2003.

following the advice of its sponsors. This system is similar to that used by most large industrial organisations. Each pupil has a photo ID with a computer chip. Students pass their IDs through the attendance monitors upon entry to the school in the mornings and afternoons. The IDs are also used to monitor attendance in each class as well as providing access to computer labs and to register books taken out of the library. They serve as credit cards for school meals and unobtrusively identify children eligible for free school meals. The registrations are processed by a central server. By the mid-afternoon a complete printout is available to tutor groups which meet in the afternoons. This will show for example that while a child arrived at school in the morning on time, that he or she might have missed attending a particular class. Computer generated letters are promptly sent to parents informing them of their child's absence. This computerised enrolment procedure saves on average up to 20 minutes a day of a teacher's time reading aloud the attendance register. In addition, computer attendance systems allow much better monitoring of children with attendance problems. Not surprisingly, schools using these systems report very high levels of attendance with some averaging 97 per cent daily attendance.

5. Lunchtime curfews

More and more schools are keeping children on school premises at lunchtime to stop them roaming the streets. At Sir John Cass School in Tower Hamlets, closing the school gates so everyone remains inside during the school day has led to a dramatic increase in retention of pupils after lunch. Lunchtime activities are organised in addition to the serving of lunch. See the case study at the end of this chapter for details.

The President of Secondary Heads' Association, Anne Welsh, said the bill for supervision at her school in Newcastle upon Tyne was £40,000 a year, but she preferred to keep her children in at lunchtime. Letting them out often brought problems with the local community she said, because people felt intimidated by a big group of teenagers roaming the streets. 'If they are allowed out in the community at lunchtime, you can spend most of the afternoon dealing with the consequences of incidents,' she said. 'It's constant hassle. People are on the telephone saying pupils dropped litter or were rude to someone. Sometimes people, especially older people, feel intimidated just because they are teenagers who may not be doing anything wrong.'[3]

---

[3] Liz Lightfoot, 'Pupils to be stopped leaving at lunchtime' (*Sunday Telegraph*, 28 March 2004).

6. Be firm on drug and substance abuse

Drug and substance abuse including under-age drinking is a much more serious problem in schools than is generally believed. An estimated 40 per cent of teenagers have tried illegal drugs. Drug dealing is a real problem, especially in inner city schools. Government guidance encourages head teachers to exclude pupils dealing in drugs and the Prime Minister has urged state schools to follow the example of some private schools, and test their pupils randomly for drugs. Abbey School in Faversham, Kent, seemed set to be one of the first to take his advice.

But drug abuse has wider effects. The Audit Commission study *Misspent Youth*,[4] a report on young offenders, found that use of drugs was one of the key causes of juvenile delinquency. Other factors were exclusion from school; poverty; poor literacy skills making it difficult to obtain a job; and bad peer group influence. Schools can and should take action to combat drug dealing. Measures such as the installation of perimeter fences with controlled access and the installation of closed circuit cameras will drive the drug dealers away. But such actions need to be accompanied by joined-up approaches to prevent drug abuse. Initiatives such as INCLUDE[5] have been remarkably successful in combating drug use. INCLUDE advocates close co-operation between the police, social services and schools. Other successful initiatives include the introduction of more sophisticated education programmes on the dangers of drug taking, using computers to simulate the harmful effects of drug taking, alcohol abuse and smoking.

7. Carrots and sticks

Phoenix High School in the White City area of the London Borough of Hammersmith and Fulham is situated in an area of considerable social deprivation. When William Atkinson, the head teacher, arrived at the school in 1995 it was in special measures and was described by the *Daily Mail* as a school in despair. The pupils were out of control, violence was commonplace and the 5+ A*–C grades at GCSE stood at five per cent. Mr Atkinson was the fifth head teacher in two years and half the staff were supply teachers.

Later in this chapter we describe the measures he took to restore order. Of particular interest is the use of reporting techniques, incentives for good behaviour and sanctions such as holding back a year students who fail to make satisfactory progress due to truancy, poor behaviour and lack of effort. The aim is to prevent a small minority of students from undermining the learning of others.

---

[4] Audit Commission, 1996 available at www.audit-commission.gov.uk.
[5] Formerly Cities in Schools. See www.include.org.uk.

8. Consider a bobby in the playground

A quarter of London's secondary schools now have a full-time Safer Schools Partnership police officer. These officers help the schools maintain order including dealing with fights or brawls between gangs. PC Jon Sivati, who is attached to the Haggerston Technology College in Hackney, is one of nine such officers in Hackney, each attached to a secondary school. And, as he explained to the *London Evening Standard* in 2004, his work is quite different from that of the average PC because he's constantly dealing with children, parents and teachers in an attempt to keep crime at bay; part custodian of the law, part educator.

> We're not here to try to arrest kids. And we're not in the schools because the schools themselves are bad. We're trying to collaborate with schools, families and all the other agencies involved in education to help the kids we think might end up in a criminal lifestyle and work with them. The job is really crime prevention, with some policing. Yet, day to day, it is the most stressful kind of policing I've experienced. My remit is to provide a safe environment for kids going to and from school. We don't want them getting beaten up on the way, or robbed at the bus stop. I constantly patrol the area in a half-mile radius around the school. This school is right in the heart of an estate [the Fellows] where there's anti-social behaviour; drugs and unemployment problems. So I'm often on the estate talking to people, or patrolling the streets – 70 per cent of the time I'm patrolling the area outside the school, keeping an eye on things.[6]

PC Sivati said that bullying was tackled on the basis of restorative justice, a new initiative which police believe can reduce offending rates. 'If a girl says "I'm being bullied", I take it up with the teachers and contact the child's family. Once I've identified the kid responsible, I contact their family, bring them all into school and make it clear that it's an offence and has to stop. It's basically a slap-on-the-wrist – but it works.' Although police officers in schools may have worrying echoes of America's more violent inner city schools, their presence can be a reassuring and helpful one for all concerned. And for the police, it helps them to build valuable relationships with young people which may help to prevent future crime.

9. Say no to bullying

Nothing is more harmful to good order in a school that the prevalence of bullying. The problem is especially worrying because the victims (especially young children) are often reluctant to report physical abuse for fear of provoking further abuse by older or bigger children. Bullying is not just a problem in boys' schools or among

---

[6] Interviewed by the *London Evening Standard*, March 15 2004.

boys; it is increasingly prevalent among girls. Nor is it just physical: it is often combined with equally damaging verbal taunts and even the abuse of mobile phones through intimidating texts. Norham Community Technology College on Tyneside is one school that has successfully overcome these problems. It has initiated a remarkable scheme to combat bullying which has been copied widely. Called 'Be a buddy not a bully', the initiative encourages older children to mentor and protect younger children. Variations of this type of action can include giving sixth formers – or Year 11 pupils if the school has no sixth form – responsibility for playground supervision.

The problem of bullying has also spawned a joint anti-bullying campaign by the teaching unions and the DfES.[7] Based on the Ofsted report on good practice and the DfES pack *Don't Suffer in Silence*, the campaign advises schools to take the following action:

- hold discussions on bullying involving staff, children and young people, governors and parents;
- keep a record of the incidence of bullying, analyse it for patterns such as frequency, people places, groups;
- regularly canvass children and young people's views on the extent and nature of bullying. Have a secure anxiety box for safe complaining;
- ensure that all children and young people are aware of the range of sanctions which may be applied against those engaging in bullying;
- involve children and young people in anti-bullying campaigns in school;
- demonstrate the power of peer support. Create and publicise schemes of peer mentoring or counselling, buddying or mediation;
- provide confidential helplines for pupils. Have an anti-bullying notice board;
- encourage the school council to play an active role in anti-bullying measures;
- provide support to children and young people who have been bullied;
- learn from effective anti-bullying work elsewhere. Have you invited colleagues from a school with effective anti-bullying policies to talk to your staff?
- create 'special safe spaces' targeted at vulnerable children and young people. Train lunchtime staff or learning mentors to identify bullying and follow school policy and procedures on anti-bullying;
- inform parents whom to contact if they are worried about bullying;
- tell parents about the complaints procedure and how to use it effectively;
- work with parents and the local community to address issues beyond the school gates that give rise to bullying.

---

[7] See the DfES anti-bullying website at www.dfes.gov.uk/bullying.

10. Get the basics right

One reason why some underperforming schools have discipline problems is that a high proportion of their Year 7 pupils has poor literacy and numeracy skills. Despite improvements in primary schools, one in four pupils still fails to reach the expected standard in English and mathematics at age 11. This is why it is so important to test pupils' literacy and numeracy in their first few weeks at the school. Tests such as the London or Richmond reading test (see Chapter 2 for details) are available to assist in this task. If half the pupils arriving at secondary school, as is the case in some schools, have severe reading problems, it should not be surprising that these pupils may also have behavioural problems. Unable to follow what is going on in class, they become bored and turned off learning. Effective remedial reading techniques are an important tool in combating the problem. Programs such as SUCCESSMAKER[8] effectively use the computer to teach reading. It is also important to train teachers in teaching basic literacy.

11. Make the curriculum relevant

Schools with discipline problems need to pay particular attention to engaging the attention of their pupils with a relevant curriculum. Schools with a large proportion of pupils from minority ethnic communities generally recognise the importance of having teachers who have an understanding of multicultural values and traditions. However, it is only recently that the Teacher Training Agency has started to have some success in recruiting in some of our larger ethnic communities. It is particularly important that schools with a high proportion of Muslim children have an understanding of the cultural values of Muslim families. The DfES has also published useful guidance on working with children from ethnic minority backgrounds.[9]

However, even more important for schools whose pupils are unlikely to excel academically is to have strong vocational programmes to teach the skills necessary for future careers whether in electrical, plumbing, car maintenance and computing work, or in growing service sector jobs such as leisure and tourism. It is important that these programmes are highly practical in content and of a high standard, so that they are not simply seen as a 'dumping ground' for low achievers. There are now some 500 Cisco and Oracle academies in English schools. These highly effective programmes provide high quality training in networking and database expertise, enabling students who successfully complete their course to obtain

---

[8] See www.successmaker.com.

[9] *Aiming High* is available at http://www.standards.dfes.gov.uk/ethnicminorities/.

highly paid jobs. There are also around 100,000 pupils aged 14–16 who spend a day or more a week at college and in the workplace, learning practical skills. Even the most difficult pupils make the connection between acquiring practical skills and getting good jobs.

12. Use sport to improve behaviour

Sport can be a valuable aid to learning and behaviour. In primary schools, most major football clubs, as well as several rugby and cricket clubs, are helping junior pupils improve their literacy and numeracy through the Playing for Success initiative. But just as schools are seeing a renewed interest in school uniforms, competitive sport is also making a comeback. During the seventies and eighties, it had sometimes fallen victim to politically correct attitudes opposed to competition. There are also far stricter guidelines on the sale of school playing fields than ever before, which won't permit sales for development, and which normally expect any proceeds from sales to be used to help improve existing sports facilities. Head teachers and their governors understand the value of competitive team sports such as football, rugby, hockey and cricket in instilling respect for others as well as enhancing personal fitness and team spirit.

13. Bin it don't drop it

The physical appearance of a school provides an excellent indication of the quality of the institution. Litter in the playground and in the corridors combined with graffiti are indicative of a poor school. They suggest little respect among staff and pupils for their school; conversely their absence is a good indicator that pupils respect their school. Although appearance is no substitute for high standards and strong leadership, a tidy, well-kept school is often a sign that these are present. Many schools have invested in carpets in the entrance halls as these are both easy to keep clean and present an excellent first appearance. They give parents and pupils a sense that this is a serious centre of learning. Signs encouraging pupils to bin their litter and not drop it on the floor, the banning of chewing gum and eating in the corridors (and especially the classroom) ensure that high standards extend to all aspects of school life.

14. Win the support of parents

Many underperforming schools blame their lack of success on the parents of the pupils. But some schools don't try hard enough to win over parents. After all, parents are a school's customers and should be treated as such. It is not enough simply to conform to the rules about an annual parents' evening or the occasional letter home with students. If parents are to be part of the solution, they need to feel involved and be engaged. We have seen how Martyn Coles, the previous head teacher of St Paul's Way School in Tower Hamlets hired Bangladeshi-speaking staff to communicate with his parents, many of whom did not speak English. He also provided English classes for the benefit of his pupils' parents. Other schools such as Kingshurst CTC encourage parents to come to the school without an appointment either to join their child for a meal or to talk to a teacher. Many successful schools provide monthly personalised reports (or even bi-weekly) to parents to tell them how their child is progressing. More and more schools now have homework books in which the parent certifies their son or daughter has completed their assignment. This involves the parent in their child's studies. Effective parent–teacher associations (PTAs) and governing bodies should also be able to help schools discipline issues.

The Academy at Peckham
Bringing the house system to Peckham

It may be something more readily associated with the exalted halls of Eton College, but the new Academy at Peckham believes that the division of pupils into individual 'houses' can be as valuable for discipline among inner city youngsters as it is among the fee-paying schools of the country's finest public schools. So the system is one of the innovations that have been brought to The Academy at Peckham in Southwark, South East London since it opened its doors in September 2003.

The Academy replaced Warwick Park School, which had been in special measures. Its emergence was one of the more positive events to occur in the aftermath of the appalling murder of young Damilola Taylor. Sponsored by Lord Harris of Peckham, there is a combined specialist focus on business and the performing arts. Peter Crook, the Principal, took up post in September 2002, which enabled him to manage the transition from Warwick Park School for a year before heading up the new Academy. He had previously been head teacher of S Peter's Collegiate School, in Wolverhampton, which undertook a very successful partnership with the Regis, later King's School in the same area, heading both schools for two years and therefore has experience of headship in very demanding circumstances.

The challenges facing The Academy at Peckham can hardly be overstated. Two-thirds of pupils are entitled to free school meals. Forty-one languages are spoken. The average pupil enters the school with the reading age of a pupil aged eight. Nearly half of all pupils are on the special needs register and five per cent have statements, many relating to behavioural issues. The local environment is a

Metropolitan Police crime 'hotspot' and murders in the vicinity are not uncommon. The centre named after Damilola Taylor is just around the corner from the school.

Taking on the challenges in Peckham

When Peter Crook took over Warwick Park, he realised that there were three major issues facing the school. They related to staffing, curriculum and behaviour. The school was not attractive to potential members of staff. In 2002, there were 16 vacancies and no advertisements had been placed to fill them. There were even five long-term vacancies at head of department level. The curriculum was inappropriate. It did nothing to encourage pupils to engage in independent study, there was little concession to the needs of the large number of African and Caribbean pupils at the school and there were no vocational elements. And the behaviour of many students caused great concern, particularly the boys.

These issues had to be tackled at the same time as the existing buildings were being refurbished and new ones built. And while the 30-month building programme offered new hope to a blighted area, it also caused considerable temporary disruption. The school had to provide lessons in 16 temporary classrooms, some of which caused health and safety concerns. The school looked like a building site, but at least staff and pupils could see new facilities starting to materialise. When we spoke to Peter Crook early in 2004, he was under no illusions that The Academy was already a 'good school' but he and his newly formed senior team were putting key strategies in place, aiming to keep the focus clear and avoid 'initiative overload'. As a priority, all staff are determined to reduce the percentage of time fire fighting and to increase efforts in eliminating the causes of those fires.

Staff development

Staffing was an immediate issue. Legal requirements meant that the new Academy inherited 58 of the 62 full-time equivalent teaching staff from Warwick Park School. Transfer of Undertakings (Protection of Employment) Regulations (TUPE) applies in such cases and this can reduce a head teacher's room for maneouvre. Some staff were suspicious of the change to Academy status, wary of the sponsor's motives and worried about pay and conditions. But Mr Crook was able to recruit 16 new staff in 2002/03 and a further 17 in 2003/04. To recruit, Mr Crook had to use every sort of recruitment strategy available, including extensive searches overseas. Thirty-one staff are now from overseas. They have qualifications in their home countries, and, through an ambitious programme led by Vice Principal Viv Walker, many are moving to Qualified Teacher Status in England. To date only three have failed to stay the course. Staffing stability is crucial to taking the school forward. Pupils and staff need to know each other, with mutual respect developed over time, which was often not possible with frequent staff turnover. Staff need time to develop their expertise. Pupils need to know they will have the same teacher tomorrow and that he or she will have marked their homework. Staff retention and development are also vital. There is a thorough induction programme for new staff. There are daily briefing sessions in school and residential sessions off site. All staff are involved in the school's development planning and serve on the relevant working parties.

Curriculum and academic monitoring

Major changes are being undertaken to the curriculum with Peter Crook now assisted by newly appointed Vice Principal, Anita Johnson. Mr Crook advocated a four-period day with four lessons of 80 minutes each. This allows pupils to study subjects in greater depth, and time wasted moving between lessons is decreased. Each department is subject to regular review. There is a renewed focus on literacy and numeracy at Key Stage 3 and on applied and vocational courses at Key Stage 4. Nine new vocational courses are being introduced including areas such as cosmetology (beauty care), automotive engineering, construction industry technologies and TV and radio journalism.

For struggling London schools, it is often vital to have a sixth form in order to attract the children of aspirational parents, whose presence can help to lift standards across the school as well as helping to attract good teachers. A new sixth form was due to open in September 2004 and it had received 73 applications by March 2004, including 14 from students at other schools.

A new 'pupil track' system now records the progress of each individual pupil, and helps to identify areas for improvement. There is now also a new and better system for reporting to parents. Instead of the traditional parents' evenings, which were not sufficiently well attended, a whole day is being set aside for liaison with parents. On these 'Academic Monitoring Days', the school closes for normal lessons allowing plenty of time for individual interviews. They are attracting 80 per cent parental attendance compared with the 37 per cent who used to come to parents' evenings.

Improving behaviour through the house system

The house system is an effort not only to improve behaviour but also to improve self-discipline. Six houses have been created, each named after precious stones – Amber, Emerald, Jade, Ruby, Turquoise and Sapphire. In effect, each is a mini-school, with

200 pupils per house, including 40 in each year group, and 20 per form tutor. There are echoes here of the single campus, multi-school approach being successfully introduced in some US schools. Each house is headed by a dean and associate dean. Students stay within their house throughout their time at the Academy. Through this network, it is hoped that this stability and the personal relationships established (including those with parents) will give a greater sense of identity and belonging.

Other methods are also important in ensuring good behaviour. Two or three members of the Senior Leadership Team are always on duty in the school and there is an 'inclusion team' of six youth workers from local estates, headed by a manager. There is a police officer on site. Mentors and learning support assistants are another important part of the picture. A merit and sanctions system has been introduced to ensure that discipline sits alongside positive encouragement. There are still many issues surrounding behaviour, but there are positive signs. Exclusions are down, though they are still used. Attendance levels are a genuine 90 per cent. Pupils have been involved in designing a new uniform and a very impressive new logo, which would have cost many thousands of pounds had it been commissioned commercially.

Mr Crook was particularly encouraged when he compared the results of two behaviour management surveys, the first in January 2003 and the second in January 2004. Generally, negative scores, such as 'fear of bullying' had halved, while positive indicators, such as 'feeling safe' had doubled. This was a sure sign that the strategies of the new Academy staff and leadership team were working. There is still a long way to go at Peckham but the foundations for success have been laid. The early experience at Peckham bodes well for the future of the Academy initiative.

A leap in performance: the Sir John Cass Foundation School story

Sir John Cass Foundation and Redcoat Church of England Secondary School is just off the Commercial Road in Stepney, in the London Borough of Tower Hamlets, at the heart of London's East End. It is located in an area of high-rise blocks, social housing and some owner-occupied houses, with its population drawn from a mix of Bangladeshi, Caribbean, African, Turkish and Eastern European communities. Because Tower Hamlets has falling primary school rolls, Sir John Cass School admits pupils from other East London boroughs as well as Southwark and Lewisham. Its pupils, however, largely reflect the area – 50 per cent are Bangladeshi, 66 per cent have English as an additional language and 75 per cent are eligible for free school meals. Although it is a Church of England school half its pupils belong to the Muslim faith.

Table 10.2 GCSE progress at Sir John Cass Foundation School 1992–2003

Year	Pupils achieving 5+ A*–C grades (%)
1992	3
1995	8
1998	22 (first 'step change')
2000	32
2001	36
2002	71 (second 'step change')
2003	79

When Haydn Evans joined the school as head teacher in 1996, the number of pupils gaining five or more good GCSE grades in the previous year was eight per cent. In 1992 it had been as low as three per cent. By 2003, the number had climbed dramatically to 79 per cent (see Table 10.2). The school was ranked as the most improved in the country for the second year running and its value-added score according to the Jesson research for the Specialist Schools Trust was +49, the highest in the country. Today, 70 per cent of pupils stay on at school post-16 and 90 per cent of the sixth form go on to university.

Improving behaviour and attendance were key first steps to the improvements at the school, and Mr Evans talks about two 'step changes', the first in 1998 and a second in 2002, which was sustained and improved on in 2003.

Behaviour is a prerequisite to improvement

Mr Evans is adamant that behaviour is the essential prerequisite to improvement. When he joined the school first, fights and poor behaviour were commonplace and Year 11 pupils were allowed outside the school during lunchtime. If they returned at all they would often be very 'hyped-up' and out of control. He and his colleagues wanted the school to improve so they set about identifying what was wrong and how to put it right. His first decision was to close the school so everyone remained inside during the school day, something the current Education Secretary Charles Clarke identified in 2004 as an important issue for schools everywhere. This led to more pupils staying in school after lunch, where previously they might not have returned. Lunchtime activities were organised and a generally more purposeful atmosphere began to prevail. Mr Evans is very keen on what he calls 'purpose' and 'pace' during the day. For example, no more than five minutes is allowed for lesson changeovers, the time it takes to move from one end of the school to the other.

To this day, the presence of the school leadership team is very evident around the school. There is an 'on call' system with senior managers available as a call of last resort to sort out any problems. There is also a 'support unit' (isolation room) for pupils who are in danger of being excluded. Mr Evans rejects the idea of having police permanently on site, however, which he feels is not compatible with the ethos of a faith school. He does, however, acknowledge the presence of external malign influences and the school is protected by CCTV and strong external security including barred ground-floor windows. Sir John Cass does not use electronic registration or smart cards but the staff are highly visible checking pupils are where they should be. Attendance now stands at 95.3 per cent something of which the school is very proud.

Parents were involved in the behaviour improvement strategy and called upon to help improve the behaviour of disruptive pupils. School uniform rules are strictly enforced. There is a rewards/sanctions system, with rewards such as prizes being given a very high profile. For the past four years there have been no exclusions, fixed or permanent, although there is now one pending. Despite the external context of the school which includes gangs and drug dealing, when you walk around the site there is a sense of order and purpose and the tidiness of the premises and the appearance and demeanour of the pupils is quite exceptional.

Boys and girls: tackling gender disparities

Bad behaviour by boys can be intimidating to girls, particularly if, as in Sir John Cass they outnumber girls significantly. At Sir John Cass, two-thirds of pupils are boys. The second major decision taken by Haydn Evans was to separate the girls' and boys' playgrounds. This was deemed necessary because of the change to the lunchtime rules, with everyone now on site. Confidence among many girls was boosted as a result, particularly in those who were very quiet, the classic 'shrinking violets'. They are also taught separately for games, PE and swimming. This is particularly reassuring for many Muslim parents who would prefer their girls to be in single sex schools. It also had the effect of helping with the issue of girls' underachievement and raising girls' performance. It was a significant factor in the 'step change' of 1998.

How becoming a specialist school helped

Under the Excellence in Cities programme, which Haydn Evans describes as 'brilliant' because of its focus on inclusion, independent learning and the gifted and talented, Sir John Cass became the local Excellence in Cities partnership's nomination for specialist status as a language college. The status was acquired in

2000 and led to the second 'step change' in 2002. Sir John Cass has an unusual profile for a language college. Many language colleges are in middle-class areas, and some are selective. Sir John Cass did not have an existing particular strength in the teaching of modern foreign languages when it applied for language college status. What it did have, however, was a very rich second language resource. Two thirds of its students have English as an additional language and 15 different languages are used by significant numbers of pupils. So, its cultural and ethnic diversity was a major asset.

Today the school offers four languages during the school day – French, German, Spanish and Bengali – and a further five in twilight sessions – Russian, Urdu, Arabic, Turkish and Mandarin. Mr Evans agrees with the premise that specialist school status has a 'locomotive effect', in other words success in the specialist language area can become a major engine for improvement across the school. Specialist status facilitated a major investment in ICT throughout the school. It also helped the school with its development planning, with building capacity, with resources and with a more flexible approach to the curriculum. Mr Evans acknowledges the consultancy support he received from the Specialist Schools Trust in this regard. He supports the specialist school community role, having strong and active links with their secondary partner (Raines School) and feeder primaries. Finally he pays tribute to the school's sponsors – the Sutton Trust and HSBC as well as the Sir John Cass Foundation – for their initial and ongoing support for the school.

Changing the curriculum

Poor behaviour cannot be seen in isolation from the nature of the curriculum. A common reason for bad behaviour and truancy is boredom. Pupils feel that lessons are not relevant to them, or to their perceptions of their future career path. Particularly in the GCSE years this can be a difficult problem. So, an important part of addressing behaviour is to examine the curriculum and the options available. Another element in the John Cass second 'step change' was the introduction of GNVQ Science. The school believes that the learning style of GNVQs suits many of its students – the 'learning by doing' and the pride taken in completing assignments. Mr Evans is worried about the Government's plans to phase them out, replacing them entirely with 'vocational GCSEs'. In answer to critics who say that the way GNVQs are counted in the performance tables has led to the massive improvement in results, he points out that GNVQs have contributed 15 to 20 per cent of the improvement. Without them results in 2003 would have been 61 per cent – still a huge rise and a result that would place the school well above the national average, let alone that for East London schools. More importantly, the GNVQs offer an appropriate and clearly effective learning style for many pupils who were not catered for by the academic GCSE route.

Another curriculum area that is key to the school's success is the 'literacy project' in Years 7 and 8. This is specifically aimed at pupils at Key Stage 2 levels 3 and 4. As we have seen poor literacy can hold pupils back in class. This in turn can be a cause of disaffection. Finally, the school makes increasing use of data and target setting and they are planning a move to the Central Management Information System (CMIS) to facilitate this further. Parents receive reports on pupil progress three times a year.

Other features of Sir John Cass help support good behaviour

Other features at Sir John Cass will be familiar to other successful schools. They have been key not only to the school's remarkable exam improvement, but also to its orderly learning environment and to its relatively good attendance record. Mr Evans believes in a participative management style and in involving the whole staff in development planning. All staff have a teaching, learning and whole-school development objective. The school has a huge professional development budget and the head teacher puts all the money he receives from the Government's Leadership Incentive Grant[10] into that. The staff is stable, retention is high and the school has been fully staffed for the past three years. The success of Sir John Cass School is a tribute to team working and distributed leadership rather than to one charismatic individual.

The Sir John Cass School has worked hard to instil a culture of independent learning. The school has 450 PCs housed in network centres. These centres are used during the taught school day, but the school is also open from 7 a.m. to 6 p.m. each day and on Saturday morning. Queues to use the network centres are a common sight. Homework clubs have been set up for every academic subject.

And a particularly important feature at Sir John Cass had been the use of learning mentors, staff who are employed specifically to support pupils' learning and social needs. Their expansion has been a major feature of the Excellence in Cities programme. There were originally 17 learning mentors at Sir John Cass, mainly graduates without a teaching qualification, funded with 'learning credits' money. This funding has now stopped, something the head teacher greatly regrets, and there are now only 11 learning mentors (this reflects a common problem when targeted funding goes into a general pot: there are losers as well as winners). The mentors work 25 hours a week during term time. They particularly

---

[10] A DfES fund designed to improve the quality of leadership in secondary schools.

support pupils with English as an additional language and less able pupils. Their style varies – some will deal with 75 students in a week spending 15–20 minutes with each and effectively 'progress checking' as many parents would do. Others might spend two or three hours with one student. Haydn Evans sees the learning mentors as crucial to the 2002 'step change'.

Haydn Evans and his team have built a school where people feel secure and confident, where there is mutual respect and where there is enthusiastic teaching. Further improvement is a 'given'. Specific plans include a new sixth-form centre, the introduction of CMIS, the development of interactive whiteboard technology and more vocational courses post-16. Mr Evans is also very interested in the possibility of becoming a Cisco/Oracle academy and is looking at the idea of federating with an underperforming school. While he freely admits that networking is not his strength and says you cannot necessarily replicate what works in one school in another, he sees the case for sharing good practice and for action based research. This is a school with a very bright future and a great deal to offer others.

Raising behaviour standards at Phoenix High School

Phoenix High School, in the White City area of the London Borough of Hammersmith and Fulham, is surrounded by a complex pattern of social deprivation. Its 400+ boys and 300+ girls are made up of 50 nationalities and 47 languages are spoken in the school. Half the pupils are eligible for free school meals but that indication alone gives an incomplete picture of the challenges facing this school. There are very high levels of mobility – only 55 per cent of pupils in Year 11 started in Year 7 at the school and this figure recently stood even lower at 45 per cent. Around 16 per cent of students come from refugee families, though this is not necessarily a problem, as some of these are quite exceptional young people. There is a traveller population. Eighty per cent of students come from one parent families and a high proportion of students spend some or all of their school career in care; many pupils frankly have chaotic home lives. Forty per cent of students speak English as an additional language. Forty-three per cent of students are on the SEN Register. Prior attainment on joining the school is mostly very poor and the majority of students entering at Year 7 are two or more years behind their expected level in reading ability. Teacher recruitment and retention was until two years ago a major issue, which is hardly surprising!

When William Atkinson joined the then Hammersmith School in 1995 it was not only a failing school, but one which had attracted national headlines. GCSEs had dipped to five per cent of pupils gaining at least five good grades. There were serious staffing problems: four head teachers had tried the job over the previous two years; the staff included many on short-term contracts. The school was renamed Phoenix by Hammersmith and Fulham Council, and was a precursor to the Government's 'Fresh Start' scheme (see Chapter 4). Along with the new name came a new uniform and William Atkinson set to work with a set of high expectations, which was crucial. He was determined that the background of pupils in the school would not be used as an excuse for poor achievement and he was determined to restore order and discipline – to 'legislate for the majority'. The improvement in terms of the educational provision was central to the school improvement process.

Early steps included requiring staff to plan lessons and hand in lesson 'pro formas' each day. He introduced lesson observations. The National Union of Teachers said no to this and threatened to walk out. It emerged that there was nothing in writing or under regulations to give a head teacher the right to go into classrooms and observe lessons, but Mr Atkinson was determined that this was crucial to raising standards. The dispute was resolved through ACAS (Advisory, Conciliation and Arbitration Service) and lesson observations took place with prior notification and feedback for staff. Many short-term and supply staff left the school and there were some competency proceedings.

Mr Atkinson, a larger than life character (who was said to be the model for the character played by Lenny Henry in the BBC series *Hope and Glory*), full of energy, enthusiasm and drive, made an early impression on the students. He recognises that being of Afro-Caribbean origin is unusual in a head teacher and this helped make an impact on the pupils. He held an early parents' meeting and 100 parents attended. He set out a basic agenda of shared expectations on each side. He held another meeting six weeks later to discuss early progress and this time 200 attended. A PTA was established. Importantly, he introduced a student and parent handbook including a 'code of conduct' and a 'code of expectation' which still exists and which is essentially a contract signed between school and parents.

By 1997, Phoenix High School was removed by Ofsted from special measures, but it took longer to improve the school's results. Since then it has been through serious weaknesses and been declared as one of eight schools in the country to face exceptionally challenging circumstances. However, when you walk into the school today the atmosphere is ordered and calm. The building is well kept and tidy. Litter is removed three times a day. The walls are used proudly to display evidence of pupil achievement including those gaining exceptional results at GCSE. The 2003 Ofsted report described the school as 'improving' and paid tribute to 'excellent leadership of both the head and governors', 'positive relationships', 'good behaviour' and racial harmony.[11] The percentage of pupils gaining five or

---

[11] *Phoenix High School Inspection Report* (London, Ofsted, 2003). Available at www.ofsted.gov.uk.

more good grades at GCSE stood at 25 per cent in 2003 and was expected to rise further. The introduction of GNVQs in autumn 2004 should lead to further improvement and the school has now achieved specialist status in science. This progress was recognised in the spring of 2004 by the award of specialist school status.

However, Mr Atkinson is the first to concede that the school still faces many complex issues and challenges. Attendance continues to be an issue and he still has to exclude pupils. He still has a very high percentage of challenging pupils and he has to keep accepting these while he has spare places. He believes very strongly that challenging pupils should be spread more equitably around the system with 'good' schools taking their share. The quality of some of the teaching is a continuing concern. Having said that, many of the strategies adopted at Phoenix have been very successful and could be helpful to other schools.

One of Mr Atkinson's early aims was to 'make disruptive pupils deviants not heroes'. He says that with any school you have to diagnose carefully what the problems are before you can tackle them – there has to be a 'bespoke' solution much as a doctor would diagnose an illness, work out the treatment and prescribe the medicine. The following strategies have been employed:

- staff, with their walkie-talkies are highly visible within the school premises and outside;
- a proper reporting system with incident sheets;
- a merit rewards system for good behaviour and results;
- peer counselling;
- a 'buddy' system where older pupils help younger ones;
- a school council has been established;
- pupils who perform badly may be required to repeat a year;
- a strong emphasis on teaching and learning;
- effective work with parents/carers;
- a differentiated curriculum is offered at Key Stage 4;
- assessment for learning.

Conclusions

Tackling indiscipline and poor behaviour are the essential steps in restoring order to any school. They are not enough in themselves to raise academic standards, but without them, such improvement is virtually impossible. Respect is key to such strategies: restoring respect in the school through uniforms and tidiness; creating a respectful environment with clear rules, good attendance, an absence of illegal drugs and a strong staff presence; and a fairly administered system of sanctions and awards, which may involve a police presence; respect too for parents, as a school's customers, by involving them fully in the life of their child's school and their child's education. But high standards and good discipline go hand in hand. The curriculum needs to address the needs of individual students, and there should be appropriate remedial help with literacy and numeracy. Innovative methods may help, such as computerised registration. But there is value too in the traditional approach to a well ordered school, as The Academy at Peckham is starting to find, with its combination of a house system with evidence that small schools, even on a single campus, can work best.

11

Inspection and audit

Before the Office for Standards in Education (Ofsted) was created in 1992, many schools never saw any national inspectors. True, there were LEA inspection and advisory services, and some were good (though others interfered needlessly in good schools). But there was no regular pattern of inspection nationally, nor was there a set of consistent standards against which each school could be judged. Ofsted was introduced after a significant change in attitudes to school improvement during the 1980s. Projects such as the Organisation for Economic Co-operation and Development's International School Improvement Project recognised that there needed to be a systematic approach to change within schools themselves. A school's lessons, procedures and use of resources became the key focus for such reforms. Educational goals were seen as important and they began to reflect the school's own priorities. Schools did not act alone and there had to be an integrated approach between top-down policy and bottom-up improvement. And change was only successful when it had become part of the natural behaviour of teachers in the school.[1] Against that background, Ofsted was introduced and its remit was continued and extended by Conservative and Labour Governments. It existed in a culture where exam results started to be published and targets became a key agent of improvement, first under the Conservatives mainly within specialist schools, and later an integral part of the Labour Government's approach to education reform.

Ofsted's early years were not without controversy, partly because of the outspoken nature of Chris Woodhead, who was Chief Inspector from 1994 to 2000. Nevertheless, by instituting a regular cycle of inspections, initially every four years, and more recently every six years, there was a valuable series of

---

[1] J. Gray, D. Hopkins, D. Reynolds, B. Wilcox, S. Farrell and D. Jesson *Improving Schools: Performance and potential* (Maidenhead, Berkshire, Open University Press, 1999), pp. 22–3.

reports produced which undoubtedly helped to improve teaching standards and gave parents an unrivalled independent guide to every school in the country. By categorising some schools as requiring special measures and others as having serious weaknesses, the process helped to identify and rescue hundreds of failing schools.

Not everything about the system was as it should have been. Many new inspectors were needed to operate the new system, and their quality was variable. There was initially no right of independent appeal if schools had genuine cause for grievance. Weak schools, once their failings were identified, often lacked the support (or the incentive) to improve. Schools were given months to prepare for a visit, creating a growing source of tension in the staffroom. The judgements of inspectors seemed sometimes to conflict with the evidence of GCSE or test results. These problems were gradually overcome: indeed, more than 800 schools were successfully improved after being placed in special measures from 1997–2004. And teaching standards rose. Ofsted itself grew in size and power: it now inspects childcare provision, further education colleges (at least courses for those aged 19 and under) and LEAs as well as schools. More recently, it has been given the responsibility to lead the inspection of children's services in local authority areas and beyond.

'Outstanding schools have always been there, long before Ofsted was ever created,' says the current Chief Inspector David Bell, who has put his personal stamp on his office. 'One of the virtues of inspection was that it set a standard of what we expected all schools to be like, as a minimum. Over time, it has increasingly set the aspirations higher than that. It has said: this is what you could be like, what you should be like. Inspection has been part of a whole series of measures that have pushed the whole education system forward. It has been a sort of cocktail effect: you can't disentangle the impact of inspection from that of a whole range of other measures. One of the key virtues of inspection, however, is that it has enabled us not just to accept variability between schools as inevitable. That variation still exists, of course. But, I think inspection sets the standard, and says it is not acceptable, at the very least, to fall below the minimum standards. And, actually, you need to be much better than that to be an outstanding school.'

Ofsted's new approach: the short, sharp shock

After ten years of inspecting schools through inspections which have involved substantial lesson observation, David Bell considers that the system needs to change. This time the change will involve more than the frequency of visits. Schools will have what have been dubbed short, sharp inspections: instead of 60 or 70 page commentaries, setting out the strengths and weaknesses of each department, there will be much shorter documents. Self-evaluation will be expected to play a greater role. And the inspectors may no longer spend a week in each school, preferring instead to focus on what David Bell has dubbed 'the central nervous system' during a two day visit. In practical terms, this means that the number of what Ofsted calls 'inspector days' – the number of inspectors multiplied by the time they spent in the school – will be halved overall, and more substantially reduced for some. A large secondary school might only have ten inspector days instead of the current 80. The reports would be more readable for parents and would be accompanied by the new 'performance profile', setting out school exam results and other key indicators of a school's success. The reports will also be more up to date, with intervals of three rather than six years between typical inspections, so more pervasive problems may be identified and rectified more quickly than before.

Mr Bell sees change as an almost inevitable evolution in the system. 'The new arrangements demonstrate a kind of maturing of the education system, as much as the inspection system,' he said, in an interview for this book.[2] 'After nearly 12 years of school inspection, we have to think again about how we can make it work more effectively. I was a bit concerned that we were beginning to enter into the territory of the law of diminishing returns: that you just keep inspecting in exactly the same way as you have always inspected, and then you wonder why you don't get the same kind of impact from inspection. We also have to take account of the cross-governmental concern about over-regulation and over-inspection. So, if you move to the kind of system that I've been describing, there will be some things that you've lost, but I think we can do inspection more efficiently while continuing to hold onto those things that have made the inspection system in this country so powerful.

'The argument for inspection in the form that it was done in the early nineties was irrefutable: we had to establish a system where you had regular independent information about all schools. Over Ofsted's first ten years, inspection has continued to provide that information. We want to hold on to the best of that: independence, regular reports to parents as consumers of education, focusing on those things that really make a difference. But, I think the time is right to move away from the larger superstructure that we have and focus on the central nervous system of the school – the three or four things that are most important in determining whether a school is good. That means deploying our inspection resource in a more limited way to give a relentless focus on things that make the most difference.'

At a practical level, this presents both challenges and opportunities for secondary schools. Fewer inspectors will descend on the school. Instead of facing an army of

[2] Interview conducted by Conor Ryan on 7 May 2004.

up to 15 inspectors in a large secondary school, spending four days looking under every nook and cranny, Ofsted is assuming, under the new system, that the same school would only face four inspectors for a couple of days. The inspectors will come every three years, instead of every six. The hope is that this leads to a more focused inspection system. Since inspections will happen with little or no notice, teachers should not be subjected to the unnecessary panic that has often preceded Ofsted inspections in the past. Inspectors have tried to discourage excess preparation, but often to no avail. Anxiety may be sharpened with a short, sharp shock inspection, but it will be spread over a few days rather than months. 'I hope that, in one sense, they stop preparing for an inspection under this new system, because I think there's no doubt that having a period of notice, even if it is only six weeks, generates a whole industry of preparation,' admits Mr Bell. 'If we are serious about trying to see schools as they are, we should be saying to schools there's not anything that should be done specifically for the purpose of inspection. What schools do need to have is a robust, up to date self-evaluation statement that captures their strengths and weaknesses. Beyond that, you really shouldn't be doing lots of extra things over and above what you should be doing anyway. I think it is a fundamental mind-shift from seeing inspection as a disruptive event within a school to something that goes much more with the natural flow of day to day activity in the school.' But the biggest challenge will then be for schools to have to take regular stock of their own strengths and weaknesses between inspections. Inspectors will be looking for evidence of robust procedures. And, if they are working well, self-review and self-evaluation should identify problems before any inspection. They should also mean that a school is always ready for an inspection, and the three days' warning, or whatever it may be, under the new system should not produce a collective panic.

However, this approach has costs as well as benefits. Inspectors will not be seeing every teacher teach, nor will they provide detailed information on how well a school tackles each subject, based on a series of lesson observations. This also places a greater onus on school leaders and governors to act when they find problems, and not wait for Ofsted to validate their concerns. Mr Bell doesn't think that the shorter inspections will prevent inspectors from identifying problems in particular subjects, but nor does he believe that an exclusive focus on lesson observation should be the priority for an inspection. 'The inspectors will still be able to decide where they go in the school,' he says. 'One of the defining characteristics of school inspection in this country has been a very strong emphasis on classroom observation. That's important, but we've just got to be careful we don't over-emphasise that. So if you want to find out more substantially about the progress that pupils are making and the quality of work they are doing, you'll not get that in a 40 or 50 minute observation of one single lesson. You'll have to look at students' work. You have to look at the examination or test results. You have to look at the value-added measures. Crucially, you have to talk to the students, and find out what they're thinking. We are saying that lesson observation will still be important, but what's more important is capturing a sense of how well the students are doing over a longer period of time than a single lesson.'

Hearing the parents

Schools will need to look at their performance in different subjects when they develop their data systems and their self-evaluation programmes. And they should also recognise the need to hear the views of parents. Indeed, one of the main purposes of inspection should be to give parents more information. 'It is right that we do consider the views of schools and what they think, it is right that we are interested in data, but it's just worth remembering that the creation of Ofsted was all about information to parents,' Mr Bell says, with some passion. 'I sometimes worry about the "producer capture" element of this. When people say: do you not think that inspection should wither on the vine with greater emphasis on self-evaluation, [I say] these things are right and they are a natural evolution, but independent inspection exists to provide independent information to parents. If we lose that, we will have lost something terribly, terribly important.' But there are fears that the new inspection system might offer them less of a chance to influence the inspectors' verdict because there is so little notice for parents' meetings with the inspection team. Mr Bell is aware of that problem, and believes that their voice can still be heard. 'There's probably not one single answer. Even with pretty short notice, it is still possible for the school to say to parents that the inspectors are coming next week and to give them an opportunity to meet the inspectors when they come. But we have found, increasingly, that parents are not turning up for the meetings.' So, the new system will probably place more store on parents' responses to questionnaires. 'The questionnaire is still quite a powerful vehicle, and there is an argument that the shorter the notice you give people to fill in a questionnaire the better, because it concentrates their minds on doing it.'

But the Chief Inspector sees parents having more opportunities to deal with the inspectors than they have at present, because of an important management change at Ofsted. Under the new system, each of Her Majesty's Inspectors – those employed directly by Ofsted, rather than by private, registered inspection companies – is likely to be responsible for a designated geographical area. So, rather than have parents just making comments at the time of inspection, the Chief Inspector hopes to provide opportunities for parents to comment at any time. A link on the Ofsted website is likely. This does not mean that Ofsted wants to start getting involved in complaints which should properly be directed to the school or governors, or even an ombudsman, but it does mean that Ofsted sees that its primary role is and has always been about informing parents. And that is a two-way process. Schools should ensure that they have equally good and responsive mechanisms for dealing with parents' complaints, so that they don't feel it necessary to avail themselves of the new mechanisms.

This raises a thorny perennial question – can and should parents trigger inspections? In fact, as the Chief Inspector revealed, it does occasionally happen. There has been at least one occasion where a number of parents wrote to the Chief Inspector, and he was sufficiently concerned about what they told him, that he ordered an inspection outside the normal cycle. 'It's a controversial issue. I remember the school being very aggrieved at me doing that – obviously I have the legal power to do it – saying that I had allowed myself to be driven by a group of parents. It wasn't exclusively because of what the parents had said. One of my reactions to the school was that it would have been a dereliction of my duty just to ignore what the parents had said. I think one of the virtues of the new system is that you will be able to build up a kind of local intelligence picture of what's going on in a school. The other benefit of more frequent inspections is that you can respond more quickly to an undercurrent of concerns that might have built up over a couple of years. That could then allow us to say we'll think quite carefully about who the inspectors are going to be in that particular school. Potentially, that means that inspections could be more responsive than they are at present.'

The rise of self-evaluation

Mr Bell strongly believes that the combination of fewer lesson observations and a new emphasis on self-evaluation should free schools from a dependency culture, where schools felt they needed the validation of the independent inspectors before tackling tough staffing issues, such as a weakness in a particular subject department. Mr Bell believes schools will welcome this change. 'I hope they'll notice the greater emphasis on school self-evaluation . . . that we're focusing not on every subject of the curriculum, as we've traditionally done, but on the key characteristics of leadership and management, on learning and teaching, the ethos of the school,' he says. 'We're saying that, if we can use our limited time to focus on those key elements, we are in a better position to make a judgement about the school, and then leave it to the school to do all the detail. One argument that could be advanced against the current inspection system is that it does generate a sense of dependency in some schools: "We need the inspectors to tell us about the state of geography or history or science," they feel. But our evidence suggests that what you really need to know about is the quality of leadership and management in the school. If you are broadly satisfied with that, then I don't think you need to know about every single subject or aspect of the school's life.' And that puts extra pressures on the head teacher, the leadership team and the governors to be prepared to tackle issues well before the inspectors visit. It also puts paid to the lie that somehow this new approach means that inspectors are 'going soft'.

It also means that inspection reports will be far less informative about progress in individual subjects. Sometimes teachers have complained that detailed judgements have been made on the basis of a few lesson observations – and little account is taken of lessons that may be unrepresentative. One result of this change is that head teachers may no longer be able to rely on Ofsted to provide the judgements they need to precipitate a change of leadership in a subject department. Of course, these decisions should not require Ofsted's backing, but the reality in many schools is that they have done in the past. 'With external validation, or without it, the responsibility for dealing with that problem does rest with the school's leadership and management,' Mr Bell insists. 'I think that saying "we need Ofsted to tell us" is a bit of an excuse, whereas if you have got weaknesses in your school, you should be getting on with it anyway. We've been quite open in saying there are some trade-offs in this new inspection process. There are things we won't have under the new system: we won't have a subject by subject account for every school, and we will not in every secondary school see every teacher teach.'

So, can self-evaluation start to fill the gaps? The leading proponent of self-evaluation is Professor John MacBeath from the University of Cambridge. He broadly supports the new regime at Ofsted and was one of the strongest critics of the former Chief Inspector, Chris Woodhead, but believes it is important that self-evaluation doesn't simply become self-inspection if it is to be effective. 'Self-evaluation . . . comes to life in the micro-context of pupils and teacher, exploring how learning works and probing the conditions that promote or inhibit it.'[3] One way in which MacBeath believes schools can see how well they are doing is by asking students to assess their work. For he argues that self-evaluation needs to focus on how pupils learn as well as on how teachers teach, and when this happens, the system is embraced more enthusiastically by teachers. Self-evaluation then becomes 'embedded' into teachers' daily practice and into the decision-making processes of school leaders. So much so that when the inspectors call, their visit is a chance to tell their story rather than a threat of being caught out. But Mr Bell recognises that the quality of self-evaluation varies enormously, and insists that while the process can help reduce the time needed for external inspection, it can never replace it. Schools need independent audit, otherwise they

---

[3] John MacBeath, 'Inside job' (*Guardian*, 20 April 2004).

become complacent. 'We have seen over the last ten years improvements in the quality of school self-evaluation, if you look at the inspection judgements,' Mr Bell says. 'But it still remains one of the weaker aspects of school management and leadership. Not surprisingly, schools are better at diagnosing their strengths than they are at diagnosing their weaknesses. One thing schools can do to improve is to ensure that self-evaluation doesn't become a massive paper-chasing exercise or a kind of systems audit. What matters in self-evaluation is the focus on the learning, the progress and the achievement of the pupils, and rigorously asking in a secondary school "How are our pupils doing?"; "What's happening in English as opposed to science?"; "What's happening to the girls as opposed to the boys?"; "What's happening to the youngsters of Bangladeshi heritage as opposed to those of Pakistani heritage?"; or whatever. It is about relentlessly focusing on the achievement of pupils, and seeing where their strengths and weaknesses are. Because then you are able to ask questions such as, "Why is it that pupils make half a grade less progress in English than science between Key Stage 2 and Key Stage 3?", for example.'

Mr Bell points out the importance of having good outside support and advice during the process. Those in a school are sometimes unable to see how outsiders might view them, which is why it is important to have a critical friend as part of the process. 'That's not an argument for armies of consultants, bureaucrats or LEA officers. Some of the most successful schools are successful because they open themselves to a whole range of other influences; one of the most crucial is somebody who is highly respected who can come in and say "Do you know how you're doing?".' Part of this process involves a greater sharing of information between schools, something that already happens in many specialist schools. And it also means being open to what the data reveals. 'Unless you know how those pupils are doing at that individual or group level, you're really not in a position to know whether you are doing as well as you might, or whether you could do better. It's a process that really has to be driven by the focus on the pupil and pupil progress. It has to be one that's not imposed from the outside, but it is one that can undoubtedly be helped by expert challenge provided from outside.'

Good governing bodies will take an interest in this process too, and will question adverse variations from the data for similar schools. But Mr Bell thinks that too many governors don't get involved with such procedures. 'At the moment we have a rather vague system where, in some schools, the governors are closely involved in the self-evaluation, and in others they're not,' he says. 'I think the self-evaluation that comes from the school should formally come from the school's governors. This would recognise the importance of the governors understanding the strengths and weaknesses of the school. On inspections at the moment, our meeting with the governors tends to be much more for a briefing purpose. During the actual inspection itself, it depends; in some schools, a lot of attention would be paid to meeting the governors; in other schools, they might say that all the evidence suggests the governors are on top of the game here, they know what's happening, we're not going to waste too much time doing it. In advance of the inspection, part of the diagnosis for the inspectors is to decide what are the issues that relate to governance.'

One effect of the greater emphasis on self-evaluation may be to reawaken a debate about the whole role of governing bodies and the type of people who serve on them. The Chief Inspector says that there are two different models: the existing one which is strong on parental and community representation, and a leaner model which more closely resembled a business board of directors. 'We have placed great store by having a large governing body in every school to represent a whole community of interests. There are lots of virtues in that, but is it the most efficient system for governance of schools? Should one look much more at a kind of non-executive model where you had far fewer but higher calibre people, and you had a much stronger business-in-the-broadest-sense orientation. On the other hand, would you lose the community dimension where there are lots of parents involved? That's a tricky one. However you have your schools governed, you have to ensure that inspectors can capture the opinions and views and effectiveness of the governing body.'

The role of data in inspections

One of the main reasons why the system of inspection and audit can change has been the growth in data, and its effective use by schools to support their improvements. Ofsted itself collects a lot of data, some of which is distributed through its Performance and Assessment Reports, known as PANDAs. In particular, this enables schools to benchmark their performance against that of similar schools. The Chief Inspector believes that the effective use of data is one of the most important reasons for success. Mr Bell welcomes what he calls 'an absolute sea-change in attitudes about data' over the last ten years, and he views PANDAS as an important step along the way. However, it is always a moot point how much data is given to schools: after all, you do not want to over do it. 'One of the dilemmas always – and it's a dilemma at school level too – is how much information you give,' he says. 'Data helps you to really focus on the priorities. So, I think schools have got more intelligent in their use of data. But there is more to be learned about the characteristics of those schools that use data intelligently to drive up standards. One of our observations would be the difference often is when schools move from the headline data – the proportion of pupils with five good GCSEs – to tracking the progress of individual pupils. That's often tied up with different approaches to the data that's shared with the pupils, so that they can track their progress and set their own targets. That's often related to the contact with the parents – rather than saying "Johnny is doing OK", you can say, "here's the data, let's see why he's doing this in history, but he's not doing so well in science". It's that whole data richness that really drives the performance up. If you look at some of the most outstanding head teachers in the country, that will come across as a common theme.'

Some schools now see data as an integral part of how they do things. Others are just beginning to recognise its importance. In those cases there may be a case for making a deputy or assistant head the school's 'data champion'. 'There is no doubt that if you are trying to galvanise effort in the first place, having a data champion for the school can be important,' Mr Bell says. However, this should only be a temporary measure. 'The downside of that is if it becomes the "deputy head's thing" or the "head's thing". You want to move from something being driven from the top to a situation where every teacher is comfortable about looking at data and how it's used. That's where it becomes a whole-school issue. The most successful schools will have data in the bloodstream of the school.' This means that, just as with ICT, every teacher needs to be comfortable with data and seeing what it tells them about the success and potential of individual pupils for whom they have responsibility.

The new inspection reports for parents will be accompanied by a school performance profile, which will tell them about the ethos of the school and its performance. But the reports themselves, though briefer, will also give parents a chance to compare how a school assesses its own performance alongside the judgement of the inspectors. Within all this, there will certainly be value-added assessments, though as we have seen, they seem set to be based on the less than helpful data provided by government statisticians, where most schools are bunched around figures that they say do not look statistically different. All this makes it of continuing importance that what is given to parents is understandable, something Mr Bell sees as crucial, too. 'I suppose my general view is that you want to provide a rounded set of information to parents about the performance of the school, and, frankly, raw examination results are a crucial part of that body of information. I think it is interesting to know, as well, the progress pupils have made. But, crucially, too, I think the inspection report provides you with that more textured picture. [It tells you] what the ethos of the school is like, what its leadership and management is like. I don't think we're quite there yet in terms of understanding the relationship between new-style inspection reports and performance profiles. But I do think that one of the virtues of going in this way is to try to package it together, so that you say to the parents: "At any moment, you can have a look at this rounded information." '

This is not without its dangers, not least that you give parents far more information than they could reasonably be expected to absorb, or more than they need. 'I always think that it's just worth reminding ourselves that what the profession needs for information purposes is not always the same as what the parent wants,' is how Mr Bell puts it. 'That's because the information you want for management purposes is often different from the information you require for consumers, who are using the service. I think we have to be very careful that we don't look at this just through the eyes of the producers. One of the things that we are proposing to do in the inspection reports in the future is to make them much shorter, which I think will be helpful. But we will be saying in the inspection reports in the future: "This is what the school thinks about the quality of its teaching, and this is what the inspectors think." '

Identifying and tackling failure

The most controversial – and, arguably, the most successful – aspect of the Ofsted inspection system has been its placing of schools which failed to meet key standards into special measures. Far from there being a lessening in the likelihood of schools being placed in special measures, the greater emphasis in leadership and management under David Bell has led to a greater proportion of schools being failed, although the overall number of schools in special measures has fallen significantly. As we have seen in Chapter 4, for most schools this has had a positive effect: with external support, and termly inspection visits, they do recover. Despite this, the critics of inspection complain about the use of special measures. The Secondary Heads Association believes that self-evaluation can replace inspections, and also complains that schools will continue to be failed or placed in 'special measures' under the new system. The Chief Inspector has little time for such complaints. 'I am certainly clear that special measures must remain. If we leave it to self-evaluation, how can parents be sure that a school in difficulty will lift itself up. After all, if it's that good, how did it get into a mess in the first place?', Mr Bell says. 'And we must also avoid any perception that somehow the accountability system has been subject to some sort of "producer capture".'

Nevertheless, there is genuine concern about inspectors declaring a school failing after a two-day visit. But, Mr Bell is clear that he believes this to be one of the trade-offs for a less onerous system, and he also rejects the idea that if something is seriously wrong in a school, it won't be obvious after a process which not only involves an inspection visit, but also an analysis of data such as exam results, and how they compare to schools with a similar intake. 'We've debated this one long and hard. On the general concern as to whether you have enough evidence to make the judgement [with a shorter inspection] that a school should be in special measures or on notice to improve, we are saying that is possible because HMI, when they visit at the moment, make judgements on the basis of a couple of days' visit. We have resisted the idea of saying: "Well, we've had the short inspection, but we're not entirely sure, so we'll get another team in." We rejected that approach, because I think you shouldn't give anyone any excuse to "bottle" their judgements. So, we are saying that, under these new arrangements, whoever is doing the inspection of the school will have the power to make the special measures judgement on the basis of what they've seen over their couple of days in the school.'

However, there is to be one important change facing schools which are not sufficiently weak to be declared failing. Under the old system, they would be declared to have 'serious weaknesses'. This can be enough for some to spur improvement, but others have simply drifted into the more serious 'special measures' category. Mr Bell thinks it is these schools which need to be treated a little differently. They will be placed on 'notice to improve', and will be visited by inspectors again after a year. 'We are still going to retain the "special measures" designation,' he says. 'That's just not up for negotiation. I don't want to change that nor do ministers. We are thinking of a slightly different system for those schools that are currently designated as having "serious weaknesses". We are proposing to introduce a new concept of "notice to improve". If you are a special measures school, you are so bad that we have got to designate you like that. But there will be schools that currently fall into the serious weaknesses category, and for them we would say at the end of their inspection, in these specific areas, you have to focus your improvement effort. We will be back to re-inspect you within a year. We think that's got a number of advantages. First of all, it will be a much more explicit statement of the areas that need to be concentrated on to improve. Secondly, I think the language is important. Rather than emphasise the serious weaknesses, you're putting the emphasis on improvement. Thirdly, from our experience over the last ten years, nothing seems to drive improvement more than the certainty of revisiting.'

Reducing bureaucracy – the tyranny of audit

There are those who complain about any inspection or external assessment. Their objections are often ideological, and are made in the face of overwhelming evidence of their benefits to schools in the last ten years. But there are others who make a more serious claim: that they are overburdened with audits and paper trails, and that this bureaucracy makes it harder to get on with the main work of a school. The best schools will have administrative staff and simple computer software to deal with these requests, but there is also an onus on central and local government to stop duplicating their efforts. In Whitehall, where this is now an objective across different departments, this is known as the 'single conversation'. The school census each January now collects far more information than before, but it should also mean fewer single requests for data. Equally, there must be considerable potential for reducing the inspection and audit trail by making the new three-yearly inspections the vehicle whereby the effectiveness of everything from a school's specialism to the way it uses its Ethnic Minority Achievement Grant can be tested, without lots of separate and time-consuming individual visits. This is something to which the Chief Inspector is sympathetic.

For example, specialist schools must apply for re-designation after four years. Schools will now be inspected every three years. With some 90 per cent of secondary schools likely to have a specialism soon, it would make sense to link the two processes, so that inspectors could validate an application for re-designation by ensuring that a school is on course to achieve its goals under the specialist schools bidding process. This is something that appeals to Mr Bell. 'I think that would be a quite sensible thing to do,' he says. 'Sometimes, the theologians of inspection worry about its purity. I'm interested, obviously, in the integrity and the rigour of inspection. But I also am anxious to avoid any unnecessary bureaucracy in schools. It doesn't seem to me beyond belief to come up with a system which did it more systematically.' Mr Bell believes it is important that all those involved in non-financial audits think about how their processes could more readily fit into the Ofsted inspection process. 'Without being naïve about inspection, many of the concerns that head teachers express to me about the bureaucratic burdens are less to do with inspection, and more to do with what they see as the multiplicity of relationships they have with central government,' he says. 'We've been talking to the DfES and [asking them] are there other things that the inspection report could do, not necessarily to gather more information, but perhaps to say that this information is of sufficient integrity that you don't need a separate audit . . . A school inspection report will tell you how a school is doing, and if you've got sufficient confidence in how the school is doing on the basis of the inspection report, you've just got to relax a bit, and not have all those separate and freestanding accountability systems. I think that's what really irritates secondary heads who find themselves in a position of being told to account in a very bureaucratic manner for relatively small pockets of money.'

However, there is a distinction between an inspection of standards and a financial audit. As we argue in Chapter 16, it is important that schools consider having a bursar to handle financial issues in a school. It is also, of course, important that they have robust independent audit procedures. There have been a few recent cases of individuals pocketing school money for personal aggrandisement, where such procedures have not been sufficiently robust or independent. Local authorities have a clear role to play, but schools which value their autonomy should see audit as a quid pro quo for having greater responsibility. Such a process might help to reduce the need for separate audit trails for each initiative that is separately funded by the government. 'I don't think it would be sensible or wise to say to inspectors that they should become accountants, but I do think there's a need for a separate discussion about reducing the audit burden on schools,' says Mr Bell. 'I'm not entirely convinced that that's featuring strongly enough in the discussions about deregulation.' Moreover, it only takes one scandal or oversight for demands to emerge for new procedures; procedures which may come to be regretted in later years. But it is a courageous politician who can resist the clamour for a new agency – with its attendant bureaucracy – in the wake of media-led outrage.

Could Ofsted do more to share good practice?

There is undoubtedly a new sense of openness in Ofsted, which has its advantages and disadvantages in schools. It has meant a more robust attitude towards weaker schools, as we have seen, but it has also meant a greater willingness to make public information obtained from schools that previous chief inspectors have felt was better kept private. Mr Bell candidly concedes that until recently, Ofsted did too little to make available to other schools the good practice it found elsewhere. 'We are enormously privileged to have access to this amount of data, and you don't compromise inspection systems by making that data available,' he says. 'We are looking much more at the dissemination of information. Recently, we've tried to ensure that in reports that have gone out, there's a much more explicit dissemination. For example, on a recent report on boys' achievement, there was a checklist at the back, so that if you were looking at gender issues in a school, you could match them to the elements of best practice. We try more explicitly in our inspection reports to cite institutions and name them, and identify case studies that others can learn from. I think we would argue that the PANDA data is the most systematic way that we do that – because we drive a lot of the comparisons by inspection.' Sample surveys are likely to become more important as there is less information available through regular school inspections about subject excellence in the future. Mr Bell defends this position: 'I think sometimes we've been seduced by the tyranny of the big number: just because we've got thousands of inspection grades, across all schools, doesn't necessarily tell you all you need to know. If you want to do a survey inspection, of, say, teaching of English in Key Stage 3, you might learn more from a smaller survey carried out by expert inspectors. So, even in this new model of inspection, we have to have a capacity to find out what's happening in schools across particular subject areas, so that we can disseminate that practice.' Another way in which Ofsted is promoting greater evidence-based reform is by allowing schools to make greater use of all its available data.

Nevertheless, none of this addresses the concern that some head teachers have that Ofsted diagnoses failure but doesn't help to pick up the pieces, having done so. There is a difference between inspection and post-inspection advice, but that is not the whole story. 'I think it is always important to have that distinction between inspection and advice, but where you are identifying outstandingly good schools, then that offers an opportunity for the other improvement networks to use that data,' says Mr Bell. 'Our job is to identify both the best and the worst – and if you identify the best, perhaps they can assist the worst . . . behind the scenes, the regular monitoring of schools in special measures is one of the key drivers for improvement. Yes, HMI are there to inspect, but, almost without exception, schools find that a powerful tool for improvement. That will continue in the new system.' He also points out that Ofsted does run action planning and good practice seminars on school improvement for schools which have just gone into special measures. They can receive help, often informally, to identify another school that has been through a similar situation and are encouraged to give the head teacher of the recovered school a call to see how he or she tackled it.

The right to complain – who is responsible when things go wrong?

The system of inspection that grew under Ofsted has been one where head teachers, local authority advisers and others work as part-time registered inspectors, often employed by private companies to conduct the inspections. In law, the registered inspector is legally responsible for the inspection, not the Chief Inspector of Schools or Ofsted. This has created its problems when things go wrong. The complaint must in the first instance be dealt with by the inspection contractor. Only then can it normally be referred to Ofsted, which allows three months for a response. If a school is still unhappy, they can refer to the Independent Complaints Adjudicator. It may be true that inspections have a 90 per cent satisfaction rating in terms of their conduct, if not the fact they are happening at all. But there must be a better way to deal with the minority of unhappy schools. This is where David Bell hopes the law can be changed so that he – or his successor – has the ownership and responsibility in law for every inspection report. (At present, Ofsted merely regulates inspections, unless they are led by Her Majesty's Inspector (HMI).) Under the proposed new system, complaints would go directly to Ofsted, and would hopefully be resolved more speedily. 'That's important because the Chief Inspector will have direct purchase over the quality of inspection,' says Mr Bell. 'It means HMI will be more heavily involved in school inspection and that will help to get greater consistency.

But we will still be using substantially independent inspectors, and they will be under the oversight and direction of HMI. Even if HMI are not on an inspection, they will have an explicit quality assurance role in the process. It ups the ante for Ofsted, because we are going to be accountable for our own reports. We have the discussion with the Independent Complaints Adjudicator all the time about when Ofsted should get involved. Our view in the current system is that it is probably right that the contractor has to deal with things in the first instance, but the downside of all that, which I hope the new system will do away with, is that by the time Ofsted gets involved, it can be incredibly late in the day.'

But even a new system won't resolve every complaint. Schools often believe they are the victims of an unfair bias, and seek to find in the inspectors' conduct justification for this belief. 'The hardest complaints of all to deal with are what I call the "he said, she said" complaint,' says Mr Bell. 'A recent inspection we overturned was straightforward because you look at the evidence base against the judgements, and you see what is right. "You said this, the evidence doesn't back you." But what happens when you're told "the inspectors didn't establish a good working relationship with the school" or "they said this to Mrs Smith when she was standing by the sink, washing her cup"? We'll never eliminate some of the glitches in the inspection system, but when we have a stronger purchase on the work of each inspector carrying out the inspection, we have a better chance of securing quality.' That also means that schools which do feel aggrieved need to ensure there is objective evidence before they complain, at least if they have any hope of their complaint being upheld.

Conclusions

There is no doubt that independent inspections have changed England's schools for the better. They have not done so in isolation, as some in charge of Ofsted perhaps used to believe. Schools have had inspection alongside testing, targets and teaching reforms, all of which have made a difference. It is sensible to reduce the notice for inspections, and to introduce more frequent but shorter visits. Six years was surely too long between visits, and a change of leadership in that period could make a huge difference for good or ill. And if inspection reports are primarily for parents, five-year-old information is of little value. But it must be hoped that in the quest for greater frequency, too much of what was good about Ofsted is not lost in the process. Parents may want shorter reports, but they also value an objective assessment about the quality of English teaching, art or PE. Schools should be able to offer it, provided they have robust and honest systems of self-evaluation in place; and so long as they are honest in public as well as in private about their shortcomings as well as their strengths. However, in the contemporary competitive climate, that is a tall order. More positively, there are signs of sensible and imaginative thinking about practical ways to reduce the burden of duplication attached to audit and an improved complaints procedure. So long as the balance between brevity and completeness is properly struck, there is every chance that inspection will continue to contribute as forcefully to school improvement over the next decade as much as it has in the past.

12

Provision for children with special educational needs

Special educational needs is a subject which provokes some of the strongest passions in education. The debate between the relative merits of special schools and mainstream education has raged for decades, but the passions of their respective advocates grow ever stronger. The government has attempted to walk this tightrope by publishing several policy statements on the subject, which have sought to encourage more mainstream provision, while retaining special schools and developing specialist units in mainstream schools. But many teachers believe that the balance has not yet been properly struck.

Pupils who have special educational needs (SEN) may have a statement of those needs issued by an LEA. Gaining such a statement means that the school will receive extra resources to care for that child; for mainstream secondary schools, where there are 78,000 pupils with statements, this can help pay the cost of extra learning assistants. Many other pupils are deemed to have special educational needs by their teachers, and may be placed on a register within the school, often in the hope that by recognising and addressing those needs, the placement is a temporary one. The Government has also tried to make it easier for pupils with SEN to gain extra help without a full statement, to try to address specific needs early. The process of statementing a child can be long and drawn out but has recently been streamlined with the goal being to complete the process within 18 weeks.

Special schools and pupils with SEN – the national picture

There are some 850 maintained special secondary schools with a total enrolment of 74,496 statemented children, or about 2 per cent of all secondary school children. Many come from poorer backgrounds: 35 per cent are eligible for free school meals (more than twice as many as in mainstream schools). Two-thirds are boys. Two-thirds of all statemented children are in secondary schools with only one-third in primary schools (though the balance is more evenly struck in mainstream schools). Most special secondary schools are quite small with the average enrolment less than 100.

A further 78,000 statemented children are enrolled in maintained secondary schools, which represents 2·4 per cent of their total enrolment. There are also 11,300 pupils with statements in independent and non-maintained special schools, their places usually paid for by their local authority.[1] But there has also been a fall in the numbers of pupils who are receiving statements, which is slightly greater than the drop in overall pupil numbers. In 2002 30,720 new statements were issued compared with 35,650 in 1997, across both primary and secondary schools.

However, a much larger group of pupils is said to have some form of SEN by their school. Almost 1.2 million pupils are recorded in the 2004 school census in this category across all schools. Of these 447,800 are in mainstream secondary schools, representing nearly one in seven pupils, or 13.5 per cent. An even higher proportion of primary school pupils is placed on the SEN register, though many more pupils should be recognised earlier if baseline assessment and foundation profiles are doing their job for those starting primary school or transferring from nursery education.

Most of the children in special schools come from one of five categories: severe learning difficulties, moderate learning difficulties, emotional and behavioural difficulties, autistic spectrum disorders and profound and multiple learning difficulties (PMLD). However, 12 types of special educational needs are used in the statementing procedure:

- Severe learning difficulties
- Moderate learning difficulties
- Emotional, behavioural and social difficulties (EBSD)
- Autistic spectrum disorders
- PMLD
- Physical disabilities
- Speech, language and communication needs
- Hearing impairment
- Visual impairment
- Specific learning difficulties including dyslexia
- Multi-sensory impairment
- Others.

---

[1] *Pupil Characteristics and Class Sizes in Maintained Schools in England* (Provisional January 2004 census data) (London, DfES First Release, 29 April 2004).

An Audit Commission survey in 2002 suggested that the incidence of different types of need was changing. It found that over the previous five years, there had been significant increases in the number of children with autistic spectrum disorders, with speech and communication difficulties and with profound and multiple learning difficulties; and significant decreases in moderate learning difficulties and specific learning difficulties.[2] In order to be statemented, children need to have a severe disability in one of these areas.

There has been considerable debate in recent years whether children with SEN are better off being educated in a mainstream school or whether they will receive a better education in a special school. Certainly, as the figures show, there are now as many statemented children with SEN being educated in mainstream schools as in special schools. But they also suggest that, while there has been some decline in special schools, the reduction has not been nearly as fast as some have suggested. There were 97,700 statemented pupils in primary and secondary special schools in 1999 (including non-maintained ones) and 91,000 in 2003.

However, procedures for both statementing and assigning SEN status vary widely by LEA. The combined figures differ significantly by school too, with some struggling schools such as Corby Community College, having statements for 12 per cent of the children on the rolls, with a further 43 per cent on the SEN register – more than half the school population in total, whereas other schools may have a combined figure of less than 10 per cent.

The sheer scale of these numbers has led some to ask whether or not the proportion of a school's children with SEN is not as important as the proportion eligible for free school meals when determining the level of social deprivation of a particular school. But the Audit Commission reported that, particularly when it came to gaining statements, middle-class parents were able disproportionately to get the extra help that goes with being seen to have SEN. Certainly, the extent of pupils with SEN is a factor in performance table positions, something the Government has more recently acknowledged.

National strategies

The Government has published several recent papers on the subject of SEN. The 1997 Green Paper, *Excellence for All Children: Meeting special education needs*[3] made a commitment to improving the statutory framework for SEN, a commitment taken forward through the Special Educational Needs and Disability Act

---

[2] *Special Education Needs: A mainstream issue* (London, Audit Commission, 2002).

[3] Department for Education and Employment (DfEE), *Excellence for All Children: Meeting special education needs* (London, HMSO, 1997).

2001 and the new *Special Educational Needs Code of Practice*.[4] However, the Audit Commission report of 2002 found that there was still much to be done. Key findings included that too many children waited too long to have their needs met; children with SEN who could and should be taught in mainstream schools were frequently turned away because staff were ill equipped and poorly trained to meet their needs and perhaps most worrying, that many special schools feel uncertain of their future role.

The Green Paper *Every Child Matters*[5] was the Government's response. It was underpinned by three main principles. First, that all children, including those with special educational needs, have the right to a good education. Second, all teachers should be capable of teaching children with special educational needs and third that all schools should play their part in educating children with SEN. This strategy was followed up with *Removing Barriers to Achievement*.[6] The paper outlines a strategy which calls for action in four key areas:

- Early intervention to ensure that children with SEN receive the help they need as soon as possible.
- Removing barriers to learning by embedding inclusive practices in every school.
- Raising expectations and achievement by developing teachers' skills is meeting the needs of children with SEN.
- Developing partnerships between special and mainstream schools.

Clearly there is a need for better, more consistent, faster and earlier identification of children with SEN. Despite the growing numbers on primary school registers, the much higher proportion of children of secondary school age in special schools is an indication of this. The lack of common procedures between LEAs, social services and the Health Service is probably the greatest cause of this, something which it is important that the new merged children's services departments start to address. There is also too little childcare for disabled children. Finally, despite some improvements in the system after the 1997 Green Paper, the procedures and the definition of children with SEN could do with greater clarity and simplification.

Specialist secondary schools with SEN expertise

One way forward is to encourage specialist secondary schools, with expertise in SEN to provide assistance to other schools in their area as part of their community

---

[4] DfES, *Special Educational Needs Code of Practice* (London, The Stationery Office, 2001).

[5] DfES, *Every Child Matters* (London, The Stationery Office, 2003).

[6] DfES, *Removing Barriers to Achievement* (London, The Stationery Office, 2004).

provision, in the same way that they currently do for specialist subjects such as language and sport. There are also 14 special schools who have specialist status and a further 30 are applying for specialist status.

An outstanding example of a specialist special school is Crosshill School in Blackburn which caters for 100 pupils aged 11 to 16, the majority of whom have moderate learning difficulties (MLD). As is the case for most secondary schools there are twice as many statemented boys as girls on roll. Mike Hatch, the head teacher of Crosshill has already shown himself to be a trailblazer as his school was one of the first special schools in the country to gain technology college status in 1999.

Working closely with mainstream schools has always been and still is central to Mike Hatch's philosophy. He believes there are enormous benefits for both parties in terms of teaching and learning, removing stigma, and recognising the range and complexities of children's needs. There are many shared agendas and much that can be learned on both sides.

He has developed the school's outward looking approach still further by looking at the needs of the community. His response to these needs was to develop an e-Learning Centre. A successful bid to the DfES, supported by the LEA, resulted in a grant of £1.5 million to develop this centre, which was opened in 2003 by Jack Straw, who is both the Blackburn MP and Foreign Secretary. There is considerable evidence that ICT can be of substantial help for children with SEN.

Ofsted has recently praised the school's 'very good relationships'. Relationships between staff and pupils and among pupils are clearly excellent. In answer to the question – what makes this a good school? – a teaching assistant responded, 'praise and respect from other children – acceptance of all different needs'. A senior teacher added 'positive pupil relationships' while a pupil added, 'It is loud in mainstream – it is quiet here.'

The atmosphere in the school is purposeful, but also friendly, something clearly appreciated by staff and pupils. An enormous amount of effort goes into work on pupil behaviour, helped, of course, by the high staff/pupil ratio. Personalised learning and a differentiated curriculum are the new buzz-words in the national education agenda. Special schools have been doing these for years and have a great deal of expertise on which mainstream schools can draw. Parents and governors welcome the way that teaching is done in small groups so that pupils are taught at a pace that they can cope with. Pupils feel more confident. 'When I came to Crosshill I found I could put my hand up and answer questions,' said one. Continuity of staff has been key to Crosshill's success. Despite the fact that six senior staff have gone on to be head teachers and deputies in other schools staff turnover is relatively low and recruitment is not a problem. There are many long-term permanent staff who know the pupils very well.

The school makes a great deal of use of teaching assistants. A teacher, in the role of 'facilitator' or 'trainer' might take a class for 15 to 20 children and 'teach' the whole class for around 10 minutes. The class will then break down into smaller groups with teaching assistants for the remaining 40 minutes. Again, this is something being replicated now, with larger numbers, in many mainstream schools as part of the workforce remodelling agenda. Teaching assistants also go to mainstream schools with pupils who attend classes there.

While raising attainment in special schools cannot fairly be measured in terms of A–C grades at GCSE, pupils at Crosshill have been working at GCSE entry level for several years. Plans for next year mean that more than half of Year 9 pupils will do some GCSE work in mainstream. The school is also looking at other external accreditation such as Trident awards for work experience and many pupils attend FE college National Vocational Qualification (NVQ) courses.

The school saw the acquisition of technology college status back in 1999 as essential to move the school forward in its use of ICT (which it regards as vital for the students' future employment), in working with mainstream schools and in recognising that children have 'pockets of ability'.

There are extensive links with other schools. For example, a pupil at Crosshill with reading difficulties might still have ability in mathematics and might be able to access a mainstream school curriculum in this area. A 'two-way traffic' of children was initially established with Queen's Park School (their specialist partner) as some of their pupils, some of whom might have been borderline in attending a special school, benefited from the special school approach in some areas. Crosshill has a similar relationship with Our Lady and St John, an arts college which also has leading edge status. Crosshill is now in Phase 2 of its specialist status. In addition to Crosshill pupils accessing the mainstream curriculum and some GCSE courses, subject leaders in the different schools work together and pupils in the mainstream setting with their own learning difficulties are able to access the expertise at Crosshill. Primary school pupils also make use of Crosshill's facilities, for example their SUCCESSMAKER programs to aid literacy and numeracy.

A key benefit of specialist school status has been the development of ICT. Crosshill has 140 laptops, video-conferencing, an 'extra net' link to other Blackburn schools and next year there will be whiteboards in every classroom. The development of the e-Learning Centre has been crucial to Crosshill's development. The facility is better than that in most mainstream schools. It offers a vocational curriculum, for example in hospitality and catering, and, according to Mr Hatch, makes Crosshill 'more than a special school'. One teacher added that 'pupils confidence in meeting the public in the e-Learning Centre helps their life skills'. The e-Learning Centre has ensured that Crosshill is seen as a centre of expertise and training centre for the whole community. Links exist not only with other schools but also with FE colleges, businesses (especially in the catering and hospitality area), the local football club and the church.

In analysing 'what makes a great special school' it becomes clear that the different elements are quite similar to 'what makes a good mainstream school'. Good leadership is certainly an essential prerequisite to both. A good special school exhibits good practice from which all schools can learn. In the case of Crosshill the school is increasingly seen as a centre of expertise on SEN from which other schools and community groups can draw. There is also an active school parents' group. In short many of its 'good features' – positive relationships, personalised learning, creative use of staff, raising attainment, specialist status, the use of ICT and working with other schools and the wider community – could be replicated as key elements in any 'great school'.

So, what is the future for good special schools? Mr Hatch fully supports the overall inclusion agenda and encourages a positive attitude towards inclusion from his staff. But he still sees the need for separate special schools like Crosshill at the present time. His ideal, both for social and educational reasons, would be a fully integrated system where schools catered for all abilities and needs – something he dubs 'education villages'. However, he makes the point that this would only work if the 'integrated/inclusive' school had specialist provision in terms of buildings, curriculum and, above all, staffing. There would need to be a 'mini Crosshill' in every mainstream school. There is still a long way to go before this vision can be successfully realised, though an increasing number of mainstream schools have been developing specialist units where pupils can have some classes, benefit from extra equipment and teachers can have the extra support they need. Around a tenth of those being placed in mainstream schools are now going to such specialist units.

The idea that there should be special schools which acquire specialist status in the particular skills required to teach pupils with SEN was developed by Baroness Ashton of Upholland, the DfES minister who had responsibility for SEN. In 2005, a pilot programme will begin which offers a new type of specialist status for special schools which have proven expertise in the following:

- communication and interaction
- cognition and learning
- behavioural, emotional and social difficulties
- sensory or physical needs.

This seems an eminently sensible idea which, instead of a rigid insistence that all pupils should be taught in mainstream schools whatever their level of disability, will create partnerships between special schools and mainstream schools to share the particular expertise required to teach children with severe disabilities. Clearly children with severe learning difficulties require teachers with special training and expertise whether in special schools or mainstream schools.

The challenge of exclusion and EBSD

Of particular relevance to this debate is whether mainstream schools should permanently exclude children with severe emotional, behavioural and social difficulties (EBSD) because they cause disruption to other children. Pupils who are permanently excluded from mainstream schools may be sent to pupil referral units – older ones drop out of education completely. As Cyril Taylor witnessed during his period of office as High Sheriff of Greater London, many of these children leave school without the basic literacy and numeracy skills required for modern jobs, making it difficult for them to find work. Some will be dependent on welfare for most of their lives; others may drift into substance abuse or become young offenders. Many will join the under-class of disillusioned citizens with no stake in our society. But, as the Government has acknowledged in its papers on SEN, every child deserves a decent education.

Part of the difficulty with the SEN debate is one of definition. Some teaching unions, particularly the National Association of Schoolmaster and Union of Women Teacher (NASUWT), are sceptical about an 'inclusion' agenda which theoretically treats pupils with severe behavioural difficulties as if they can be integrated as easily as pupils with physical disabilities. Yet an increasing number of parents expect just that. They would see anything else as unfair to their child.

We have to distinguish between what is possible and appropriate for those with physical disabilities and moderate learning or behavioural problems, and those who have severe emotional, behavioural and social problems.

Of course, no school should turn a child away for want of wheelchair access, Braille translation facilities, or a suitable hearing loop. And good special needs assistants can help overcome most learning difficulties. There has been a lot of extra money for such provision through various Access Funds – and there should be more. New schools should automatically make such provision as standard.

However, many young people with severe forms of EBSD need alternative provision to make progress. (And the same is often true with severe forms of autism.) If the Government's commitment to 'personalised education' is to be realised, every child must have an education appropriate to his or her needs, whether that is in a mainstream school, a special school or a combination of the two. And if they simply can't cope with mainstream education, despite the best support, the right alternatives should be there. Not making such provision fails them individually and lets down their classmates whose own chance to learn is being constantly disrupted.

As a result of the Government's policies to provide better support for excluded pupils, there has been a big growth in the number of pupils in pupil referral units, from 8,260 to 12,010. Some of those new pupils are shunted from one exclusion to the next, having little chance of a decent education in the process. Some secondary schools can and do provide excellent support, but many with spare capacity already struggle with a host of other problems. Those like Corby Community College are taking more than their fair share. And while the quality of pupil referral units has improved, there are not enough appropriate long-term places for pupils with severe behavioural problems.

It may not therefore be enough simply to promise that special schools will continue, or that special schools can gain a new form of specialism, welcome though such commitments may be. We may need new special schools for pupils with EBSD. This can be expensive, but it might be a more effective way to spend some of the £1.7 billion a year being spent on SEN in mainstream schools at present. Better data is needed about how this money is spent to start a sensible discussion. Of course, too many EBSD special schools in the past had an appalling record, one reason why some closed. And Ofsted still reports that teaching is unsatisfactory in a fifth of such schools. So we may need new types of special schools and more specialist units, which don't repeat past mistakes. Possibly new types of City Academies with a small number of pupils could be developed for pupils with EBSD.

Conclusions

Providing a good education to pupils with SEN is costly. Depending upon the severity of the statement, the additional funding for statemented pupils varies from £2,000 per year per pupil to as much as £20,000. That makes it all the more important that problems are diagnosed early, and appropriately. We need better information about the reasons why one in six pupils is diagnosed with SEN (without statements) – and, for example, the numbers for whom remedial literacy or numeracy support at an earlier stage might have made the difference. While the Government has sensibly sought to provide more help to pupils without statements when they need it, the statutory statementing procedures can still be too slow and bureaucratic. There may be a case for a fast track statementing procedure for children with severe EBSD whose needs were not properly recognised in primary school. Good schools might be persuaded to support more children with emotional and behavioural problems if additional funding was available. This would be better than what happens at present with many excluded children with EBSD being assigned to underperforming schools with vacancies so that these schools have far more than their fair share of children with these difficulties.

But such provision will not meet the needs of every child. We need to see more new types of provision – new special schools, new specialist units, and new types of specialist school – to ensure that every child has the personalised education that is at the heart of current education policy. The needs of the individual child must come before the interests of any lobby, be it for greater integration or greater segregation. Clearly considerable progress still needs to be made to ensure that all our children with SEN receive a decent education.

13

Schools helping schools: the value of partnerships

Of the 253 secondary schools in England where fewer than 25 per cent of their pupils achieved at least five good GCSE grades in 2003, 82 had been designated by Ofsted as requiring special measures and a further 63 as having serious weaknesses. Of course, not every school below this standard is technically 'underperforming'. Some have a relatively high value-added score when comparing the ability and academic standard of their intakes with their performance at GCSE. Nevertheless, the nation cannot ignore the plight of the over 150,000 children in these schools. Many will leave school at 16 unable to read or write to a reasonable level or without basic numeracy skills. They will lack the minimum skills which modern jobs require.

Some underperforming schools are failing their pupils so badly that they should be closed; either permanently or re-opened as an Academy under completely new management with private sector support. However, many can raise standards dramatically if given the right support and if their leadership is strengthened. This chapter looks at the remarkable story of how many previously underperforming schools are now providing a good standard of education through the help given to them by a higher performing school.

This type of collaboration takes many different forms. Some school to school links are quite informal, often as part of the community programme required by the specialist schools programme. Others are hard edged federations such as those organised by S Peter's Collegiate School in Wolverhampton with the Regis School; by Ninestiles School's federation with the Waverley School in Birmingham; by Cornwallis's federation with Senacre Technology College (which is not an officially designated specialist school) and Oldborough Manor in Kent; and by Thomas Telford's recent link with the Madeley Court School in Telford. Yet others are part of the Specialist Schools Support Programme under which over 150 lower performing specialist schools are receiving help from other, higher performing specialist schools.

There is clear evidence that these partnerships are raising standards, indicating that school to school partnerships are often more effective that other more formal approaches, such as Fresh Start. As Susan Elkin put it in a report published by the Specialist Schools Trust in 2002:

> The key words are collaboration and partnership. Schools should no longer view each other as competitors. Although every school needs its own distinct ethos, the main aim is common to all. All schools should exist to ensure that all pupils get the best possible education. That is why collaboration makes sense – and why it works.[1]

This is also very much the view taken by the current Government, and ministers are actively encouraging partnerships and federation. Let us first examine some examples of where schools have federated.

Federations of schools

These federations were given legal sanction by the 2002 Education Act which allows for the creation of a single governing body or a joint governing body across two or more schools and originally provided substantial additional funding, although this has subsequently been reduced.

The Lichfield Federation

The pioneer for a federation of schools was the unique partnership developed under the outstanding leadership of Peter Crook of the successful S Peter's Collegiate School in Wolverhampton with the nearly failing Regis School in the same town. Under this arrangement, the LEA closed the Regis School in 1998. It was simultaneously reopened as a new voluntary Church of England School with all of its pupils and most of the staff transferring to the new school. The new school, called the King's School, joined S Peter's School in a federation of the two schools under the aegis of the newly created Lichfield Foundation. The site of the Regis School and its buildings were purchased by the Lichfield Foundation from the LEA but this wise local authority chose to invest these funds in the new school by refurbishing the buildings. The story started in 1996 when Roy Lockwood, Chief Education Officer of Wolverhampton discussed the difficulties of the Regis School with Mr Crook. Enrolment in Regis had fallen by a half with no first-choice applications. Attendance was poor and only 21 per cent of pupils were gaining five good grades at GCSE. By contrast, S Peter's was a highly over-subscribed Church of England Technology

---

[1] S. Elkin, *Working Together to Share Success* (London, Specialist Schools Trust, 2002).

College with over 80 per cent of its pupils gaining five good grades at GCSE, having risen dramatically from 36 per cent in 1989 when Mr Crook was appointed.

Initially there was discussion of merging the two schools while retaining two sites. Mr Crook was completely opposed to that. He believed the two schools were geographically too far apart from each other to operate satisfactorily as a split site school. The suggestion he made was far more radical and original: to form a foundation and to bring both schools into it so that each could benefit from and help the other. This was strongly supported by Wolverhampton Council as well as by the Bishop of Wolverhampton and the Diocese of Lichfield.

Mr Crook agreed to be seconded that year to Regis to prepare for its change in status. During his first week at the school, he had a conversation with an 11-year-old student who said: 'I know you because you used to teach my cousin at S Peter's,' adding with unconscious pathos 'and I know why you are here. It's because we are rubbish.' Then there was David in Year 11, a very tall, bored African-Caribbean boy who was hanging about listlessly in the lunch break. 'Why don't you play football?' Mr Crook asked. 'Because we haven't got a ball,' was the reply. The upshot of this conversation was that the new head teacher dramatically increased the provision of sport in the school.

The old school had suffered from poor discipline. Mr Crook appointed Bobby Woods as his behavioural consultant. An imposing physical presence, Mr Woods, together with the other staff, rapidly restored order to the school. After long and arduous negotiations and with the benefit of immense goodwill on all sides, Regis was closed in 1998 to be reopened as the King's School under the leadership of Tim Gallagher, the newly appointed head teacher.

During the next three years, the school was transformed. All pupils were given a new school uniform. Better relations were established with the local community. The two schools appointed a number of staff to work jointly in both schools. Facilities were renovated and a curriculum focus on the arts was nurtured. Today, King's School has achieved arts college specialist status. Its results are rapidly improving – 51 per cent of pupils gained five good grades at GCSE in 2003. The school is now over-subscribed and received a glowing Ofsted report. The two schools continue in partnership where value is added by collaboration. This is secured by the Director of the Lichfield Foundation, working with both head teachers, governing bodies and LEA.

Improvements at Cornwallis School that led to the South Maidstone Federation

The story of the King's School is not unique. There are many similar examples of the power of collaboration. When Michael Wood took over the headship of the Cornwallis School in Kent in 1985, it was in many respects a traditional secondary modern. Kent had and still has a selective system under which the top 25 per cent of the ability range are selected by the grammar schools. The school was held back by the modest expectations of the LEA, parents, staff and pupils.

In 1989, just two per cent of Cornwallis students gained five or more grades at GCSE. By 1995 this figure was 45 per cent. It became one of the first technology colleges in 1994. Today with a close working relationship with Microsoft it is a leading proponent of the use of IT in learning, especially the use of laptops connected by wireless links to the Internet. In 2003, 68 per cent of its pupils achieved at least five good grades at GCSE. The school had no sixth form until 1992 but now has 320 sixth formers studying a strong mix of academic and vocational subjects. The school has just had its first Oxbridge acceptance.

In short, Cornwallis School has moved from a curriculum designed to inhibit pupils to one which makes demands on them and expects them to achieve. It is one of a small group of secondary modern schools in Kent to make this transition. The challenge now is to roll this out to other schools, not necessarily to 'replicate' Cornwallis but to apply some of the strategies which have worked.

For the past year Michael Wood has been Chief Executive of the South Maidstone Federation. As well as Cornwallis School, this includes Senacre Technology College and Oldborough Manor Community School. Both schools are 11–16 secondary modern schools with, until recently a quarter or fewer of their pupils gaining five or more good grades at GCSE. Both are under-subscribed with approximately 500 students, each with low staying-on rates and they had previously offered very few vocational opportunities to their pupils. So, in many ways, both are where Cornwallis was ten years ago. This is a natural grouping both in terms of experience and geography and it has been encouraged and supported by the LEA which wants to see its schools working together.

Approval has been sought from the DfES to become a 'hard federation' with the funding which goes with that status. But there has already been considerable progress. The federation has four main aims: to raise attainment; to raise staying-on rates post-16; to increase the schools' intakes; and to improve vocational provision. One of the federation's first concrete activities was to introduce a GNVQ Key Stage 4 science course at Senacre taught by staff at Cornwallis for students unlikely to gain 5+ A*–C grades at GCSE. The Cornwallis science department has worked closely with the science department at Senacre. The second was that Cornwallis now leads the teaching of music across two schools and advises the third as neither of the other two had qualified music specialists.

The head teacher of one of the schools is leaving and a new 'Head of School' has been appointed who will report to Mr Wood and work in tandem with him, while having a considerable degree of autonomy on a day to day basis. Mr Wood also acts as a mentor to the head teachers of the other schools and works closely with them and their leadership teams. There is a new Executive Governing Body consisting of the Chairman and Vice Chairman of Governors from each school and chaired by the Chairman of Governors from Cornwallis. An additional deputy head has been appointed to develop the post-16 and vocational curriculum in all three schools, with a successful bid to Kent County Council and the Learning and Skills Council for at least £250,000 for capital development to enable the introduction of work-related courses. These are early days but Mr Wood is optimistic that progress is being made. He expected an upward movement in results in both partner schools in 2004.

Thomas Telford School–Madeley Court School partnership

Perhaps the most inspiring example of collaboration between schools is the partnership between Thomas Telford School in Telford, Shropshire with its neighbour Madeley Court School. As we have seen, for several years, all Thomas Telford's pupils have achieved five or more good grades at GCSE – and most achieve ten good grades. Ninety-seven per cent of its pupils stay on at age 16 with an average point score of 36.5 at A Level. Thomas Telford is a particular proponent of using IT to improve learning. All of its Year 7 pupils learn to touch type upon entry and every child has access to a computer.

The school has developed a highly popular online curriculum to prepare pupils for the GNVQ qualification in ICT. This has been so successful commercially that nearly 1,000 secondary schools are using the curriculum. With the proceeds of the licensing fees, Telford has both sponsored and is establishing two Academies in Walsall and Sandwell. It has also sponsored around 70 specialist schools. In 2003 Telford agreed to federate with the nearby Madeley Court School which was in special measures with less than 20 per cent of its pupils gaining five or more good grades at GCSE. The arrangement is known as a 'loose federation' since each school retains its own separate governing body. There is a Federation Board consisting of the head teacher and chair of governors of Thomas Telford and the head teacher and chair of governors of Madeley Court School, plus two representatives from the LEA, plus an independent Chairman, former HMI David Woods.

Objectives and targets are set out in a service level agreement. In general the three aims are to drive up results; improve standards; and refurbish the site. Funding has come from several sources for the improvements at Madeley Court School. Thomas Telford School's business arm has put in a third of a million pounds and the school's entire 'leading edge' programme grant of £180,000, is being used in the Federation. There is also a Federation Grant of £365,000, a one-off grant for the three years. And, additionally, the Youth Sport Trust has been very helpful with the school's bid for specialist status. The school is being jointly sponsored for specialist school status by both Telford and Dr Peter Ogden.

A new head teacher, Vic Maher, has been appointed at Madeley Court. His first task was to prepare a radical redesign of its curriculum at GCSE level, which previously was focused primarily on academic subjects. There is now a wide range of vocational subjects teaching the pupils the skills they will need for employment. Seventy-five pupils at Madeley Court attend some of their classes at Thomas Telford and there are a number of joint staff appointments with online curriculum links between the two schools. Already, attitudes towards Madeley School have changed. Many of the pupils unable to get into Thomas Telford are now applying to Madeley. In just one year the number of first-choice applications grew from 63 in 2002 to 189 in 2003. The school is now over-subscribed.

Ninestiles School's Federation

Elsewhere in this book we described the remarkable progress made by Ninestiles School under the leadership of Sir Dexter Hutt. As we have seen, Ninestiles School improved its GCSE performance from just 6 per cent achieving five or more good GCSE grades in 1988 when Sir Dexter became head teacher, to 73 per cent in 2003. It has one of the highest value-added scores in the country with 29 per cent better actual results than predicted from its intake. Ninestiles agreed to federate with the Waverley School in 2001 and with a second school, the International School, in 2003.

Sir Dexter has responsibility, as the Chief Executive, for strategic oversight of all three schools. His own deputy head teacher, Christine Quinn, was appointed as head teacher of Waverley with Sir Dexter being her line manager and mentor. As Susan Elkin put it:

> A federation of schools can give a number of advantages. Faculties can work together across the two schools, schemes of work can be shared and combining reputations shores up schools against failure. Collaboration allows you to make changes fast. Wheels do not need re-inventing. Working closely with a successful school helps to establish a 'can do' culture and a belief that anything is possible, providing the recurring resources are available.[2]

In 2000, the year before Christine Quinn took over, only 14 per cent of Waverley's GCSE students had achieved 5+ A*–C passes. Just three years later, the

---

[2] S. Elkin, *Top Performing School Starts by Managing Behaviour* (London, Specialist Schools Trust, 2004).

figure in 2003 was 51 per cent. An Ofsted inspection declared the school to be rapidly improving. 'I couldn't have done this alone,' says Christine Quinn. She believes this dramatic improvement demonstrates the value of federation as a path to school improvement. Ninestiles' second partnership with the International School achieved equally impressive results with a reported rise in the proportion of youngsters gaining five good GCSE grades from 9 per cent in 2003 to 32 per cent in 2004. Ms Quinn was asked by Sir Dexter Hutt to take over International. Her first step was to implement behaviour for learning, the system successfully developed at Ninestiles. 'The behaviour has to come first, because improvement and raised standards cannot happen without it,' Sir Dexter says. 'There is a lot of excellent vision at International School,' he adds. 'The job now is to find practical ways of bridging the gap to achieve that vision. Getting the behaviour right is the crucial first step.'

These case studies show the potential for federations in school improvement. However, it should be noted that all four of these examples are strong federations with only one or two partner schools. Other loose federations which involve less robust structures, or many schools, have not enjoyed such success.

The same lessons can be drawn from the partnerships organised by the Specialist Schools Trust under its Specialist Schools Support Programme. Under this arrangement, leading specialist schools are helping underperforming specialist schools to improve their results. There are now over 150 such partnerships and the number is growing rapidly. Only a modest amount of funding – £9,000 per year – is available to help pay for the cost of the partnership. However, results have been encouraging and the scheme is being expanded. A further development in this partnership ethos is the changing of the guidelines for schools bidding for re-designation as a specialist school. Re-designating schools will be encouraged to list as their secondary school partner an underperforming school; the objective being that over the four years of designation that school will be helped to achieve specialist status.

Other partnerships can reduce mutual suspicions

Such links are not the only sorts of partnership to develop in recent years. Two particularly valuable schemes have been the provision of grants to grammar schools and independent schools to work with other schools either to help them to improve or to expand their curricular opportunities.

Four years ago, Ripon Grammar School feared it might be forced to close. Anti-selection campaigners had collected enough signatures to force a vote about its future. But local parents surprised the campaigners by backing the grammar school's case by a two-to-one majority. More interestingly, the battle drew the 450-year-old school closer to Ripon College, the 530-student non-selective specialist technology college located just across the Clotherholme Road in the North Yorkshire city. It also encouraged ministers to consider supporting other similar partnerships in other selective areas.

While the two schools had worked together before the ballot, they have worked more closely since as the college helped the grammar school to win the vote. 'Rather than seeking to disentangle what we'd already got, we decided to look to each other's specialisms,' Ripon College Principal Paul Lowery said. 'That spirit of working together has been quite refreshing.'

There are joint staff-training sessions between the two schools. And this is a two-way process, with computer training taking place at the college. The libraries are integrated, so all the students can use both. There is also a lot of interchange in the sixth form. Over a third of the grammar school students come to the college for information technology, psychology and law classes, while the college's students go to the grammar school for humanities, classics and some science lessons. Students from Year 7 at Ripon College and Ripon Grammar School also joined together to explore citizenship issues through geography and science with the help of the authors of the best-selling *Horrible Science* and *Horrible Geography* books.

Alan Jones, head teacher of Ripon Grammar shares Mr Lowery's views. 'There's been an excellent blending of the traditional and the modern,' he said. 'Local schools working together can provide new opportunities in different but complementary ways.' Perhaps the icing on the cake is that Ripon College's results are now among the fastest improving in the country. A remarkable 44 per cent of pupils gained five good GCSEs in 2003 compared to just 8 per cent in 1998, a huge achievement for a school with a secondary modern intake.

Scores of independent school partnerships have also been developed since 1998, covering all aspects of the curriculum under the Building Bridges initiative. For independent schools, they are a chance to demonstrate their charitable purpose. But they have also built new bridges between two sectors which have traditionally been suspicious of each other. A new innovation announced by the Education Secretary Charles Clarke in May 2004 is that the Learning and Skills Council will be able to provide funding for pupils in comprehensive schools to take A Level courses in certain subjects at an independent school if there is no provision for those courses locally. The new Charity law which will require independent schools to demonstrate public benefit will provide a spur to such partnerships.

Partnerships are the way forward

We have come a long way since the mid-nineties when schools were immensely competitive, believing somehow that excellence had a finite limitation and that if one school was successful, it would be at the expense of another school. As David Blunkett, who pioneered the community role of specialist schools, said in his Annual Lecture to the Technology Colleges Trust on 5 November 1997 at the Whitehall Banqueting House:

> The success of one school will not be to the detriment of another. I have never believed that the more you expand excellence in some schools, the more you are likely to dilute what is happening in others. There is not a finite amount of excellence that has to be confined in a safe place lest someone else steals it.

Partnerships between schools should be encouraged at all levels. Perhaps sometime in the next decade when all schools have become specialist there will be a range of different specialisms in each urban area, both giving parents a wider choice of schools as well as requiring each partner school to provide expertise in their particular subject specialisms to nearby secondary and primary schools.

Partnerships and federations are a way of sharing best practice, building bridges and expanding choice. Whether between schools in a town, across the country, or across borders, there is no doubt that with the growing potential of ICT, they will grow ever more important in the future. And they are very much a part of the contribution which good schools can make to helping others raise standards.

14

Turning the rhetoric of school choice into reality

School choice is the holy grail sought by many politicians. While teachers are often sceptical of its benefits and possibilities, there is undoubtedly a huge appetite among parents for a greater say in choosing their child's school. An opinion poll for *The Economist* in April 2004 found that 76 per cent of parents felt it was very or fairly important to them to have greater choice over which state school their family attended.[1] However, the political promise of greater choice is often hard to translate into reality on the ground. Parents may be happy to send their child to the neighbourhood primary school, where polls suggest they are also happier with the standards on offer. It is in secondary education that the difficulties most often arise. Official statistics from the DfES show that parents appealed in 22,410 cases in 2002 because they missed out on their preferred primary school. And 69,020 appeals were lodged over secondary school places – affecting around one in ten 11-year-olds. Only a third were decided in the parents' favour.[2] This is one reason why seven per cent of parents have their children privately educated and one in ten children in London goes to an independent school.

The desire for choice often comes up against the complex system designed to ensure fair access to schools. While 164 secondary grammar schools in England still select their intake entirely by ability, most schools use other methods to decide which children to admit. Two criteria are most common: the distance a child lives from the school (proximity) and whether or not they have a brother or sister already attending. The sibling criterion tends to be less controversial than distance. There are, after all, good social reasons why families might wish to have their children

[1] *The Economist* April 7 2004. Yougov questioned over 2000 voters by Internet for the poll.
[2] See the full data at www.dfes.gov.uk/rsgateway/DB/SFR/50000470/19-2004rev.pdf.

attend the same school. But distance is problematic. It creates catchment areas which can become socially exclusive. House prices near a good school can attract a £40,000 premium. If the school is in a middle-class area, it can be out of the reach of those living in more disadvantaged circumstances who simply live too far away. Conversely, the rule can turn neighbourhood schools in socially disadvantaged areas into poor schools simply because they lack the social and academic mix which we have seen is so important for good standards. Moreover, as the majority of schools acquire a specialism, it becomes even harder to justify admitting students solely on the basis of distance. Otherwise, the child who might benefit from a language school is denied that opportunity simply because their neighbourhood specialist school happens to be a technology college, and the language college is already full of children living within a mile and a half of its campus.

Diagnosing the problem is easier than delivering solutions. Several ideas are being considered in the run-up to a likely general election in 2005. The Conservatives have proposed a 'pupil passport', a sort of voucher which could be used to cover the full cost of educating a young person for a year in a state school or in a low cost independent school. The party suggests that they would improve the number of school places by preventing the reduction in surplus places in popular schools and by gradually prohibiting schools from using distance as a criterion to decide whom to admit. In some ways, the scheme is based on the voucher system which has been used with varying degrees of success in the USA. Aguably the most successful scheme has been in Milwaukee, Wisconsin where the vouchers are targeted on families with low incomes (though the Milwaukee scheme has been tarnished by the discovery that one of those setting up a new school under the scheme had a criminal record and that another school provided no lessons while taking the cash[3]). In that £75 million programme, schools cannot charge more than the £3,200 maximum value of the voucher. Crucially, there is a lottery to decide who gets in where a school has more applicants than places. The Conservative proposals also assume that popular schools will be able to expand to meet demand, and that they will want to do so.

But there are troubles with such a system. First, many parents will wish to apply to the same popular school which may be unable to cope with the demand. Even if the popular school can expand its number of places, this may cause a neighbouring school to become unviable through insufficient enrolment or the popular school to become too large. This is why there are school organisation committees (drawn from local schools) who decide between them where new places are needed and who recommend closure of unpopular or failing schools.

---

[3] Stephen Phillips, 'Voucher cons hit model scheme' (*Times Educational Supplement*, 16 April 2004).

Second, parental popularity can be a passing phase. It is remarkable how quickly a good popular school can decline when confidence in it is lost, perhaps through an unsuccessful leadership change. Money spent on expansion can end up being wasted and the cost effect on less popular schools could be very damaging for their pupils. But the biggest challenge of all is that popular, over-subscribed schools will still have to decide which children they admit. The challenge is not to provide choice for the few but to ensure that every child can enrol in a good school.

The Government has argued that the expansion of specialist schools is essential to delivering more choice for parents. But to do so with ten different specialisms on offer, it needs to give parents the chance to choose between these specialisms. One way it could do so – and this is a system which could also work with a voucher system – is to look to a system that City Technology Colleges have been legally required to use since their inception. This is banding by academic ability to ensure that schools achieve a comprehensive intake. It is possible to include with a banding system arrangements to accept children from both an inner and an outer catchment area. The law allows other options at present. Church schools can allocate places to members of the religious denomination for which the school is intended to cater. Most such schools cater for Anglicans or Catholics, although some Jewish, Muslim, Greek Orthodox and Sikh state schools have opened in recent years. Specialist schools can also give priority to pupils deemed to have a particular aptitude in certain subjects.

Priority by aptitude

It is legal for specialist schools to choose to offer a tenth of their places based on the aptitude of their pupils in certain subjects, though only around seven per cent of specialist schools choose to exercise this right. Where the system operates, admissions policies for specialist schools can give some priority to pupils who might particularly benefit from the school's specialism. The School Standards and Framework Act 1998 allows every school with a specialism in certain subjects to give priority to up to ten per cent of pupils who can demonstrate an aptitude in the relevant subject. Tests for aptitude must be related to the specific subject in which the school has a specialism and which is one of the subjects specified in the Education (Aptitude for Particular Subjects) regulations 1999.[4] Those subjects are:

- Modern foreign languages, or any such language;
- The performing arts, or any one or more of the performing arts including music;
- The visual arts, or any one or more of the visual arts;

---

[4] Available at http://www.legislation.hmso.gov.uk/si/si1999/1999 0258.htm.

- Physical education or sport, or one or more sports;
- Design and technology;
- Information technology.

There have been no similar regulations for more recent specialisms. Admission authorities – which are LEAs or individual voluntary-aided and foundation schools – determine how aptitude is assessed. They must ensure that tests do not assess general academic ability and are free of racial or gender bias. They should only assess aptitude for the subject in question. The Chief Schools Adjudicator, who decides on admissions issues when disputes with admission authorities arise, has ruled that schools who wish to select by aptitude must use either a well-established test or for sports and arts, where there is no such test, objective assessment by a qualified person independent of the school. To avoid breaching the *School Admissions Code of Practice*[5], schools are advised to check that the ability profile of those selected matches the ability profile of all applicants, and that the testing is adjusted if not.

There has been much controversy about the difference between ability and aptitude. The Labour Government changed the law so that no schools that were not already selecting on the basis of general academic ability could use that as a criterion in future. That position could change again under a future Conservative government, but it remains the legal position in 2004. The Chief Adjudicator, Philip Hunter has set out how he sees the difference:

> We can find a way through this by using the word 'ability' in the same way as we use 'achievement'. Ability is assessed using the normal tests used in schools and elsewhere – GCSEs, musical instrument grades, swimming proficiency certificates and so on. These are tests to find out what people can do. However 'aptitude' then means a gift or a talent. It denotes a potential or propensity to develop an ability given appropriate teaching or preparation. In other words aptitude + preparation = future ability. It is also important to find a means of assessing a specific aptitude that does not trespass into assessing ability or general aptitude. Aptitude tests are hard to come by but there are a few that have been developed for some subjects. There are tests for languages that rely on the propensity of children to recognise the meaning of non-familiar languages. Tests for aptitude in music assess the propensity of children to recognise pitch, rhythm, harmony and texture. Tests in spatial awareness can identify aptitude for design and technology. But be warned. Even these tests have a tendency to select general as well as specific aptitudes. Schools can correct for this by making sure that the pupils selected are spread across the ability range but that is an extra stage to go through. Aptitude tests for sport are being developed but not yet established. There are no aptitude tests

---

[5] DFES, *School Admissions Code of Practice* (London, The Stationery, Office, 2003). The code can be read in full at www.dfes.gov.uk/sacode.

yet for the arts. Here it seems reasonable to rely on the assessment of qualified coaches, directors or teachers.[6]

Given the difficulties which can be associated with determining attitude, many schools have chosen instead to develop a system which both allows them to offer a greater degree of choice to parents and ensures that they can achieve a broadly comprehensive intake of students. This is what is known in the law as 'fair banding'. In fact, it used to be operated across inner London by the Inner London Education Authority until its abolition in 1990, and survived in some boroughs afterwards. But it is perfectly within the law for any individual school to operate in this way. And if such a system were more widely adopted it has the potential to improve parental choice.

Banding

The Government's *School Admissions Code of Practice*, which is legally binding on schools and education authorities, makes clear that admission authorities which admit the first 10 per cent of children on the basis of aptitude may band the remaining 90 per cent. Alternatively, they may choose to band children first and then admit 10 per cent of each band on the basis of the relevant aptitude.[7] But they do not need to select any pupils on the basis of aptitude in order to introduce banding. Any school may decide that they want to allocate all of its places by putting all applicants into a series of at least three – and, in some cases, as many as nine – different ability bands. These bands can also be further refined by teachers when placing students in their initial ability sets for different subjects.

A school is permitted to use 'fair banding' by the School Standards and Framework Act, which means that banding must be used to ensure that a school's intake mirrors the ability of its applicants. The legal requirement is:

> the admission arrangements for a maintained school may make provision for selection by ability to the extend that the arrangements are designed to secure–
>
> (a) that in any year the pupils admitted to the school in any relevant age group are representative of all levels of ability among applicants for admission to the school in that age group, and
>
> (b) that no level of ability is substantially over-represented or substantially under-represented.[8]

---

[6] This and other judgements by the Chief Adjudicator can be read at www.schoolsadjudicator.gov.uk.

[7] *School Admissions Code of Practice* Annex A, A69.

[8] Section 101, School Standards and Framework Act 1998. Available at http://www.hmso.gov.uk/acts/acts 1998/1998 0031.htm.

While any school can decide that it wishes to introduce banding – and this will be a decision made by the governing body – schools planning to introduce banding must publish statutory proposals. They must allow other local schools and the education authority, as well as local parents, to give their views. The proposal is a notice alerting interested parties to the fact that the school intends to introduce banding, though it is not necessary to go into the detail of the proposed banding arrangements in the notice. However, it would make sense to be able to offer local newspapers, for example, good reasons why a school is introducing the new system, and an explanation of how the system could prove to be fairer for pupils. That may not prevent all objections: parents who have moved into what they thought was a catchment area for a popular school could resent the new admissions arrangements if they felt they reduced the chances of their child obtaining a place there. The details of the banding will be subject to the statutory consultation and the right of referral to the adjudicator, in the same way as other admission arrangements. However, provided the system is drawn up fairly, it ought to be possible to deal with any objections. And if banding were to be adopted much more widely – perhaps with official government encouragement – it would become far easier for individual schools.

How does banding work?

Under fair banding, all applicants are asked to sit a test of ability. Admission authorities – which can be individual schools – must themselves decide which tests to use. But when they do so, the law says they must ensure that they do not discriminate against children on the grounds of race or gender. Many specialist schools use the National Foundation for Educational Research (NFER) non-verbal reasoning test. Having sat the tests, the children should be ranked according to their results and placed in bands on the basis of their rank. It will be for admission authorities to decide how many bands they have and what proportion of pupils to place in each band – always having regard to the need to ensure that no level of ability is substantially under-represented or substantially over-represented. For example, if a school were to have three ability bands, it could decide to place the top 25 per cent ranked pupils in the top band, the next 50 per cent ranked pupils in the middle band, and the bottom 25 per cent ranked pupils in the bottom band. Alternatively, it might place pupils in five bands of 20 per cent, with the top 20 per cent of ranked pupils in the top band, the next 20 per cent in the second band, and so on.

Whatever number of bands is chosen, the proportion of applicants placed in each band must be mirrored by the proportion of applicants offered places from each band. In other words, if a school places the top 25 per cent of applicants in the top band, the middle 50 cent in the next band and the bottom 25 cent in the bottom band, then it must offer 25 per cent of its places to pupils from the top band, 50 per cent of its places to pupils in the middle band and 25 per cent to pupils in the bottom band. Banding schools cannot apply another test of ability once pupils are allocated to bands, so they cannot admit pupils in rank order of merit within bands. A banding school must admit all its applicants unless it has more applicants than places available. Where that is the case, it will have to apply its published over-subscription criteria. One way in which this can be achieved is through the use of catchment areas. But, as we have seen, this is increasingly being seen as encouraging a postcode lottery in admissions. This is where it can make sense to use a system which supports both local children and those living in a wider radius from the school.

Giving priority to non-local children

Some specialist schools simply wish to serve their local neighbourhood. But, as the choice of specialist schools increases, others believe that a balance should be struck between the needs of children living in the immediate vicinity of the school and those from further afield. Having a catchment area or areas does not mean that children from outside the catchment area cannot apply to a school under the Greenwich Judgement (see below). Parents can express a preference for their child to attend a particular school wherever they live. This is not affected by the existence of a catchment area or areas. However, where a school is over-subscribed, it can give priority in its admissions to those children who live within the catchment area or areas.

One way to achieve this could be to have two catchment areas. Local circumstances will vary. However, some specialist schools have decided to adopt an inner and an outer catchment area. The first catchment area might set a distance to facilitate the admission of children living in the immediate vicinity – perhaps those in a two mile radius, and the second area could cover children over a wider area, perhaps over a five mile radius. The inner area would cover all children living within two miles of the school, while the outer catchment area would cover those living between two and five miles from the school. Half of the school's places could be reserved for those in the inner catchment area or whichever proportion is preferred.

Admission authorities are responsible for drawing up their own catchment areas, but they should ensure that they reflect the diversity of the community served by the school. This means that the admission authority should carefully consider the potential impact of their arrangements on ethnic minority families and should also monitor the effect their arrangements have. The law – as decided by what has become known as the Greenwich Judgement – says that catchment areas should not be set so that a child is given priority simply because they live in the local authority where the school is situated.

On the buses: getting to and from school

However, simply setting fairer rules for admissions may not be enough. Getting to and from school is a real issue. And this is where it is important that schools and pupils have access to a decent system of home-to-school transport. Some schools run their own buses. Others depend on services provided by LEAs or contracted by their LEAs to private operators. But the public services are hindered by archaic rules which can make it difficult for pupils to access buses unless the LEA says that they should do so. The law expects children under eight to walk or cycle up to two miles to school, and older children to walk three miles. Only if no suitable school is available within these prescribed areas are children entitled to free transport to a more distant school. Apart from special needs, free buses are therefore often limited to rural areas or those attending distant denominational schools.

The result has been that a growing number of children are driven to school by their parents, exacerbating the school run. In 2001 39 per cent of primary school children were driven to school, up from 22 per cent in 1985. By contrast, the proportion walking to school fell from 67 to 54 per cent in the same period. Only 6 per cent used a bus in 2001, a drop from 9 per cent in 1985. Among secondary pupils, where distances travelled are greater, there was a similar pattern. The proportion walking fell from 52 to 43 per cent and the proportion being driven rose from 10 to 18 per cent, though bus usage did increase a little from 29 to 32 per cent.[9] If many of these cars were off the roads, there would be less traffic congestion, which has economic, environmental and social benefits, and children would travel to school more safely, reassuring parents worried about their children's safety.

A draft transport bill was published in March 2004, which is intended to give the go-ahead to as many as 20 English local authorities (and six Welsh ones) to charge school-bus fees to those children who are not entitled to free school meals. This would include many who could travel free under existing legislation. These experiments, which are likely to start in 2006, could last for up to three years. Each year LEAs spend £675 million on school transport, including £300 million on children with special needs. But for a small additional outlay – perhaps as little as £200 million a year – a universal subsidised bus scheme could be introduced which might be linked with new measures to enable students to attend schools

---

[9] Figures provided by the Department for Education and Skills.

beyond their immediate neighbourhood. This is an idea which is being promoted by Sir Peter Lampl, Chairman of the Sutton Trust, an educational charity. He argues that you could keep costs down and use buses more efficiently by staggering school start times, which might see classes starting earlier for many pupils, an approach which would also fit in with studies showing that pupils concentrate better in the morning. As Sir Peter points out, in the USA elementary schools start at 9 a.m., middle schools at 8.15 a.m. and high schools at 7.30 a.m. Many buses could then run two trips in the morning and the afternoon. Such a staggered system already operates in parts of West Sussex and on the Isle of Wight.

The Sutton Trust also notes that the top 200 performing state schools nationally (mainly grammar schools) are largely the preserve of the well off: just 3 per cent of their pupils are entitled to free school meals compared with a national average of 15 per cent. A combination of fairer admissions and accessible school transport could start to change this profile.

Expansion of popular schools

Expansion of popular schools is another option that can increase school choice. Both the Government and the opposition say that they want this to happen. But the ultimate decision is left in the hands of the local School Organisation Committee. This body, which operates in each LEA area, was established in the 1998 School Standards and Framework Act as a replacement for a system which left decisions with the LEA and, ultimately, the Secretary of State. It also has the responsibility for deciding on when new secondary schools should be established. In 2003, new regulations were passed designed to make it easier to set up new schools where standards demand it. Nevertheless, the procedures that schools must follow before expanding are complex.

The law says changes can be made to existing schools either by the LEA or the governing body of the school itself, where it is a voluntary-aided or a foundation school. But most significant changes require a school to publish statutory proposals and have them approved by the LEA or the School Organisation Committee. In some cases, where another admissions authority objects to the School Adjudicator, the final decision will be made by the Adjudicator. Since 2003, the Learning and Skills Council has had the right to make changes (subject to the final approval of the Secretary of State) to school sixth forms, which has put extra pressure on 11–18 schools to maintain and expand the size of their sixth forms. When new schools are proposed, LEAs must mount a competition process. This is intended to give voluntary bodies, faith groups, trusts and parents the opportunity to propose new models of school which may be different from those that an LEA might propose.

So, a popular school which wants to expand the number of pupils it admits each autumn – the standard number – will need to go through a long process. It must consult for several months before making any proposals, particularly with other schools in the area, parents and teachers who may be affected, the LEA and other interested parties such as the Diocese. The governors or LEA must then publish its plans, allowing a further six weeks for representations to the School Organisation Committee (or the LEA who must forward any objections to them). A shorter time is allowed for failing schools. The Committee will then make its decision. The government has promised to reduce the bureaucracy as part of its five year plan in 2004,

Conclusions

School choice may be the holy grail of politicians. But delivering it to every parent is another matter entirely. As we shall argue in Chapter 15, the limitations of school vouchers, which are fashionably suggested as the answer by some, are clear. The basic problem is that the system does not have the capacity to allow every parent to have the school of their choice. However, with the expansion of specialist schools, there is a chance for politicians to grasp the nettle of school choice. A start has been made by proposals for the partial deregulation of school transport, which suffers from ludicrously bureaucratic rules that exclude far too many children. Politicians must be braver and more radical in making school buses the norm for both primary and secondary school children. But a second shibboleth must also be overturned: that of the neighbourhood school. It is eminently sensible and environmentally wise to encourage local neighbourhood primary schools, and to try as far as possible to enable youngsters to have one within walking distance of their homes. By contrast, the rules on secondary admissions perpetuate a system which can only loosely be described as comprehensive, and where too many schools are the prisoner of their catchment area. As we have seen, a first step for many head teachers turning around failing schools is to try to improve the social mix of the school, by appealing to more middle-class families. If admissions are determined by the distance one lives from a school and by whether your sister or brother also goes there, the only parents who have real choice are those who can afford to live nearby. A much more equitable system would involve banding, where places were available both for local children and for those living further away. Their intake would reflect a full range of abilities. And, crucially, with good school transport and active recruitment outside the immediate neighbourhood, every school would be open to pupils of all backgrounds. This is the logic of moving most schools towards specialist status: without some form of banding and wider catchments, it cannot create the choice that is promised.

15

Lessons from abroad

The phrase 'not invented here' is one often used as a criticism by those who oppose attempts to replicate in this country educational innovations which have proven successful abroad. The reasons they give for their opposition are that our children are different from those in other countries, our school system is different and above all such innovations will not be popular with either parents or teachers because our culture is different. This attitude is clearly too simplistic but its prevalence should be recognised by those wishing to learn from relevant experience abroad in raising educational standards. It may not be helpful for the English school system to look to, say, Japan, but many other countries have more similar backgrounds and experience.

This chapter will study the differing systems of primary and secondary education in the USA, France and Germany and discuss whether there are lessons to be learned from their experience. Let us first consider recent developments in the USA. State funded US public schools, especially in urban areas, face enormous problems, which are often aggravated by concentrations in poverty and social deprivation, as well as the ethnically segregated nature of many public schools. There is much we can learn from the many initiatives currently being trialled in the USA in order to raise standards.

American public schools: the original comprehensives

The concept of large, all-ability neighbourhood schools admitting pupils with a wide range of ability from a relatively narrow catchment area was first developed in the USA. Indeed, its ethos and philosophy ran directly contradictory to the framework established by the 1944 British Education Act (the Butler Act) which planned a tripartite system of grammar schools (with their admissions being determined by ability), secondary moderns and technical schools. Largely as a result of the unpopularity of the 11 plus examination which determined entry to grammar schools, the concept of the American style comprehensive school became increasingly popular in England and they were introduced widely in the sixties and seventies. Harvard President James Bryant Conant's 1959 book *The American High School Today* (see www.beacon.org/k-12/high-schools-intro.html) was especially influential. But that is not the end of the story. There has been a close relationship between policy developments in the two countries since.

Magnet schools and specialist schools

British specialist schools and their predecessors, the City Technology Colleges (CTCs), owe their very existence to the development in the seventies and eighties of the American magnet schools. These schools were originally developed for the purpose of racial integration; the idea was that concentrating resources in a particular school as well as choosing a particular academic focus, such as science, would attract pupils from different social backgrounds and thus be an alternative strategy to busing to achieve racial integration. They were also partly developed as a result of concerns about the academic standards achieved by 'one size fits all' comprehensive schools. Magnet schools are typically 14 to 18 high schools which specialise in a particular field of study such as mathematics, science or the performing arts.

At their peak there were many hundreds of them and a considerable number of excellent schools such as the Bronx College of Mathematics and Science still exist. Many were so outstanding in their academic performance that they became highly selective. Others are so popular that they choose pupils by a lottery. It is ironic that the broad concept of magnet schools, though first developed in the USA, have become so popular in England through the development of specialist schools, yet the whole concept now attracts little attention in many areas of America. Opposition from local school boards and unions, both of whom perceived magnet schools as a threat to their influence, played a big role in hindering their expansion. In addition, not all magnet school experiments were successful. In Kansas City, for example, magnet schools were mandated by the Federal Judge as a way of integrating the public school system. Sadly this initiative did not achieve its objectives (see www.cato.org/pubs/pas/pa-298es.html).

From magnet schools to charter schools

The charter schools, which are now a common feature of the American school system, are a development of the original magnet school principle. There are around 3,000 charter schools currently in operation across 37 states and serving

685,000 students, and the movement has developed during the 1990s as various state legislatures mandated their establishment. Their numbers continue to grow as more states back the movement.

Charter schools are non-sectarian public schools which are free from many of the regulations that apply to other public schools. In return for this freedom, they must agree a 'charter' or performance contract which sets out the school's mission, programme, goals, students served, assessment methods and ways to measure success. Charters are typically granted for three to five years, which may be renewed. Charter schools are accountable to their sponsor – usually a state or local school board – to produce good results. Increased autonomy comes in return for this accountability. One of the more popular – and controversial – providers is the private sector Edison Schools, a publicly owned profit making company which has about 25,000 students in its charter schools.

Charter schools are usually newly established schools, both primary and secondary, often occupying leased school buildings set up under an agreement with either the state or the local school board under which the organiser receives all the theoretical per capita funding per pupil authorised by the school budget – that is the total school budget divided by the number of pupils. The movement's success has been mixed. Some charter schools have been successful in raising standards; others have not and have had their funding agreements revoked.

One of the difficulties is the lack of a coherent curriculum framework similar to that used so successfully by the original City Technology Colleges initiative in the UK, and now by the Academy programme. This is because education in the USA is primarily the responsibility of the 50 individual states and not of the Federal Government. Even within individual states, school boards exercise considerable power and independence, thus making it difficult to have a simple framework for charter schools even within one state. This is why companies like Edison, which provide their own programmes for all their schools, have been able to grow.

Charter schools have nevertheless considerably improved levels of accountability for American schools, since like specialist schools in England, renewal of their agreement depends upon delivery of improvement in standards. And this is one lesson which we can and should share with the USA. Both the new Academies, through their funding agreements between sponsors and the DfES, and specialist schools, through their bids for both the initial award and the renewal of specialist status, should continue to be accountable for their results or lose their status. Some schools would become complacent without the re-designation process.

Successful charter schools reinforce the lesson of many of our own schools that it is possible to achieve significant improvement in failing schools in socially disadvantaged areas, providing that the vested interests opposed to change such as some teaching unions or bureaucratic school systems, have their powers curtailed.

LEA and teaching union opposition to the establishment of CTCs in the 1980s made their expansion difficult. Fortunately, there is a more positive attitude being shown by many LEAs to the development of Academies today, with UK cities, like their more forward-looking US counterparts, seeing the benefits that autonomy and real accountability can bring towards improving schools.

Vouchers

If magnet schools and charter schools have largely operated within the parameters of the public school system in the USA, with contracts normally drawn with states and cities, the development of school vouchers has taken the debate one stage further. Many US educational reformers are attracted by the idea that parents should be given a voucher which is equivalent to the value of the theoretical per capita sum spent on state schools and be allowed to take that voucher to any school, whether public or private or religious, to pay for the education of their child. In an ideal world, this should produce a massive increase in choice as well as subjecting schools to the accountability of the market. However, despite the many years during which vouchers have been discussed and a number of small-scale experiments, the most interesting of which is in Milwaukee, Wisconsin, there has so far been no successful large-scale test of vouchers in the USA. A reasonable large-scale experiment with vouchers is just commencing in Washington DC.

One reason why the Milwaukee experiment has been more interesting than others is that it is very carefully targeted at youngsters from disadvantaged backgrounds. The value of the voucher is fixed and schools cannot introduce 'top up fees' by charging more than that sum. But, the main impact of most voucher schemes in the USA, where public schools cannot be run by the churches, is to enable parents to gain free or subsidised places at fee-paying religious schools. That is not an issue in the UK, where we have a long tradition of supporting church schools on a similar basis to other state schools. Indeed, the present government has sought to expand this tradition to support more Christian, Jewish, Muslim, Orthodox and Sikh schools.

But unless vouchers are limited to poorer families (as has been the case in most voucher experiments in the USA), they would give middle-class families, who already pay for their children to attend private schools, a massive financial windfall. In the UK, where 580,000 children from middle- and upper-class families attend 2,300 private schools, an unrestricted voucher scheme would require an increase in the overall education budget of £2.1 billion. It is certainly questionable whether this would be the most efficient use of limited taxpayers' resources.

Under the present system of local management of schools (LMS), established by Kenneth Baker in the 1980s 'money follows the pupil'. Of the total school budget

87 per cent is delegated to individual schools for spending determined by the head teacher and governors *and* the funding of a school is directly linked to its number of pupils, with schools in general being funded on a per capita basis. Most of the balance is spent by LEAs either on special needs or school transport. There is therefore already considerable accountability built into the system.

But the most difficult issue is admissions. It is all very well promising parents that they will be able to choose where to send their child, implying that the existence of the vouchers will in itself produce sufficient places to guarantee choice.

Even without vouchers, the number of parents not getting their chosen schools has risen. In part, that may reflect the fact that there is much better information these days about schools. But it also makes it hard to see why simply transferring that money to a paper voucher would necessarily improve choice. Many parents would still be unable to gain admission for their children to the schools of their choice since these schools are already or would become substantially over-subscribed. In such circumstances, schools would still either have to use the admissions criteria described in the previous chapter or resort to some other form of selection, which would be unlikely to benefit the poorest pupils. Without massive capital expenditure on the popular schools to increase their capacity or investment in new schools, many parents would be disappointed in exercising their voucher at the school of their choice.

Concurrent with the introduction of LMS, British schools have been made even more accountable by having their examination results published both locally and nationally. However, until recently there has been a significant weakness – failing, underperforming schools with falling school rolls, instead of being closed and reopened under new management, were propped up by special subsidies. This policy has changed. Underperforming schools in England now must either improve or risk closure, sometimes to be re-established as an Academy. Well over 100 failing schools have been closed since 1997.

There is a third objection to vouchers in the USA, which constitutionally forbids the funding of religious schools by the taxpayer. The American system does not therefore have the detailed scrutiny applied in this country to the establishment of new religious schools. Without this safeguard, giving parents vouchers could stimulate schools set up by extremist religious sects. In order to prevent this in the UK, schools funded by vouchers would be required to teach the National Curriculum as well as meet minimum standards with inspection by Ofsted.

Lessons from the state of Georgia

Under the inspirational leadership of Governor Zell Miller, who also served as a US senator, the state of Georgia transformed its schools in the nineties.

One initiative of particular interest has been the development of the P–16 Initiative introduced in Georgia in 1995 – P stands for pre-school learning of basic literacy and numeracy skills, especially in the rural areas, through the establishment of preschool learning centres; 16 stands for the last year of a four-year undergraduate degree course.

A key requirement of the P–16 Initiative is that elementary schools (equivalent to primary schools here) must work with middle schools; middle schools must collaborate with high schools; and high schools must work with further and higher education. David Blunkett, who met Governor Miller in London in 1997, introduced an element of this thinking when he required specialist schools to spend a third of their extra funding on supporting their feeder primary schools.

HOPE Scholarships and the funding of links between high schools and universities

Governor Miller provided the funding for links between high schools and further and higher education by launching his HOPE Scholarship Lottery. The first state lottery to be launched in the South, this lottery now raises substantial sums each year for the HOPE Scholarships. Under this initiative, all resident Georgia students who achieve and maintain a B average in high school, are given free tuition at a Georgia state university, providing they maintain this average. They are also required to mentor high school students while at university. A number of other American states have P–16 or K–16 or K–20 initiatives (K = Kindergarten). Several states also have versions of the HOPE Scholarship idea.

The development of close links between schools and universities in the UK could be mutually beneficial to both of them. The Specialist Schools Trust has already launched a number of initiatives to do this, including the sponsoring of 15 science specialist schools by GlaxoSmithKline in co-operation with Imperial College, the sponsoring of a similar number of schools in West Yorkshire by NM Rothschild in partnership with Leeds University, and the sponsorship of 15 London Schools by Goldman Sachs working closely with the London School of Economics. Among the benefits of these partnerships are continuous professional development for school teachers with access being provided for them to take post-graduate courses, sometimes online; the identification of gifted and talented children at an early age and the provision of courses for these children both on Saturdays and in the summer; and finally support of teachers in subjects such as science where technological developments are rapid and teachers need to be retrained in the latest scientific developments.

There has also been an encouraging development in the number of links between inner city schools and leading universities like Oxford and Cambridge, based on the summer school concept, initially developed by the Sutton Trust, and now funded by government through the National Academy for Gifted and Talented Youth.

Testing

Although the USA lags behind the UK in the use of national examinations such as GCSE and A Levels, as well as the Key Stage national tests in primary schools and secondary schools, the USA has developed expertise in mass testing including the Scholastic Assessment Tests (SATs) and Advanced Placement Tests used to enable the most able to take college level courses while still at high school. These tests have been developed by the College Board (www.collegeboard.com) and the Educational Testing Service (www.ets.org). They are taken primarily by students aged 16 and 17 and are used by universities in their selection of students. Many UK universities are concerned about the difficulties in assessing applicants based solely on A Levels. And the introduction of SATs is one measure which has been considered. A recent study by the Sutton Trust[1] shows that the use of SAT style tests in the UK would provide a useful supplement to A Levels in determining the potential of pupils to benefit from a university education. Some states are also introducing tests similar to the British Key Stage tests.

Raising performance in New York City

Some US cities have been more successful than others in raising standards. Programmes such as those developed in Chicago, for example, have been better advanced than those in New York City, which faces an extraordinary combination of poverty and social problems; lack of accountability; entrenched unions and undue concentration of power in school boards. This heady brew has led to disturbingly low levels of achievement. New York's Mayor Bloomberg and Schools Chancellor Klein have initiated radical reform of the system, including bringing accountability into the school system. Schools must produce annual reports giving details of the performance of their children including attendance and standards in literacy and numeracy. Third graders are no longer automatically promoted to the fourth grade if their literacy level does not justify this. The previous three tier system of bureaucracy with local, regional and city school boards has been streamlined, saving $250 million a year in bureaucratic office jobs. The Mayor and Chancellor are also seeking to reduce the size of schools, many of which have 3,000 or 4,000 pupils, into smaller units with funding provided by Bill Gates.

---

[1] *Aptitude Testing for University Entrance: A literature review* available at www.suttontrust.com.

Table 15.1 Ethnic mix at Louis D. Brandeis High School compared with other New York City Schools (*Source*: Louis D. Brandeis High School 2004)

	Louis D. Brandeis High School (%)	All NY City schools (%)
White	2	16
African American	37	35
Hispanic	59	35
Asian and others	2	14
	100	100

It will take time for these reforms to show results as the problems facing New York City schools are so immense.

Perhaps a typical such school is the Louis D. Brandeis High School situated on the west side at 84th Street. This school is led by an outstanding principal, Dr Eloise Messineo, supported by an able team of administrators and staff. The school has 2,338 pupils. The majority of its students are from an Hispanic background and over a third are of African American origin. Just 2 per cent of the pupils are white and a further 2 per cent Asian (Table 15.1). Black and Hispanic pupils traditionally underachieve in American schools, while Asian pupils typically do better in exams than their white counterparts. Attendance at the school is 77 per cent, still poor, but significantly better than two years ago when it was 71 per cent. Eighty-three per cent of pupils are entitled to a free lunch compared to 54 per cent for all New York City schools.

One of the school's biggest problems is mobility and drop out. Only 189 of the 1,000 pupils who enter the school at age 14 graduate from the school four years later – less than 20 per cent.

Traditionally, New York City schools were more poorly funded than those in the wealthier up state areas. But in recent years the proportion of the total funding available to spend in schools actually spent inside the schools has risen dramatically. Overall, New York City has a school budget of $12 billion for 1.1 million children or a theoretical average of $11,000 per pupil. Parochial schools, mostly Catholic, typically charge $4,000 per head. Brandeis currently receives $9,500 for direct costs, or 87 per cent of the average total available, a devolution figure close to the UK average. This is a considerable increase over the total in 2001 when it was just $7,968 or 72 per cent. It should also make it easier for New York schools to recruit teachers – the city suffered shortages more acute than those in London, because of huge differentials in salary with better paid teachers in richer districts outside the city.

One of the techniques used by Brandeis High School, which some English schools are starting to consider, is the use of safety officers, though not in the same numbers. Brandeis has 15 such officers, who are seconded from the Police Department to maintain order in the corridors, provide security and supervise entry. An increasing number of English schools are now using this approach with an estimated one quarter of London schools having a resident police officer. Brandeis has also benefited in recent years through a support group of artists and musicians recruited by Diane Volk, a distinguished New York City lawyer, now devoting much of her time to helping schools. With her encouragement opera singers and other musicians regularly come to the school on a voluntary basis to work with the students. This has improved the commitment of pupils to learning. Another, more controversial measure, is the provision at the city's expense of a crèche for some 18 children aged three months to four years. The crèche is for the benefit of children of the school's pupils, the youngest of the mothers being 14. By providing a crèche, the school has succeeded in keeping the mothers in school. There are 40 such nurseries in schools around the city. These are all small steps in turning around one of the biggest school systems in the USA.

On the other side of Manhattan, in Harlem, one can find St Paul's Catholic School for 300 pupils aged four to 13. The school was founded by the philanthropist Bill Ruane who personally led a campaign to renovate several nearby blocks of rundown housing. The school occupies buildings donated by the Catholic Church, on land which was originally intended to be used for the Manhattan Cathedral. The school charges its parents only $2,500 a year. But since many families cannot afford even those fees, Mr Ruane pays them himself. He personally supports 68 children as part of a wider bid to regenerate the local area and improve the lives of the local community. There is calm and order in the school, led by its outstanding principal, Agnes Sayaman. The school emphasises reading skills using Renaissance Learning's Accelerated Reading programme. If such a good education can be provided for only $2,500 compared to a typical $11,000 a head in city schools, questions must be asked about the wisdom of the US constitutional ban on any aid to such church-led parochial schools. It will be interesting to see how the current case on this issue before the United States Supreme Court will be resolved.

Cisco and Oracle academies

Another successful technique to raise standards in inner city American schools has been the introduction of Cisco and Oracle academies in schools, with several thousand such academies having been established so far. These academies train 16 to 18-year-olds in computer skills leading to the award of industry standard diplomas. Students who pass these tests are able to obtain well paid jobs in the

IT sector. W.C. Overfelt High School in San José, California, has a very successful Oracle academy which is over-subscribed and has contributed to improving test scores at the school. Most of its 1,728 students are Hispanic, with a significant number of Filipino or Vietnamese. Courses typically last a year and have rigorous online assessment. The Cisco Certified Network Associate (CCNA) diploma has 280 hours of formal instruction, part of which is online with the remainder being laboratory work. Cisco academies are very popular in the USA and worldwide with 6,000 academies having been established. Cisco academies have been introduced into some 300 English specialist schools with considerable success. A similar initiative has now been agreed with Oracle, with sponsorship of 80 such academies in specialist schools.

Learning from French schools

In France, education is required for all children from the ages of six to 16, but a very large proportion, nearly 90 per cent of students, transfer at age 15 or 16 to a *Lycée d'Enseignement Générale et Technologique* or to a *Lycée Professionnel* or *Lycée Technique* to study for the baccalaureate. Each type of *lycée* prepares for different types of *baccalauréat* (*bac*) namely *général* (academic), *technique* (technology or specialised field like social care, basic accountancy, secretarial skills etc.) and *professionnel* (vocational). Success in this examination at age 18 entitles students to enter university. It is a goal of the French Ministry of Education that 80 per cent of all French students will pass the baccalaureate. Currently, the proportion of pupils passing the *bac* is about two-thirds.

The French state education system is centrally administered by the French Ministry for Education.[2] It is well funded and generally standards are high. The state system is complemented by a large network of private schools which account for 15 per cent of pupils (13 per cent at primary level, nearly 20 per cent at secondary level). Whatever their background, pupils attending *l'ecole republicaine* and the vast majority of partially state-funded private schools are expected to follow a curriculum devised at national level by the *Ministère de l'éducation nationale* and delivered locally by teachers who are themselves trained and selected through a set of national (for secondary) or regional (for primary) competitive examinations. Children are required to do more homework than in English schools and have high expectations from their teachers.

---

[2] Key information about the French system is provided in English on the French Ministry of Education website (www.education.gouv.fr) if you search for 'State of education', and French Entrée (www.frenchentree.com) which offers an introduction to French state education.

Like German schools, French schools require each child to achieve a minimum standard before moving to the next level. This system of *redoublement* or retaking a year is not unusual in French education and the system is designed to allow pupils to do this without stigma or hindrance to their future potential. There are perhaps lessons to be learned between the two nations as we develop a system of allowing students to take exams such as their Key Stage 3 tests or their GCSEs when they are ready. So far, this has typically meant students doing a few GCSEs a year or two earlier than their peers. In the future, the chance to do such exams later may have important implications for the organisation of classes.

The French education system is divided up into nursery schools for ages two to five (*écoles maternelles*), primary schools for ages six to ten (*écoles primaires*) and secondary schools for pupils aged 11 to 18. Students at the secondary level start in the *collège* or junior high school where they stay until they are 15. At age 15, students sit a written test (*brevet des collèges*) in French, mathematics, history and geography. This acts as the entrance examination to a *lycée*. Poor performance in this test does not exclude students from higher education as this test serves as an end of secondary certificate of achievement in the aforementioned subjects.

French *lycées* are akin to a US high school or English sixth form college. It is perhaps the most respected part of the French state education system and leads to the prestigious baccalaureate which gives automatic entry to university. Most pupils enter the general and technology *lycée* (*Lycée d'Enseignement Générale et Technologique*) which prepares students for the general or technology baccalaureate or a technical diploma (*brevet de technicien*). Approximately one-third of 15 to 16-year-olds enter the *lycées professionnels* which prepare students for vocational and technical diplomas. There are also a number of *lycées professionnels* and *Centres de Formation d'Apprentis* (CFA) leading to vocational certificates.

Students in *lycées* study a broadly based curriculum in at least six main subjects including at least one foreign language. Students who opt for more vocational studies during secondary education may apply either to enrol in a vocational *lycée* (*lycée professionnel*) or a technical *lycée*. These students study for either the *Brevet des Etudes Professionelles* (BEP) or the *Certificat d'Aptitude Professionelle* (CAP) or even the *Baccalauréat Professionnel*. These options have proved very popular in recent years (especially the *Baccalauréat Professionnel*, which was precisely created in order to improve traditional perceptions of vocational qualifications as second rate) and have led to successful employment in a vast range of trades, commerce and industry.

Students in *lycées* with particularly high standards may prepare for entry into the *Grandes Ecoles* by studying for another two years after their *Baccalauréat Général*. These unique higher education institutions, roughly comparable in prestige to universities such as Oxford, Cambridge and Imperial College, have great standing and their graduates dominate the professional class in France.

Another interesting special focus of *lycées* is their teaching of foreign languages, usually English, German and Spanish. Many *lycées* have *sections européennes* which teach one or several subjects of the *bac* through the medium of a foreign language.

The key issue to consider from the French system of education is perhaps the breadth required by the baccalaureate examination which requires study in six subjects. There is also a more coherent system of vocational education with the *lycées professionnels et techniques*. Finally there is a far greater emphasis on the teaching of foreign languages.

LC–SE Project

Following a meeting between Jacques Lang, the then French Minister of Education in 2001 with the Specialist Schools Trust, over 100 English language colleges were linked with a similar number of French *lycées* with *sections européennes*. This became the LC–SE Project.

There is a general consensus between the English and French schools that for a successful partnership, there needs to be a particular focus. One way to do this is to move beyond the traditional exchanges of letters and e-mails by penpals in the two schools to look at topics that can support the curriculum more directly. Successful projects have covered towns, festivals, historic events, the monarchy, music, films, geography and the environment. Whatever the topic, the organisers believe it tends to work best if it is agreed by the pupils themselves.

There are several important benefits from such international links. For a start, developing links across borders broadens the mind and erases geographical and cultural barriers. They are also an imaginative use of ICT, making it possible to 'travel' abroad without taking a physical journey. Educational partnerships play their part in helping pupils to become more sociable, more flexible and more able to adapt to a changing world. And the possible inclusion of a third partner from another European country, which some schools have developed, can further foster an awareness of European culture, particularly significant in the light of the expansion and growing importance of the European Union.

This pioneering partnership between French and English schools has been so successful that the Trust is now seeking to establish a four-way partnership between English, French, German and Spanish schools. There is substantial funding available through the European Union's Comenius and Lingua projects but sadly so far, English schools have been unable to access this funding. This is because of the way funding of schools in England relates to the narrowly drawn additionality rules which require European Union funding to be restricted to projects jointly funded by both the individual country and the European Union. It is hoped that officials in both the UK Treasury and the European Union will agree that the English specialist school language colleges funding meets the matched funding requirement and this encourages the development of many links between schools in the four countries.

Learning from German schools

The current German school system was radically changed in the 1960s. Being an industrial country with almost no raw materials, Germany is largely dependent upon a skilled workforce and its educational system reflects this concern. But while the vocational system remains a strength of the system, there has also been considerable angst in Germany recently about the country's poor showing on international surveys of secondary school standards.

German children start school at age six when they attend primary school (*Grundschule*) for four years until they are ten. According to their talents (as recommended by teachers) and their preferences, children at age 11 transfer to one of four types of secondary school. All the different types of school require the study of at least one foreign language. Most students learn English but some learn French or Russian – particularly those in East Germany. A particular aspect of German schools is that students who perform poorly have to repeat a year.

There are four main types of school.[3] The *Hauptschule* is geared towards students who wish to do an apprenticeship (*Lehre*) when they have finished school, and is attended by around 22 per cent of students. Thus the main emphasis is on teaching practical skills. Students attend *Hauptschule* for six years from 11 to 16 and then transfer to an apprenticeship while attending a further education college. The *Realschule* offers a broader, more general education than the *Hauptschule*, but has a similar proportion of students, though some *Länder* (or provinces) have tried to combine the two – and schools offering both strands now educate nearly one in ten German students. Students may learn a second foreign language and are expected to work more independently than in a *Hauptschule*. However, in comparison with the *Gymnasium*, the *Realschule* offers a more vocationally orientated education. Students attend the *Realschule* between the years of 11 and 16 and then transfer to a further education college (*Berufsfachschule*) while also serving as an apprentice. Students who attend the *Gymnasium* (similar to an English grammar school) attend school from 11 to 18

---

[3] For more information on the German education system, visit www.inca.org.uk, from where statistics used in this section were drawn.

or 19 to study for the very daunting *Abitur* diploma, similar to the French *Baccalauréat*. Nearly 30 per cent of pupils attended a *Gymnasium* in 2000. The *Gymnasium* is intended for students who wish to study at university or technical college (*Fachhochschule*). Considerable emphasis is put on academic learning and students can specialise in certain areas.

In 1969, a new type of school, the *Gesamtschule* (comprehensive school) was introduced but it has not been adopted universally in Germany. Fewer than one in ten pupils attend them. Education policy is determined at the German *Länder* level. The 16 *Bundesländer* in Germany each have their own Ministry of Education and exercise considerable autonomy. There are 203 comprehensive schools in North Rhein-Westphalia but only three each in Bavaria and Baden-Württemburg.

The simple, most important lesson for the UK to learn from Germany is the excellence of its vocational training or its so-called dual system. Of the students who finish post primary school 70 per cent go to work as an apprentice in a company, workshop, private business or industry. However, unlike most other countries, the training that 16-year-olds gain at the workplace is supplemented by part-time enrolment at a vocational school (*Berufsschule*). The so-called dual system in Germany which combines work experience with specialist theoretical knowledge is one of the principle reasons for the highly skilled German workforce.

The dual system has the advantage, unlike the UK, of giving high status to vocational training, possibly because it dates back to the craft skills taught by the guilds in the Middle Ages. Transfer of German practice into an English setting is not straightforward, but the Government would be well advised to study the German dual system in depth before trying to accomplish too much within the single diploma which was expected to be proposed by the Tomlinson Review of 14–19 education, due to report by the autumn of 2004.

Conclusions

In some ways, the UK is at the cutting edge of school reform. Our levels of accountability are generally higher than those in other countries, and our systems of testing and inspection more advanced. Other countries understandably look to us for lessons in how to improve their own systems in this regard.

But there are areas where we can learn from others. Developments in literacy and numeracy, for example, were strongly influenced by the experience of Australia and New Zealand, and there is much shared practice between our nations. The charter and magnet school movement in the USA has influenced diversity in the British school system, through specialist schools, CTCs and

Academies. But we should be wary about embracing a national system of school vouchers, when the results of limited experiments in the USA are as yet unproven. There is much that we can share with each other about urban school reform, where the challenges are similar, if magnified in places like New York. And policymakers can benefit from avoiding reinventing the wheel.

Some aspects of the French and German systems are particularly worthy of examination, not least as the Government seeks to reform 14–19 education. The clearest is the value of a good vocational education system, where equal status is provided not by trying to create a 'parity of esteem' or a commonality of content for a shared diploma, but where the practical nature of the vocational is regarded as no less valuable than the theoretical nature of the academic. There are merits in the baccalaureate approach, which some UK schools have seen replicated in the International Baccalaureate. But one area which is more controversial, yet surely demands further inquiry, is the question of whether students should be able (and expected) to repeat years when they fail to achieve an expected standard. Clearly, such a system can present problems, particularly where failure is repeated. But with the system moving towards a more flexible attitude of taking tests and exams when students are ready, these are questions that government should consider.

16

Good schools manage their finances well and learn how to raise sponsorship

Spending on England's schools has been rising in recent years. In secondary schools it is now approximately £5,000 per head including all grants. Head teachers and governors have also gained greater control over their budgets. Many secondary schools have budgets of around £5 million a year, greater than many businesses. Secondary schools could be categorised as medium-sized employers; indeed, in rural areas, they may be the largest local employer. There is more money available for capital building and repair projects, particularly in secondary schools, than for several decades. Yet budgeting remains a difficult and challenging business. There is never enough money to do everything that schools would wish. Moreover, although school incomes have been rising faster than inflation, so have staff pay bills, as performance related pay and shortened incremental scales put pressure on costs. There are new expectations for support staff, who have acquired a long overdue salary scale to go with their new status. And while ICT may be saving time and enabling more interesting lessons, it has brought rising expectations, new maintenance costs and new staffing needs. How do schools cope with these changes? How do they maximise opportunities for innovation and income? And are there other ways to bring revenue into school budgets?

Spending in schools has grown, but where has it gone?

Until 1999, schools had got used to funding being restricted. If they were lucky, there might be enough money to cover the annual teachers' pay rise. Governments even phased in the pay increases to help them balance the budget. There had been occasional spurts of spending to coincide with general elections, but money was tight. There was little to spend on extras, like computers or books; repairs often had to be put off; and new buildings were rare. The school stock was badly in need of a major overhaul. There had been some improvements: local management of schools (LMS) had given every head teacher and the governing bodies greater control over how just under 80 per cent of total school spending was used. This allowed savings to be made when broken windows needed replacing. There was more choice over who did the catering or managed the playing fields. Grant-maintained schools had been given greater budgetary freedoms, so much so that some claimed they had an unfair advantage over the majority of schools. But for most schools, budgeting was about a difficult balancing of the books.

Between 1994–5 and 1999–2000, total current spending on schools rose from £18,981 million to £19,623 million in real terms, an increase of just over three per cent in five years.[1] Once Gordon Brown introduced three-year spending reviews in 1999, things began to change. There were increases of between five and six per cent a year (after inflation). These will continue until 2005–6, after which they are set to fall back to around 3·5 per cent a year. Total spending on education in England is set to be £63·9 billion in 2007–8 compared with £29·8 billion in 1997–8. The result is that actual spending per pupil will be £3,000 more than ten years previously. Capital spending is also rising rapidly: barely a billion pounds a year was being invested by central and local government throughout the late nineties. More than £6 billion will be invested in 2007–8.[2]

Yet many schools find it hard to reconcile these figures with the difficulties they face each year balancing their budgets. Of course, they do see where new buildings have been built or when new staffing posts have been created. But the changes in their revenue seem less dramatic. There are good reasons for this. The main change has been in teachers' and head teachers' pay. The average teacher's pay rose from £23,197 in 1997 to £29,365 in April 2002, 13 per cent above inflation (or an additional £172 per pupil in real terms a year).[3] This reflects the introduction of performance related pay, which gave experienced staff increases initially of more than £2,000 a year followed by at least two payments on the upper pay spine. But there have been other changes too: the pay scale for new teachers has been shortened from seven to five years, giving many teachers larger incremental increases below the threshold for performance pay. Starting salaries have risen and there have been extra one-off incentives for some specialists. More teachers have been recruited too, sometimes to address rising rolls. There has been a new leadership scale, with some head teachers (though not many) able to earn in excess of £100,000 a year. And there have been significant increases in the

---

[1] Figures from DFEE and Ofsted, *Departmental Report 2000* (London, The Stationery Office, 2000).
[2] Figures from *Hansard* 18 March 2004. Available at www.parliament.uk.
[3] Figures from Conor Ryan, 'How are we doing? Very well actually' (*Times Educational Supplement*, 28 November 2003).

weighting payments given to those living in or near London. There has also been a big growth in support staff, with more teaching assistants and secretaries in most secondary schools. Add to this higher national insurance and pension contributions; and with salaries making up in excess of 80 per cent of most school budgets, staffing costs have eaten much of the extra money.

A second factor has been the growth of targeted funding. The Standards Fund, which replaced the old 'grants for education support and training (GEST)' were worth £3,288 million in 2003–4[4] compared with £356 million in 1997–8. While the money was initially carefully earmarked for programmes from learning support units to staff professional development, there is now more freedom for schools in how they use their budgets. Attempts to shift some Standards Fund budgets into the general pot in 2003–4 were one reason why some schools faced budgeting difficulties: the Standards Fund budget was often targeted at deprived schools. And that has created another problem: schools with largely better-off intakes have not seen as much extra money as those with a greater preponderance of poorer students or those with language difficulties. A third factor has been the growing costs of new technology, which is part-funded through Standards Fund grants. Not only are all schools connected to the Internet, many have broadband access, video-conferencing facilities and interactive whiteboards. Teachers have had to be trained. Maintenance contracts are needed. There are increasing numbers of terminals and desktops (the latter also received specific government funding). Spending per pupil on ICT in secondary schools was £69 per pupil in 2003 (it had peaked at £81 in 2002) compared with £46 in 1998.[5]

Direct funding: challenges and opportunities through LMS

However, it is worth balancing these factors with some aspects of the budget that schools will have noticed most. Around 87 per cent of school spending now goes directly to schools, compared with 79 per cent in 1997. That has meant that some things once provided by the LEA must now be purchased by the school. But it also gives head teachers and governors greater freedom over nearly £2.5 billion worth of expenditure each year. Add to that the introduction of the School Standards Grant and formula capital, which is worth around £180,000 a year to the typical secondary school in 2004 – and schools have around £530 per pupil of extra spending to use directly on their priorities each year. This has not been a benefit

---

[4] Figures from *Hansard* 26 Feb 2004, includes local authority contributions where appropriate.

[5] *Survey of Information and Communications Technology in Schools* (DfES, 2003). Full survey is available on the Internet only at www.dfes.gov.uk/rsgateway/DB/SBU/b000421/index.shtml.

seen by all schools: grant-maintained schools, many of which became foundation schools after the 1998 School Standards and Framework Act, had their budgets frozen in real terms for several years until other schools caught up with them in terms of funding per pupil. Some are only now seeing their budgets rise. And the Government's decision to change the formula by which it distributed local government funding limited the increases seen by many schools, particularly in London and the South East, so much so that some faced serious budgetary difficulties in 2003–4. Add to that the fluctuations caused by falling rolls, and it is easy to see how the increased funding can be so readily absorbed by so many schools.

What should schools spend their budgets on?

Benchmarking can be a useful way for schools to compare what they spend on different aspects of their budget with what similar schools are spending. For example, the typical school will spend around 80 per cent of its budget on staffing, but when that proportion starts to creep up towards 90 per cent the school could face real difficulties if staffing costs grow unexpectedly or when faced with the need to hire extra supply teachers due to illness or other factors. Schools can also see whether their investment in professional development or ICT is reasonable or not. They can gauge how much they are spending per pupil on school meals or maintenance and repairs: it can help to see how others are doing to judge whether contracts are offering good value for money. The DfES offers schools benchmarking software online (at www.dfes.gov.uk/valueformoney) which enables such comparisons to be made easily. Schools which are putting out to tender services such as school meals or cleaning, need to prepare detailed specifications to avoid a contractor not delivering all that is expected of him. They need to develop effective measures of performance to assess the quality of delivery. They should also look at poten- tial alternative suppliers so that proper comparisons can be made and value for money assured. The DfES website also provides schools with guidance on consistent financial reporting, which is encouraged by both the Audit Commission and Ofsted.

Some schools find it useful to save money by setting up purchasing consortia with other schools – this might include a secondary school and its feeder primaries, for example. The consortium approach can produce efficiencies and economies of scale, saving schools money. LEAs have been forced to become more competitive because schools have more choice over services, and they are not the only provider. For example, computer maintenance contracts are now fairly evenly split between LEAs and other private providers. Schools should always seek alternative quotes to keep the LEA or any existing provider on its toes. The National Grid for Learning has also made it easier for schools to save money by buying some supplies online, though doing so can require some changes to a school's approach to spending.

Leave it to the bursar?

The increase in direct funding has put more responsibility on the shoulders of head teachers and governing bodies not only to balance their books, but to ensure that they are upholding the highest standards of financial probity. Budget-making is a challenging task for any school. But day to day budgetary control and management of a typical secondary school's multi-million pound budget is equally important. There are around 5,600 bursars in English state schools[6] (some go under the name of business managers and some are shared by larger primaries) according to the DfES.

One such school is St Joseph's Catholic Comprehensive School, providing education for students aged 11 to 18 in Swindon. The school had been grant-maintained in the past and is now voluntary-aided. A brand new £20 million school is being built, which is due to open in early 2006. But as a voluntary-aided school, it has also had to raise significant resources through the Diocese. The school is also applying for specialist school status. Its deputy head teacher, Ann Parry, is also the school's business manager and bursar. She comes from a business background.

'My responsibilities are for all of the issues at St Joseph's related to finance, premises, health and safety and administration,' explains Mrs Parry. The school has a £4·2 million budget, a fairly typical sum for many secondary schools these days. 'To expect a head teacher without any of the background training – or who may have had it only as an add-on to his academic training – to run that sort of budget is very short sighted. Having in the role of bursar someone who has financial qualifications and experience is very useful. Without the finance, the rest of what schools do just doesn't happen.'

There are many advantages to a school having a bursar or business manager. It is clear who has the lead responsibility for producing the annual budget and managing the daily flow of expenditure. More importantly, there is one person who can take responsibility for co-ordinating fundraising and bidding from different national and local pots. Large secondary schools are run like businesses, and are expected to produce business-type accounts, cash-flow and budget monitoring statements, as well as forecasts of what will happen in the future.

---

[6] *Statistics of Education: School Workforce in England* (including pupil: teacher ratios and pupil: adult ratios) (Provisional January 2004 census data) (London, DfES Statistical First Release, January 2004).

Mrs Parry has been a business manager at St Joseph's since 2000. She worked in a similar role at another school for eight years before that. But her background was as a financial controller in industry, a background which made her ideally suited to the combination of responsibilities she has as deputy head teacher at St Joseph's. She is part of the group responsible for the new building, but the responsibility does not all fall on her, as the Catholic Diocese is also involved and has its own expert to help out; there are also project managers co-ordinating the new building with whom she works closely. A specific part of her role was to gather figures and information to support the school's bid to the DfES.

As the school was preparing its specialist bid (due in October 2004) for Business and Enterprise status, Mrs Parry convened a steering group to help raise sponsorship. In April, she reported that there were five partners on board, though details of their contributions had not yet been finalised. A local Swindon-based firm, Great Western Enterprises, proved particularly helpful in providing links to local businesses.

Having a dedicated business manager eased the burden on other colleagues, as Mrs Parry explains. 'We did start by having the head of Business Studies as the main person to run the bid. But when she left, I was asked to take over because I can spend more time facilitating the whole thing. Of course, the bid has to be owned by the whole school, and we've got teachers in different areas helping with different parts of it. But you have to have somebody who can pull it all together.'

Bursars work with figures all the time and they can see the fluctuations in the budget, and respond if necessary. They will be on top of the information coming in from the LEA and the Learning and Skills Council. Mrs Parry sees her role also as analysing other information on issues like workforce reform, which could impact on the budget for several years to come. She talks to her colleagues who are bursars in other schools, to identify possible new opportunities and potential future costs. She can also assess whether the school is getting the best deals possible in its contracts for building or computer services, or school meals. 'The strategic planning of the budgetary process is actually the main part of the job,' she says. 'It is done as you would do it in a business. In fact, it's an easier piece of planning than in a business, because in a business you have to try to predict future sales, whereas we know what our income is going to be. So your budgetary procedure relates far more to levels of expenditure, particularly staffing, which means that you have to work very closely with those colleagues who are responsible for timetabling or leading teaching and learning.' A good budget planner will be able to avoid any deficits at the end of the year, because problems can be anticipated well in advance.

Schools rely on a wide range of suppliers for everything from computers and textbooks, to ground maintenance and cleaning. Having a bursar should mean that schools are able to shop around more for the best value suppliers. They also have a good network of fellow bursars who share intelligence on good and bad suppliers. 'We have the ability to look much further afield than other schools might to get much better value whether its our electricity and gas supplies, or any sort of capital or building works. We can also produce our own specifications to get exactly what we want. Last year, we put in a brand new telephone system. By talking to lots of different companies, we were able to put together exactly what we wanted, and then go out to tender for that. We've now got a system that suits us down the ground.'

Mrs Parry's presence has lifted a burden from the school's head teacher. Naturally, he wants to know what's happening with the budget and has clear ideas about where things should be spent, but he leaves the detailed budgetary work to Mrs Parry.

Nationally, the number of bursars started to grow when schools went grant-maintained, because schools began to have far more control over their budgets (more than they did through the still relatively new local management of schools) and they had to deal with a national agency, the Funding Agency for Schools. As we have previously stated, although St Joseph's is now voluntary-aided it was previously grant-maintained. But Mrs Parry, who is also very involved with the National Bursars Association, believes it is not just former grant-maintained schools which are seeing the benefits of a bursar. 'When I came to Swindon in 1993, bursars were the norm in local secondary schools. But their job at that stage was mainly to interpret the LEA information and run the school's purchase ledger. Their role wasn't really proactive. But in those schools that went grant-maintained, the role of the bursar changed. Schools started to employ people from outside education to fulfil the new, more demanding system. You needed that knowledge to do the accounts. You were producing real business accounts in state schools for the first time.'

While grant-maintained schools became foundation schools or voluntary-aided schools after the 1998 School Standards and Framework Act, not only did the bursars stay, but the Government encouraged other schools to start employing them. As a result, the National Bursars Association has grown by around 50 per cent in the last six years. The latest school staff census suggests that with 5,600 bursars in English schools, there has been a healthy increase of 1,500 since 1997. Larger primary schools are also employing bursars. The introduction of Fair Funding, which increased the proportion of all school budgets that went directly to schools and its transparency, has meant that all schools now have far greater financial and accounting responsibilities than before.

The Government's workforce reforms mean that schools need to employ a large support staff to take over the 25 administrative tasks which are no longer deemed to be the responsibility of the teacher. Mrs Parry has responsibility as the line manager for all the 70 full- and part-time support staff at St Joseph's (that includes staff employed directly by the school as cleaners and dinner ladies). The school has 72 teachers, though they are largely full-time. ICT has had an enormous impact on the bursar's ability to do the job. Financial projections and budgeting are far easier not only with SIMS but also with programmes like EXCEL.

Tapping the available pots

We have seen how the Standards Fund has grown tenfold since its establishment. However, fewer and fewer programmes within the Fund require the sort of competitive bidding that characterised earlier programmes. Money for spending on performance pay or projects within the Excellence in Cities programme, for example, is allocated according to formula, which may take account of a school's size and its poverty indices. However, there remain a number of programmes which successful schools should consider, firstly for the potential they have to improve its standards and standing; and secondly, for the additional resources that can go towards making the programme a success.

One head teacher who has been successful at winning on several different fronts is Peter Beavan, who heads Norton Hill School, in Midsomer Norton, Somerset. The mixed comprehensive, with 1,300 students aged from 11–18, gained specialist status as a technology college in 1999. In 2004, it was awarded training school and leading edge status and it also received money from the Teaching Environments of the Future fund, a DfES programme to encourage innovative school design. The school has additionally raised money to build a new Astroturf sports pitch.

Mr Beavan is candid about the range of reasons why Norton Hill went for specialist status. 'We couldn't sit back and wait for the local authority or the DfES to do something about the quality of the accommodation and provision at the school. It was clear that IT and technology were particularly poor. So, we were attracted by the financial benefits of being a specialist school. But we were also attracted by the potential involvement of the local community in what we were trying to do. We welcomed the idea of having targets in certain subjects, and we particularly wanted to raise standards in the areas associated with technology status: mathematics, science, technology and ICT.'

The requirement of bidders for specialist status in 1999 was that they each had to raise £100,000 from business before receiving any funding from the Government. (It has subsequently been reduced to £50,000.) Mr Beavan and his chair of governors drew up a plan, which identified the local companies which might contribute. They sold the idea to the companies and were pleased to receive a positive reaction. They raised the money in three months. Mr Beavan wrote the bid himself, pulling in ideas from his staff on what it should contain, though he maintains he initially had limited support from his LEA.

This process has, he believes, made it easier to prepare more recent successful bids. 'Putting in bids and having a longer term, coherent and planned vision for the school, all of those things grew out of the specialist school process. It took the leverage of the technology college status to get closer monitoring and targets.' The result has been better results: 47 per cent of students gained five good GCSE grades in 1999, and 70 per cent did so in 2003 (75 per cent did so in 2002, but there was a weaker intake group in 2003).

Fundraising is now an integral part of the school's approach, and is something which is expected to supplement the school's annual main budget. In the financial year 2004–5, the school has in addition secured £350,000 from the Teaching Environments of the Future fund; £135,000 through its specialist status; and £35,000 each for its new training school and leading edge status (both of which start in September 2004). It has also got £5,000 for work as a 'lead practitioner' on workforce remodelling for the Specialist Schools Trust. A sum of £580,000 has also been raised in cash and kind from government funds, trusts and the Football Foundation for a new Astroturf pitch and changing rooms. These extra funds enable the school to spend more on buildings and equipment, something Norton Hill sees as a priority. 'I don't think you'd find another local school that has spent as much of their own money – or money they have raised – on accommodation,' adds Mr Beavan.

Perhaps one reason why they had such success in an area which other schools have found difficult is that Norton Hill serves a fairly distinct community within Midsomer Norton, a self-contained Somerset market town. But another is probably the cultural change which occurred in the school when it prepared for a ballot to apply for grant-maintained status in the mid-nineties, which was strongly opposed by the LEA. 'We narrowly lost the vote, but we came out of it much stronger, and with a robust view that we were not going to rely on the local authority, we were going to go out and do things like this for ourselves.' Mr Beavan has a bursar at Norton Hill, but believes that where fundraising is concerned, some potential supporters will feel 'fobbed off' unless they can speak to the head teacher.

New revenue streams: sponsorship

There has been some controversy about the extent to which some schools have relied on external sponsorship to help with specific projects or the overall budget. But provided that the sponsorship is handled carefully, there is no reason why it should not be of real benefit to the school as well as the sponsor, who has chosen to be identified with the school. The Specialist Schools Trust has worked with hundreds of schools to help them gain the sponsorship that is a requirement of specialist status. The Trust estimates that new specialist school bids now raise over £30 million a year from the private sector in the form of sponsorship. While this may be a small proportion of the education cake nationally, it is focused on individual schools in ways which bring them maximum benefit. Schools applying to become specialist schools must raise £50,000 each before they can access additional funding from the Government, including a one-off payment of £100,000, which helps the school buy new equipment and facilities, and an extra £129 a pupil each year (a sum capped for schools with between 1,000–1,200 pupils).

Sponsors range from wealthy and generous foundations, often developed by large companies or philanthropic business people, to small local businesses. Examples include the Garfield Weston Foundation, which funds not only educational projects, but works in other areas such as health, the arts and the environment. The foundation has donated more than £3 million to the Brooke Weston City Technology College in Great Oakley, Northamptonshire. It has also supported 400 specialist schools and is now sponsoring two Academies. The Philip and Pauline Harris Charitable Trust has so far supported, to the tune of £4 million, two CTCs, two Academies including the Academy at Peckham (see Chapter 3) and four specialist schools, with the intention of supporting many more. Some schools have developed additional revenue streams by selling products that they have developed. The money both helps their own budget and is sometimes used to sponsor other schools. Brooke Weston has a separate trading arm, CTC Trading Limited, which markets online vocational and academic courses to over 130 schools nationally. It organises lettings to business of its theatres and meeting rooms for conferences and other events. And it lets sports facilities, including two Astroturf pitches and a sports hall to local sporting organisations and the wider community. This trading helps to generate extra money for the school and some of the profits will be used in a partnership with Corby Community Council and Northamptonshire County Council to help sponsor a new Academy in Corby.

But the lesson from schools that have been successful at raising sponsorship and trading is that this cannot be a part-time activity, simply tacked on to a teacher's responsibilities to be covered in any spare time they might find. Gains are only made when the proper staff resources are invested in doing the job properly. Working with sponsors is a skilled, time-consuming management role. Sponsorship in education involves building a new relationship between a donor and the school. A school should not be surprised if a sponsor wants to see their name in the local paper, in order that the firm is associated with their generosity to the community. That's fair enough. But there must be no direct commercial benefit to the sponsor: so sponsorship by the local hardware store could not be conditional on the school agreeing to buy all its supplies from that store in the future. Offers must be unconditional in that sense and not linked to future purchases of the sponsor's goods or services.

Some sponsorship can be made 'in kind'. This is where a sponsor wishes to donate something they produce or sell to the school, rather than providing cash. This might involve new computers or desks. Similar principles apply to such arrangements. But a school's relationship with a sponsor can go much deeper than an exchange of money and a bid of good publicity for the donor. The most successful arrangements involve other activities such as visits by senior staff to the school, mentors provided, visits by teachers and students to the firm, work experience and other activities. Some businesses encourage their employees to become school governors. BAE Systems (formerly British Aerospace) involves its staff as sponsor-governors in schools, and sees this as bringing a business perspective to the governing body and an excellent way of developing the interpersonal skills of its staff.

The Specialist Schools Trust suggests seven sensible sponsorship steps which a school should go through in the process of identifying, approaching and responding to sponsors.[7]

1 It is important to set out in simple and professional (though not necessarily glossy) terms what your school is trying to do and why it is worth investing in your school. The best documents are targeted, perhaps using a direct letter from the head teacher and chair of governors to local firms. Each letter will have certain key points, such as a summary of a recent Ofsted report or improving exam results, in common.

2 Draw up a list of about 20 names of potential sponsors: focus on companies with school connections, perhaps through parents, governors or past pupils. Local chambers of commerce, education business partnerships, Rotary clubs and the Specialist Schools Trust are all good sources of information.

3 Make initial contact, with a short letter to the chairman or local managing director, accompanied by the targeted introductory guide to the school. Follow your letter up after a few days with a phone call, suggesting a meeting, but don't be too pushy or hasty.

4 Once a potential sponsor has agreed to meet, make sure you are clear about what you can and cannot offer in return for sponsorship. Read DfES bidding guidelines for specialist school status, for example. Sponsorship should normally be adding something to the school.

---

[7] *Seeking Sponsorship: A guide for schools* is available from the Specialist Schools Trust, www.specialistschools.org.uk.

5 Be prepared before you meet the sponsor. Depending on the nature of the meeting, you may want to have a chat or to back it up with a short POWERPOINT presentation. Whatever method you use, be clear about why it is in the sponsor's interest to invest in your school.

6 Invite the sponsor to visit the school, perhaps to visit a classroom and meet staff if your first meeting was in the sponsor's offices.

7 Get the offer in writing, and respond in writing. The DfES website offers some good advice on pro-forma wording. This is important to avoid any later misunderstandings and is required for specialist school bids.

17

New ways of learning using ICT and structural change

When schools first started to acquire computers, they were often treated like new toys, and were rarely integrated into mainstream lessons. An enthusiast on the staff was often given the task of looking after the technology. Even as schools became linked to the Internet, following a major drive in the late nineties, the position was slow to change. However, the new century has brought a rapid expansion in the applied use of ICT throughout the curriculum. Most secondary schools have seen how interactive whiteboards can transform lessons – when used, it should be said, by an effective teacher. School trips can sometimes be virtual instead of physical, though nobody wants to lose the thrill of the latter. Classes can be shared across counties and continents. Video-conferencing, combined with broadband technology which all schools are supposed to have by 2006, is making this possible, just as some schools can expand their curriculum with the technology, offering masterclasses provided by universities or lessons delivered from public records offices, museums, galleries or zoos. None of this is a substitute for an effectively planned and well-delivered lesson. But the technology makes it possible to bring that lesson to life in ways that might once have required a field trip.

These developments are not without their challenges. The content available on the Internet has improved substantially in the last five years, though its limitations are still obvious. Programmes like Curriculum Online are helping bring the material together and to relate it to the National Curriculum, though it can still require a teacher to be sufficiently hard headed to separate the wheat from the chaff. Using the technology means that students need access to computers, not just in the school, but at home afterwards. The computer:pupil ratio has improved: there was one computer to every 8·7 secondary pupils in 1998 whereas a typical secondary school now has 160 computers to use for lessons, apart from those used for administration, so, the ratio had risen to 1 : 6·5 in 2003.[1] That ratio still makes it difficult to integrate the technology into even the majority of lessons. All secondary schools now have an Internet connection – 17 per cent had no connection in 1998. But not all are yet through faster broadband links, though the 2006 target seems likely to be met. Teacher confidence has improved, but one in four teachers still say that they are not confident using ICT to teach their subject, despite having had some training to help them do so. And while students are increasingly confident using the Internet as a research tool, that has brought its own problems. Cheating and copying from websites have led to calls for a drastic reduction in the amount of coursework that is credited towards public exams. There is much talk in the education world about the 'transformational' potential of new technology. Only a few British schools have reached that level. But their numbers are increasing all the time, not least with the development of new Academies and the expansion of specialist schools.

Changing the way classes are organised

It has taken some time for schools to think through the implications of new technologies for their working practices. In part this is because the rapid growth in technology was accompanied by a slower improvement in content. Additionally, broadband access was relatively slow to spread. Both of these deficiencies meant that ICT seemed more like an interesting appendage rather than an integral part of lessons. That has started to change: schools are trying to integrate ICT into the majority of lessons. And as we have seen in Chapter 7 some such as George Spencer Foundation School in Nottingham now regard ICT as simply another (albeit sophisticated) tool for learning, not much different in theory from pen and paper. Nevertheless, ICT can be much more than a twenty-first century biro. National studies may have been unable to measure any direct link between school improvement and the advance of ICT, but there is impressive evidence from individual schools about the difference that can be made.

Two schools in Grimsby, in North East Lincolnshire offer a good case in point. Lessons are being taught by the best teachers in Tollbar Business and Enterprise College to pupils in Wintringham School. Interactive whiteboard technology, together with video-conferencing ensure that the classes are participative, and advanced skills teachers help to ensure that they enable students to gain the most in particular subjects. The two schools are different. Tollbar takes 1,900 students

---

[1] *Survey of Information and Communications Technology in Schools* (London, DfES, 2003). Full survey is available on the Internet only at www.dfes.gov.uk/rsgateway/DB/SBU/b000421/index.shtml.

aged 11–19 from villages around Grimsby; its students live in largely privately owned housing. ICT has been an important and integral part of the school's curriculum, and there are nine separate ICT suites which teachers can use for classes. In 2003, 51 per cent of pupils gained five good GCSEs, in line with the national average, but well above the LEA average. Wintringham School, by contrast, faces challenging circumstances: 28 per cent of pupils gained five good GCSEs in 2003, though this was a considerable improvement on 2002, when just ten per cent of pupils had reached that standard.

Through the initiative, pupils have their own individual computers for remote lessons. They have had to adjust to a changed classroom environment, where participation is not with a teacher in front of the class, but online from another school. The project is being evaluated by researchers from Edge Hill College, whose initial report noted that there were some teething problems, which any schools trying a similar approach could learn from. It was important to position desks in a way that ensured that every pupil could see the screen. Pupils then needed to learn the new 'rules of engagement': there was some initial shyness about knowing when or how to contribute in class, and whether they were being spoken to or not. These problems were overcome and the researchers reported that: 'Pupils are becoming far more comfortable with the uniqueness of the situation in which they find themselves.'[2]

More importantly, perhaps, is the question of what impact these new lessons have on what children learn. As the researchers say: 'It would be relatively easy to be seduced by the technology employed in this project; but it is only as impressive as its use.' Initial findings were encouraging here. The new approach was particularly helpful in Wintringham, where pupils showed significant improvements when compared against end-of-unit assessment criteria. Yet such partnerships have important implications for the relationships between staff at both schools.

The researchers say there are three possible approaches. In the first, both schools would have equal responsibility for the planning, delivery and assessment of the programme of activities. In the second, which they call a 'support teacher' model, the teacher in the 'sender school' (in this case, Tollbar) would assume responsibility for planning, delivery and assessment, while their counterpart in the 'receiving school' (Wintringham) would be kept informed, as well as helping manage the class and deliver the lesson, re-enforcing pupils' learning. A third approach would give the teacher in the receiver school a limited role, effectively controlling behaviour and providing technical assistance. The researchers say that

[2] K. A. Crawford, J. Price and K. Ryecroft, 'Using new technologies to deliver real-time interactive lessons between an LEA pathfinder secondary school and a school facing challenging circumstances: interim report' (Ormskirk, Edge Hill College of Higher Education, January 2004).

the second model is being used in this project, though, in ideal circumstances, they think the first model might prove most effective.

What is interesting about this approach is that it combines pedagogy and new technologies effectively. The advanced skills teacher, as we have seen, is growing in importance, particularly in those schools that have been brave enough to resist opposition from the National Union of Teachers towards their employment. In this case, they are a vital part of the programme, and their lessons embody the spirit of the advanced skills teacher ideal, sharing their expertise with other schools. The technologies are also being used to best effect, too. Other schools have used video-conferencing to deliver lessons in subjects where staff are in short supply. But in all cases, the lessons are reinforced by a knowledgeable teacher, who can help construct and plan classes, and answer students' questions.

The rise of the independent learner

ICT cannot only change the way classes are taught, it can also change the way students learn. Public services are increasingly being encouraged to adapt themselves to individual circumstances. This personalised approach is now being applied to learning in many schools. The idea is that pupils should be enabled and encouraged to become independent learners, finding out more for themselves through research, often on the Internet, solving problems and developing an ability to reason. But the concept is still not properly understood outside educational circles, and has still not been fully defined within them.

What it is not – and should not become – is a *laissez-faire* approach to education, such as that which left thousands of youngsters unable to read or write, and which left youngsters to learn (or more likely, fail to do so) through osmosis. Instead, it is a recognition that each pupil has particular needs and there is only so much a teacher can do through formal lessons, and that if students are to have a full understanding of their subject, they must be able to do their own research, to read around the subject or to do projects that help increase their knowledge. It is linked to the idea that they should be able to think through problems or issues, and not simply be passive recipients of what the teacher includes in his or her lessons. But it is not a substitute for good teaching: indeed, one aspect of good teaching is the ability to help students to manage their learning, and this includes instilling an understanding of what techniques work best to help individuals with research or revision. In one sense, none of this is new. Simply because it has its own neologism doesn't mean it is not based on long-standing pedagogic best practice. But it now can harness the potential of the new technology. If it works, this could make a huge difference to many pupils. However, for it to work, there must not only be the right resources; there must also be changes in teaching practice, in how schools are organised and in the expectations of parents, pupils and schools.

A new model of school organisation: the Chafford Hundred story

If we are to envision the school of the future, we must look at the effects not just of ICT, but also of wider structural changes. The Government's commitment to investing significant capital resources in secondary education presents real opportunities to change the way schools are structured. This need not be just about having more classrooms properly wired up, or providing extra whiteboards and laptops. It could do something far more radical, and enable a whole new type of school to emerge. The Government has been promoting 'extended schools' which offer their facilities to the whole community, and go beyond the traditional school timetable. Some schools have gone further, and their popularity is testimony to an holistic approach to education, which is both practical and visionary. Chafford Hundred Campus in Thurrock, Essex combines a secondary, primary and nursery school in a single building which also includes a library and community facilities. If any school were to be the poster boy for 'lifelong learning', this would be it. Situated close to the giant Lakeside shopping centre, the campus opened in 2001 for pupils. The secondary school has had the benefit of starting afresh with Year 7 pupils, who were due to sit their National Curriculum tests in 2004. There were 430 pupils in the secondary school by spring 2004, with a capacity of 600 when the school is full.

Alison Banks came to Chafford Hundred after a career of 30 years in teaching, including two headships, one in Salford and the other at the Beacon Community College in Crowborough, East Sussex. She moved from leading an 1,800 split-site comprehensive to heading a smaller one-site school. Her school has had to build its reputation without the benefit of national exam and test results. It has also had a relatively small budget and staff, reflecting its smaller size. The budget was only £2 million in 2004, and there was a staff of 27 teachers and 17 full- and part-time support staff. But it had ambition, something which Ofsted recognised when its inspectors visited the school in May 2003. Their inspection report concluded:

> Chafford Hundred Campus Secondary is a new school based in an impressive new building. It has established itself as a popular choice of pupils and parents. Standards are above those seen nationally for pupils in Years 7 and 8. Teaching is good. The leadership is very good and has clear vision for the school's further development.[3]

---

[3] *Chafford Hundred Campus – Secondary School Inspection Report* (London, Ofsted, May 2003). Available at www.ofsted.gov.uk.

The school is a one building, three-storey campus which works off a central atrium, a large shared space with plenty of glass and daylight. The design is energy efficient, providing warmth in winter and cool in summer through inbuilt natural features. As such, it is more like a modern civic building or shopping mall than a school. As Mrs Banks explains: 'It was about getting across to parents in particular, and Thurrock people in general, that this was something different from their traditional view of school. It is a neighbourhood learning centre.' Of course, in today's troubled times, security is a big issue. So, while the centre may be open-planned, the primary school is not open access, though the secondary school is, and there are adult classes and community activities throughout the day. Computer passes are provided to restrict entry, so members of the public can't wander in uninvited. CCTV cameras also help protect the children. Nevertheless, people can walk in off the street to the atrium and its library. The school is not fenced off and it tries to strike a sensible balance between the need for good security and the importance of community access to a local learning facility.

The school's intake reflects its local community. Most parents work in the retail, service or logistics sectors. But while the work may not provide large salaries, virtually everybody has a job, so just six per cent of pupils are eligible for free school meals. At the same time, Mrs Banks feels there is no strong education-ally aspirational culture. Hardly any parents have been to university. The school has 15 per cent of pupils drawn from different minority ethnic communities. Like many schools, in-term intakes are also significant, something that can pose a par-ticular problem for schools seeking to guide pupils through an individualised curriculum from the start. The school's intake is average by national standards, but there are large numbers of pupils at either end of the ability spectrum, present-ing different challenges. A third of pupils are on the special needs register in Year 7, though with help and support, this proportion is greatly reduced by Years 8 and 9. The school also has a significant number of pupils with physical disabilities and mobility problems, for whom the school's modern lifts are important.

Is small beautiful: does size matter?

One aspect of Chafford Hundred's approach that may have implications for the future development of schools is its size. We have become used to the 1,000–1,500-student comprehensive; and mergers have often been expected where secondary schools fall well below this size. But experience abroad has suggested that smaller schools can be more successful at teaching students, and as we have seen, some schools here have adopted a house system (see Chapter 10) precisely to deal with the problems of anonymity and isolation faced by some pupils in over-large schools.

Mrs Banks says there is an important vision behind her innovative approach: 'We've gone for a small school, which we believe is the way that the school of the future will develop. It is very different from the very large comprehensives of the seventies. I can see that a larger school might have allowed for greater curriculum choice and diversity in the past, but, with ICT, we don't need that model any more. Our small size allows us to cater for children as individuals in their neighbourhood.'

This means that all the pupils live within easy walking or cycling distance from the campus, something the school believes is also important for the environment, as it lessens the school run. When they come to school, they get individual attention, with half-hour tutorials at 8.30 a.m. once a week. Each tutorial group consists of between four and six children with two adults; if a child has an urgent personal need for a confidential discussion, that can usually be managed because there are two adults there, and one can break off to give them that support. Otherwise, the groups follow routines such as checking planners and journals. The groups are cross-age groupings, so that children in Year 9 might help those in Year 7. Mrs Banks meets every parent with their child before they are admitted: this has nothing to do with selection, but helps the school to know what sort of provision it will need to make to treat every child as an individual. They each get an individual learning plan with personal targets.

More controversially, the school's small size also means a sharp move away from the convention that every secondary teacher must concentrate on their particular subject, and do nothing more. Other schools have broken this convention where shortages dictated it: with science teachers taking maths classes, for example. But the philosophy of the Chafford Hundred school is that teachers should be much more generalists, particularly with pupils at Key Stage 3. This fits in with the school's integrated curriculum, based on a model developed by the Royal Society for the Arts, which emphasises competences rather than individual subjects. None of this means students are not being fully prepared for their GCSEs. Indeed every pupil started taking ICT vocational GCSEs in Year 8, at the age of 13. Of these 70 per cent started vocational business studies GCSEs at the start of Year 9. Many of them have also completed GCSE languages modules, as part of a fast-track languages group.

'We're trying to enable children to become managers of their own learning, and to move away from the nineteenth-century model of school subjects, towards one with greater evidence on skills and competences,' says Mrs Banks. 'So, our curriculum is much more like that in primary schools, in the sense that the pupils have one teacher for most of the week, particularly in Key Stage 3. The integrated curriculum decreases and an optional specialised curriculum increases as pupils approach their GCSEs.' Students have five options in Year 9 for example, which though it takes a large chunk of their week, does not represent the majority of lesson time. Plenty of pupils take GCSEs two years early. In Year 10, the curriculum is more individualised with 12 choices, but the school is trying to avoid having blocks which would prevent it tailoring each pupil's timetable to his or her own individual needs. 'There are always timetabling problems,' admits Mrs Banks. 'But the issue is whether you start with a structure and you expect children to fit that structure, or you start with the children's needs, and make the structure and timetable fit them. The latter is more difficult, but we don't do things because they are easy.' Unlike some schools we have seen in earlier chapters, there are no house groups, for example, because even that would be seen as administrative convenience at the expense of pupils' individuality.

Making use of ICT

ICT is central to how the curriculum is delivered at the school. There is a wireless network, and in the near future every pupil and every teacher will have their own laptop computer connected to central servers through wireless links in the ceilings of classrooms and corridors rather than by fibre optic cables. By summer 2004, 330 out of 430 pupils had laptops, and with some sharing, a very ICT-rich approach to teaching and learning was being delivered. 'We see ICT serving children's needs,' says Mrs Banks. 'We're working towards the provision of one laptop per pupil. But our approach means not just using laptops, but also mobile phones and personal digital assistants (PDAs). Whatever it is the children are using, we want to use it to help their learning and help their communication. We see our role as preparing them to use new technology in all its forms. So we have set up a platform which enables children to access all their lesson plans, online journals, targets and any relevant materials. The whole system has a single ID pass which allows both parents and children to access it from home. So we are doing away with homework books and having instant online reports for parents any time they want to read them.'

Since the school was due to become a Business and Enterprise College in September 2004, it was planning changes to its timetable. An extra half hour was being added to the school day, from Monday to Thursday, to enable every child in Key Stage 4 to spend one day a week doing work-related learning. From Year 11, students would also be able to start courses at the two nearby FE colleges, where most will go for sixth form studies. 'For us, it's about kids doing really practical things in their learning, including community service and work in business,' explains Mrs Banks. The placements, which are spread over five terms, will be carefully linked to the school's curriculum and the individual pupil's interests. One term will be spent in an ICT environment, and students will be expected to complete a case study and produce a piece of software or design a website. A second term would be linked to business studies, with a case study on the nature of a particular business or a draft business expansion plan expected at the end of the placement. The third term would reflect the preponderance of retail jobs in the Lakeside area, but also the fact that most students will have jobs with a customer service element. An NVQ or similar qualification in retail and customer care is being developed with a local college. The other two terms would allow options much more geared to the interests of the individual pupil: 'It might include catering or social care, or even the music business if that's where the kid wants to start a career,' says Mrs Banks.

Like any good school, there are plenty of extra-curricular activities, and the school is full on Saturday mornings. There are after-school clubs until 5 p.m. and a breakfast club for early attendees, but pupils often come back to use the library and get involved in youth activities on the campus, though the school is closed at that stage. In the evening the campus is a hive of local community activity, hosting breastfeeding classes, a gospel church, a karate club and a local councillor's surgery at different times in the week. There's even been a wedding reception on campus.

There are joint projects where the secondary children work with the primary children. 'As an example, a reception class went on a trip to the zoo,' adds Mrs Banks. 'Secondary arts club children went with them. When they got back, the younger children came to the secondary art room to do a collage of their favourite animal from the zoo. The secondary children worked with them on this.' When the school first opened, its small size meant that it had to rely on a lot of joint staffing. The initial budget was just £700,000. But after the school started to grow as new year groups entered, PE and music staff worked across both schools, while primary teachers and assistants helped to introduce the Key Stage 3 strategy in the secondary school, drawing on their experience from the Literacy and Numeracy Strategies.

But that was easier said than done. 'That's not because of a change in our philosophy,' explains Mrs Banks. 'It's simply because we have had huge difficulties trying to structure this in a way which is legal. There are massive problems with the regulations.' There are rules designed to allow 'federated schools' to work together, but Mrs Banks believes their scope needs to be extended to allow schools to work together with shared staffing and shared budgets. Trying to manage a site with a nursery, primary and secondary school, as well as a public library and adult and community facilities can be particularly difficult because of the existing restrictions, which clearly need to be looked at again if the extended school concept is to be taken to its logical conclusion. Far from applauding this innovation, Thurrock Council has cited national regulations to break up joint arrangements at Chafford Hundred Campus because legally two separate schools are involved. The only legal way to do it would be to have one school, not two, as some 3–18 Academies have done. This seems perverse. After all, if schools want to share staff and budgets, why shouldn't they be able to do so, provided that the governance is sound?

Even a model school has its problems

The school has also come up against some of the most difficult problems of secondary education in England today. As a Community school, its admissions are determined by the LEA, which operates a strict catchment area and sibling rule. Yet, it is hugely popular, receiving up to 485 preferences for 150 places in September 2004. This has put pressure on the school to expand its intake, inevitably creating tensions with the head teacher and governing body, since one the school's most innovative features is its relatively small size. 'If the campus is successful – it may be too early to say – they should build another campus two miles up the road,' says Mrs Banks. 'The LEA has already increased our intake from 120 to 150 a year and wants to increase it to 180. I can understand that the authority wants to respond to the parental demand for places. But the current plans include taking the primary school out of this building and relocating it to give the space for the larger intake. They want to solve the problem by making us a bog standard comprehensive school. I think that will destroy what we are trying to do.'

One area where the school takes a less structured approach than some of the other schools we have seen is on discipline. It prefers to blend aspects of programmes like Discipline for Learning and Assertive Discipline with what teachers think will work well for individual pupils. There is a high proportion of pupils with emotional, behavioural and social difficulties (EBSD). For them, the school believes its individualised approach can prove particularly helpful, not least the personal tutor system where teachers are paired with 'learning support tutors' (teaching assistants). 'A personal tutor takes full responsibility for each individual child, including liaison with the family and helping the child overcome any learning difficulties,' says Mrs Banks. There is a behaviour group in the school, which develops individual action plans for children whose behaviour causes concern. The students' campus council also plays a role through peer pressure. Ofsted said behaviour was good, despite a minority of boys who caused concern. The school believes their post-Ofsted action plan has led to dramatic improvements since then. The school doesn't rule out exclusions, but there has only been one permanent exclusion since it opened. And Mrs Banks thinks there is a stronger motivation to learn in the culture of the school which reaches even those who do cause trouble. 'The kids want to learn, and if I exclude a kid, they often do want to come back to school. I had one boy who I had temporarily excluded, and he was desperate to come back to school. He was so overjoyed when I said he could come back.'

It hasn't been easy for teachers to develop what amounts to a new curriculum. Fortunately, those recruited have proved to be enthusiastic about the cross-curricular approach, despite the fact that it presents them with enormous demands to their workload. 'They have had to write their lesson plans from scratch, and buy new materials, which does mean a lot of extra workload initially,' says Mrs Banks. 'The fact that we've gone for an integrated curriculum, which very few other schools have done, means that we had to invent it for ourselves. But the teachers find it rewarding and enjoy it. Some have commented that it's the most rewarding teaching experience they've ever had in their lives.'

Many of the innovations at this school may come to be reflected in other secondary schools, though their approach to the curriculum may seem like a step too far, at a time when subject specialisms are being promoted so actively by Charles Clarke. Either way, Chafford Hundred has made a real effort to think about what the school of the future should look like. And, because it has had the advantage of being able to start afresh, it has had greater freedom in that endeavour.

Conclusions: lessons for the future

Chafford Hundred could be a test bed for how the Government sees the future of education developing. Smaller units – which are reflected also in house systems – are likely to be embraced as pupils are expected to have more personalised timetables. Schools will inevitably need to work much more closely with others, if they are to benefit from each other's specialism. Sixth forms already recognise that only through a consortium approach can they maximise choice. On the other hand, within colleges, there is growing recognition that 14–19 education is a more distinctive phase of learning, where at the very least, separate pastoral care is vital. For a struggling school, a sixth form can mean status and respect from parents. But many schools recognise that the dedicated 16–19 sixth form colleges can provide a greater choice for students, hence the development of consortia. Pressure from the Learning and Skills Council to offer value for money will provide a strong, if not always welcome, spur.

Whether the integrated curriculum is the way forward is more questionable, though it is undoubtedly popular with students at Chafford Hundred. Certainly subjects like maths and science are likely to be popularised by the option of an applied approach. But while the integrated curriculum may be deliverable at Key Stage 3 – and Chafford Hundred pupils are a year ahead of their Thurrock peers on national tests – it is far more problematic for 14–19-year-olds. Work-related learning is certain to become a more meaningful experience than the week of work experience that children have known until now; and the approach adopted here is one which others are developing too. But the 14–19 curriculum presents new challenges and contradictions that have yet to be resolved. The Tomlinson idea of mixing entry level, foundation, intermediate and advanced qualifications, both academic and vocational, in a single diploma, has its bureaucratic attractions, but it also presents dangers. It is unlikely to lessen the clamour that exams have got too easy which greets the publication of results each summer. But it is also questionable whether a single diploma allows the flexibility to deliver the right options for every pupil: after all, the mantra of 'parity of esteem' has meant that vocational GCSEs and A Levels became less practical than the exams they replaced. Moreover, at a time when the Government is also seeking to promote apprenticeships for 14–19-year-olds, the single diploma could stifle their development. Some schools have unilaterally adopted the International Baccalaureate, which at least ensures that academically minded advanced level students receive a rounded and specialised education. But there are fears, which are rejected by comprehensive heads who deliver the IB, that it could prove too difficult for many who currently take A Levels. If that is so, it may still offer a better starting point than trying to create a new diploma by committee which tries to please every lobby simultaneously.

Either way, the curriculum of the future will be determined in part by the demands of the new 11–14 and 14–19 phases. That will shape the way schools are organised. One thing on which there is growing agreement is that students should sit exams when they are ready to do so. If they can do Key Stage 3 tests at 12 or 13, they should be allowed to do so. If some GCSEs can be completed at 13 or 14, so be it. By the same token, some students may want to do GCSEs a couple of years later than is now currently the case. After all, the proportion of students achieving NVQ 2 or five good GCSEs increases by 30 percentage points between the ages of 16 and 19, often thanks to college courses.

What is more certain is that ICT has started to change the role of the teacher. Workload agreements are relieving them of administrative tasks, and teaching assistants are increasingly on hand to support their lessons. But it is ICT that offers the greatest potential for change. As we have seen, some schools already recognise that if the way pupils learn is as important as how teachers teach this has implications for the future of teachers. There will be more specialisation: some teachers will be good at developing contents, others at managing the pupil's learning. Some lessons will be delivered by master teachers through video-conferencing. Specialist classes are likely to move into half-day concentrated blocks to avoid the disruption and loss of learning caused by constant movement. Interactive ICT will be an integral part of most lessons and school life. None of this means that teachers will become redundant; on the contrary, it will mean that their role becomes potentially more demanding and no less important. But it does mean that the Victorian (or even the late twentieth-century) classroom may soon be an historical curiosity.

18

Can we transform our schools?

We are in a time of transition in schools. But we are only part-way through the transformation of the school system. Only half of our 16-year-olds obtain five good grades at GCSE yet Digby Jones, the Director General of the CBI says that soon 80 per cent of the jobs in the UK will require five or more good GCSEs or their vocational equivalent. Transition can bring its own difficulties (as well as opening new possibilities) for children moving from primary to secondary schools. It is hardly less traumatic for the education world as it moves from old to new ways of working. There are schools which have embraced the implications of change with enthusiasm: we have seen some in these pages. The use of data to transform pupil attainment has become near-universal. But there is also a sense of foreboding among many others about what the future holds. Teachers worry about what their role will be – a fear that can lead to reluctance to incorporate new technologies into learning processes and suspicion about the enhanced status of classroom assistants. The Government has promised an unprecedented building programme of repair and renewal, but how many schools will grasp this as an opportunity to make their buildings more fit for their contemporary purpose, rather than simply a chance to repair past damage?

Both major political parties wish to see more choice for parents and greater independence for schools. The Government wants to achieve this by the rapid expansion of specialist schools and Academies. It also sees a greater role for foundation schools, those which replaced grant-maintained schools in 1998. The Conservative opposition has published radical proposals which it claims would greatly extend school choice by giving parents the equivalent of a voucher worth £5,500 a year to buy places in state schools and cheaper private schools. But by removing much of the planning from the system, not least over admissions, it could create more choice for some and less for others, even if its ambitious plans for expanding school places are realised. We have argued that while specialisation can certainly increase choice, urban schools need to take in pupils from a far wider radius than at present to ensure that places in good schools are not just restricted to those who can afford to live close by. We suggest that this can best be done through banding and the use of wider catchment areas and that it will require a considerable improvement in home-to-school transport. But we do not believe that a free-for-all on selection would achieve such equity; indeed the likelihood is that it will widen divisions rather than reduce them. Nor do we believe that the answer lies in making successful schools much bigger since this may lead to lower standards in those schools and damage efforts to raise standards in other schools.

Choice is only part of the story . . .

Choice is no panacea for schools that are struggling. It can help to lever up standards, when it is combined with the panoply of information that has been developed in recent years, such as inspection, pupil-level data, testing and performance tables. But struggling schools still need to have a variety of strategies in place if they are to recover. They must be able to tackle poor discipline, and while we acknowledge that head teachers should have the freedom to exclude unruly pupils, we also recognise that the best heads work to prevent pupils reaching the stage of needing to be excluded. Clear strategies of sanctions and rewards are important, so long as they are fairly and consistently applied. Good discipline, as we have seen, is the first prerequisite to attracting a better mix into a school which has through its failings been disproportionately attracting lower achieving pupils. The success of the latter depends to some extent on a school developing a strong aspirational group of pupils and parents as well as strong leadership.

Good leadership and good teaching are at the core of successful schools. This does not emerge by accident. It needs strong teacher and leadership training, and good continuing professional development. It needs good schools to work in partnership with others to share their best practice. Good leaders need strong middle managers, as even the most inspirational head teachers acknowledge, if they are to make their mark and their schools are to succeed. And school workforces are changing, with a much wider group of people contributing to their success: teaching assistants, computer experts, secretaries all changing the pattern of the typical school workforce, and enabling teachers to focus on their core tasks. There is also a need to improve the effectiveness of our governing bodies. At the same time, pupils are being encouraged to use ICT and new learning techniques to become more independent and inquiring learners. But these developments also have major implications for the future of teaching: we have seen some heads arguing that two types of teacher will emerge. One will help develop lessons and curriculum materials. The other will facilitate and teach lessons, often leading others in the process. These implications are potentially far-reaching.

Specialism is becoming near-universal . . .

Changes are not only happening to the nature of teaching and learning, they are also affecting the way schools are run. Within a few years, nearly all schools will have specialist status with many of the remainder likely to become Academies. With that expansion, it will be important that the strengths of the specialist movement are retained and built upon. They should not be diluted because their success owes much to the challenge that is built into the process. So, schools must still be able to lose their specialist status, if they show no signs of making the progress they promised, though the hope must be that few need to do so. But there must also be new rewards for those that succeed. The Government abandoned the School Achievement Awards in 2003, but has not replaced them. The Awards were certainly too wide in their scope, and had been distorted by a desire to reward a maximum number; moreover they took little account of the vagaries that a particularly weak intake can inflict on a school's result in a single year, distorting an otherwise seamless climb. Nevertheless, it is right in principle to reward the best, and to learn from their success. And this is where the Government needs to consider the next phase of secondary reform.

Academies – formerly City Academies – are an important statement of the value of independence and specialism combined. Their nature is a hybrid between the freedoms that come with being an independent school and the controls of admissions and other issues that result from depending on the government for most of their funding. But they are also showing themselves to be innovative in their approach to timetables and the curriculum, and they may become test beds for the future of education in this country. Labour is planning 200 Academies if it is re-elected, but Academies are expensive, and can cost as much as £36 million each. It will be important to ensure that the other 3,000 secondary schools, many of which need to be rebuilt, receive the support they need to modernise and develop. Nevertheless, the replacement of 200 underperforming schools in this country by Academies presents a unique opportunity to ensure that every child receives a decent education.

The new possibilities of partnership

The growth of specialism and Academies can, with the right infrastructure, improve choice. But just as important is their potential to lift standards not only in designated schools, but also in others that are struggling. And there is surely more that can be done to share the expertise of the best specialist schools and Academies with other schools. We have seen in earlier chapters how imaginative partnerships, such as that developed by Sir Dexter Hutt at Ninestiles with the Waverley and International Schools in Birmingham can become truly transformational. There need to be more opportunities and encouragement for such innovative collaboration. The best specialist schools should not only be able to aspire to the Leading Edge programme or training school status; there should be a greater opportunity automatically available to the most successful specialist schools, so that they can receive extra funding to spread the secrets of their success and to partner schools which could benefit from their support. For if one thing is clear from the success of the great schools we have seen in this book, it is that they need great leaders and excellent teachers; and the best thing they can contribute to the development of higher standards elsewhere is peer support. The development of local clusters of specialist schools working together to raise standards is an exciting prospect.

Already proposals have been made to allow successful specialist schools when they apply for re-designation to have a fast track procedure to greater independence. There are plans for successful specialist schools to be able to offer a second specialism building upon the success of the first with additional resources. They will be able to become training and leading edge schools. If they do not already have voluntary-aided or foundation status they can consider becoming foundation schools able to directly employ their own staff and appoint their own governors. If they are currently limited to 11–16 provision they should be able to provide post-16 courses providing there is a local need for additional provision.

Promoting innovation while striking the right balance

The best schools are also those that are often best able to innovate, advance the curriculum, develop successful teaching and learning strategies, and in doing so to get the most out of their students and teachers. Society rightly demands minimum standards from our schools, whether in a curricular entitlement for every student, or through targets and inspection. Yet, schools themselves are usually the best equipped to advance successful strategies for their improvement. This is why so much of this book has focused on how schools have solved common problems, recovered from failure, advanced beyond the average and achieved high standards in innovative ways. We have seen some schools that have used new buildings, ICT or new ways of organising their affairs to challenge traditional perceptions, and move beyond the Victorian models which still inform much classroom practice today. Equally, we should be careful not to throw the baby out with the bath water.

Some of the fads that emerged in the sixties and seventies have been deeply damaging. The Literacy and Numeracy Strategies have started to recover lost ground in primary schools, but many secondary schools still have to deal with too many pupils who do not have basic literacy or numeracy skills. It is still shocking that nearly seven million adults cannot read and write properly, though the number is finally coming down. Simply announcing that every school should be free to do as it pleases will not help those who are still struggling: there is an important role for policymakers in developing and building on these strategies to reduce the numbers who are still failing. Similarly, failing schools have not recovered by themselves. They have been helped by partnerships with other schools, but they have also been spurred by demanding post-inspection targets and continued attention from Ofsted. It is a fallacy to imagine, as some on both the left and the right do, that simply leaving such schools to the market will ensure their recovery.

The details matter . . .

One thing that successful head teachers always say is that the details matter. Sometimes the broad brush of the political debate can ignore this truth. Yet, as we have seen throughout the book, there may be no single 'magic bullet' which produces success, but there are lots of details which can make a difference. We have spent a lot of this book talking about the importance of data and targets, and their potential to help individual students to improve. This has been crucial to specialist schools since their inception in 1994 and is very much a common feature of successful schools. It means not just striving to reach the average from a position of struggle or failure; it is also about moving from good to great, from average to exceptional. The current fad of dismissing all targets and statistics as bureaucratic or deceptive could prove deeply damaging if it were treated seriously by schools or policymakers. Nevertheless, there have undoubtedly been too many targets and initiatives, and too many which have distracted from the main business of schools. Their reduction is welcome. The proposed 'single conversation' between schools and an educational mentor representing both the LEA and the DfES would enable schools to spend their time on raising standards rather than chasing a myriad of different grant possibilities. And the best targets are those developed by schools themselves, with the challenge and support of independent external advice. But any suggestion that schools should be encouraged to abandon targets would not only set back the cause of school reform immeasurably, it would be deeply damaging to the life chances of thousands of young people.

The use of data is not all that matters. We have seen, for example, how a longer school day and a five-term timetable have made a big difference to some schools. And we have argued that bursars can help schools to manage their money more effectively, and that schools should benchmark their financial performance with others. But equally important to the development of greater success in the system is the development of collaboration through partnerships with other schools, both primary and secondary, at home and abroad.

There was a time when partnership was simply a vaguely aspirational element of the education system: it was a good thing, it felt right, but, with the exception of some of the education business links developed in the 1980s, it didn't always achieve a lot. For some, partnership brought with it too much paperwork, with too little to show for it. Partnership has been a watchword of the Labour Government since 1997. There have been independent–state school partnerships, links between grammar schools and secondary moderns, a new community focus to specialist schools, links between universities and inner city schools, college–school partnerships for 14–16-year-olds, and the development of extended and full service schools. Yet perhaps the most important, and potentially most lasting, development has been the growth of federations and consortia. Where two or three schools come together to share facilities, improve flexibility in their timetable, swap best practice or train staff together, there is something more enduring. Moreover, such partnerships can bridge the divide in a way that few other partnerships can, because they are based on each partner giving and receiving. It is a two-way process. With the law now enabling Learning and Skills Councils to buy sixth-form provision in minority subjects from the independent sector, the notion of independent–state school partnerships is maturing. With the development of federations of strong and weak schools, there are real gains to be made in improved educational standards. Moreover, the development of ICT means that such links can be virtual as well as physical.

Partnerships, as we have seen, can also play a big role in easing the transition from primary to secondary school. By organising activities for feeder primaries, schools can prepare youngsters for the trauma of moving from a small school to a larger one; they can help pupils to familiarise themselves with their new surroundings from an early stage. And they can ensure continuity in what is taught, rather than going over old ground in Year 7.

The biggest advantage of the partnership approach is that it is not top down. The nature of the partnership can vary enormously. In each case it is about a professional dialogue – teachers learning from their colleagues. This is not say that there will not sometimes be a hard edge to the relationship: a strong school helping a weak school to recover may symbolically evoke notions of equality, but the nature of the partnership will be dictated by the schools' different circumstances. Rather it is to see that, if we are to overcome the remaining challenges of weak and failing schools, to extend choice and opportunity, or to take full advantage of the new technologies, then such partnerships must not only endure, they must become the norm for schools.

Developing 14–19 education

Perhaps the biggest challenge facing secondary schools, colleges and universities this decade will be over the 14–19 curriculum. Problems with the new A Level system, and a weakness in vocational education, have created a climate for long-term change in 14–19 education. The Government's 14–19 Working Group has recommended a new four-stage diploma, which would offer students stepping stones from 'entry level' (pre-GCSE) qualifications through to advanced level qualifications. Students would be required to take English, maths and computing through to the sixth form, as key skills rather than academic subjects. They would be able to take different stages of the Diploma when they are ready to do so, sitting intermediate (GCSE-standard) exams, for example, earlier or later in their lives than at present. There would be both academic and vocational options available throughout. There has been a mixed reaction to the Diploma, and the Government had not explicitly accepted this model by the summer of 2004, as Tomlinson's final report was awaited.

There are other options. Some schools, including Impington Village College, featured in Chapter 8, have adopted the International Baccalaureate. There is an argument that this could become the main route for sixth-form studies, offering a combination of breadth and strength, while the new practically oriented apprenticeships, launched in May 2004, could become the main vehicle for vocational education.[1] By contrast, others believe the case for change is overdone. Professor Alan Smithers, of the University of Liverpool, believes that it is a mistake to try to force young people to take compulsory subjects or groups of subjects beyond the age of 16. He also argues that the 'spread of interests is too wide to be contained within the one qualification'.[2] And the trickier issue is what to do with vocational subjects. Is it right that vocational qualifications should automatically be part of any new overarching diploma? The argument for inclusion is that this will create a 'parity of esteem', placing vocational and academic qualifications on an equal

---

[1] See C. Ryan, 'Don't dumb down the Baccalaureate' in *Bac or Basics: Challenges for the 14–19 curriculum*, ed. C. Ryan (London, Social Market Foundation, 2004).
[2] A. Smithers 'An array of awards beats a Baccalaureate' in *Bac or Basics: Challenges for the 14–19 curriculum*, ed. C. Ryan (London, Social Market Foundation, 2004).

footing. There is certainly a good case for increasing the range of applied qualifications on offer, particularly in subjects like maths, science and ICT. And the Government has already made clear that it expects a third of youngsters to take Apprenticeships. It has also formally introduced Young Apprenticeships for 14–16-year-olds, where young people can learn a trade for two days a week. However, the danger of trying to fit practical subjects into a complex academic and bureaucratic framework is that the practical elements are compromised in favour of paper-based assessments.

It is certainly the case that many more students would benefit from the International Baccalaureate approach than do so at present, so why not give far more positive backing to its use from the top, but leave it to schools and colleges to decide whether to offer the IB or A Levels, or both. As we have seen, many schools already enter pupils for some GCSEs a year or two early; and colleges often work to develop level 2 qualifications after students have left school with insufficient good GCSEs. So, there is certainly a case for making exams much less age-related. However, it will be important that this does not make it impossible for parents to make a fair judgement about a school's exam performance. Something more easily understood than the current DfES value-added data is clearly needed. The idea that students should be actively encouraged to see their exams and achievements as a stepping stone towards the next stage of their learning has a lot to commend it. The new apprenticeships will be a valuable component of the new framework.

Yet the public debate misses these changes

These changes are the ones that are already affecting schools across the country – or will do so in the future. Yet the public discourse seems largely unaware of these changes. This book is primarily intended as an examination of what makes good and great schools, the techniques that successful head teachers use, and the ways that they have improved standards and discipline. But it also gives a picture of how our schools have changed over the last decade – and continue to change – which should help to inform the public and political debate about educational policy. The picture we present is neither a rosy view of a perfect school system nor one of a system in crisis that some argue requires a completely fresh start. But it is one of a system where a substantial number of state schools are improving significantly; it is one that is embracing the challenges of change; and it is one where pupils are gradually getting a better deal.

Next steps

English education has come a long way in the last 15 years, but it still has a long way to go. The improvements which have been seen by many schools show what is possible; the persistent tale of underachievement shows that not everyone has yet benefited from such possibilities. What we do know, however, is that there are many great schools which have already begun to harness the possibilities of technology with practical and effective new ways of working for the benefit of all their students. We know that data, when used intelligently within a school setting, can have a powerful impact on ambitions. We have seen how new ways of working, of timetabling, and of organising school buildings can improve the processes of teaching and learning. We know that specialism can be a powerful spur for improvement, and that with the right strategies, once failing schools can be turned around successfully. All this shows how many in the education system have, as a result of reforms introduced by successive governments, begun to address and overcome the challenges of underachievement and the possibilities of new technology. The goal for English secondary schools over the next decade must surely be to effect a similar transformation throughout the education system so that every child wherever he or she lives will be able to attend a good school.

Appendix 1: How to calculate the value added of a secondary school

David Jesson

Almost all secondary schools recruit their pupils at age 11 just after they have taken their Key Stage 2 tests. These tests provide each pupil with a 'level' of attainment in English, mathematics and science.

When pupils arrive at secondary school it is usual for these 'prior attainments' to be collected on a spreadsheet to provide useful information for teachers and others in forming the appropriate teaching groups for each pupil. A very useful measure is provided by the 'average level' at which each pupil is working – obtained by adding up the levels achieved and dividing by how many tests the pupil took at Key Stage 2.

Each school has, therefore, a list of pupils' names and their previous Key Stage 2 test results. These lists describe the 'intake' measure of the pupils entering each secondary school – and their average value tells us quite a lot about how able each school's pupils are compared to those entering other secondary schools. In recent years it has become common practice to refer to these 'intake' measures by their points score equivalents using Table A1.1. All schools should be able to provide parents and other interested parties with this information very easily.

In 2003, for example, most secondary schools had an 'average Key Stage 2 points score' around 25.5, but over the country as a whole this ranged from a low of 21.0 to a high of over 30.0 points. In general schools with 'low' Key Stage 2 points scores are found in relatively disadvantaged areas while schools in more favourable areas tend to have higher scores. These numbers enable schools (and parents) to see where

Table A1.1 Point score attributed to Key Stage 2 levels

Key Stage 2 levels	1	2	3	4	5
Points score	9	15	21	27	33

their own school stands in comparison with all other secondary schools – as far as their pupils' attainments at age 11 are concerned.

Five years later when these pupils have taken their GCSE examinations each school's performance is calculated using the percentage of those on roll who achieved five or more A* to C passes – this is known as an 'output' measure for each school. This percentage has been going up in recent years and in 2003 the national average performance was close to 53 per cent of all pupils gaining this level of performance at GCSE.

The most natural thing is then to see how schools with different 'intakes' fared in their GCSE outcomes. It is this which provides a very simple way of deciding 'how well' a school has done in turning the 'intake' it had into 'output' five years later.

There are a number of simple ways to do this – all of which depend on a 'picture' of how schools' performance at GCSE compares with their 'intake' at age 11.

Figure A1.1 shows how the GCSE performance of every non-selective mixed secondary school in the country is linked to its 'intake' score. It shows the percentage of pupils in each school who were expected to obtain five or more A* to C passes on the basis of the 'average Key Stage 2 points score' for that school. (Girls' and boys' schools have their own lines as explained below in 'Single-sex schools'.)

Figure A1.1 shows in a very general way that schools with 'high' intakes tend to obtain high levels of GCSE performance – while schools with 'low' intakes tend to score rather less.

Whether schools do actually achieve these levels of performance is an important question – Figure A1.1 provides a framework onto which each individual school's

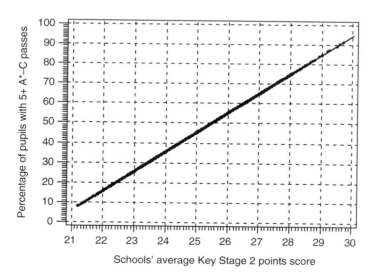

Figure A1.1   Value-added chart linking expected schools' performance to 'intake' for mixed schools

outcomes can be placed, and used to tell if its performance is 'above', 'below' or 'close to' the 'expected' value.

Schools which lie above the line are described as having 'positive added value', while those below the line as having 'negative added value'. In each case the diagram gives an indication of the percentage of pupils 'above' or 'below' what would be expected if the school was 'doing as well as expected'.

For many schools this procedure will show that they are performing at or about as expected (within a few percentage points on either side of the relevant line), but for others their performance may be 'well above the line' – meaning that they are adding substantially to the value obtained by similar schools. In a similar way if a school's performance places it 'well below' the line it shows that that school is achieving very much lower value than similar schools.

Clearly this provides very important information about the way any school has performed; the example in Table A1.2 shows how it works in practice by comparing the performance of two schools. One of these achieved over 60 per cent of its pupils with five or more A* to C passes and the other just 46 per cent. (Simple league tables would only provide this information – from which we might infer that the first school has done very much better than the second. However, this remains to be seen!)

Figure A1.1 shows that School A with 61 per cent A* to C passes was 'expected' to achieve 74 per cent – this is shown by School A's point being well below the middle line on the graph. School A achieved 13 per cent less pupils with 5+ A*–C passes than other similar schools.

School B, in contrast, achieved 46 per cent A* to C passes while 'similar' schools achieved around 31 per cent – so in School B's case the school achieved 15 per cent more pupils gaining five or more A* to C passes than similar schools.

Translating this into numbers of pupils: in School A some 24 pupils (13% of 186) did not achieve the performance they might have been expected to obtain, while in School B an additional 24 pupils (15% of 156) did achieve this level of success. Clearly School B is providing a better outcome for its pupils than School A, even though a higher percentage of School A's pupils obtained 5+ A* to C passes.

This shows just how important to parents, pupils and others the results of these

Table A1.2   Performance of two schools

School	Year 11 size (no. of pupils)	School type	Intake points	Pupils with 5+A* –C passes (%)
Leafy suburb (A)	183	Mixed	27.9	61
Inner city (B)	156	Mixed	23.5	46

evaluations are. League tables do not give the most important messages about schools' performance since they ignore the 'value' which each school adds to its pupils. The simple methods outlined above can be applied to any comprehensive or modern school in the country.

Parents and others interested in the performance of grammar and independent schools may like to know that similar frameworks are available for evaluating them. The only difference is that the outcome measure (the percentage of pupils achieving five or more A* or A passes) is one chosen to be relevant to such schools which normally select only highly able pupils.

More technical information – formula for calculating the expected outcome of any mixed secondary school

The main GCSE outcome of interest is the percentage of pupils with 5+ A* to C passes. To calculate the 'expected' 5+ A* to C passes for any non-selective school:

Expected %5+ A* to C passes = 50.5 + {9.9 × (School average KS2 pts – 25.5)}

Example of calculations for School A
Expected %5+ A* to C passes = 50.5 + {9.9 × (27.9 – 25.5)}
50.5 + {9.9 × 2.4}
50.5 + 23.8
74.3 (rounded to 74%)
School A achieved 61% and so 'underachieved' by 13%.

Example of calculations for School B
Expected %5+ A* to C passes = 50.5 + {9.9 × (23.5 – 25.5)}
50.5 + {9.9 × – 2.0}
50.5 – 19.8
30.7 (rounded to 31%)
School B achieved 46% and so the additional value added was 15%.

Single-sex schools

Where pupils attend a single-sex school it is important to use the chart shown in Figure A1.2 for finding out how well its performance compares with similar schools. This is because of the fact that girls outperform boys nationally at GCSE – they gain about 10 per cent additional five A* to C passes. This means that girls' schools 'should do better' than mixed schools with similar ability pupils while boys' schools are likely to 'do worse'. (The distance between the lines is around

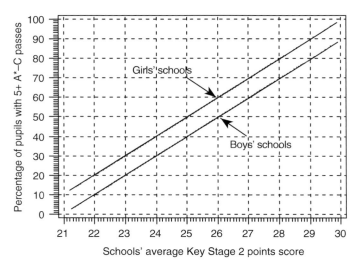

Figure A1.2 Value-added chart linking expected schools' performance to 'intake' for single-sex schools

10 per cent, showing that girls' schools' performance is around ten per cent higher than boys' schools with similar pupils.)

This chart is used in exactly the same way as the earlier version – simply find out the schools' latest percentage of 5+ A* to C passes and its Key Stage 2 points score and plot the point on the chart. If it is above the appropriate line the school is 'doing better' than expected and if it is below, then it is 'doing worse' than expected.

Schools' performances which are within a couple of percentage points either side of the line are given the benefit of the doubt and are described as 'doing as well as expected'.

Appendix 2: Survey of best practice in leading specialist schools

As part of the research for this book, we asked a number of leading specialist schools – with the help of the Specialist Schools Trust – to tell us what made them great schools. The schools we chose were those which either had good absolute scores, had seen substantial recent improvements, or which had good value-added scores. We then asked the Institute of Education at the University of London to help us to analyse the findings. Dr Anthony Green, who teaches sociology of education and research methods, and his research student, Ayo Mansaray looked at the returns from the schools. Here are their findings.

Aims and objectives:

- To collate the quantitative results of returned questionnaires on 'Best practice in leading specialist schools'.
- To analyse the data obtained for suggestive trends of common/divergent strategies and approaches adopted by leading specialist schools.

Main findings

The data from the questionnaires were collated and analysed using the following broad categorisation:

- Leadership, management and support staff
- Tests and target setting
- ICT and innovative teaching
- Behaviour and discipline
- Ethos
- Parental involvement

- Networks
- Extra-curricular provision.

Leadership, management and support staff. Schools indicated that strong leadership and good management were developed through careful delegation and less hierarchical management structures with staff development a priority. Support staff were valued and deployed in various capacities, from taking over clerical and administrative tasks to active involvement in teaching and learning. The data clearly suggests that Remodelling has had an impact on organisational arrangements within the respondent schools.

Tests and target setting. Target setting was widely used by schools and many used published cognitive/ability tests. Assessments were part of an ethos of target setting which enabled schools to monitor and tailor teaching and learning. ICT was also an important facilitator in the management of target-setting data.

ICT and innovative teaching. There were substantial variations among schools in the level of ICT provision, e.g. number of laptops available for pupils and teachers. Nonetheless, the majority of schools reported using ICT extensively across the curriculum. There were several examples of 'innovative' ICT use in teaching and many used ICT to extend the learning opportunities offered to pupils by developing Internet based resources. Non-traditional awards were embraced with enthusiasm by a number of schools although some schools remained sceptical of their value.

Behaviour and discipline. The vast majority of schools had well-planned strategies to maintain good behaviour and high standards of discipline. In general, schools either implemented a 'bought in' programme or devised their own. Most strategies emphasised rewards rather than sanctions.

Ethos. Responses suggest that vision, good leadership and a general 'can do' attitude were important in creating an ethos of achievement. Many remarked on the positive changes that attaining specialist school status had brought about.

Parental involvement. There were plenty of examples of active parental involvement in school affairs and evidence of schools trying to bridge the home–school divide. The data suggests good home–school relationships require active participation on both sides and this may be lacking in a number of cases.

Networks. The data indicates that schools form networks with several agencies such as universities, colleges and most commonly with other schools in the local area. Some schools were found to have extensive links and involved in large networks. The findings suggest that while networks are important to schools, in terms of sharing good practice and introducing new knowledge, much more research is needed to examine the nature and benefit of networks to specialist schools.

Extra-curricular provision. The provision of extra-curricular activities was taken very seriously and schools offered a range of activities to both pupils and the local community. Sports colleges were well placed to offer their facilities and services to the local community. Many of the schools opened late into the evening, at the weekends and organised activities during the school holidays.

Methodology

In the summer of 2003 there were 938 specialist schools. Of these, 384 were selected to take part in the Specialist Schools Trust's survey on 'Best practice in leading specialist schools' using three criteria ('club membership'):

1 Schools that achieved 70%+ 5 A*–C GCSEs in 2003
2 Schools that had improved their raw GCSE performance 10+ percentage points since 2000 (2003 minus 2000 results)
3 Schools that had a value-added score of 10+ points. This was calculated using Jesson's formula and published ranking of Specialist schools (Jesson 2004).

Questionnaires were sent to schools on a compiled list via post/e-mail. It was a semi-structured questionnaire consisting of 27 open and closed ended questions. The total number of questionnaires returned was 88[1]; the response rate was 22·92 per cent. While this is low, it is not uncommon for a geographical dispersed sample (Chiu and Brennan 1990). However, a few words of caution regarding what we are able to infer from the data and the results presented in the following analysis are in order. The design of the survey and the targeted sampling means that while we can glean insights from self-reporting schools regarding their practices, we cannot conclude that these same practices and/or techniques are responsible for their 'success' relative to other schools that either were not in the target group or did not respond. The data cannot tell us if the trends identified are unique to 'leading specialist schools' or in fact common to non-specialist schools as well. Such an answer would require a different kind of survey technique. What we can infer are the differences and similarities within the respondent sample and with much caution beyond that to the larger population of specialist schools initially invited to respond. In this too we must be careful, as with any survey with

---

[1] All tables presented in findings are based on an actual sample of 75, as single sex schools were excluded from the main analysis.

a small response rate, the characteristics of the respondents may to some extent be atypical, for example, responders may be more motivated and willing to discuss their work than other comparable schools who did not respond. Although we cannot be sure of the characteristics of the non-respondents, it is likely that the respondent schools represent those schools most motivated about being a specialist school and to that extent self-selecting enthusiasts.

A substantial proportion of the data analysis reported has involved simple numerical comparisons derived from relatively unambiguous questionnaire items where coding is likely to be reliable. However, much of the data is in open text form and needs more elaborate and time-consuming qualitative analysis than resources permitted to assure confidence in the reliability and validity of the results, so far. Indeed, further work is likely to reveal an even more complex picture than emerges below.

Leadership, management and support staff

Previous research by the NFER (Rudd *et al.* 2002) indicates that leadership and management style/structure are important factors in leading specialist schools' success. This survey confirms those findings. A particularly interesting result of this survey is the important and diverse roles that support staff have in these schools. The findings resonate with Rudd *et al.*'s (2002: 52) investigations, and importantly suggests that what they termed as 'innovative use' of support staff is in fact more widespread.

Leadership and management

In responses regarding leadership within their schools, head teachers often mentioned 'teamwork', 'mutual support' and clear lines of responsibility. One school had conducted an 'audit of leadership team by a consultant' and several said that members of senior management went on leadership training courses. Offering good opportunities for professional development to staff was felt to be a mark of good leadership. Delegation of responsibility was often cited and in some schools there was 'rotation of responsibilities' between individuals or teams. For some, 'shared leadership' meant 'keeping the team small' and having frequent meetings. This idea of 'shared' management is taken to its logical conclusion at Kirk Hallam Community Technology College, as the head teacher explains:

> A shared Senior Management Office – I share the office with both Vice Principals and the benefits in terms of regular communication, daily review of progress, sharing of ideas, speed of decision making, unity of purpose etc. are overwhelming (we do have a 'drop-out space' when it all becomes too much for any of us or we need to work in peace).

The need for 'leadership teams' to be involved 'in a range of collaborative programmes' was emphasised. Several respondents said that head teachers or senior management undertook coaching of younger/junior management staff. This was expressed as a preference for 'growing their own' senior management and internal promotion where possible. As one head commented, '[we] have moved away from traditional hierarchies – [and] promoted staff when they are ready not when they have "served their time" '.

There appears to be a discernable pattern in the responses. The comments suggest a move towards more devolved forms of management and delegation of responsibilities either to individual departments or teams. One respondent called it a 'corporate' style. A 'flatter' management structure, more suited to what one head teacher described in their school as 'continuous improvement' and a 'culture of change' based on high levels of trust. However, such 'flatter management' requires sustained engagement which some schools foster by direct involvement of the general teaching and support staff (e.g. 'management residential'). A few schools recommended leadership teams 'who actually teach'. In addition, there is an increasing specialisation of management functions linked to the Remodelling policy that has enabled schools to create new management roles/positions (see below). However, several heads mentioned that a less hierarchical management structure does not obviate the need for clear lines of accountability, 'clear responsibility frameworks which are supported by robust data and information' are vital in such an environment.

Recruitment and retention

The majority of schools pointed to good quality continuous professional development as a strategy for staff retention, with one offering 'MBAs' to its staff. Several cited the maintenance of good links with local universities and other providers of Initial Teacher Training (ITT) providers as part of their recruitment strategy, with many of the teacher trainees returning to work at the school. In particular, some had begun to offer Newly Qualified Teachers (NQT) pay from June/July for the following September start. The importance of organised induction for all new staff was recognised, as well as NQT support programmes, one head teacher reported holding an 'induction residential'. For a lot of the schools, creating a convivial atmosphere for the teaching staff was very important, this varied from 'free lunches', 'teas, coffees during the break', 'promised clerical support', 'parents' evening start at 4.15 p.m.', 'protected non-contact time', 'gifts', to 'financial rewards above the going rate'. Several mentioned using the Graduate Teacher Programme (GTP) as part of their strategy of recruitment, as one head teacher admits, 'recruitment remains difficult and without the GTP we would be understaffed'. The reputation of the school was cited as an attraction for new staff. While there were differences, most schools stressed an integrated approach to staff retention and recruitment, linked to core aspects of school policy, as illustrated by this quote:

> CPD for all staff, no cover and no duties for teachers, interactive whiteboards in all class-rooms, using ICT to support teaching and learning, remodelling the workforce so that teachers have the capacity to focus on the detail of student achievement which underpins the raising of standards.

Support staff

Support staff were clearly an important resource for schools, both as part of their general approach to teaching and learning, strategies of teacher retention and recruitment. From the data, several patterns are evident in regards to the use of support staff.

Support staff are increasingly been deployed to take over administrative, assessment and clerical tasks within schools, a common response was that the 'widespread use of support staff for admin, thereby allow teachers to teach'. One school had an 'attendance officer'; in another school support staff did all the exam administration. Significant mention was made of the involvement of support staff in pastoral care.

The impact of the Remodelling policy was palpable, as one head teacher reported, 'under re-modelling of the workforce additional hours by support staff to take on admin tasks of teachers so they can focus on core task of teaching and learning'. While this was common to the majority of schools, several stressed how support staff could enrich teaching and learning in terms of support for the core curriculum subjects and ICT, for example at Bishop Rawstorne C of E Language College:

> This process began with a colleague undertaking a DfES Best Practice Research Project on the effective training and deployment of support staff and has since progressed under the re-modelling agenda. ICT Technician, Science Technician and Technology Technician are all trained to work alongside pupils to support their learning. Some Teaching Assistants are developing roles in specific subject areas, some have been trained to deliver the Progress Units, and some are looking to secure the standards for Higher Level Teaching Assistants. All support staff take part in Professional Development Days, keeping the focus for all the adults in the community on teaching and learning. Participation by all colleagues – site, administration, Teaching Assistants, Teachers and Governors – in the Well Being Programme is helping to provide cohesion, understanding and a shared sense of purpose.

Learning mentors/assistants and teaching assistants were also important in providing support to less able pupils as well as supporting schools' gifted and talented programmes, after-school clubs, homework clubs and the like. Many said that they nurtured their support staff, providing them with opportunities for career development, either towards Qualified Teacher Status or specialisation (e.g. higher level teaching assistant, TA foundation degree/NVQ etc.). In fact, some acknowledged support staff as potential teaching recruits. Support staff were also being used at more senior levels, one school 'employs a professional Business Manager who is part of the senior leadership team', while another school's approach illustrates how support staff and community links can feed off each other.

> [Teaching assistants] are used to support learning in classrooms, both in support of students with SEN and of classes generally. We have incorporated the skills of the wider community and professional arts practitioners into our work, to the great advantage of both students and staff throughout the school. These support staff range from peripatetic music teachers, to drama practitioners, dance animateurs, artists in residence, a theatre manager with administrator and technicians. We employ dedicated technicians and administrators in Art, Music and the Performing Arts.
>
> (Stantonbury Campus North)

While the general tenor of the responses suggest that support staff are increasingly being used in innovative and flexible ways within these schools, it must be noted that there remains some variation in the extent to which schools are adapting and adopting these practices. While the majority of schools are using support staff for administration and clerical and classroom support, a significant number are clearly moving forward with the Remodelling agenda, creating new roles and positions for support staff, as teaching assistants, learning mentors, etc., giving them more responsibilities to plan, teach, assess and monitor pupil progress. In several schools teaching assistants were used as 'cover supervisors' and this is linked into those schools' 'no cover' policies for teachers. Support staff are clearly a vital and flexible resource for schools.

Tests and target setting

Ninety-four per cent of responding schools said that they used tests of reading and numeracy tests for incoming Year 7 children and 96 per cent set specific targets for achievement in each subject/child or year group. The two most commonly used tests were the NFER's Cognitive Ability Tests (CATs) and the Middle Years Information System (MIDYIS) tests. The importance of systematic target setting was a theme of many responses and was bound up with other school policies, such as the deployment of support staff to administer and input assessment data, and the use of that data to target 'booster classes' and 'intervention groups' etc. Similarly, schools stressed the importance of ICT in enabling them to collate, monitor and use data for target setting. However, it was more than a technological exercise; it was about senior members of staff taking the lead as one respondent explains:

> The Head teacher interviews and sets targets for all Year 11 in September each year. This is followed up by each member of the senior leadership team mentoring one Year 11 tutor group to monitor progress towards their targets.
>
> (Greenwood Dale School)

Target setting was often mentioned in the larger context of 'individualised learning programmes' that it supports, in concert with good ICT provisions, and at the systematic level of the school where departments were set targets. Thus, in general respondents' statements suggest that target setting was used at the pupil and departmental/school level and consequently was ingrained in the ethos of a number of schools (see also 'Ethos' section below).

ICT and innovative teaching

Figure A2.1 clearly shows that staff in virtually all respondent schools have received some kind of ICT training. While a clear majority of schools had broadband access to the Internet, 29·3 per cent did not have wireless internet access.

In terms of ICT provision, there were huge variations in the number of laptops available to teachers and pupils and in the number of classrooms with white-boards (see Table A2.1 for average figures). One school did not have any laptops for its teachers while several had enough for one each. Again, while several

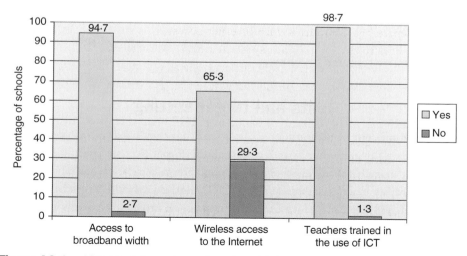

Figure A2.1   ICT provision – broadband and Internet access and training in ICT

Table A2.1   ICT provision – laptop and whiteboard availability

Median[2] number of laptops available to teachers per school	Number of laptops available to pupils as a ratio	Median number of classrooms with whiteboards per school
40	1 : 60	10

schools had scores of laptops for pupils, quite a few (16.7 per cent) had none. The same variability was apparent in the use of whiteboards. The data suggests that the scale of provision is quite uneven, but that schools are planning to expand the number of laptops and whiteboards available in the near future.

Schools were enthusiastic about ICT and the possibilities it presented for enriching teaching and learning, often in directions that they felt to be 'innovative'. ICT permeated most aspects of the curriculum, from dance to English. Schools approached ICT in a number of ways, most often using it to extend or augment their teaching and learning capacity, to do what they did better. The main variation between schools lay in the level of integration of ICT with other aspects of the curriculum. The ubiquity of broadband Internet access ensured 'e-learning' featured in several responses. However, this meant different things to different schools. For one school:

> Extensive and flexible use is made of laptops to promote e-learning. Laptops are allocated according to need, i.e. to a whole year group, departments or to individual pupils. Our network allows individual access to the Internet from 8 a.m. to 5.30 p.m.

While in another, it was access and provision that was stressed, '[our] Learning Resource Centre has computers with Internet access, it is staffed throughout the day for students to drop in and complete research'. Others mentioned how ICT enabled staff to work more efficiently, for example as one head teacher comments, '[we have] 400 workstations around the whole site. All staff enter reports on an electronic report system so that data is immediately available'.

Several schools also pointed to aspects of ICT that were not as reliant on Internet technologies, for example '[we have] a wide range of applications in the arts, such as video-editing, radio and TV suites, music technology, digital animation and [a] range of multimedia, including website design'. Schools named an array of software programs that they used in concert with their drive towards 'individualised learning'. Some schools claimed that ICT software allowed them to

---

[2] This measure was adopted because of outliers in the sample.

create individual 'learning programmes' that matched pupils 'learning styles' and other attributes. The use of 'interactive whiteboards' (IWB) was commonly referred to as an 'innovative' teaching technique. Many schools emphasised an integrated approach towards ICT as illustrated by Landau Forte College:

> All students have their own user area with industry standard software, access to ILS packages; email, broadband Internet access and access from home to their user area via the College website. ICT is used for learning across the curriculum and through specific courses – students can work independently to produce work both inside and outside of College – facilities for work are made available before and after College and during students holidays.

Clearly, while schools are enthusiastic about ICT some comments indicate that lack of funds is still an important constraint.

> We are constantly introducing new techniques and ideas and are a Test Bed School for ICT. We would like an IWB [interactive whiteboard] in every teaching space but the site and budget makes this difficult. We have developed a comprehensive school intranet which has personalised packages for each child to access. We are developing the school website further with the aim of providing 24-hour school access to learning.
>
> (Wood Green High School College of Sport)

It must be remembered that the effective use of ICT rests on the quality and knowledge of the teaching staff, who must be prepared to continually update their skills in order to deliver on the potential of ICT, as the approach of Stantonbury Campus North school suggests:

> We have an increasing emphasis on the use of film as [an] artefact for student expression and assessment of student work. We are investigating this as 'soundscape' in music. We are working in partnership with the British Film Institute (BFI) and Cine Club. We are running collaborative INSET for teachers on the use of digital film technology in learning. To enable this work we have committed ourselves to the provision of 10+ laptops, with Windows Movie Maker and Adobe Pinnacle 8.

This approach also demonstrates the benefits to staff and students of forging links with outside agencies like the BFI. The case of S Peter's Collegiate School, a voluntary-aided technology college, shows that 'innovative' practice in ICT can be comprehensive and ambitious in scope:

> As part of our Phase Four development plan, we are developing a Managed Learning Environment (MLE) using ICT, which enhances the delivery of the specialist subjects in addition to other vocational subjects at S Peter's and across partner schools. The aim of this development is to promote independent learning through the use of an ICT learning platform at home as well as in school. Staff are currently creating new and exciting

e-learning material with online assessments, which not only supports learning, but also allows for a more imaginative and dynamic approach to classroom delivery by the teacher.

Non-traditional awards and innovative teaching

Eighty-eight per cent of respondents said that they used 'innovative' teaching techniques including the use of non-traditional awards. What 'innovative' meant to each school was quite different. For many, it meant techniques relating to ICT as discussed above, for others it meant having 'philosophy for children', 'whole-brain teaching', 'thinking skills', one school offered 'financial services qualifications', quite a number offered 'Microsoft' and 'Cisco' courses, another 'in conjunction with a local company' is delivering courses as part of the modern apprenticeship. A large proportion offered BTEC, NVQs in a range of vocational subjects, sports coaching awards, vocational A Levels and vocational GCSEs. In one school, they 'share assessment criteria with students'. For the Bishop Walsh Catholic Performing Arts College, 'innovative' teaching means:

> The school is also training staff in the use of TEEP (Teacher Effectiveness Enhancement Programme) techniques. This Warwick University based initiative brings together the areas of multi-sensory learning, lesson planning, classroom management and the use of ICT (among other things) to ensure maximum impact in the classroom. The school is also exploring international links with the Canadian based Learning Through the Arts initiative. This strand of thinking fits exactly into the schools vision as an arts college and promotes the use of Performing Arts Teaching and Learning styles to improve students learning in all areas of the curriculum.

For the Ashcombe School, it means offering something different to their students: 'Our Chinese programme – quite a number of students now studying Chinese at university based on a three study visit to China followed by lunchtime lessons. No public examinations used.'

Sports colleges, in virtue of their specialism, were more likely to report the use of non-traditional awards, as elaborated below.

> We have a strong range of vocational courses on offer and are constantly looking for ways to recognise and celebrate achievement of all kinds through external accreditation such as ASDAN, JSLA, CSLA for example; locally and nationally recognised awards such as Jack Petchey, Shining Through, Princess Diana, Red Cross, NCB and our own awards, certificates and other forms of recognition[3]

> (Langdon School)

---

[3] ASDAN, Award Scheme Development and Accreditation Network; JSLA, Junior Sports Leader Award; CSLA, Community Sports Leader Award; NCB, National Children's Bureau.

However, there was a countervailing tendency for some schools to eschew non-traditional awards. This attitude is summarised by the head teacher of Thomas Mills High School:

> Apart from adjustments made following Curriculum 2000, our 11–16 is largely unchanged and our students do not study for qualifications which have dubious credibility. Instead our focus has been not to search for quick fixes, rather to improve the teaching of our existing curriculum to all pupils.

In conclusion, it is evident that self-reported 'innovative teaching' is closely connected in many cases with ICT and willingness of schools to adapt. However, in many schools the use of non-traditional awards/examinations does not seem to be viewed as a viable element of innovative teaching and learning.

Behaviour and discipline

Figure A2.2 clearly indicates that the majority of schools employed multi-faceted strategies to maintain order and good standards of behaviour. Again, it is interesting to note the importance of support staff in this regard. From the qualitative responses, one gets a sense of the diversity of the strategies used: from 'anti-bullying counsellors', 'parental conferences', 'merit systems monitored through a tracker system', 'peer mentoring', several using 'assertive discipline',

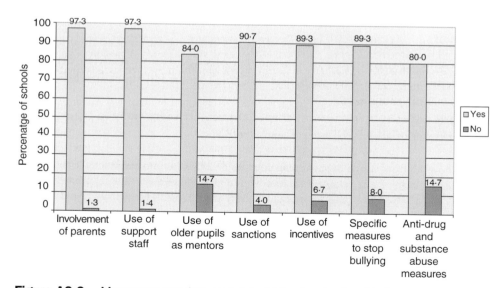

Figure A2.2 Measures used to maintain high standards of behaviour and discipline

'star points system devised by pupils', 'reward culture' and 'positive behaviour' to 'all staff have behaviour management training'.

There are two clear tendencies: one, for schools to use a named behaviour approach or 'programme', with the Assertive Discipline programme being the most popular; the other, for some schools it was more important that they designed their own local programmes based on consultation with pupils and parents in light of their particular circumstances. As this head teacher firmly advocates:

> [We do] everything – but not 'bought in' programmes – we like to make our systems very specific to our context. The emphasis is on 'can do' and rewards rather than punishments. We give praise for success and achievement a very high profile. We are, however, quite prepared to act swiftly and rigorously if there is a problem – for example we have encouraged the police to bring drug-sniffer dogs into classrooms and I closed the school early for a public meeting when we had extreme problems with security that the LEA and police were not assisting us with.
>
> (Wood Green High School College of Sport)

However, despite the aforementioned differences, most schools agreed that while rewards were preferable to sanctions, the latter were still needed. This balanced approach, encompassing many aspects shown in Figure A2.2, is exemplified by the work of Trinity Catholic High School, who incidentally devised their own programme:

> [We use the] Damascus programme – a school-based and -developed behaviour and social inclusion initiative characterised by a reward structure. Pupils are involved in an explicit course at the start of the programme and then mentored for up to five or six months. Students are set graduated achievable targets, recognised by a range of certificates, the affirmation of the headmaster, and the clearing of the child's record of negative letters and reports so that a 'fresh start' at the school is possible. The programme seeks to educate the pupils in relation to their behaviour as opposed to managing their behaviour. The range of incentives are in place to offer recognition, to reward good work, and to act as tangible extrinsic motivation with the hope that this will be transformed into an intrinsic process by the end of the course. Incentives to all students include merits, the praise box, department certificates, effort and excellence awards, headmaster's awards, Jack Petchey nominations, happy days, letters of congratulations, attendance certificates, achievement assemblies and achievements [are] publicised to parents and via notice boards. Older students act as 'Guardian Angels' to younger students with behavioural problems or learning difficulties. There is a parent reading scheme and there are literacy support volunteers. There is a regular confidential survey of all students in relation to bullying.

What the findings indicate is that schools consider the maintenance of discipline and high standards of behaviour a serious concern and that they have developed varying approaches towards this end. A significant number have opted for established behaviour management programmes while others have and continue to develop their own individualised programmes suited to specific local contexts and pressures.

Ethos

When asked to describe what were the key factors in attaining a school-wide ethos of achievement, a plethora of suggestions were made. 'Team work', 'strong pastoral support', 'clear messages', 'clear vision' were referred to and the use of target setting was also commonly cited. Others said a 'focus on standards – not becoming submerged in other issues' and 'consulting pupils on how to improve over the coming years recently has engaged them as has large extra-curricular opportunities'. Several accentuated what they believed were their strengths such as their 'inclusion policy' or raising the achievement of ethnic minority children and boys. The response from Landau Forte College gives a comprehensive flavour of both common and individual factors that schools described as important.

> High aspirations and expectations; focus upon effective learning with high quality teaching; modular curriculum – quality of planning, and use of assessment; celebrating and rewarding success; the impact of the Personal Tutorial System and involvement of parents; the continuous day; the five-term year; the dedication, professionalism and commitment of the staff; building relationships and treating students with dignity and respect; providing a stimulating and well cared for environment; providing access to resources and facilities including ICT – before, during and after the formal College day; wide range of enriching and extension opportunities beyond the subject curriculum; work-related learning and enterprise activities; sheer hard work!

Interestingly, a few schools mentioned the importance of 'display' for creating and communicating a sense of achievement through displays of artwork, performances and events (e.g. assemblies) within the school.

Many schools described how attaining specialist status had changed their working ethos. Some reported that it had engendered a sense of 'excitement' and 'enthusiasm' as was well as enabling overdue capital investment on infrastructure projects. By others' accounts, it raised the 'self-belief' of the school and the 'encouragement to strive harder'. Several said that becoming a specialist school emboldened them to take 'risks' and one head teacher described it as a 'seminal' turning point, while a new member simply stated, 'no exam result evidence yet, but it feels different'.

Parental involvement

Eighty per cent of schools said that parents had an active involvement in the school, in 14.7 per cent of schools they did not. Behind the statistic lay noteworthy differences in the level of participation and involvement. One school has made tutors' comments available online for parents to peruse. Parents 'organise events, e.g. quizzes, presentations' and educational activities and are 'encouraged to support children's learning by using the Learning Resource Centre (open on Sat–Sun)'. One head teacher tells us that 'a number of parents are involved in supporting sport in the School and have been taken on a part-time basis as coaches. They have also been able to gain recognised qualifications'. Most reported well attended PTAs, who often raised 'considerable' sums of money.

> Very good relationships with parents – involvement in decision making, continual communication of expectations and encouraging participation and use of the school, massive expansion of adult education and sports provision, and a smiling, family-friendly ethos – we never turn a parent away.
>
> (Westleigh High School – a College of Technology)

There is less information on the 14.7 per cent of respondents who said that parents did not have a direct involvement in the school. Negative responses often go unelaborated. However, one school frankly reported that: 'Parents are very difficult to motivate at this school. We often feel we achieve what we achieve despite apathy about their children's education.' In this case, the head teacher clearly locates the lack of involvement on parents' perceived apathy. We do not have any more information about this particular case but the figure itself and the few remarks document 'cool' and possibly antagonistic home–school relationships. This should give cause for concern and requires further investigation.

Networks

Schools formed several partnerships or more appropriately networks with horizontal links to other 'partner' specialist schools, colleges, consortia and individuals, vertical links with formal organisations such as the DfES, the Specialist Schools Trust (SST), local businesses, national bodies, universities, etc. arts colleges referred to their links and knowledge of the 'creative industries' while sports colleges were more likely to report local community links.

The data[4] shown in Figure A2.3 helps us to assess the assumed importance of certain kinds of links and suggests that while partnerships with other schools and contacts with the SST are important, the involvement of business is markedly less so. The open ended responses paint a more complex picture. For example, most

---

[4] The 'no' category is missing for the first column because respondents either did not respond or wrote 'non-applicable'.

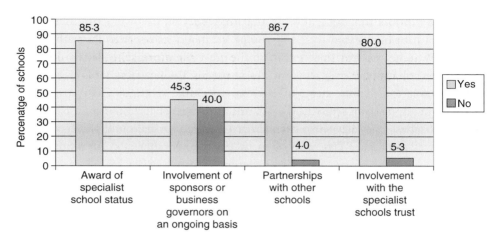

Figure A2.3 Strategies considered important in making great schools

schools valued the link with the SST although in practice the level of involvement was not of the same order as that reported between collaborating schools.

The comments also capture the infrequent, sporadic but nonetheless important links schools form on a case basis (e.g. writer/researchers in residence, see also the Stantonbury Campus North school in the 'ICT and innovative teaching' section). One would expect specialist schools to have highly developed networks and this is indeed the case. S Peter's Collegiate School represents a highly embedded school, with plenty of horizontal and vertical ties. A lead school in the Wolverhampton consortium:

> S Peter's Collegiate School is actively involved in a number of collaborative curricular partnerships with other secondary schools and industrial companies. This includes two inner city schools that are currently underperforming or facing challenging circumstances. . . . Collaboration with the LEA and industrial partner. We initiated and still lead a cross-phase consortium, promoting Integrated Learning Systems in mathematics. This has expanded significantly and has produced real learning and pedagogical gains. INSET for maintained and independent schools.

One school mentioned that, 'A Peer Mentoring enterprise with pupils from a school in serious weaknesses has enabled our own pupils to appreciate the positive learning environment we have created. We hope to build on this.' This suggests that what was often described as 'sharing expertise' may mask the hierarchical nature of such relationships. It was interesting that when one looks at the few who responded saying that they did not believe that partnerships with other schools were an important strategy, the same schools in a different question go on to document how they liaise with primary/middle schools. This possibly indicates that some schools did not consider the links they had with other secondary schools, or with businesses as necessarily as 'strategic' as connections with feeder schools. Whether or not this is indeed the case for more schools would need further investigation. It was also unclear in the data whether schools were more likely to collaborate with non-specialist or specialist schools. The data clearly documents networking activities by schools and suggest that partnerships, especially with other educational institutions, are very common and business links less so, or at least not as developed as the former. More research is needed to explore in depth the consequences of different kinds of networking activities and ties for schools.

Extra-curricular provision

The vast majority (89.3 per cent) of schools did more than ten hours of extra-curricular activities and 10.7 per cent did between five and ten hours a week. However, most schools reported long opening hours and organised a range of extra-curricular activities for pupils. In addition the regular use of facilities by the local community was mentioned. Unsurprisingly sports colleges were most likely to mention local community use of facilities. Many schools pointed out that extra-curricular activities did not simply mean 'after school' but weekends and holidays too. Opening outside the working week or late was often linked with increasing participation from the local community. The qualitative response suggests that although most schools did not use an extended day (69 per cent), as a rule, they did maintain long opening hours. The example of the Langdon School illustrates well the nature and extent of extra-curricular activities to be found in the respondent schools.

> Although our normal school day is 8.40 to 3.30 p.m., we extend this provision through our extensive Out of Hours Programme of before school, lunchtime and after school, weekends and holidays activities which include academic, sporting and cultural activities. We have a Saturday School running for 30 weeks per year for our Partner Primary Schools and a two week Summer University open to all Langdon students. We have Saturday classes for Year 10 and 11 coursework and revision and Year 9 SATs revision a well as three day Easter Revision School for GCSE and SATs. Sporting activities, which include School and Community Clubs, run after school, at weekends and during all school holidays. As part of our extended schools work we also have activities on site provided by our own Inclusion Team and the Family Support Project during most school holidays, as well as weekend activities for students and families.
>
> (Langdon School)

Interestingly, they mention using a five-term year, which is rare among respondent schools. In fact, only 9.3 per cent claimed to use a non-standard term of either five or six terms; the majority of schools used the three-term year.

Conclusions

In summary, the findings suggest that there are indeed a range of common strategies and approaches adopted by leading specialist schools: in ICT, behaviour and discipline, leadership and management and much else. Conversely, there are differences, where particular schools adopt strategies and approaches specific to their local context, history, pupil intake and ethos. Interestingly a cross-tabulation of the survey data points towards noteworthy variations among the responding leading specialist schools, in terms of key indicators such as percentage of 5[+] A*–Cs, post-16 staying-on rate, the percentage going on to university or other post-secondary education and permanent exclusions. Arising from the cross-tabulation schools fell in to three groups which were[5] club membership, school specialism and whether the school had a sixth form. This preliminary analysis suggests these are important issues for further investigation. More analysis is needed to examine and locate the potential qualitative differences between these groupings. Moreover, this alerts us to the fact that differences among specialist schools may be as significant as those between them and non-specialist schools. Furthermore, the possibility of identifying activities and practices that are promising for future worthwhile trends is beyond the scope of this kind of data or analysis. Thus, that finding out whatever 'value' specialism per se contributes to the success of these schools would require more comparative quantitative and qualitative work to tease out.

References

Chiu, I. and Brennan, M. (1990) 'The effectiveness of some techniques for improving mail survey response rates: a meta-analysis', *Marketing Bulletin* 1(13–18), 1–7.

Jesson, D. (2004) *Educational Outcomes and Value Added by Specialist Schools: 2003 Analysis*. London: Specialist Schools Trust.

Rudd, P., Aiston, S., Davies, D., Rickinson, M. and Dartnall, L. (2002) *High Performing Specialist Schools: What makes the difference?* Slough: National Foundation for Educational Research.

---

[5] Gender was of course a potentially important variable but the sample of single-sex schools was very small, as a result they were removed from the analysis.

Index